Lives of Women
IN
RUSSIA
AND
EASTERN EUROPE

Live&Work
IN
RUSSIA
AND
EASTERN EUROPE

Jonathan Packer

Published by Vacation Work, 9 Park End Street, Oxford
Web site http: //www.vacationwork.co.uk

LIVE AND WORK IN RUSSIA AND EASTERN EUROPE

by Jonathan Packer

Copyright © Vacation Work 1998

Jonathan Packer has asserted his moral right to be identified as the author of this work in accordance with the Copyright, Design and Patents Act 1988.

ISBN 1-85458-190-2 (softback)
ISBN 1-85458-191-0 (hardback)

No part of this publication may be stored, reproduced or transmitted in any form without the prior written permission of the publisher.

Publicity: Roger Musker

Cover Design by Miller Craig & Cocking Design Partnership

Typeset by WorldView Publishing Services (01865-201562)

Printed by Unwin Bros Ltd.
The Gresham Press, Old Woking, Surrey, England

Contents

General Overview

INTRODUCTION

What is Eastern Europe?.. 20
Geographical and Economic Structure – Eastern Europe – The Baltic States – Borderlands – Central and Eastern Europe – CIS – Pros and Cons of Moving to Eastern Europe – Some Do's and Don'ts.. 20

RESIDENCE AND ENTRY REGULATIONS

The Current Position – Visas – Categories of Visa – Health and Safety – Applying for a Residence Permit – Work Permits – Entering to Start a Business – Entering with Retirement Status – Identity Cards – Tax Numbers – On Arrival – Embassies and Consulates.. 29

PREPARATION AND ARRIVAL

Crime – Personal Safety – Getting There – Transport – Sources of Information – Preparation – Multi-Trip Insurance... 36

SETTING UP HOME

Property and Accommodation. – Hotels – Renting Property – Buying Property – Offshore Mortgages – Land Registry – The Preliminary Contract – The Property Contract – Payment – Expenses – Buying a Plot of Land – Planning Permission – Paperwork – Property Taxes – Insurance...................................... 46
Removals – Checklist Before Moving – Removal Companies – Cargo and Freight Forwarders – The Import Procedure – Useful Addresses – Importing Cars.. 51

DAILY LIFE

The Languages – Learning the Language – Language Schools and Courses.. 56
Schools and Education – The Education System – Study and Exchange Schemes for Russia and Eastern Europe... 59

The Media and Communications: Books and Newspapers – Communications – Post – Telephones – Radio and Television.. 63
Transport and Utilities – Cars – Insurance – Electricity, Water, Gas............ 65
Health – The Health Service – Reciprocal Health Care Agreements – Health Insurance – Social Security – What to Take.. 68
Money and Finance – Convertible Currencies – Bank Accounts – Money Transfers – Procedures for Transferring Money – Financial Advice – Resident Accounts – Opening Your Account – Credit Cards – Banking Procedures – Offshore Banking – Summary.. 73
Taxation – Expenses – The Tax System – Income Tax – Tax Returns............ 80

WORKING IN RUSSIA AND EASTERN EUROPE

Employment – General Background.. 83
Employment Contacts – UK Newspapers and Representatives – The Internet – International and Local Press – Directories – Libraries – Research Services – Recruitment Agencies – Consultancies – Teaching (Britain, USA) – Useful Addresses – Tourism – Voluntary Agencies – Internships and Exchange Schemes – NGOs – Qualifications – Other Contacts and opportunities... 84
Business and Industry Report – Business Opportunities – Business and Employment in Russia and Eastern Europe.. 102

The Baltic States

BALTIC REGION

Introduction – Geography and History... 107

ESTONIA

Introduction.. 109
Living in Estonia – History – Geographical Information – Climate – The Language – The Currency – Getting There – Travel Agencies – Residence and Entry – Work Permits – Residence Permits – Customs – Courier Services – Accommodation – Utilities and Communications – Electricity – Telephones and Post – Transport – Daily Life – Health Service and Hospitals – Banks – Books – Newspapers – Cultural Background – Religion – Song Festivals – National Holidays – Useful Addresses.. 109
Working in Estonia – Economy and Trade – Employment – Advertising – Employment and Business – English Teaching – Tourism – Voluntary Work – The Tax System – Doing Business.. 116
Business and Industry Report – Sources of Information.............................. 118

LATVIA

Introduction.. 120
Living in Latvia – History – Geographical Information – Climate – The Language – The Currency – Getting There – Trains – Travel Agencies – Residence and Entry – Customs – Courier Services – Accommodation – Utilities and Communications – Electricity – Telephones and Post – Transport – Daily Life – Health Service and Hospitals – Education – Banks – Books – Newspapers – Television – Radio – Cultural Background – Religion – Entertainment and Social Life – Food – Useful Addresses............................ 120
Working in Latvia – Economy and Trade – English Teaching – Teacher Agents – University Teachers – Tourism – Voluntary Work – Doing Business.. 127
Business and Industry Report – Useful Addresses................................ 129

LITHUANIA

Introduction.. 130
Living in Lithuania – History – Geographical Information – The Language – The Currency – Getting There – Travel Agencies – Residence and Entry Regulations – Customs – Courier Services – Daily Life – Accommodation – Utilities and Communications – Transport – Cultural Background – Useful Addresses... 130
Working in Lithuania – Teaching – Teacher Agents – Tourism – Voluntary Work – The Tax System... 134

Russia, Belarus and Ukraine

RUSSIA

Introduction – Russia and the Soviet Union – The Commonwealth of Independent States – Reform in Russia – Early History – The Nineteenth Century – East and West – The Russian Idea of the State – Geography – Cities and Population – Language and Religion.. 140
Travel – Travel Agencies – Airlines – Charters – Transport and Communications – Coach – Railways – Removals and Freight – Onward Connections – Import Procedures – Customs – Courier and Delivery Services................. 144
Residence and Entry – Visa Support Services – Travel Advice................ 150
Daily Life – General Background – The Alphabet – The Language – The Language Deficit – Language Courses – Culture Shock – New Russians – Old Russians – The New Poor – Getting Around – Utilities and Communications – Post and Telephones – American Express Offices – Western Union – Issues Facing Expatriates – Books – Health Care and Hospitals – Other Health Issues – Personal Safety.. 152

Employment – Getting a Job – Recruitment Contacts – Teaching English – Tourism – Voluntary Work – Taxation and Insurance – Finance – General Taxation – Personal Taxes – Corporate Taxes – Employment and Tax – Health Insurance.. 160
Business – Doing Business in Russia – Market Summary – Currency – Background to Doing Business – Current Trends – Doing Business – Hospitality – Social Life and Social Attitudes – Business Ethics – Taxation and Business Advice – Business Taxes – Useful Contacts... 167

BELARUS

Introduction... 173
Living in Belarus – Residence and Entry Regulations – Useful Information.. 173
Working in Belarus – Useful Addresses... 173

UKRAINE

Introduction... 175
Living in Ukraine – Geography – History – Residence and Entry – Getting There – Travel Agencies – Hotels – The Language – The Currency – Customs – Education – International Removals and Freight – Cultural Background – National Holidays.. 175
Working in Ukraine – Business and Industry Report............................ 179

Central and Eastern Europe

Central Europe

Introduction... 183

CZECH REPUBLIC

Introduction... 184
Living in the Czech Republic – People – Geographical Information – Cities and Regions – Prague – Brno – Getting There – Hotels and Travel Agencies – Residence and Entry Regulations – Embassies, Consulates and Tourist Offices – Accommodation – The Language – Language Schools – Media and Communications – Public Holidays...
Working in the Czech Republic – Business and Employment – Immigration – Employment – Specific Contacts.. 184
Business and Industry Report... 189
193

SLOVAKIA

Introduction...	195
Living in Slovakia – The State – The Language – The Currency – Getting There – Accommodation – Residence and Entry Regulations – Utilities and Communications – Transport – Health Service and Hospitals – Banks – Useful Addresses – National and Religious Holidays..	195
Working in Slovakia – Teaching Contacts – Tourism Contacts........................	199
Business and Industry Report...	200

HUNGARY

Introduction...	202
Living in Hungary – Political and Economic Structure – Government – Politics – History – Geographical Information – Cities and Regions – Getting There – Residence and Entry Regulations – Embassies, Consulates and Tourist Offices – Accommodation – Removals – Import Procedures – The Language – Language Schools – Telephones – Driving – Public Transport – Schools and Education – Banks – Healthcare – Culture – Useful Addresses – Public Holidays..	202
Working in Hungary – Employment – Business and Industry Report...............	209

POLAND

Introduction...	212
Living in Poland – Political, Economic and Geographical Structure – Entry and Residence – Useful Addresses – Getting There – Currency – Geography – Climate – Daily Life – Accommodation – Utilities – Removals and Freight – Import Procedures – The Language – Transport and Communications – Getting Around – Health and Hospitals – Shopping – Public Holidays............	212
Working in Poland – Business and Employment – Specific Contacts – Economy..	220

South Eastern Europe

Introduction...	224

ALBANIA

Introduction...	225
Living in Albania – Language and Population – Government and Politics – Geography and History – Communism – The Climate – The Language – The Currency – Getting There – Visas – Customs – Utilities and Communications – Health – Accommodation – Getting Around – Cultural Background – Useful Contacts..	225

Working in Albania – Economy and Trade – Employment – Doing Business – Business and Industry Report.. 229

BOSNIA-HERZEGOVINA

Introduction.. 231
Living in Bosnia – Climate – Residence and Entry – Currency and Customs – Getting There – Communications – Books and Maps – Embassies and Useful Addresses... 231
Working in Bosnia – Business and Industry Report – Commercial Contacts... 233

BULGARIA

Introduction.. 234
Living in Bulgaria – History – Residence and Entry – Getting There – Travel Agencies – Removals – Health Service and Hospitals – Culture and Daily Life – Embassies and Tourist Offices – Public Holidays.. 234
Working in Bulgaria – Business and Industry Report – Employment – Commercial Contacts... 238

CROATIA

Introduction.. 240
Living in Croatia – Political, Economic and Geographical Structure – Pros and Cons of Moving to Croatia – Getting There – History – Economy – Government – Currency – Population – Geography – Climate – Cities and Regions – Accommodation – Renting and Buying Property – Hotels and Agencies – Utilities – Removals and Freight – Import Procedures – The Language – Courses – Transport and Communications – Getting Around – Travel Agencies – Banks – Health and Hospitals – Manners and Customs – Social Life – Public Holidays.. 240
Working in Croatia – Business Background – Employment – Tourism – English Teaching and Language Schools – Business Contacts – Running a Business – Business and Industry Report – Zagreb – Other Employment Contacts – English Language Schools – Residence and Entry – Embassies and Consulates... 255

FYR MACEDONIA

Introduction.. 260
Living in Macedonia – History – Geography – Climate – Culture and Language – Communications.. 260
Working in Macedonia – Business and Industry Report – Useful Addresses... 262

MOLDOVA

Introduction.. 264
Living in Moldova – History – Visas and Customs – Travel Agencies – Culture and Language – Religion – Communications... 264
Working in Moldova – Business and Industry Report – Useful Addresses.. 266

ROMANIA

Introduction.. 267
Living in Romania – History – Residence and Entry Regulations – Getting There – Travel Agencies – Accommodation – Currency and Customs – Culture and Daily Life – Embassies and Tourist Offices – National Holidays.... 267
Working in Romania – Business and Industry Report – Employment – Commercial Contacts.. 270

SLOVENIA

Introduction.. 272
Living in Slovenia – Pros and Cons of Moving to Slovenia – History – Geography – Getting There – Visas and Residence – Customs and Currency – By Plane – By Boat, Road and Train – Communications – Accommodation – Travelling Around – Culture and Daily Life – Embassies and Tourist Offices – Public Holidays.. 272
Working in Slovenia – Establishing a Company – Employment – Income Tax – Business and Industry Report - Useful Addresses.................................. 276

YUGOSLAVIA (MONTENEGRO, SERBIA)

Introduction.. 278
Living in Yugoslavia – Politics – Economy – Geography – Business and Trade – History – Climate – Population – Visas – Currency – Getting There – Communications – Cities and Regions... 278
Working in Yugoslavia – Business and Industry Report – Sources of Information.. 282

The Caspian and Central Asia Region

The Caspian and Central Asia Region

Introduction.. 286

ARMENIA

Introduction.. 288

Living in Armenia – Geographical Information – Residence and Entry Regulations – Useful Addresses.. 288
Working in Armenia – Business and Industry Report................................ 289

AZERBAIJAN

Introduction... 290
Living in Azerbaijan – History – Geographical Information – The Language – The Currency – Getting There – Travel Agencies – Hotels – Residence and Entry Regulations – Customs – Utilities and Communications – Health Service and Insurance – Schools and Education – Cultural Background – Useful Addresses.. 290
Working in Azerbaijan – Business Contacts – Courier and Freight Forwarding Services.. 293

GEORGIA

Introduction... 294
Living in Georgia – Residence and Entry Regulations – Useful Addresses.... 294
Working in Georgia – Economy and Trade – The Tax System – Doing Business – Business Contacts... 295

KAZAKSTAN

Introduction... 297
Living in Kazakstan – Residence and Entry Regulations – Useful Addresses.. 297
Working in Kazakstan – Economy and Trade – Business, Legal and Recruitment Contacts.. 298

KYRGYZSTAN

Introduction... 299
Living in Kyrgyzstan – Geographical Information – Residence and Entry Regulations – Useful Addresses... 299
Working in Kyrgyzstan – Economy and Trade.. 300

TAJIKISTAN

Introduction... 301
Living in Tajikistan – Residence and Entry Regulations – Useful Addresses.. 301
Working in Tajikistan – Economy and Trade... 302

TURKMENISTAN

Introduction... 303

Living in Turkmenistan – Residence and Entry Regulations – Useful Addresses...	303
Working in Turkmenistan – Business and Industry Report...........................	304

UZBEKISTAN

Introduction...	305
Living in Uzbekistan – Geographical Information – The Language – Residence and Entry Regulations – Useful Addresses...	305
Working in Uzbekistan – Economy and Trade – Business Contacts................	306

APPENDICES

I – Personal Experiences – Former Soviet Union...	309
II – Personal Experiences – Central Europe..	315
III – Personal Experiences – Eastern Europe..	327

MAPS AND CHARTS

Central and Eastern Europe and the CIS..	18
The Baltic States...	106
Russia, Belarus and Ukraine...	138
Central and Eastern Europe..	182
Caspian and Central Asia Region...	284

Acknowledgments

The following organisations and individuals have contributed by giving their time and attention to the author's many enquiries and queries during the year in which this book was written. To all the rest of those who responded to my letters or questionnaires also, thank you very much.

In particular, thanks are due to Artur Szustka and his family, David Marshall, Tatiana Trifanova, Steven Penney, Danute Karpaviciene, Maila Saar, Yana Khrustovskaya, Alexander O. Chebotarev, Mansur I. Zokirov, Yuri Malyshev, Deana Mash, Uvaid Z. Oripov, Olga Nikishina, Silvana Durasevic, Tanya Styrkas, Ian Leach, Anatoly Karibov, Konstanca Drakulovska, Alan Gallop, Rok V. Klancnik, M. Rajnic, Mariola Trebus, Kamol Kh. Makhmoudov, Peter Y. Soukhov, Czeslaw Jermanowski, Andrzej Rode, Joan Pearson, Marlen Taffarello, Gábor Tarr, Keith Pitteway, Judit Bak, Kornelia Murphy, Riita Balza, Claire Jarrold, Mari Liigand, Peteris Janovskis, Monika Pasková, Pauls Gusts, Genovaite Balseviciene, Kevin Christie, Nicole Miller, Sue Harrison, Richard Creagh, Natalia Belokon, Corinne Sharpe, Chris Rocki, Ben Harris, Mr Pluyko, Nurgaisha Jecksembiyeva, Sadykov T. Salmenovich, Joanna Kopel, Maria Kropiewnicka, Mike Bugsgang, David Shepherd, Tanya Kouznetsova, Anthony Goodwin, Branko Strok, Brian Woollard, Julia Berg, Piotr Rabczak, Romana Gasperein, Grenville Yeo, Paul Colston, Phil Hooley, Vladimir Yuryev, Janna Belousova, Alica Früwaldová, John Charles Lopez, Keith Bates, Jeff Toms, Paul Humphreys, Ian Rushmer, Karolina Novotná, Maria Skirgailo, Pavel Rybin, Natalia Hladilova, Irina Deineko, Alexander Soukharev, Marina Vladimirova, Jaroslaw Kopczyk, Dr Sergei G. Kulik, Mikhail Jurievitch, Natalya Rostovtseva, Martin Oravec, Milena Margetic, Valnea Bressan, Marcin Klosniau, Jana Randrüüt, Lea Noorma, Magdalena Wakulicz-Jacynska, Marija Barbic, Marc Jeffery, Branka Raijkovic, Attila Hetey, Csabu Rona, Marianna Müller and Piroska Szalay, Leszek Oledzki, Anica Kolmanic, Irina Sokolova, Roman Kacin, and most of all to Reiko Okada for the ways you helped me too.

Telephone area code changes.
On April 22nd 2000 there are to be a number of changes to certain area telephone code prefixes in the UK. The most important of these is that the current 0171- and 0181- prefixes for London will both be replaced by the prefix 020-, followed by 7 for current 0171 numbers and 8 for current 0181 numbers. Also affected will be Cardiff (numbers will begin 029 20), Portsmouth (023 92), Southampton (023 80) and Northern Ireland (028 90 for Belfast; contact directory enquiries for other numbers in Northern Ireland.

In addition, as from the same date, the numbers for various special services including freephone and lo-call numers will begin with 08 and all mobile phone numbers will begin with 07. Telephone operators are planning to ease the transition by running the current 01 numbers in parallel with the new 02 numbers until the spring of 2001.

Foreword

This book is for all those thinking of living and working in Russia or the CIS (Commonwealth of Independent States) countries, or of moving to Central and Eastern Europe (CEE), or visiting any of these countries on a long-term basis, or anyone travelling there – for business or pleasure – who will come more closely into contact with these countries and their people.

If you are interested in the background to living and working in Azerbaijan, in English-teaching opportunities in the Czech Republic, or a general overview of living, working and doing business in Russia, you will find all of this information here, and for all of the countries of Eastern Europe and Central Europe, and Central Asia as well. Getting visas and contacting tourist and information offices will be some of the first steps you can take; and everyone visiting these countries should also do their own research and make their own preparations before they go. This book can be a starting-point, the beginning of a story which you will complete yourself.

You will find the main names and addresses here – of embassies and tourist offices in Britain and the United States and for each of the Central and Eastern European/Central Asian countries – and a wide variety of other information considered from the point of view of business travellers, working expatriates and shorter-term workers in the region.

It is hoped this can be of interest to all those from Western Europe and North America – and indeed anywhere else – who has a practical interest in living, working or doing business in Russia, Eastern Europe, Central Europe or Central Asia.

Living and Working in Russia and Eastern Europe

Live and Work in Russia and Eastern Europe is the first publication of its kind which aims to bring together this wide range of information on all these destinations, for workers, volunteers, businesspeople and others. It gives the essential background to everything from residence and entry to the way of life, culture and history. There are twenty-seven of these countries which are considered in all, in this vast region stretching from the Baltic and the Mediterranean to the Pacific Ocean.

This is a wide range of destinations, and hopefully, it will be used by a wide range of readers as well. Nowadays many may be thinking about moving to the CIS/CEE, or of doing business, or going there to take up an executive posting, or just to get a job. From a business point of view, most of these countries are now on the up, after a difficult transitional period, but we can see that their dream of a rapid transformation to western standards of prosperity has yet to materialise in many.

There will be many more years – even decades – to come before most of these countries can reach their goal of modernisation and a more prosperous economy. This in turn will help to bring a more stable and democratic way of life.

Doing business will be the reason many go. For those investors ready to take a risk in some of these emerging markets there is still great potential; and others have reached a stage of development where the business and investment opportunities are less risky, and more long-term. Certainly, many large and small businesses will be trying to find ways of doing business here.

Other managers and/or personnel or human resources departments of larger organisations will be responsible for posting staff to Russia/Eastern Europe/CIS. There are staff now in all the main cities of the region, working in a wide variety of professions, or sent there by British or American companies. These personnel managers themselves may not have much direct experience of living in the places they are dealing with. They will need the kind of direct sources of information and advice to be found in this book.

Live and Work in Russia and Eastern Europe has been written for all these people, from recruitment professionals to individual jobseekers. Then there are young people – on a year off perhaps – in search of a more adventurous place to live and work. For them, this advice and background information will be most important – but also enough money to see them through the first difficult days. Whatever your point of view, you should find something here of interest. So, if you are in need of interesting contacts and useful advice, read on!

How can this be done, in such a diverse region and for so many countries? The answer is to make this book not the definitive answer to all your problems, many of which – by definition – cannot be anticipated or predicted. Life is always more complicated than our various prescriptions for it, and this applies as much to this kind of work-and-travel book as to anything else. But the idea which is most important is that this is a starting-point, a way of setting out.

Jonathan Packer
Oxford, April 1998

NOTE: While every effort has been made to ensure that the information contained in this book was correct at the time of going to press, some details are bound to change – particularly wages, exchange rates, government policies, political situations and telephone numbers. The information given here is intended as a guide, and readers are advised to check facts and the credentials of organisations for themselves. You may also find out more about living and working in Russia and Eastern Europe yourself. If you have any additions or corrections – or any ideas or contacts you would like to see included in future editions these contributions will be very welcome. Please fax or write to the author c/o *Live and Work in Russia and Eastern Europe*, Vacation Work, 9 Park End Street, Oxford OX1 1HJ, UK; fax 01865-790885.

Russia and Eastern Europe

General Overview

Introduction
Residence and Entry
Preparation and Arrival
Setting Up Home
Daily Life
Employment

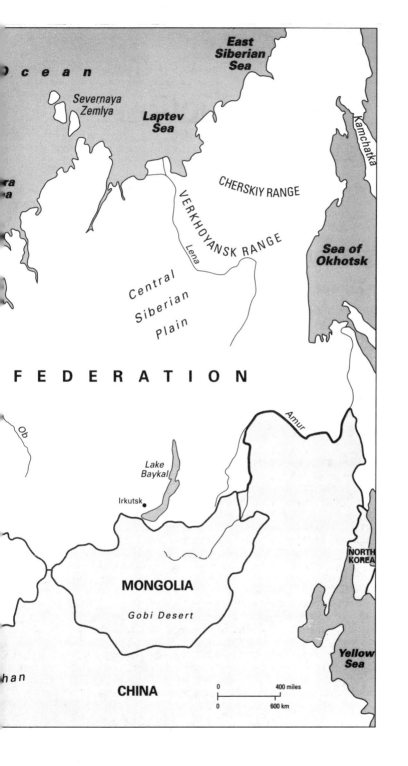

Introduction

What is Eastern Europe?

This is a diverse region – really many regions – and includes Russia and its neighbouring countries in Central Asia as well. In recent history, these have in common mainly their reemergence from communism. There are also more complex strands of history and culture which unite many.

Geographical and Economic Structure

Eastern Europe

No longer is there a simple division between East and West. Countries such as Poland, the Czech and Slovak Republics, and Hungary see themselves as Central European. The three Baltic States to the north are keen to identify themselves with the West. The former Yugoslavian countries, Serbia and Montenegro, Croatia, Bosnia-Herzegovina, Slovenia and F.Y.R. Macedonia, along with Albania, have their own 'Balkan' history. Some want to be in Central Europe (Slovenia and Croatia) and others see themselves as belonging to this wider region, the South-East, a newer and less prejudicial term for the Balkans. Slovenia has close historic ties with Austria and Italy. There are also states which come more directly under Russian influence, like Belarus and Ukraine (although the latter also has some real independence from Russia). The Russian Federation itself stretches far into Central Asia, and to the Pacific coast; and its Central Asian neighbours from Azerbaijan to Uzbekistan are part of a 'commonwealth' known as the Commonwealth of Independent States or 'CIS' but are also independent and sovereign countries, like the members of the former British Commonwealth.

There is a 'former British Empire' and a former British Commonwealth (today known simply as the 'Commonwealth') and the former Soviet Union was a similarly artificial construction, something between a modern nation state and an old-fashioned land-based empire. Its disappearance has seen the rise of competing nationalisms, not least in Russia itself, where formerly there was one official ideology. These national tensions are expressed least acutely in the Central European countries which have moved more easily to a market economy, and aspire to membership of the European Union in the near future – and are more obviously expressed the further east you go.

The history of Eastern Europe is a story of shifting borders. Each state has its own minority communities (like the Russians of the Trans-Dniester Republic, who seceded from Moldova, which seceded in its turn from the former Soviet Union and was unwilling to be part of what became Ukraine). This state within state of some 200,000 people even has its own minority communities as well. There are people here who have been left behind by the tides of history: a microcosm of the situation in the whole of the former Soviet Union.

Pointing You in the *Right Direction* at the Crossroads of Europe

Electronics, Energy, Retailing, I.T., Manufacturing, Telecommunications - in whatever sector you operate, the opportunities offered in the developing markets of Central Europe and Asia are as numerous and varied as the countries represented within this vast region.

Doing business is different. In order to maximise your operational effectiveness you will need to have a thorough understanding of the markets and people you will be dealing with; you need to be aware of the cultural differences and how to turn them to your advantage and be able to develop totally new approaches to communication and negotiation. You may also need to learn a new language!

The Centre for International Briefing provides the most comprehensive range of country, regional and business briefings available anywhere. Programmes are designed for expatriates taking up long and short term assignments, for business travellers as well as for those operating as home-based managers with international responsibilities.

- **Scheduled and Customised Briefings for all countries in Central & Eastern Europe and Central Asia**
- **Comprehensive country specific and regional Business Overviews**
- **Intensive Tuition in all languages**
- **Intercultural Awareness and International Team-Building Workshops**
- **Fully residential in the 12th Century Farnham Castle**

Further details from the Marketing Department:
Tel: +44 (0)1252 720416/9 Fax: +44 (0)1252 719277
E-mail:cib.farnham@dial.pipex.com or on our web-site located at
http://www.cibfarnham.com

THE CENTRE FOR INTERNATIONAL BRIEFING
The World's Leading Training Centre for International Effectiveness

state of some 200,000 people even has its own minority communities as well. There are people here who have been left behind by the tides of history: a microcosm of the situation in the whole of the former Soviet Union.

Some of these divisions will not last. Others are more stable. Poland, for example, has its post-war borders which are much further to the west than the historic Polish state, and has no claims on its lost teritories in Lithuania, Belarus or Ukraine. It is now in Central Europe, or the 'West', and much more firmly established as a modern nation state than at any time in its history. In fact there is a great desire in each of these countries – stable or otherwise – simply for economic and social progress; and mainly to avoid the conflicts which have afflicted them in the past (and which could arise again in the patchwork of ethnic communities and nationalisms left behind by the collapse of the Soviet Union, and of former Yugoslavia).

In Russia itself, economic reform and reconstruction is a greater priority than nationalism – which is however making a come-back – and there is a kind of nostalgia for communism and the influence which the Soviet Union and its Tsarist forerunner used to wield in neighbouring countries. Then there are various Russian minorities in many of these other countries of Eastern Europe and Central Asia. Some have stayed on – like the British settlers in India – and some are going home. But Russia is still the most influential country in the region.

So far as democracy and economic development are concerned, there is also a gradation from east to west (as there is in the kinds of nationalism which are expressed). Poland, the Czech Republic, Hungary, and Slovenia have developed closer economic ties with the European Union; Croatia and the Baltic States are not far behind. Prosperity has come to Russia itself, at least to certain sections of the population, although democracy is not as yet so firmly established. Less successful have been the Slovak Republic, Serbia, F.Y.R. Macedonia, Bulgaria and Romania, with the policies of the Serbian government the most destabilising factor in the region, and its intransigence in relation to its province of Kosovo.

Ukraine and Belarus are also relatively poor and underdeveloped; and are another potential focus of instability between Russia and the West – as are all the countries of Central Asia – Kazakstan, Turkmenistan, Kyrgyzstan, and Tajikistan. Along with Uzbekistan, Armenia and Georgia south of the Caucasus Mountains, these have found the transition from the centralised Soviet system to a diverse market economy most difficult (although there are substantial natural resources, like minerals and oil in many). The Caspian oil boom could change this, as it is currently changing Azerbaijan, and could be a factor for progress, or renewed regional rivalries.

It should be re-emphasised that these all now regard themselves as independent and sovereign states; and this process of economic development and reconstruction is the background against which work and expatriation in these countries should be seen – something we return to in some of the country chapters which follow. There are many new opportunities for international workers – in everything from consultancy to volunteer work – and also a challenge: to live in a country whose history and way of life are often very different from the experience of most Western Europeans or North Americans, even those who have lived abroad before.

This pattern of employment and expatriation is also very different. Again, there is an alignment from east to west. The countries of Central Europe are those where there is the broadest range of job opportunities; and a less pronounced economic and cultural difference. The further east we go the greater we feel this cultural difference to be.

Employment

From the point of view of those interested in working there, these countries also have certain features in common. Expatriate workers can be roughly divided into those who are sent there by large companies or organisations, and are therefore paid at more or less 'international' rates – with even some allowances for the stresses and strains of living so far away from home – and others in more 'normal' areas of employment who work for local organisations – or in the local context for western ones but are paid at local rates. There are some areas of work – such as English teaching – which fall between these two categories. Many others are volunteers, who will be paid very little or even pay for this privilege.

Other expatriate workers are doing valuable work in training and consultancy, helping to put the local economy back on its feet; or looking after the casualties of social change, the poor and underprivileged, where provision is often inadequate. The growth in future will be – as it already is in Central Europe – in the 'middle' range of jobs, teaching, secretarial, retail, technical, and managerial positions, as these economies develop, again on an axis from east to west.

In the broader jobs and business context, the main area for growth is the infrastructure: roads, railways, airports, telecommunications, financial services and administration. Manufacturing industry and distribution are being developed, often in collaboration with foreign companies, as are service industries like food distribution and retailing. There are opportunities here for the more adventurous or commercially minded in many sectors like mining, gas, and engineering, airlines and road transport, information technology and telecommunications, and all the other areas where there are partnerships between 'western' and local firms.

Challenging conditions (where accommodation is often cramped and bureaucracy a major problem) mean that volunteers – as well as some of these other business people and expatriate workers – will often be of a more adventurous nature. Experts are needed in consultancy and development, who should have a real experience in and understanding of their field as well as the right qualifications. There are openings, too, for those who are more entrepreneurial, who know how to make new contacts and can start a business and make it grow.

Moving to Eastern Europe

For more about this, see the chapters in this *General Overview* on *Residence and Entry*, *Setting Up Home* and *Daily Life* which follow this one – and the individual country chapters in the following regional sections of this book. Taken together these will provide a full picture of living and working there.

The Baltic States

In the westward-looking Baltic States, the signs of the recent Soviet past are everywhere, in the barrack-block style public housing and the uniformity of railway stations and airports which are not very different from those in neighbouring Russia. There are many other things these countries have in common with their eastern neighbour, in their recent and more distant past, not least a significant population of Russian immigrants. But this is all changing. The Baltic States have all drawn a line under their recent Soviet experience and are trying to get away from this rather negative image. However, the economic conditions these nations are emerging from are really not very different from those in Russia, and much more like those in Belarus and Ukraine – even if the aspiration of Estonia, Latvia and Lithuania is to belong to the European Union in the near future.

Borderlands

Estonia, Latvia, Lithuania, Ukraine, Belarus is somehow the order of westernisation and prosperity in this group of emerging countries along this border with Russia – with Estonia at the head of this queue for European Union membership. A similar league table or 'order of merit' could be drawn up for all the countries in this book, which have a relation in these economic terms to each other, and also to this process of transition or 'westernisation'. These countries are Estonia, Latvia, Lithuania, Belarus, Ukraine, Russia, Albania, Bosnia-Herzegovina, Bulgaria, Croatia, FYR Macedonia, Moldova, Romania, Slovenia, Yugoslavia, the Czech Republic, Slovakia, Hungary, Poland, Armenia, Azerbaijan, Georgia, Kazakstan, Kyrgyzstan, Tajikistan, Turkmenistan, and Uzbekistan.

Each one is an independent country with its own sense of itself and its history, and an (often disputed) national identity. Like the Baltic States, each has its own separate culture and traditions, and a sometimes disputed history. The countries of the borderlands between East and West are the Baltic States, and Belarus and Ukraine, but each in its own way is a 'borderland' between past and present, the old and the new.

Central and Eastern Europe

Many are not in Eastern Europe at all in fact, and the worst thing you could say on arrival in Poland or Hungary is that you are now in Eastern Europe: this is Central Europe, which is rapidly becoming part of the West. These issues are best understood in their historical and cultural context, and we return to this is some of the country chapters which follow. Sidestepping for the moment the thorny question of where Eastern Europe actually is, we can move swiftly on to the question of what it is like to live there...

The Commonwealth of Independent States

It is worth reemphasising that the Soviet Union (like the former Yugoslavia in all but name) is a state which no longer exists. This is now the Russian Federation, part of the Commonwealth of Independent States, which are just that, independent, although many economic and cultural ties with Russia still remain. See the chapter on *Russia* and *Caspian and Central Asia* for more on this.

Pros and Cons of Moving to Eastern Europe

A general impression of Eastern Europe based somehow on crime and communism, cold weather and a frosty welcome will be wide of the mark. Some countries are poor, but the opportunities for western visitors tend to be correspondingly great. Pricewise, you could exchange your modest residence in the UK for a 150-room château in Poland for instance; and the labour to do it all up will still be much cheaper than in Britain. Problems are mainly logistical, which will make living in towns more practical than the countryside, although in many of the more stable countries you can find a life away from it all even in the country which would suit the more adventurous elderly or retired resident. For most expatriates like these, Western Europe has its own traditional 'sun-belt' of course, which is a more probable destination. But Croatia and Slovenia too could soon join this club of Mediterranean countries which welcome longer-term visitors as well as many tourists from Britain and northern Europe.

Central Europe in general is becoming more prosperous (much as Spain and Portugal, when they emerged from their years of dictatorship, also enjoyed a cultural and economic boom). Real estate prices in the cities are high; and city centres are being redeveloped, sometimes with little regard for their heritage and history. These Central European countries look the best bet for those who would prefer a lifestyle and a location which is 'closer to home' and where there is the least sense of cultural difference, although this is sometimes greater than people expect. This is where most Britons and Americans, who may have married a resident of these countries, or be working for an international or local company, will end up. The closer economic ties, with the entry of Poland, the Czech Republic, Hungary, Slovenia and also Estonia into the EU in 2002 or shortly thereafter, are also strong factors which favour these countries. The strong historical links between Britain and Poland in particular are also a positive factor, making this a popular and welcoming country for citizens of the UK to move to, as it is for Americans who have their own ethnic ties with many Central and Eastern European countries – the 'CEE', which is shorthand for Central and Eastern Europe, and not a political grouping as such, like the 'CIS', the Commonwealth of Independent States.

As a general rule, conditions become more difficult the further east you go. Historically and culturally, too, these are more remote locations where the way of life will be most different. But the transition to democracy and/or capitalism – which has gone much further in some countries than others – will also provide useful openings for anyone considering developing business or commercial connections in CEE/CIS, or who are working in specialist fields like information technology, consultancy, manufacturing, the oil industry, and so on. In Russia in particular, but latterly also in Azerbaijan – which is currently experiencing the same kind of invasion of western expatriates and businessmen – there are many opportunities where a commercial or technical skill will help; or in many countries more everyday forms of employment (notably English teaching) which will not make you a lot of money; but are a way of getting closer to the country and the people.

This boom also has its downside. It has already helped to make Moscow and St Petersburg two of the most expensive cities to live in in the world; and it is having a similar effect elsewhere. The stereotype of communism and bureaucracy still finds a very real expression in many countries: it is a state of mind as much as a system, and means that many locals are more afraid of doing something wrong than achieving something new. Also, there is a sharper dividing line here between the go-getters and the people who are just getting by, the real or aspiring *nouveaux riches* and others who are making their way up the ladder, and the ones who have been left behind. For many, their standard of living has hardly changed since the nineteen-eighties; and for many things have got worse. There is not the enthusiastic endorsement of all things western nowadays which many visitors found in the immediate aftermath of communism, when many countries were turning their back on Russia.

Things are more complex today, and many of the local people you meet will also now have had the opportunity to travel abroad, or even to live and work in western countries. This was the greatest culture shock of all which the collapse of the Berlin Wall (in 1989) and of the Soviet Union (in 1991) set in train. For many a kind of cynicism has set in about a life in the West which is not – as many had imagined – all about international jet-setting and an easier life (one new version of the old communist 'bright future') but a place where work also gets done and life can be difficult too. Preconceptions – in both directions – still abound, even as the previous Cold War division of Europe has broken down and a more ambiguous world order has emerged, or reemerged. And of course, relations between Britain and the West on the one hand, and Russia and the East on the other have always been more complex and many-sided than this black-and-white picture, and go much further back than the twentieth century, black propaganda and the Cold War.

There are longer histories which are being rediscovered throughout the CEE/CIS (which is not as artificial a geographical unit as it might seem, even today). In every country in this vast region there is a new or subtly different sense of nationhood, a nationalism which may be expressed violently (as in former Yugoslavia) and in a relation of rivalry with its neighbours; or much more peacfully, and in other, more inward-looking ways. In this way a whole new network of relationships between these newly independent nations has emerged, which somehow went underground or were suppressed under communism. Relations between Russia and the West may sometimes be difficult; but these are also being developed in new ways, no longer on the basis of ideology – as this was understood in the post-war period – which also ended in 1991 – but on ideas of culture and nationalism which have much deeper roots.

So, in Baku, capital of Azerbaijan, some of its more aged residents will remember the time when British troops came there, and the dilapidated mansions which housed the first wave of oil magnates and business tycoons still remain, as the new entrepreneurs are moving in. Everywhere in these countries which are today discovering their independence there is an eagerness to learn more about the time before the Iron Curtain came down, and what it means to be an Azerbaijani, or a Pole, or a Ukrainian; and so some of the international links which until recently had been suppressed – for example with emigré communities abroad – have also been rediscovered; and are making their contribution to an economy which now has to stand on its own feet. All this has created a generally positive climate in which to live and work there.

From the business point of view, these opportunities tend to decrease, at least in scale, where this tendency towards 'normalisation' is most pronounced, and some destinations will suit those of an entrepeneurial disposition more. This may be a good reason to move to Ukraine, or Lithuania for example. In fact some of the least developed countries in the region – in these comparative terms – may be where the greatest business opportunities lie. Others who prefer a more settled way of life may choose countries like Poland, Estonia or Slovenia which in their economic development are more like the West. There may be fewer business and trade opportunities in the Czech Republic for entrepeneurs than in its less economically advanced neighbour Slovakia for example; and a more difficult transition to a market economy is being made in countries like Slovakia which were more dependent on heavy industries and their centrally planned economies. But there may be more opportunities today to set up partnerships or joint-stock companies here, and for international capital to gain a greater (although a riskier) return.

From the point of view of finding employment, there are many more foreign residents in the former than the latter kind of country, and a higher standard of living in the Czech Republic, say, making this a much more attractive and more stable place for most to live and work than its eastern neighbour. Those thinking of living and working or doing business in any of these countries will have to weigh up the advantages and disadvantages like this – and then you should make a choice which is based on your interests – which may be cultural or economic, or more probably a mixture of several factors like these – of a country whose way of life and and cultural circumstances suit you most.

The potential for business and trade may be most important to you, or the language and the people. However you decide – or if this choice is forced upon you as it will be for many expatriates who have been posted there – you will certainly have to adapt to a different way of life and culture. If you are living, working or doing business in Russia or Eastern Europe – or anywhere in this CEE/CIS region – you should certainly approach your trip not with the feeling that you know everything before you go, but in a spirit of openness and with a readiness to meet new challenges and find out more.

Some of the advantages are listed below, in addition of course to your own personal motivation and experience which we suggest is most important. But it is as well also to be prepared for what you will find. One disadvantage is the bureaucracy which is legendary in Russia, and a legacy of communism almost everywhere – again there is often a scale from west to east, with Central Europe the least bureaucratic and most 'open' of the regions covered here. It can take up to six months to get a residence permit in many countries. Even if you speak the language you will often need an intermediary with local knowledge who can help you to make these kinds of arrangements. The luckier expatriates will find their company or organisation will do much of this background preparation work for them. But bureaucracy – and finding out how to deal with it – will be a problem for all those wishing to live and work in Russia and Eastern Europe.

These disadvantages have to be weighed against the local hospitality, which is traditionally more highly valued than in Britain or the United States. Then there are the advantages of discovering a new way of life and a different culture; the greater opportunities for work in many areas; and the many opportunities which will be open to those who return home with experience of living in the region. Then there is the food, the language, the culture... These are some of the many reasons to consider living and working in Russia and Eastern Europe, or to visit for a shorter time on a preparatory 'holiday'. Some other pros and cons are listed here.

Pros:

These are generally all extremely hospitable countries.

Apartments and property may be cheap to buy, especially outside the cities.

Services are developing in the cities popular with expatriates.

Central Europe is now catching up with its more sophisticated EU neighbours.

The unspoiled picturesque charm is one of the many attractions of the countryside. A distinctive local culture can be appealing.

Although prices, especially property and rental prices, have increased over the past few years, the cost of living generally is lower than in Western European countries.

New investment means there are now a wider range of international job opportunities, especially in Central Europe and Russia.

There are business opportunities in a wide variety of areas.

Tourism has meant that travel between Britain or the United States and most of these destinations is now a lot easier and less expensive.

Learning a new language will be an asset in future.

Cons:

Despite these opportunities, openings for foreigners in locally-run industries or businesses are often limited.
Housing conditions usually do not meet UK or US standards.
Rental prices, especially for foreigners, can be very high.
Wages locally are low compared with Britain or the United States.
Dealing with bureaucracy will be a test of forbearance and fortitude.
Especially in remoter regions, communications and transport facilities will be poor or non-existent.
The climate, even in the south, can be cold and extreme in winter.
Those expecting a luxurious lifestyle will find this way of living here to be very expensive.
Social life, especially family life, can also be closed and inward-looking.
Travelling around can be difficult; and crime is sometimes a problem.
Development, especially in Central Europe, is making these countries less distinctive and more like other 'western' countries.
Essential services like hospitals are often not up to UK or US standards and in some places non-existent.
Prices are rising fast, and imported goods are usually expensive.
English is not yet widely spoken, except by young people and in the business or tourism communities.

Here are also some do's and don'ts also for all those thinking of moving temporarily or permanently to Central and Eastern Europe and Russia, to do business or to live and work:

Do:

Show patience when dealing with bureaucracy.
Be adaptable, and try to recognise the strong points as well as the weak points of the local way of life.
Meet people from outside your own country or circle of business or work acquaintances.
Have a readiness to meet unexpected situations or events.

Don't:

Underestimate the difficulties of living in Russia and its neighbours.
Go there if your spouse or partner is unwilling to meet these challenges.
Expect to find suitable accommodation easily.
Go without suitable preparation and knowledge of the country.
Look always for differences between this country and your own.

Residence and Entry Regulations

The Current Position

The bureaucratic love of paperwork is strongly in evidence in all of these countries; and can exacerbate some of the painfully slow and plentiful demands involved in your application for a tourist, work or residence permit. Sometimes (as in the case of Russia) the issuing of visas has been made more complex as a matter of policy, in response to the perceived slights to its own citizens when they apply to enter Britain or the USA. Not only a work but also a residence permit will be required by those working there. Otherwise a business visa (or multi-entry visa if you are travelling around) will be most suitable if you are doing business; with a tourist visa perhaps the most convenient to apply for in the first instance as less paperwork will often be needed.

Applications should be made at the various government departments or the local town hall or police station as appropriate, with enquiries to be made beforehand to the relevant embassy or consulate (these are also listed for each country). Embassies will usually be able to make most of these arrangements before you go. Get a copy of the rules and regulations in English (if you can) from the embassy before you go. Their trade or commercial department will often be able to help, and supply further information about employment or business. British and American embassies in the country concerned, and their own commercial departments, are other useful sources of information.

Apart from a residence permit and a tax number, prospective residents will also require an identity card, which will usually by law be carried by all citizens as well as by foreigners resident in the country. Application forms for these should be available at your nearest Embassy or Consulate on the spot; and then you should submit these completed forms to the local council or city administration in good time (within 72 hours of arrival in some cases) which may then take its time processing them. Two or three trips may be required for you to get your residence visa, and that you go along with your visa sponsor. This is someone from the organisation or the private individual who gave you your letter of invitation.

Visas

British and American visitors will usually need a visa, but not for some countries like Poland and Estonia (see the relevant country chapter for details). Those entering a country where a visa is required should make their application to the nearest consulate of the country concerned. Short-term visits can usually be extended by up to six months by applying to the local equivalent of the Home Office or Ministry of the Interior and their visa registration office once you are in the country; branch offices can be found in some cities – there will certainly be an office in the capital – and the US or British Embassy will supply information. To renew your visa, you will also need your visa sponsor (the person or organisation which invited you) to write a letter requesting that you extend your stay; and remember if you are planning to extend your visit and you do need a visa that your passport must be stamped on entry so that the authorities will be able to determine the date of entry; and you may need other documents like currency declaration forms.

In Russia and its neighbours, the UK *Foreign and Commonwealth Office* advises that you declare all foreign currency and valuable items such as cameras, computers, jewellery etc. on arrival at customs and that you 'ensure that your visa is valid'. If it is not you will be at the mercy of the local border guards or police when you leave, who may see this as an opportunity to solicit a bribe – and probably anyway there will be some payment to be made if it is a question of leaving the country when your visa has expired. All of this may seem strange at first to people who have not travelled in the region before – or only across the more 'open' borders in some other parts of the world – and does not now apply in most of the Central European countries. It represents also the major barrier in many countries to the development of tourism; which is why an agreement between all the countries of the CIS and the EU, the United States, Japan and the other major trading areas of the world is needed which will facilitate both tourism and trade generally. Economic growth – if this continues in the next century – should favour the development of this kind of more equitable and open world order. But until then, this new global village – so far as travel and tourism are concerned – does not exist; and the rules remain.

What to do when faced with all this bureaucracy? The answer is to be as careful and punctilious as possible, and to follow all the rules and regulations with as good grace as you can. This will ease your crossing into the country – and expedite all your dealings with authority when you are in it. When faced with an over-zealous border guard the best way is not to complain and complain... but just to grin and bear it. This applies to many forms of authority and is what the locals have learnt to do. But when you do complain put your complaint forcefully and politely. Pulling rank – if you are a British or American citizen – and going to the front of the queue of hapless locals at the border crossing or wherever – is not unknown either. In any emergencies, your British or American Embassy – whose number or, better still, a business card you should always have – is there to help.

'Lost/expired visas in Russia can be replaced, but it is a lengthy and complex procedure and heavy fines can be levied,' the Foreign Office says, and: 'you will not be allowed to leave Russia without a visa.' Extending your visit can also require several visits to the visa registration office (known in Russia as the *UVIR*). This applies equally to all the Commonwealth of Independent States countries, which are Belarus, Moldova, Ukraine, Armenia, Azerbaijan, Georgia, Kazakstan, Kyrgyzstan, Tajikistan, Turkmenistan and Uzbekistan. If you have received a visa on the recommendation of a local sponsor, a private individual, hotel or business, the loss of your documents may also cause them problems as well, so keep duplicates, if you can, of everything.

Categories of Visa

There are basically three categories of visa so far as entering any country in the region is concerned (in those countries where a visa is needed of course, mainly across the CIS and South-Eastern Europe). If you have a reliable local contact who is prepared to join several queues on your behalf, you can request a private visa based on their invitation, and the fact that they are looking after you while you are there. If you are doing this, allow several months for the application to go through; it can take that long. A tourist visa can be organised through a travel agency or local approved hotel, and is usually quite easy to arrange. Hotels can do this, but this is where locally based travel agents or your own local or specialist travek agency come into their own and should be able to do this for you. But you can also do this yourself, by contacting and then visiting the relevant embassy – which in all these cases is what you should do first.

Many readers of this book will probably choose a business visa, based on a business invitation from a company; and the Foreign Ministry can grant this, based on your need to visit the country and the ability of your sponsoring organisation to look after you (it will have to be recognised by the local city council or national government). A single entry visa is valid for just one country, e.g. Russia. Then, if you are travelling throughout the former Soviet Union/CIS or to several countries, multiple entry visas are useful; and will allow you to cross several borders, and then retiurn home, without any further formalities. Allow at least a couple of months for this from the time when you make your application, although travel agencies can often expedite matters. Then, if you are travelling by land across a third country where visas are required (e.g. through Ukraine to Russia) or even stopping off at an airport there – and you do not have a suitable multi-entry visa – you will probably need a transit visa as well. Check on this with the embassy of the country or countries you are travelling through. It is worth emphasising what is also spelt out below, that the best time to make telephone enquiries or to visit the embassies of all these countries in in the morning, which is when visa departments are usually open.

Then there is your residence permit. Applying for this residence visa – as it is also sometimes known – directly from the UK or US can be time-consuming, but usually less so than if you wait until your arrival – and this is still the best way if you can do this – and make the decision to live and work there – well in advance. Others will have to do it on the spot. Britons and Americans will certainly need a residence visa or permit to get a work permit which you will also need if you are working – these are not the same thing. If possible, find someone already living there (a national or foreign resident) who is willing to act as your referee and help you through the procedure. You may also need some passport-sized photos, your passport (or copies of the relevant pages), proof that you have some kind of housing or accommodation which has been arranged, your letter of invitation or details of your local private or company sponsor (who may also have to provide a copy of their own registration certificate proving that they are registered if this is on behalf of a company); also a letter of 'authorisation' from your own company or employer saying or 'authorising' who you are, and that you work for them; some evidence of good financial standing (like your bank account or income details); and a medical certificate. We can see now the advantages of doing your preparation in advance! This, along with your fee – and stamped addressed envelope if you are doing this by post – is a general checklist for the kind of information you will have to provide for all visa applications, and everything you should need for a residence permit.

One tip when applying for your entry visa, by the way, is to make the dates of your visit begin a little earlier and end a little later than your actual intended visit. The dates are not exact ones but dates between which your visit is valid; and this will allow some leeway at both ends in case of any delays.

It is useful not to put off getting the residence visa until you have actually arrived, as you will avoid becoming embroiled in the local bureaucracy at this later stage; it is not unknown for British or American nationals to be forced to return to their own country to apply from there, or to travel to the nearest embassy of the country concerned in a neighbouring country to do this. Preparation in all aspects of your visa application – whether this be for tourism (usually the simplest way to enter the country), for business (this visa is usually more expensive), or for residence – is the key; and doing this as far as possible in advance. Last-minute or express applications tend to cost more. The Foreign and Commonwealth Office presently advises against all travel to Albania, the Chechen Republic (in the Russian Federation), and Tajikistan, and only recommends travel on essential business to Bosnia and Herzegovina.

Health and Safety

For medical and innoculation advice (it will do no harm at all if you have a vaccination certificate) you should contact your doctor/GP. Up to date FCO travel advice for Britons is displayed on BBC2 (Ceefax, p.470 onwards) and can be accessed at the Internet address http://www.fco.gov.uk/:

Foreign Office Travel Advice Unit, Consular Division, FCO, 1 Palace Street, London SW1E 5HE; tel 0171-238 4503/4; fax 0171-238 4545.

The FCO produces a number of leaflets, including *British Consular Services Abroad, Checklist for Travellers, International Road Haulage, Backpackers and Independent Travellers, Do's and Don'ts in Russia* and *Do's and Don'ts in Eastern Europe,* available from the address above.

Applying for a Residence Permit

Once safely there, those who have not already made their residence permit arrangements and intend to live and work in the country should apply as soon as possible, and preferably immediately, to the local police/town hall/ministry for the application form for the document which confers residence status on the holder. This period may be as little as three days or as long as a month. You are advised to contact your local embassy or consulate first, which will be able to give advice; and you should register your presence in the country with them as well. The best way for UK citizens to apply for this is first to go to the local British Consulate. For a small fee they will certify in a letter that you are a British citizen, or supply any documents you need, and if you have no prison record certify that this is the case, and so on.

Next, take your passport, the consular certificate, some passport photos, a copy of your most recent bank statement, and all the invitations and other documents required – included a declaration which you should make as to your anticipated earnings for tax purposes – to the ministry or visa administration. They may process the residence permit in just a few days, although it will probably take longer. This is often a card bearing the applicant's photograph and signature (and sometimes thumbprint) which must be carried with the holder at all times for possible inspection. The consular authorities warn that foreigners may also have to apply for yet another identity card after six months of residence, which must be presented to the police on demand.

For visitors, of course, carrying a stamped passport containing the correct visa stamps will do just as well: you are advised to carry a copy not the original with you for these general ID purposes. The police or militia may however give you 12 hours to produce your real ID card or passport at the police station if you do not have it to hand and if they suspect you are living in the country illegally for example; and may detain anyone who does not have this card or suitable ID on them indefinitely, or until they can get hold of this. On all these occasions, the more documents you have of an official-looking kind, letters of invitation, or even the business card of the local British/US ambassador or some other notable local worthy – all this may expedite your dealings with officialdom. As soon as you arrive, the FCO advises, you should 'jot down the address and telephone number of the local British Embassy,' and keep this with you. Their opening hours 'tend to follow the local pattern.' Full medical cover and 'being security conscious' are important too, they say.

When the time comes to renew your residence card you will need to give proof that you can support yourself for the coming year, e.g. current bank statements showing a regular income, or a letter from your employer. After following this process for a number of years, residents may become entitled to a longer-term, five or ten-year permit, which means you have more or less become a permanent resident of the country.

Work Permits

These are required by all British, European Union and American citizens not otherwise entitled to work, for example by marriage to work in these non-European Union countries (which will change as some become members of the EU, making life easier for Britons and usually more difficult for Americans). Otherwise, anyone planning to work for a temporary period of less than one month is often not required to have a work permit as such, but must gain a suitable written consent from the Ministry of Labour or equivalent in the area in which he or she wishes to work. This kind of temporary work is usually covered by a business visa if you are not permanently resident in the country. The UK or US Embassy will often be able to provide contact for these offices or the relevant ministry for anyone who has difficulty in locating where to obtain this permission and can supply lists of local lawyers etc.

Others who intend to work on a long-term basis will need their work permit. For this they must be able to present proof of having a job, e.g. a contract of employment from the prospective employer and the approval of the Ministry of Labour, as well as the range of other documents mentioned above under *Applying for a Residence Permit*. Similarly to Britain or the United States, this procedure can be long and laborious for foreigners (although none of the countries mentioned in this book has an equivalent of the Green Card lottery for those wishing to work in the United States). Applications are made to your nearest consulate at the same time as the request for the initial residence visa: the contract of employment will be sent to the local employer, who must then submit this usually to the Ministry of Labour for approval. The entire procedure is likely to take a few months; and so preparations should be made well in advance. On the spot, you should enquire at your local British or American Embassy first.

Although some more reckless travellers who only want to work in Russia or its neighbours temporarily, go there first, find a job, and then apply for the work permit later, this is not recommended. Perhaps this works better if you are closer to home – that is to say in a more sympathetic country which does not require a visa to enter in the first place, like Poland or Estonia. Applications for work permits in Russia and throughout the former Soviet Union tend to be fraught with a great many more difficulties; and a labour market which is actually badly in need of the expertise which Britons or Americans can bring it is still quite difficult to enter. Basically, the local authorities must be convinced that the job for which you are applying could not be done equally well by a national of that country; and this decision will depend heavily on a variety of factors, including the amount of unemployment (often high) in the particular area. Furthermore, in some countries, employers are restricted by law as to the number of foreign nationals they can employ.

Entering to Start a Business

A special permit in addition to your residence permit will often be required by those entering to set up their own business. Perhaps a business visa will be enough in some cases, and the best way to go about it; but professionals going there to work (e.g. doctors and lawyers) must first have their qualifications checked by the relevant professional body, which will grant permission to practise based on the authenticity of these qualifications and whether they are considered equivalent to the local ones. Although a work permit as such is usually not needed by the self-employed, many of those who fall within this group will be have to obtain a licence before setting up a business, just as the locals do. They will usually have to do this with a local partner, often in the form of a joint-venture company, and be careful about starting a small business in some countries where crime is rife.

Entering with Retirement Status

Anyone who intends to retire to this region will have to provide pension details and proof that they have sufficient funds with which to support themselves without working there. This information must be provided when applying in the UK for your residence authorisation and is certainly better organised from the UK (or USA) before departure.

Identity Cards

These are a way of life in all these countries (as in the rest of continental Europe) where even today an internal passport as well as an international passport is often required by residents too; and previously official permission was needed even to leave their local area. A British or American passport will normally be enough in most of your dealings with officials – who will often assume that you are simply a tourist – but one of these ID card is useful for you too. It entitles the holder to apply for a local driving licence, for instance, and can be used in lieu of a passport when registering at hotels and for identification purposes, even for travel within the CIS countries and elsewhere, making your life easier and sometimes cheaper, as you may be able to pay for some local items at local rates. Applications and enquiries should be made, as in all these matters, to the local British or US consulate first.

You will need to produce your passport, a few photos, and the residence card, as listed generally above. Once you have completed the application form (available from the Consulate) take this, along with the above mentioned documents, to the the local city or district council. It will be their responsibilty to certify the authenticity of your address and to stamp the card, which will take anything between one day and one month to process.

Tax Numbers

A tax number is essential for work, to do business, or to buy anything substantial in Russia and its neighbours. Everywhere, the tax system has been or is being completely revised and brought more into line with the British or European systems, in employment as in other areas. On arrival in Russia, for example, an individual has 30 days to register with the Tax Authority if he or she is working there; and usually a tax return also needs to be submitted within 30 days during your first year of residence. Generally, taxation tends to be individual, with few allowances for married couples, and you will need to complete all the relevant formalities if you wish to buy anything like a house, land, or a car. The relevant permit is available to tourists or residents on presentation of a current valid passport at the local tax office. You will be given a temporary fiscal number which will be replaced by a permanent number and card after a few months. The fiscal number will then appear on all your tax returns and on any formal documentation involved in the buying or selling of property or on any business transactions.

On Arrival

Remember to register your name and address at the local British or American Consulate or Embassy as soon as you arrive. Once a UK/US national has obtained a residence permit, he or she is entitled to the same rights as a national of the country concerned, with the exception that he or she is not allowed to vote in local elections – but will retain this right at home. UK nationals living abroad still retain the right to vote in UK elections and remain British citizens, even though they are resident in a foreign country. The same applies if you are from the United States, of course, r any other country, and the embassy will supply information about maintaining this right and voter registration etc., and local political organisations (f there are any!), as well as churches, societies and clubs and so on for expatriates, and will have information about your various rights and responsibilities as a resident, businessperson or worker in the country concerned. They should certainly be contacted near the beginning of your stay.

If at any time you decide to leave the country permanently, then simply lodge your residence card at the local police station or at the same local city or regional administration office – address available from the embassy – which you visited when you arrived.

Embassies and Consulates

The relevant embassy and consular addresses in Britain and the USA are included under *Useful Addresses* in the various country chapters which follow this *General Overview*. These embassies and consulates can advise on all aspects of tourist, business and residence visas, work permits and preferences in granting these permits, and so on. In all of these dealings a reliable local contact, usually your visa sponsor, can be an invaluable source of help and advice; and may be the best person to approach the visa registration authorities on your behalf.

But your Embassy or Consulate will be used to dealing with the kinds of problems which arise for visitors and residents – and can deal with many of them as well. In an emergency they can help with your repatriation. This should be your first port of call in your contacts with offialdom.

Preparation and Arrival

Living there may not be as hard as it seems – especially if you have some experience of the region, or have lived abroad before. But when you go there to live, there are some practical matters you need to be aware of – which are covered here, and for many of the individual countries in subsequent sections of this book. You will find for each country an impression and some practical advice regarding residence, and entry, and daily life in all these varied and fascinating places. Travel experience is a major plus; and see some of the *Personal Experiences* which are *Appendices I, II and III* to this book as well. This is really how it is to live and work in these Central and Eastern European and Former Soviet Union destinations, from the point of view of other travellers who already done this, and have their own advice to offer.

These longer-term visitors – including you, the readers of this book – are sometimes lumped together under the category of business travellers, but include many on assignment or living more permanently there. They need more than the image of an intrepid traveller, setting off with little more than a spirit of adventure, and half a squash ball to plug the sinks, weighed down by essential supplies – and the cans of baked beans which at least one correspondent to our publication still recommends – along with all the other appertenances of adventurous travel in the Former Soviet Union – as recommended in Eric Newby's intrepid *Big Red Train Ride* among other travel stories.

It is not like this today; and this is an image which most business travellers in the Commonwealth of Independent States simply will not recognise, as they are whisked from the chaos of the airport in hire cars or limousines to their chandeliered hotel (and these can be some of the most expensive in the world). Service with a smile has come for those who can afford it in all these places; and there are other surprises, in Moscow and beyond: the international restaurants, shopping malls, lively night life, museums to visit, impressive metro, and always at least an adequate local transport system with trams and trolleybuses; as well as streets clogged with traffic, a haze of pollution sometimes, and all the more unwelcome signs of modern life.

There are down-and-outs and beggars in Moscow today, but not so many as on the streets of Washington or London today – not that there is no poverty here, but the police regularly round up drunks and vagrants. In any case in winter many will die. All the advertising hoardings seem to make one statement: that it is better to have money, and to buy, that life is for living now, that consumerism is here to stay and the old order is gone. In city centres, there are some impressive modern buildings, too, alongside the Soviet-era architecture and drab housing estates.

Visitors will find something like this throughout the former Soviet Union, and also its neighbours to the west. The shopping streets of Prague and Budapest are like those of any European city. Some of the other capitals – like Zagreb or Ljubljana – are still quieter; but the signs of investment, in building work and redevelopment, are much in evidence everywhere. Other cities, like Minsk or Kiev exist in a kind of twilit world between the old and the new, and there is less in the way of attractive old architecture or new hotels.

There are some sights to see; and a daytime tour through the city will be one way to get your bearings. There are islands of the past in a sea of uniformity, and you will find an Old Town in many places like the one in Tallinn, where the pre-communist buildings have been preserved through long years of oppression, war and redevelopment programmes (not unlike those in Britain in the fifties or sixties). Many of these private houses are now being refurbished. In Warsaw, where the Royal Palace was destroyed during the last war, this building has even been rebuilt, brick by brick, according to what remains of the original plans, and sometimes an illusion has been created like this of an old quarter, in cities which were almost entirely destroyed by earlier conflicts or by communism.

The same thing has happened in many places, a kind of vogue for reconstruction which was also a part of communism, an ethos which is expressed in Soviet-style museums of the countryside recreating peasant villages, in dance and folklore, or an idyllic version of history – which find an echo in our own Disneylands which idealise a fictional past. Some of the socialist-realist art also looked forward to a brighter future – the difference being that these communist theme parks are now falling apart. And so the illusion was created of a national identity which was prospering under Soviet or Russian rule.

Almost everywhere this pattern has been the same. What was truly old or old-fashioned has been destroyed; and what was kept was changed or recreated. Only the churches are an exception, going back much further in time, and are beacons of an older spirituality which many of the locals are rediscovering. These have somehow managed to survive unscathed – sometimes as museums – and are once again serving their original purpose. Other signs of cultural identity are also being rediscovered, and a history which is much more complicated than the struggle between capitalism and communism.

Much of what is going on now looks forward and not back: a kind of rejection of the past which finds its purest expression in the phrase 'business is business'. Mobile phones are everywhere – and are often the most reliable way to get in touch with colleages when local telephone services can be unreliable – but cardphones have also come to Central Europe, and many of the big cities. Faxes and computers are on sale, often at exorbitant prices. And there are the trams with brightly painted advertising – for Coca-Cola or the BBC – as well as crowded trolleybuses, apartment blocks with their array of satellite dishes, tree-lined squares (usually without their statue of Lenin) and domed churches.

The major cities in Russia and Eastern Europe can offer the international jet-setting lifestyle which can be found in many other countries around the world, but it can be a shock to go into the countryside or the suburbs, where life has a different pattern and seems to carry on much as before. Everywhere, living conditions can be difficult. Often there is a striking contrast between this apparent poverty in town and country – and the more affluent urban lifestyle. For some visitors from perhaps more modest backgrounds in the West the greatest culture shock can be to meet this world of ostentatious consumption and wealth for the first time. But bringing that half-a-squash ball is probably still a good idea.

These are all aspects of the astonishing transformation which has taken place over the last ten years: from a kind of generalised poverty, for nearly everyone, to extreme wealth, but only for some. We come to the world of the 'new Russians' – stereotyped once again as a band of mafiosi and criminals – 'gangster capitalism' as it has been called – and a main subject of British newspapers when they deal with Russia and its neighbours, as it is a topic of many a hushed conversation among expatriates there. Alongside the pauperisation which is probably the longest-lasting effect of communism, and which exists side-by-side with this reversion to Tsarist excess, this is the greatest contradiction of life in Russia post-1991.

Most will only glimpse these troubles from afar. But again, this is a strong image in our minds of life in Eastern Europe, of a dark and somehow sombre place where there are spies and secret assignations, like the setting for some latter-day Eric Ambler novel and other spy fictions; along with the more modern television reports on orphanages in Romania or Albania, or the wars in Bosnia and Chechnya... But these selective images will certainly not be enough to prepare anyone for the complexities and contradictions of life in Warsaw or Budapest, Moscow or St Petersburg today.

Poles and Czechs will already be bristling with indignation to read this conflation of their life in the rest of Central and Eastern Europe with this half-sketch of modern Russian life. This is another incomplete picture perhaps, and this difference between Central and Eastern Europe is also very important. Life is certainly not the same in Russia as it is in Poland, say, or even the Baltic States. We can round off this brief introduction with the consideration that life in Central Europe, and some other countries like Slovenia or Croatia, is increasingly not so very different from our own.

Still, there is a truth to this feeling of 'eastern' adventure and opportunity. People are living dangerously in Russia and its neighbours, and living life to the full. There is money to be made, and in the aftermath of the Soviet Union many made their fortunes in illegal or semi-legal ways, using the power and connections they already had under the previous dispensation. This something which it is as well to be prepared for, but one which can cause perhaps the greatest misunderstanding when it comes to visiting these countries of Central and Eastern Europe and Former Soviet Union: crime.

Crime

No, business is not all in the hands of the mafia; and this assumption, which some might bring to a trip to Italy, say, or Colombia, will not aid you in your business activities here either. But as these are all formerly communist countries where business – until the late 1980s at least – was itself an entirely illegal activity, inevitably this developed without some of the legal checks and balances which exist in the West.

In one way, small businesses started on a small scale as people needed to buy and sell things simply to survive – a kind of car-boot economy – meaning the buying and selling of personal possessions, second-hand trinkets or clothes, or keeping valuables like gold stored away for a rainy day. On a larger scale, business people could be jailed for starting an enterprise like this – this was the prerogative of the state – or for importing and exporting goods illegally – and so on – all crimes under communism but entirely legitimate fields of activity today. This was 'economic crime' so called, and this was how many quite legitimate businesses originally got off the ground. People went to prison for it; and in the minds of many Russians even today there exists a strong association between capitalism and criminality: the legacy of decades of propaganda and economic mismanagement, when property really was theft.

This is not just all an invention of the West. And if doing business really makes people feel as if they are doing something illegal and illicit, many will often begin to behave in a criminal fashion as well. Russia was never quite the homogenous and orderly society it pretended to be, even in Soviet times. The nearest parallel could be with America during the time of the Great Depression – which had a parallel and deep effect on the development of the American identity. (The nearest time in British history is probably the seventeenth-century English Civil War). The result in modern Russia, according to some, was the creation of a kind of

'Soviet' mentality (*homo sovieticus* the writer Alexander Zinoviev called this mainly Russian phenomenon) which itself was slightly criminal...

This ethic has transmuted or simplified in recent years – with the sudden arrival of capitalism – into an idea of getting rich quick, or at any cost. Perhaps communism and 'gangster capitalism' are both two sides of the same coin. But – however it started – from the point of view of readers of this book – this small minority of Russian mafiosi and small-time criminals – who have their counterparts in many Eastern European countries – is best avoided if you can.

Special caution is required when you are travelling to do business in Russia, the CIS, and much of Eastern Europe where your business partners are not established and widely known to be reputable, or well-known personally to you. Caution is needed when you make a business contact for the first time. The important point for anyone doing business there – is to establish a respectable track record in your opposite number, and some evidence of personal integrity – and your Russian business partners will also be seeking signs of this in you; and your integrity and standing should be important to them as well.

What is the best test of this integrity, that someone you are dealing with is above board? Transparency and openness are good signs; and many organisations exist to run checks on this for you; these can be tests of the legitimacy or otherwise of the person concerned, plus other knowledge acquired 'through the grapevine' confirming that their reputation checks out at least. Sometimes personal knowledge through a friend of friends who will vouch for their honesty can be better than a company search and any amount of documentation. Be alert to what seems to you to be suspicious behaviour, as instinct can be a good guide too. When you think about it, everyone doing business in Russia and former Soviet Union, and to a lesser extent in some of these other countries, needs to be working for a large organisation to back them up, or to have an entirely reliable local contact or friend who they know is 'on their side'. It is easy to see how this general atmosphere – which is still, to a certain extent, one of mistrust – can shade into criminality.

For a brief check-list of advice, also see the *Business Risk Avoidance in Eastern Europe* booklet published by *Lufthansa* (Lufthansa Eastern Europe, FREEPOST CL 2075, Fenton Way, Basilson, Essex SS15 5BR) and some of the other publications referred to in the chapter which follows this one.

Personal Safety

The Foreign Office (FCO) in Britain offers advice to travellers and has a special line to call (tel 0171-238 4503) which warns of everything from petty theft around railway stations, for example in Budapest which it identifies as a blackspot, and more general problems in Albania or Chechnya. There is a great difference of degree in these two scenarios. Hungary is an enjoyable and safe country to visit. Albania (at present) is not, and you should use your common sense in some of these matters.

In general, you should keep all your valuables out of sight, and avoid carrying branded luggage or camera bags for example. Travellers may 'dress down' if they wish and try to avoid being identified as a rich foreign visitor in this way – although in many of the towns and cities of Eastern Europe there is another approach. and everywhere you go you will find locals who are well-dressed – in suits or designer gear – so you will not stand out if you try to emulate them, and are wearing a suit, shirt and tie or smart clothes.

According to Julie Broom of *British Airways Holidays*, 'any unusual offer of help should be treated with suspicion.' (This might apply to your business dealings too). Many pickpockets use the tried and tested tricks (known in Dickensian London) of distracting your attention while a partner rifles your pockets while an accomplice strikes. 'Stay calm,' if you have to deal with any unusual situations like this. 'Figures of apparent authority' also cannot always be trusted, according to the *FCO*. In many of these countries, the policeman you may mistrust the most is the helpful, friendly one; and vice versa. The FCO warns visitors to the Czech Republic to 'beware of bogus plain-clothes policemen who may ask to see your foreign currency and passport.' Some gullible tourists have handed over money to these strangers never to see it again.

'If approached, decline to show your money but instead offer to go to the nearest police-station,' they advise. Money-belts are probably a good idea – but be prepared to hand over even these if you are the victim of a mugging. Some visitors find some other, less conspicuous way to conceal the cash they carry with them. Also, handbags are noticeable, carrier bags are not – and quite difficult to get hold of there so take some with you. Travelling with a suitcase will make you stand out less than if you have a backpack; and one good way to remain unnoticed in some places is simply not to talk too much in English, or to be too loud or overbearing in your behaviour.

Generally speaking, you should have a neat appearance not too dissimilar from that of the locals; and even if you look like a foreigner in Russia, there are so many nationalities here, from Volga Germans to Estonians to Afghan or Nigerian students and so on, that most people going there will look like someone who lives there, and need not stand out too much.

Beware of airport and bus terminals, railways stations, and crowds. This is where the local pickpockets and other small-time criminals hang out. Be alert at all times when you are out and about, and carry an amount of money with you you can afford to lose. Avoid changing your money in the street – and thus participating in the one trade that is definitiely run by the mafia – but rather go to the many exchange kiosks, or a bank. These are plentiful, and usually charge less than in Britain or the United States, making it worthwhile for you to keep most of your money in pounds, or more usually in dollars. At the airport – or coach terminal if you are arriving on a budget – make sure you have somebody to meet you, or that there is a car or hire car waiting, anywhere further east than the Central European countries; or at the very least that you know there is an airport bus service (maybe it doesn't run at night). You should have made arrangements for accommodation in advance if you are arriving for the first time.

Getting There

Information on airlines, coach and rail travel, car hire and travel agencies and some agencies which specialise in each of the countries mentioned in this book are covered in each of the individual country chapters. Many have their own national tourist offices which are an invaluable resource for all visitors and should be contacted as well for general background information on travel there. Some useful general publications are: *Advice and Information for the Business Traveller to the Russian Federation and C.I.S. Countries* published by *Worldmark* (tel 0171-799 2307); the longer and more detailed book *Russia Survival Guide* by Paul E. Richardson (Russian Information Services, 89 Main Street, Suite 2, Montpelier, VT 05602, USA; tel 802-223-4955; fax 802-223-6105; e-mail 73244.3372@compuserve.com; http://www.friends-partners.org/rispubs/) published in the United States but also available in Britain; Lufthansa's *Go East* guide (available from the airline) and their *Information Services Eastern Europe* series of booklets on the Eastern European destinations and travel.

Also useful are the general brochure entitled *Independent Traveller into Russia and Beyond* from Intourist (219 Marsh Wall, London E14 9PD; tel 0171-538 5965; fax 0171-538 5967); the *City Breaks* brochure available from the Central Europe specialist *Fregata Travel* (13 Regent Street, London SW1Y 4LR; tel 0171-451 7000; fax 0171-451 7017; 117A Withington Rd, Manchester M16 8EE; tel 0161-226 7227; fax 0161-226 0700); and a variety of other brochures and information available from travel agents, airlines and tourist offices which you may wish to contact. National tourist offices will be able to refer on any enquiries you have about residency or business which they cannot deal with themselves.

Transport

In a recent survey for *Lufthansa*, a staggering 92% of business travellers to Eastern European destinations suggested that transport services were deficient or should be improved. Nearly half (45%) agreed with the proposition that there were few airline choices and 61% said they felt they needed to be met at the airport by a local representative rather than taking a taxi (52%) or hiring a car (10%). Of those that did take a taxi, nearly two thirds (64%) said they were overcharged, with travellers at this end of the market resolutely avoiding the use of local buses (46% said they had never used them). The most frequent destination for business travellers from Britain to the region was Poland (49%) followed by Hungary (44%) and the Russian Federation (41%). Those that hired a car to get around were 'happy driving in different surroundings;' but 42% 'encountered bad road conditions;' and only a few (19%) 'would choose to drive in the city.'

Sources of Information

Lufthansa publishes a general map of the *New Markets of Eastern Europe and Asia* (which can also be obtained by subscribers to *New Markets Monthly* – see below) and business travellers, and long-term residents should also consult the local English-language press, details of which follow in the chapters for each country; as well as the more general guide-books and independent travel books which are available. Get a list in advance of expatriate contacts and clubs from the local UK or US Embassy if you can. Travel articles appear from time to time in the UK 'quality' press and Sunday newspapers with occasional destination reports for the more popular destinations like Prague or Budapest.

New Markets Travel is a supplement aimed at both the business and general traveller published by *New Markets Monthly* (tel 0171-628 4442; fax 0171-628 4443). *The European* (in its news pages), *The Financial Times*, and especially *The Wall Street Journal* cover news and financial matters but also travel for business or more generally to Eastern European destinations.

Airlines, Car Hire, Coaches and Trains
See the country chapters which follow. The advertising sections of the daily and Sunday newspapers devoted to travel, and magazines like *TNT* (distributed free in London, or contact 14-15 Child's Place, Earls Court, London SW5 9RK; tel 0171-373 3377; fax 0171-373 9457; e-mail enquiries @gtntmag.co.uk), as well as *New Markets Monthly* (address below), all contain details of airlines and special offers for Russia and its neighbours.

Travel to Central Europe and Moscow has become much cheaper in recent years; and the many airlines can be contacted direct. In the individual country chapters there are also some details of car hire, coaches, trains and travel agencies, and also see the *Car Rentals* section below for car hire contacts in many East European countries.

Preparation

The Centre for International Briefing: Farnham Castle, Farnham, Surrey GU9 0AG, tel 01252-721194, fax 01252-719277, e-mail cibfarnham@dial.pipex.com, Web-site at www.cibfarnham.com – provides fully residential scheduled and customised briefings for all countries in the world to prepare executives and their families to live and work overseas and for those coming to live and work in Britain. Customised business overview briefings are also available for frequent business travellers and home-based international managers. Each programme provides in-depth information on country background including politics, economics and social issues. Current advice on the business and working environment, as well as the practical aspects of living in the destination country is provided by recently returned expatriates and those with current business interests in the specific region or country, with the opportunity to develop negotiation and communications skills for more challenging locations. Intensive tuition for all major world languages is also available at every level.

The Centre for Professional Employment Counselling (CEPEC): Lilly House, 13 Hanover Square, London W1R 9HD, tel 0171-629 2266, fax 0171-629 7066 – provides a careers counselling and resettlement service for corporate-sponsored professional expatriates returning to the UK. Their counselling service covers career, personal and financial matters to determine the client's career direction and options. Enquiries to the Client Services Manager. It is a useful contact, also, for employment agencies and search consultancies. These are listed in the *CEPEC Recruitment Guide*; and many have dealings with Eastern Europe.

Corona Worldwide (The Women's Corona Society): The Commonwealth Institute, Kensington High Street, London W8 6NQ, tel 0171-610 4407, fax 0171-602 7374 – is a voluntary organisation with branches in the UK and overseas (including Eastern Europe) which provides, among other services, either postal or personal briefings for women and men about to live or work abroad. The postal briefing is in the form of a series of booklets containing all the practical and domestic details needed to prepare for setting up home in a new country, including climate, clothing, educational and medical facilities, housing, household requirements, food, leisure activities etc. Publications includes this 'Notes for Newcomers' series (£5) and 'Living in a Muslim Country'. The society also runs day-long or telephone briefings on how to adapt to a new lifestyle and culture; and write for details of their many other services. Their annual magazine lists contacts and addresses, as well as some reports from people who are already working abroad.

Expatriate Management Ltd: St Clements House, 2 St Clements Lane, London EC4N 7AP, tel/fax 0171-280 7732 – handles the administration of expatriate employees for companies, but also organises orientation and training courses. Prospective expatriates should enquire about a briefing.

Going Places, 84 Coombe Road, New Malden, Surrey KT3 4QS, tel 0181-949 8811, fax 0181-949 6237 – was formerly part of 'Employment Conditions Abroad' (and is not connected to the travel agency of the same name); it provides half-day, one-day, and two-day training courses for individuals, couples and company delegates, varying from country to country and meeting specific requirements. The cost is around £1,000 for a one-day course.

Returned Volunteer Action: 1 Amwell Street, London EC1R 1UL – does not send people to work abroad but does give advice and information to those considering working overseas, mainly to volunteers and charity workers. It is an independent organisation of those who have worked abroad on project workers or as volunteers in development projects; and aims to ensure that the experience of volunteers is put to good use after their return, both through contacts with British community groups and through feedback to overseas development agencies.

Liberty International (UK) Ltd: 11 Grosvenor Street, Chester CH1 2DD, tel 01244-351115, fax 01244-351116, e-mail liberty@chester.itsnet.co.uk, http://www.itsnet.co.uk/grouptravel/liberty – offers full destination management services, including conference and meeting organisation, hotel reservations, excursions, guides and tour services, study tours and special interest groups in the Baltic States, Russia, Bulgaria, Romania, the Czech Republic, Hungary and Poland.

Moores Rowland Chartered Accountants: Clifford's Inn, Fetter Lane, London EC4 1AS, tel 0171-831 2345, fax 0171-831 6123 – provides a range of services for expatriates including executive briefings, pre-assignment planning, tax compliance, remuneration, tax, social security and other issues.

Overseas Business Travel Ltd: 8 Minories, London EC3N 1BJ, tel 0171-702 2468, fax 0171-488 1199 – is a company which offers a visa service, discounted air fares and special hotel rates in the region.

Overseas Business Travel Ltd

In London
- Unrivalled experience in business travel
- Specialists with Romania, Bulgaria, Russia and All East European Countries
- Special Deals on flights and accommodation
- Visa service and visa support
- Russian and Bulgarian native speakers

In Moscow and Almaty
- Provides Internal CIS travel
- Hotel Bookings – Invitations
- Airport Transfers – Car and Driver
- Full office facilities
- Interpreters and translators

Head Office: 8 Minories, London EC3N 1BJ **Tel:** 0171-702 2468 **Fax:** 0171-488 1199 e-mail: OBUSTRA1@AOL.COM
Moscow office:
125047 Moscow, Triumphalnaya Square, 2 Tverskaya Jamskaya Dom 6, Russia, CIS
Tel: +7 095 250 22 31 Fax: +7 095 250 22 64
Almaty Representative: Daribai Kamzoldaev Tel/Fax: +7 3272 222615

IATA

The Russia House Ltd: 37 Kingly Court, Kingly Street, London W1R 5LE, tel 0171-439 1271, fax 0171-434 0813 – organises visa procuration, travel, and exhibitions, trade meetings and seminars, with many other services for Russia and its neighbours, and has offices in London, Edinburgh, New York, Stockholm, Hong Kong, Brussels (from September 1998), Moscow, St. Petersburg and Tbilisi.

Also see the invaluable (but also expensive at £250) *Price Waterhouse* publication *Managing Expatriates in the CIS* containing a survey of expatriates already living in the CIS countries and useful background information ranging from accommodation to tax matters (for Russia, Azerbaijan, Kazakhstan, Ukraine and Uzbekistan – Price Waterhouse International Assignment Services Europe, Southwark Towers, 32 London Bridge Street, London SE1 9SY; tel 0171-939

3000; fax 0171-378 0647). They also have an International Assignment Services department for Russia.

English Contacts Abroad, PO Box 126, Oxford OX2 6UB – also offers a background research and reports service for businesses, expatriates and individual business people interested in living and working in the CEE/CIS region.

The *Centre for International Briefing* (see above) organises two-day briefings for companies and their staff for a range of Central and Eastern European and former Soviet Union countries including a country profile, language and communication, living conditions, the business and working environment and so on, for both 'new and experienced expatriates'.

With a range of background information like this, business travellers and expatriates can travel to Central and Eastern Europe with some knowledge of the working and living conditions which await them.

Multi-Trip Insurance

For frequent business or other travellers there are many European (usually covering Europe west of the Urals) and worldwide multi-trip insurance packages available. Ask whether the company has local representatives, or a single number to contact; and of course check the various exclusions which are listed in the various leaflets. Ask how does the policy works in Russia and Eastern Europe. Is hospital treatment local, or are those requiring assistance are flown home?

BUPA TravelCover: PO Box 2878, Russell Mews, Brighton BN1 2NZ; tel 01273 866150; fax 01273-866191; or tel 0990-858585. See above. *BUPA* also offer international health insurance – see the following chapter for details.

Club Direct Insurance Services Ltd: Dominican House, St. John's Street, Chichester, West Sussex PO19 1TU; tel 01243-817766 or 01243-787838.

Hamilton Barr Insurance Brokers Ltd: Hamilton Barr House, Bridge Mews, Bridge Street, Godalming, Surrey GU17 1HZ; tel 01483-426600.

Interzug Leisure Ltd: Sanford House, 37 Medwin Walk, Horsham, West Sussex RH12 1AG; tel 01403-270463; fax 01403-270465.

Journeys Travel Insurance: Majestic House, 122-132 High Street, Staines, Middlesex TW18 4DA; tel 01784-457657; fax 01784-460440.

Wexas International: FREEPOST, London SW3 1BR; tel 0171-589 3315; fax 0171-589 8418. Ask for their multi-trip annual traveller insurance leaflet.

Worldcover Direct: PO Box 555, Cardiff CF5 6XH; tel 01222-675121; fax 01222-6751431; e-mail headoffice@worldcover.co.uk; http://www.worldcover.com). Up to 93 days cover per trip.

Gap-year students (and anyone up to the age of 39) may contact *Inter Assurance Ltd.*, The Courtyard, 16 West Street, Farnham, Surrey GU9 7DR, tel 01252-747747 fax 01252-717788, about its Options extended stay policy for those taking trips of between four months and one year. Their free 'concierge service' allows messages to be relayed home and offers other assistance.

BUPA TravelCover International Travel Insurance, PO Box 2878, Russell Mews, Brighton BN1 2NZ, tel 01273 866150, fax 01273-866191, is 'specially designed for residents of all countries outside the UK, USA and Canada' and thus may be very suitable for readers of this book. You can request a booklet from the address above. Finally, for those considering renting out their UK property while on assignment abroad, getting the right insurance for your home here is one point to consider. *ABG Schemes Ltd.*, Companies House, Briton Street, Bampton, Devon EX16 9LN, tel 01398-331061; fax 01398-331918, has insurance policies for UK-let properties, as do *John Watson (Insurance Brokers) Ltd.* – see under *Insurance* in the *Property and Accomodation* section below.

All complaints about insurance in the UK should be addressed to the insurance company in the first instance; or to *Lloyd's of London* (Complaints and Advisory Department), 1 Lime Street, London EC3M 7HA; tel 0171-623 7100.

Setting Up Home

Property and Accommodation

Hotels

The survey conducted for Price Waterhouse mentioned above (*Managing Expatriates in the CIS*) found that in 1997 41% of the companies operating there used hotels and 'temporary accommodation' to house their staff for periods of more than one month. There tend to be two kinds of hotel throughout the region: good, if impersonal and expensive ones which are run on modern lines; and old-fashioned ones which seem to belong somehow to the previous system; and where you will certainly need that roll of toilet paper and a universal plug for the sink. Hotels which have been part-renovated may be a kind of schizophrenic mixture of the two, with 'normal' hotel rooms on the upper floors, and the unrenovated ones below.

These are two different worlds which have a kind of uneasy coexistence, as in Russia and its neighbours the way of life itself seems to fall into two distinct categories: the old and unreconstructed on the one hand, and the new and ostentatiously capitalist on the other. For those who like their creature comforts the four and five-star hotels are like their equivalents anywhere in the world, and often run by the same internationally known hotel chains. A sense of adventure and a readiness to meet the unexpected will be required by those staying in more modestly priced accommodation.

Renting Property

There are apartments and houses for rent in all the main cities of these countries, both through commercial agents and private owners. But even for those who are intending to live there permanently or long-term, it may be a good idea to stay in a hotel initially, before renting or buying, to get acclimatised, and to give you plenty of time to find the right property. You may not enjoy trailing around from one unsuitable and cramped flat to the next, but you will get used to local property and rental prices which are likely to go up when it is realised that you are a foreigner. One way to do it is through a reliable local contact if you want to pay the same price the locals are paying, or through an agency. The embassy may have a list of suitable addresses.

You may find that the reality of Russian, or Polish, or Czech life doesn't quite meet your expectations, but this is no reason to settle for second-best; and the main compromise you may have to make is over the size of your apartment but not over comfort or security Look for an entryphone or code, or a concierge, even armed guards in blocks of flats where the rich live, good outside lighting, and a parking space with a 24-hour guard or attendant – even if of all of this may make you feel less, not more secure. If you have made these arrangements in advance. Bringing some of your own furniture may be a good idea, though this can be very expensive, but many rented flats will be furnished to acceptable standards. There may be some curiosity about a foreigner moving in, which can be dispelled perhaps if you introduce yourself to your neighbours, or let it be known that you are not a millionaire, and are a westerner of more modest means. Knowing some of your neighbours or people who live in the area is a very positive factor in all of this; and the personal recommendation or 'friend-of-a-friend' approach may contribute to increasing your feeling of personal safety.

Allow plenty of time. Many expatriates choose to live out of a suitcase for six months or even a year. The lucky ones will find their company provides accommodation for them, or will refurbish their flat. One common problem arises when expatriates expect every amenity which is available at home; but the heating should be up to scratch at least (and may be difficult to switch off, so check the windows and ventilation). Renting can mean a less permanent commitment, allowing you time to make up your mind about where you end up living in what is after all a strange and unfamiliar environment. Many who have offered their advice to the author of this book have said they have moved, once, twice or three times, before finding the right apartment. So renting will often be the only option, and will also suit single people and those in less secure professions, like English language teachers and others.

Generally, rentals are recommended for all categories of resident, as the charms of hotel life can quickly fade; and you will be more a part of your local environment and community if you truly live there more or less as the local people do. But the disadvantage of rentals everywhere in Eastern Europe and beyond is that they often seem to be extortionate for what you get – especially for foreigners – at whatever standard you have chosen. You may feel you are being ripped off when you are paying $500 a month for your dingy flat when your neighbours pay $50, or often much less; or $5,000 for a not-quite-luxury apartment in Moscow. These are at the lowest and highest ends of the price range for apartments for westerners.

Buying Property

This is recommended only for people with experience of the country in question, and its way of life. Especially in Russia and its neighbours there are many mortgage schemes offered by banks with a less than secure financial basis; here cash purchases are the norm, or you are recommended to approach a UK (or US) company in the first instance, which on the basis of a regular income or your existing home may be able to offer a mortgage, and there are many property bargains for a home, or land, or for long-term investment to be found outside the major city centres.

Owners or potential purchasers should use a local financial adviser, or one with experience of dealing with the country. Some advertise in *New Markets Monthly*, see above, or the local English-language press; or contact the British or US embassy. Any non-resident property owners using an off-shore mortgage should be sure to have an appointed fiscal representative in the country, as this is likely to be required by law; and to check on the tax situation there. Readers should refer to the section on *Offshore Mortgages* which follows.

You will need a variety of documentation which your specialist lawyer or financial adviser will advise you on, including a copy of the land registration documents or deeds: this is the only way to be entirely sure that you are not buying a property which owes back rates or buying from a vendor who is behind with his or her own mortgage payments. In many countries the new purchaser becomes responsible for these, and the bank which is providing the vendor's mortgage will probably have the right to take possession of the property and to sell it to repay the debt. A lawyer is primarily employed to check on the work of the local agent from the local administration responsible for these matters, and will not do this himself – and in some ways the purchaser is paying twice for the same service – at least the latter has an independent point of view to fall back on and is then sure that all the necessary safeguards and precautions have been observed.

Obviously, for the sake of diplomacy, it is preferable to employ a separate lawyer to that of the vendor, as it is quite likely that, at some point, interests will clash. A list of English-speaking lawyers may be provided by the *Law Society*, 113 Chancery Lane, London WC2A 1PL, tel 0171-242 1222; they no longer have an international lawyers' list; but they can give you a contact for their equivalent association in the country concerned. Alternatively, a list of local law firms is often available from your embassy. Contact the British or American Embassy in the country concerned.

Offshore Mortages

Offshore property mortgages are now available through many British building societies which have moved into offshore mortgaging; one such is *Abbey National* with many local high-street branches, and in Jersey (PO Box 545, Abbey National House, Igonville Place, St Helier, Jersey). Your local high street branch should be your first port of call. Another is the *Halifax Building Society.* also at *Halifax International (Isle of Man) Ltd.* at PO Box 30, 67 Strand Street, Douglas, Isle of Man. The Halifax, like most high street building societies and banks, has leaflets on offshore mortgages, and other financial matters like international payments, which will be worth consulting. *Lloyds Bank Overseas Club*, which offers a range of services, is based at the Offshore Centre, PO Box 12, Peveril Buildings, Peveril Square, Douglas, Isle of Man IM99 1SS; tel 01624-638104; fax 01624-638181.

Land Registry

The local official responsible for property purchase should first of all investigate the seller's title to the property and the land. One problem which is quite specific to the region is competition between various local and national administrations and an often deficient legal framework which means that your first step will be to ascertain exactly which official, department or ministry is responsible for this (sometimes these will be local or national privatisation agencies). All property sales and purchases must be registered at the relevant property registry, and often with several other organisations; and before signing a final contract a title check should be made to confirm the legal ownership of the property (it is surprising how often this is not actually registered in the name of the seller) and to reveal any unpaid property taxes or mortgages.

Good independent advice will mean you can find out whether there are plans to develop a factory or to construct a busy main road close to your property, and the impact of other local developments; this is something which a lawyer will check again for you at a later stage as well; and is a standard part of the service a locally based lawyer with international connections should provide.

The Preliminary Contract

If the land registry check passes smoothly, then the lawyer will proceed to draw up a preliminary agreement for sale. Although the law may not require a preliminary written agreement for property purchase, it is advisable to have one, as it may well save trouble later on in the purchasing procedure. For instance, if a deposit is demanded, this preliminary contract can provide that the deposit be returnable in the event of the vendor defaulting and the transaction falling through. It should also give a date for the new owners to move in, and other similar matters, as well as specifying whether the balance of the purchase price is payable in full and immediately or by instalments.

The Property Contract

The legally-binding property contract or transfer deed is usually signed by both vendor and buyer in the presence of the relevant local official. It often takes weeks before it has gone through the system and is ready to be signed: if you are abroad and it is inconvenient to return for the signing, you can appoint an agent to act on your behalf. The agent can be any trusted friend, need not be a local national, but must officially be granted a special power of attorney entitling him or her to sign on your behalf.

Once the property document has been signed it remains only for a notarised copy of this document to be submitted to the land registry office or equivalent in order for the new owner's name to be inserted on the registry deed; and probably also for the property to be registered with the local tax office for eventual payment of annual rates and taxes (low, but rising in most countries, encouraging many locals now to sell). Depending on the complexity of the property purchase in question, the whole procedure will take anything from between two and six months to complete.

Payment

Providing that a property has been bought with foreign currency or legally imported currency and that the purchase has been registered at the local land registry office, the home owner should usually be entitled to repatriate the proceeds of any future sale of the property in sterling or dollars, subject only to tax clearance. The money coming from offshore companies in Britain nowadays will certainly be liable to the same tax in Britain as any other income, making the tax advantages of this somewhat less than they have been. The same should hold true for any 'non-speculative capital gains accruing on the disposal of the investment after the relevant taxes have been paid,' the authorities say. Income from rent may also be transferred back to the UK, providing that the purchase price has been paid in full and that the owner is up to date on his or her local tax payments. For these and many other reasons, you should avoid cash purchases and all suggestions of under the counter payments where you can.

Expenses

A variety of fees will arise separate to the actual purchase price of the property. The most substantial of these include the administration fee and/or the registration fee; both costs should be calculated relative to the registered value of the property, which may be less than the purchase price. New property owners will also be liable to pay a purchase tax (see local country chapters for details), especially if you are buying the property from a company, or a transfer tax if you are buying from a private seller. The percentage is on the value declared in the transfer deed mentioned above; and under-declaration of this value may result in penalties, and potentially in increases in any capital gains tax to be paid on subsequent resale.

Having bought the property, you will become liable to various local rates or property taxes; and should certainly establish what these are in advance as they can differ from region to region, even within each of these countries.

Buying a Plot of Land

When considering buying a piece of land to build on, you will need to bear in mind that all land will subject to an increasing plethora of rules and regulations, and the various plans and rules pertaining to local land usage are kept at the town hall or local adminstration and should be available to the general public as well as your tax adviser or lawyer where, once you have ensured that the piece of land which you are interested in is not designated purely for agricultural use, and that it has been approved for building purposes – and you have done a little research into the legal background to this and whether this is regarded as it is in some countries but not in others as being secure – you may proceed to apply for a building or development permit – and have made sure most importantly that you are paying the right price.

Planning Permission

It is essential that anyone planning to buy a plot of land on which to build their own home, or hotel, or buildings for business use, or as an investment, first applies for planning permission from the local town hall or local administration. Although ten years ago this was virtually impossible – when land and property were generally in public ownership – as today agricultural land still is in Russia – the introduction of first, workers' cooperatives and then private enterprise has resulted in a myriad of badly-designed developments in many places which have led to local councils drawing a far tighter rein on property development. There are some unusual real estate acquisitions to be had in Eastern Europe, in all the flotsam and jetsam left over from the previous regime, and many which will lend themselves to redevelopment.

Paperwork

A special permit will be needed to buy development land – and probably a local business partner. Anyone else intending to purchase a plot of land or residence will be required to complete a number of forms, usually in duplicate and triplicate. On completion of this, and of any building work – or for any renovations – the land owner will have to work through another minefield of paperwork, so you really have to take professional and locally based advice.

It should be reemphasised that local experience – and not just some general advice – is what you need most if you purchase land, property or a business in Russia and Eastern Europe.

Property Taxes

For more information about property and other tax matters you can contact the appropriate consular offices in the UK or USA; or a local tax adviser on arrival – which the British or US embassy or consulate can recommend.

So far as the relocation of employees is concerned, any housing allowance you receive in excess of your actual rental will be taxable; but relocation allowances or expenses paid by an employer for removals and relocation costs from the UK and USA will usually not be; this applies also to a settling in allowance (in

Russia, up to one month of salary, with an additional allowance for dependants and family). The tax situation is also something which employers as well as employers should consider when staff are being transferred to any of these countries.

Insurance

A new owner or tenant should always arrange appropriate insurance for a new property. Apart from being a sensible precaution, third party insurance for property is now becoming a legal requirement.

Anyone who has purchased property from a previous owner may find the seller's insurance may be carried on to the next owner. However, the new owner will have to check whether the policy is transferable, or indeed whether they wish to cancel it in order to take out a new policy. Many will prefer to use an insurer in their own country for theft, property and other insurance requirements; one such policy for expatriates from a firm with extensive experience in the region is offered by *John Watson (Insurance Brokers) Ltd.*, 72 South Street, Reading RG1 4RA; tel 0118-956 8800; fax 0118-956 8094. 'We already have a large client base in Moscow, together with policyholders in Kazakstan, Kyrgyzstan, and Uzbekistan, to name but a few,' they say; and are 'used to dealing with claims from all corners of CEE (Central and Eastern Europe) and beyond.' *ABG Schemes Ltd.*, Companies House, Briton Street, Bampton, Devon EX16 9LN, tel 01398-33106, fax 01398-331918, offers insurance policies for UK-let properties.

Removals

For those who have bought a second home or residence, the procedure for importing personal effects and furnishings will usually be similar to that for other shorter-term residents, except that the home owner is generally also required to draw up a declaration that he or she will not sell, hire out or otherwise transfer ownership of this property within a twelve-month period. as well as these imported goods. Apart from this, the procedures for importing goods or personal effects will be much the same for all longer-term or permanent residents; and when the Czech Republic, Estonia, Hungary, Poland, and Slovenia have joined the EU, VAT will supposedly then be more or less harmonised in all these countries too. Until then, and throughout the region, if you are buying anything to take with you, such as a fax, fridge or personal computer, it can still be sold to you VAT-free if the goods are delivered direct to the remover as an export shipment from the dealer. Tax will be paid on arrival, the duty you pay for importing the item.

The first concerns though, of most people who are moving to an unknown or more distant destination will be the practicalities involved. Moving to Russia or Eastern Europe will bring its own specific problems, but we can begin in a practical way with a general checklist for what to do and things to get done beforehand. You should also contact the embassy concerned, and several international or specialist removers.

Checklist Before Moving

Confirm dates with mover
Sign and return contract together with payment

Book insurance at declared value
Arrange a contact number
Arrange transport for pets if necessary
Dispose of anything you don't want
Start running down freezer contents
Contact carpet fitters if needed
Book mains service for disconnection
Cancel all rental agreements
Notify dentist, doctor, optician, vet
Tell your bank and savings/share accounts
Inform telephone company
Ask PO to re-route mail
Tell TV licence, car registration, passport offices
Notify HP and credit firms
Make local map for friends/removal company
Clear the loft
Organise your own flight etc.
Plan where new things go
Cancel the milk/newspapers
Clean out the freezer/fridge
Find and label keys
Address cards to friends and relatives
Separate trinkets, jewellery and small items
Sort out linen and clothes
Put garage/garden tools together
Take down curtains/blinds
Collect children's toys
Put together basic catering for family at new house

The *British Association of Removers* can provide advice on choosing a removal company; and members offer a financial guarantee through the Association if they go out of business. Write to *BAR Overseas* at the address above. *Resident Abroad* magazine has articles of interest to all expatriates, with details of planning and preparation, personal finance and investment services; and other practical information. Subscriptions for one year from Europe are £53; and they also publish a 'Survival Kit' (£9.95 in the UK): *Resident Abroad Survival Kit*, FREEPOST SEA0524, Haywards Heath, West Sussex RH16 3BR; tel 01444-445520.

Removal Companies

Removal companies can take much of the hassle out of moving if you choose the right one; you should consider one with worldwide experience or local connections in the country you are moving to as transport – especially to the countries of Central and Eastern Europe, and into Russia – can be difficult. See the useful list of international removal companies below.

Cargo and Freight Forwarders

Then contact several companies for a quote, and any advice or tips they may have; as well as some specialist cargo or freight forwarders for the region. Some advertise in *New Markets Monthly*, 45 Beech Street, London EC2Y 8AD; tel 0171-628 4442; fax 0171-628 4443; e-mail new.markets@btinternet.com. All forms of transport in Russia and its neighbours are still an emerging market, with UK and US companies showing an interest and getting involved, as they are in distribution and many other transport-related areas. A useful contact in this respect is the *International Trade and Exhibitions Group* which organised the *TransRussia '98* trade fair in Moscow, for those 'transporting cargo in and out of Russia and the CIS and involved in air, rail and sea transport and cargo handling.' They can presently be contacted on 0171-286 9720, or by fax on 0171-286 0177; e-mail transport@ITE-Group.com; and they may forward a copy of their most recent exhibition catalogue.

For smaller packets and parcels, there is the Royal Mail; or if you have little confidence in local postal services there are specialist courier services for countries in Eastern Europe and the CIS from Albania to Uzbekistan like *Inter-Logistic Ltd*: tel 0181-569 0616; fax 0181-569 0605. Their address is Unit 7, Craufurd Business Park, Silverdale Road, Hayes, Middlesex (also with an office in Azerbaijan: *Inter-Logistic PLM*, Apt 60, 111 Nizami Street, Baku 370010). They have a fast courier service for urgent packages and correspondence (and see under *Freight Forwarding and Courier Services* below).

When you are moving, remember to make the photocopy of the first five pages of your passport, with the visa and details of your sponsor or sponsoring organisation, and give this to the removal agents, as they will need to present it, with any other documents they require, at the customs office when they enter with your shipment of goods; and they may have to make arrangements with other countries along the way.

It is a good idea also to take out comprehensive insurance for your goods or possessions in transit. Your removals or freight company can advise about cover and make arrangements on your behalf; or you can ask another company for a quote.

These charges are also something which a good removals company or freight forwarder with experience of the country can advise on, and also the value of the goods in the country concerned, in other words how much it costs to buy there. This is another question you can ask your removals, freight forwarding or courier company.

The Import Procedure

This consists first of all of compiling a signed inventory, to be written in the local language, of the goods to be transported there. This should then be presented to the relevant consulate with a completed customs clearance form and it should be stamped there, usually for a fee. The basic procedure is outlined below:

1. Make two copies of a complete inventory of all the items to be taken, valuing all of the items at their cuurent value, and not their cost. Even if there are some things you want to take now and others which will not follow for several months include all of these on the inventory as once the list is compiled, it usually can't be added to later. Remember to include the makes, models and serial numbers of all electrical items, for example, and you will usually need copies of a declaration that you are the woner of the goods, a declaration of ownership.

2. The customs clearance form must be completed. This should be available from the relevant consulate or embassy – or the British or US embassy can advise if you are already in the country.

3. You may also need to present either a copy of your residence permit or details of your property or residence there at the embassy.

4. A full passport with visas – and photocopies of the first few pages which have been stamped at the consulate – will also be required.

Although it is obviously more economical to transport all of your possessions in one go, you will be allowed to import all household goods subsequently in as many trips as are required. But the more you take at the beginning – if you are really going to live in the country – the better.

Useful Addresses

International Removal Companies:
Aarmada European removals and storage: tel 0181-347 5281; or Southampton 01703-641191.
Allied Pickfords: 490 Great Cambridge Road, Enfield, Middlesex BN1 3RZ; tel 0181-366 6521. A worldwide network with many branches in Britain. *Avalon Overseas*: Drury Way, Brent Park, London NW10 0JN; tel 0181-451 6336. Branches in Aberdeen (01224-709200); Birmingham (0121-233 9330); Glasgow (0141-226 5717); Manchester (0161-945 9685); Northampton (01604-27605); Oxford (01865-240130); Southend (01702-432565); and Southampton (01703-339115).
Britannia Removals: Britannia House, Alington Road, Eynesbury, St. Neots, Cambridgeshire PE19 4YH; tel 01234-272272; fax 01480-218430.
Britannia-Finches of London Ltd: Serin House, Hindsley Place, London SE23 2NF; tel 0181-699 6766; fax 0181-291 3478.
Cargo Forwarding: 96 London Industrial Park, Roding Road, London E6 4LS; tel 0171-474 1000 or 7000; fax 0171-474 3000. Birmingham (tel 0121-373 3331); Edinburgh (0131-669 1886); Manchester (0161-248 8700; fax 0161-225 9372); Norwich (01508-471491). A worldwide service with door-to-door or door-to-depot rates on request and storage facilities.
Clark & Rose Ltd: Barclayhill Place, Portlethen, Aberdeen AB12 4LH; tel 01224-782800; fax 01224-782822.
Cotswold Carriers: Unit 9, Worcester Road Industrial Estate, Chipping Norton, Oxon OX7 5NX; tel 01608-642856; fax 01608-645295.
Crocker International Removals, Unit 3, Cornishway South, Galmington Trading Estate, Taunton, Somerset TA1 5NQ; tel 01823-259406 or 277404; fax 01823-334091.
Crown Worldwide Movers: Freephone 0800 393363, with offices in Aberdeen (01224 583770); Birmingham (0121-212 9499); Bristol (0117-982 1219); Edinburgh (0131-557 2000); Glasgow (0123-644 9666); Heathrow (0181-897 1288); Leeds (0113-277 1000); London (0181-591 3388); Manchester (0161-273 5337); Montrose (01674-672155); Newcastle (0191-261 4562); Oxford (01235-833898); and Swansea (01792-463844).
Four Winds International Group: Wyvern Estate, Beverley Way, New Malden, Surrey KT3 4PH; tel 0181-949 0900; fax 0181-949 1300.
Harrison & Rowley: 34-36 Foster Hill Road, Bedford MK40 2ER; tel 01234-272272.

Harrow Green Removals Group: Merganser House, Cooks Road, London E15 2PW; tel 0181-522 0101; fax 0181-522 0252; e-mail 106035.2157@compuserve.com. Full removals service, and they can also make arrangements for pets.
Interpack Worldwide Plc: FREEPOST (NW5715), 1 Standard Road, London NW10 0YR; tel 0500-003613; fax 0181-453 0544. 600 offices around the world and services including pet shipping, full / part house contents, motor vehicles, air freight and storage.
Luker Bros (Removals & Storage) Ltd: Shelley Close, Headington, Oxford OX3 8HB; tel 01865-762206.
Pink & Jones Ltd: Britannia House, Riley Road, Telford Way, Kettering, Northants. NN16 8NN; tel 01536-512019.
Robinsons International Moving and Storage: Nuffield Way, Abingdon, Oxon OX14 1TN; tel 01235-552255. They can send a brochure on *International Moving*. Branches in London: tel 0181-208 8484; fax 0181-208 8488; Basingstoke: tel 01256-465533; fax 01256-24959; Birmingham: tel 0121-449 4731; fax 0121-449 9942; Bristol: tel 0117-986 6266; fax 0117-986 2723; Manchester: tel 0161-766 8414; fax 0161-767 9057; and Southampton: tel 01703-220069; fax 01703-331274.
T.C.P Worldwide Freight Services Ltd:- 24-hour freephone 0800-614645 and worldwide removal service.

Freight Forwarding and Courier Services:
Lakor Ltd: 2 Sen-Somona Str., Astrakhan, 414014, Russia; tel 007-8512-390257; fax 007-8512-390258. Sea transportation Caspian Sea, River Volga, Astrakhan-Iran; and forwarding of cargoes via Astrakhan.
The Russia House Ltd. (Courier Service): 37 Kingly Court, Kingly Street, London W1R 5LE; tel 0171-439 1271; fax 0171-434 0813. A once-a-week service for letters, documents, parcels and money London-Moscow-London.

Car Hire Companies:
AVIS: UK, tel 0990-900500; http://www.avis.com. Azerbaijan: +994-12-975333; Belarus: +375-172-347990; Bosnia-Herzegovina: +387-71-641780; Bulgaria: +359-2-981-4960; Croatia: +385-1-444436; Czech Republic: +420-221-851225; Estonia: +372-6-388222; Hungary: +361-1-184-685; Latvia: +371-722-5876; Lithuania: +370-2-724-275; Macedonia: +389-91-222046; Poland: +48-22-6504869; Romania: +40-1-2104344; Slovak Republic: +421-7-521611; Slovenia: +386-61-1612153; Ukraine: +380-44-2942104; Yugoslavia: +381-11-43-3314.

Importing Cars

Anyone thinking of importing a foreign-registered car into any of these countries should first of all consider the drawbacks: the inconvenience of having a right-hand drive car in a country which drives on the right and the inevitable tortuous red tape that the import procedure gives rise to. If you decide to do this, you must apply for an import licence from the appropriate ministry, and first seek advice from the consulate or embassy.

Daily Life

One key to unravelling the daily life in all the countries of the region will be the ability to speak the language reasonably well, or at least to have some phrases which will help you get by and make yourself understood. So, the first part of this chapter is about the language and language learning

The Languages

The language which will be most useful in Russia and most of its neighbours is Russian, even if Belarusian – or Belorussian – and Ukrainian and so on are now taught widely in local schools in these newly independent places, and the other countries of the CIS are busy asserting their cultural as well as political independence. For more about this language and the basics of its alphabet and phonology see the country chapter on *Russia*. The paradox of life to the west of this CIS region in Central and Eastern Europe is that Russian here is often the least helpful language even though it is spoken by many, especially older people. This is seen today as the language of the former occupying power.

But if you do speak Russian – and somehow make your western origins clear – this often frosty reception will thaw; and people in many areas are meeting Russians once again, not as occupiers this time but as tourists.

A similar situation holds true in former Yugoslavia, where Serbo-Croat (or Croato-Serb) is still almost universally spoken, although there are other languages there, like Albanian, Macedonian, or Slovenian (which may themselves have a disputed status). This language – like the country today – has been divided and what were previously western and eastern dialects now have 'national' status. The language spoken in Croatia is called Croatian nowadays, and in Serbia, Serbian.

Turkish is important in Central Asia – and even in the Russian federation – where the various Turkic languages can usually easily be understood by Turkish speakers. This gives those with experience of Turkey (and who speak its language) a great advantage if they are thinking of moving on to Azerbaijan or Uzbekistan for example. This is one factor (another is religion) which is favouring trade relations between this *Central Asia* region and Turkey.

But you can survive in Poland, or Hungary, or Azerbaijan, without speaking their respective languages. Local people are often pleased to have the chance to practise their English (making English teaching one work opportunity which many 'EFL' teachers are taking advantage of). Indeed, English teaching is booming in many of the countries featured in this book.

And everywhere, the German cultural influence is strong, making this the best second language after English to learn, if your shorter stay in Central or Eastern Europe does not make it worthwhile learning more than a few phrases of the local language. These 'minority' languages will certainly not be very useful outside the country – and in some cases are not always spoken very widely within it, or in different dialects. Linguistic boundaries in Eastern Europe in the past have also been very fluid, meaning that some Russian speakers see the national languages of neighbouring countries as merely imperfect versions of their own (just as some 'standard' speakers of English look down on the Scottish version of the language for example). But these are really all separate languages; and the main (Slavonic) family of languages in the region has many branches, just as English is also one of several Germanic languages, like Dutch or German.

Against these nationalistic trends has been the great centralising influence of Russian, which was spread through the former Soviet Union through a very centralised schools system as well as through the mass media. This was previously favoured over other local languages; and spoken in exactly the same way almost everywhere – with some national and regional variations – a linguistic situation which is not unlike that of the United States.

Learning the Language

Living and working abroad usually means learning another language. In many international careers, and in your daily or business life, speaking the local language can be a decisive advantage seen from this very practical point of view, as well as one of the opportunities which living in another country can bring. Those best able to adapt to their new life and living conditions in Russia and Eastern Europe will be the ones with some knowledge of the language.

The question is, where to start – and it should certainly be with the idea that learning the language is not some kind of grim necessity, but a positive opportunity which you should welcome. Then, readers may choose to visit their local library or bookshop to find courses like the *Teach Yourself...* books (Hodder & Stoughton, London, usually under £20) for Russian and many Eastern European languages, which each come with a cassette, and which should be used ideally with other, more basic courses or a teacher. *Colloquial...* is a similar and slightly more expensive 'interractive' series covering most of the countries featuring in this book (Routledge, 11 New Fetter Lane, London EC 4P 4EE; 29 West 35th Street, New York, NY 10001. A long-standing and popular series is *Teach Yourself...* (Hugo, generally priced at around £35). The well-known *Linguaphone* courses can be ordered by telephoning 0800-282417. These are suitable for beginners, and are organised around useful vocabulary and phrases, as well as grammar.

You should remember when you learn in this way that simple repetition of phrases – which may of course be useful in themselves – is not the main aim of your study. You are endeavouring to discover, in a practical way, how the individual sounds of the language are made, and how they relate to each other, as well as its basic structures, usually not very different from English and other European languages – although there are often more inflections in some languages outside the 'European' family, like Estonian – with its fourteen case endings and special verb-forms – or Hungarian, or the Turkic or Central Asian languages mentioned above. A useful companion book which explains some of these issues (and an indispensible referencee for all those who will teach English as a foreign language) is *A Mouthful of Air* by Anthony Burgess (Hutchison). This can tell you why we should learn foreign languages, and how these can be studied in a practical way. There is also a chapter on learning Russian.

There are many phrase-books on the market, but these are generally less useful as many try to transcribe the phrases into the Roman alphabet, without enough explanation of how these sounds are made. In fact, there is an International Phonetic Alphabet which would much more helpful to those who really have to use these phrases. *Berlitz* publishes some phrase-books: Berlitz Publishing Co. Ltd., Peterley Road, Cowley, Oxford OX4 2TX; as do *Lonely Planet* – PO Box 617, Hawthorn, Victoria 3122, Australia, tel 03-9819-1877, fax 03-9819-6459 –

and *Rough Guides* – 1 Mercer Street, London WC2H 8QJ – which specifically apply to the region. The *Cortina Institute of Languages* – 19 Newton Turnpike, Westport, CT 06880 – publishes a series of *Traveler's Dictionaries* at around $5.95, as well as interactive courses with a cassette which are available only in the USA and Canada.

Private or home tuition, or study in your local college or university, are other options – or some combination of these. Contact with native speakers of the language will also help. Notices in your local university or English language school in Britain or the United States as well as the various cultural institutes and emigré clubs etc. could be your way to track them down, perhaps offering English language conversation in exchange for some language lessons. Some countries, like Estonia and Poland, provide special classes for foreign workers and their families – and some companies in the USA and UK include language courses as part of their training and preparation programmes.

Language Schools and Courses

See the following country chapters and contacts, or *The Earls Guide to Language Schools in Europe* – published by Cassell, Wellington House, 125 Strand, London WC2R 0BB – which details over 1,000 schools in Europe including Russia, the Czech Republic, Poland, and so on (with most in Western and Central Europe). There is cross-referencing by subject specialism and some useful information on many of the schools listed.

Berlitz (U.K.) Ltd,9-13 Grosvenor Street, London W1A 3BZ, tel 0171-9150 909, fax 0171-915 0222 (also in many cities across Europe and the USA) – has native-speakers to teach almost any language. The Berlitz method was one of the first to combine the study of grammar with speaking, and will be suited to those who prefer a rather more formal approach to learning.

Eurocentres, 56 Eccleston Square, London SW1V 1PQ, tel 0171-834 4155, fax 0171-834 1866 – is a non profit-making organisation which provides language courses in various European countries for periods of up to six months. The minimum age is 16. All teaching is conducted in the language concerned, with extensive use of language laboratories, computer-assisted language learning, and audio-visual materials.

The Eurolingua Institute, Eurolingua House, 2 Nelson Street, Congleton CW12 4BS, tel/fax 01260-271685 – is the largest pan-European organisation of its kind, providing unique opportunities for people of all ages and from all walks of life to learn languages in the countries where they are spoken. Combined language learning, study, activity and holiday programmes are offered in the UK, Russia and the USA. You may live and learn on a one-to-one homestay basis with your personal tutor, or participate in a group programme.

inlingua School of Languages, 28 Rotton Park Road, Edgebaston, Birmingham B16 9JL, fax 0121-456 8264 – can offer a wide variety of courses in all the major European languages – and many rarer ones. There is an extensive range of possible courses, and prospective participants should, in the first instance, write to the Information Centre at the above address.

The *Centre for Information on Language Teaching and Research (CILT)*, Regent's College, Inner Circle, Regent's Park, London NW1 4NS, is the organisation in Britain which provides information on the available range of resources for the study of many of these less well-known languages, including many in this CEE/CIS region. At the same address the *CILT Library* also has a range of documentation on courses: tel 0171-379 5110. A list of their publications can be obtained by sending an SAE to the above address.

However you learn, it is advisable to make a start before you go.

Schools and Education

How and where to educate their children is the question facing many of those who have been posted to this region; and can be a source of great concern to some. The answer, in many places, can be in the local schools – where your children will learn most by being with the local children – especially the language. Young children will pick this up surprisingly easily easily. For older children, some extra tuition will be needed, but they also may enjoy this challenge and prefer to take the opportunity to study in a local school. This may be more difficult for them, but many parents say that it is your own attitude, and how this communicates itself to your offspring – and whether or not you yourself have a positive approach to fitting in and integrating into the life of these countries – which counts for a lot.

Russians and others who come to the USA, and even the UK, often complain of the poor standards of education away from home, and are disappointed when their own budding maths geniuses find themselves in the more laid-back atmosphere of our own student-centred primary schools where the aims may be rather different. This more progressive idea of education has not quite caught on in Russia; and there is a much stronger notion that children are there to learn – and learn poetry and songs by heart for instance – and have this knowledge imparted to them by a teacher who knows what he or she is talking about – – and even if they don't they should be listened to respectfully!

The coming of more modern teaching practices is also having a beneficial effect though, and in schools in Poland or Hungary today you will find often limited resources but an approach combining the best of both worlds – the progressive and the traditional. This is the mixture which often prevails in Russia and Eastern Europe today where – some readers may be surprised to learn – standards in schools are often high.

You can consider the local state sector as one option, especially for younger children. They will usually adapt quite easily if the parents take a positive approach to the whole process – and this applies to your more motivated older offspring as well, who made need some extra language tuition. An article by *The Times* correspondent in Moscow (14.9.97) entitled 'Why I'm sending my daughter to a Russian school' appeared recently which highlighted some of these issues and may be reassuring to some nervous parents. The author's friends expressed horror at the thought, but his experience at least was a 'relaxed and friendly' one, and the staff (more highly valued than teachers in the West in the community at large, if not as well paid) at School No.57 in Moscow, were 'dedicated' and 'believers in lots of homework and good presentation.' School dinners are 75p.

Although the local education system is probably perfectly adequate – despite shortages of textbooks and materials – and this can also be one good way for you to integrate your family more closely into the community where you live – the curriculum will obviously not follow quite the same pattern as the UK or US ones. This will create difficulties, if a child in the middle of an A Level course, for instance, is suddenly uprooted to Poland, and expected to do well in Polish examinations. Many children of those working overseas will find themselves back in Britain in public schools or 'crammers'.

Other parents choose to send their children to rather more congenial-sounding international schools; which often have a strongly British expatriate or American cultural flavour. Here students from many countries (including the local one) often study for exams like the International Baccalaureate; and will also learn the local language. These international schools can – like some public schools – be somewhat isolated from the outside world. But standards in the best are high, and your children will have a more international outlook than if they studied back home in the UK or USA.

There will be different solutions for different families. Those who can afford it sometimes choose to keep their children at UK boarding school for the simple reason that they do not wish to to disrupt their education. Others believe they will receive a better one. But the chance to mix with the locals – especially of you are not moving too much from place to place – may well be more interesting and productive in the long run, and is well worth considering.

The availability of these international schools is one important limiting factor in all this, when expatriates are assigned to the CIS and Eastern European countries and want their children to come too; but there are more and more of these latterly, as far afield as Almaty, Tashkent and Baku, although not generally outside the capitals, or in provincial Russian cities. Contact them well in advance, as there can be a waiting list.

The Education System

Within each of these countries, the education system has often undergone a radical transformation in recent years (see above). But even under communism, this was always open to all classes and to people of all abilities. It was never exactly 'comprehensive' in the British sense, though; and often organised according to the German or French model, with many secondary schools specialising in a particular vocational or other subject, like languages or engineering.

It should be emphasised that in Russia and all its neighbours there is a deep and inherent respect for study and education not always found elsewhere. And in each of the newly independent countries of the CIS, a series of laws has been passed which now favours the indigenous language and their own national history; and the number of children learning Russian as a foreign language has dropped dramatically in nearly all of them. Most local schools are now opting for English or German as their second language. Today, also, both state and private education exist side by side – with some locals opting to educate their children in English public schools which are now rather fashionable among the *nouveaux riches* of these countries, so if you want your children to mix with the children of the richer Russians you can send them to Britain to study!

Study and Exchange Schemes for Russia and Eastern Europe

The *ASSE* programme gives school students in Britain the opportunity to spend a year in some Central European countries, living with a local family and attending school there. This is for sixth-form students aged between 16 and 18. They can provide details of possible placements and have representatives on the ground to assist students once they are there. Contact: *ASSE UK*, PO Box 20, Harwich, Essex CO12 4DQ; tel 01255-506347. In addition, teachers interested in exchange programmes should contact the *Central Bureau*, 10 Spring Gardens, London SW1A 2BN. Internationally, the *European School Exchange Database* also has a list of schools seeking partners throughout Central and Eastern Europe: contact the *Centre for International Education (CEVNO)*, Nassauplein 8, 1815 GM Alkmaar, The Netherlands; tel 31-72-118502; fax 31-72-1512212.

There are a number of such schemes for those already studying or intending to study at a British university and wishing to spend up to a year at college in Russia or Eastern Europe as well. The *Central Bureau* in London should be contacted (see address above) or your UK university. The *Erasmus* scheme is part of the EU's Socrates programme, intended to encourage cooperation between universities as well as student exchanges which will apply to those countries which have joined the EU in the near future. Students and UK institutions should contact the *UK Erasmus Students Grants Council*, The University, Canterbury, Kent CT2 7PD; tel 01227-762712. This scheme will change in 1999. There are also Central Bureau offices at 3 Bruntsfield Crescent, Edinburgh EH10 4HD; tel 0131-447 8024; and 1 Chlorine Gardens, Belfast BT9 5DJ; tel 01232-664418.

There are now a number of vocation-orientated student exchange schemes in the UK and USA, similar to BUNAC or Camp America, which will be of interest to young people; and some other voluntary exchange schemes are detailed in the various country chapters.

AIESEC (French acronym for *International Association for Students of Economics and Management*), 29-31 Cowper Street, London EC2A 4AP, tel 0171-336 7939, fax 0171-336 7971 – offers students and recent graduates within accountancy, business administration, computing, marketing, economics, and finance the opportunity to take placements in diverse working environments through its Work Abroad programmes. Placements last between six and seventy-two weeks in any one of its 87 member countries around the world (including this region).

AIESEC US, 135 West 35th Street, 20th Floor, New York, NY 10020, tel 212-757-3774 – operates a similar scheme in the USA. Again, the main precondition for an overseas placing is membership of an AIESEC chapter in an American university, and the need to ensure an equal number of work exchange positions for foreign students in the US, which limits numbers.

Association for International Practical Training (AIPT), 10400 Little Patuxent Parkway, Suite 250, Columbia, MD 21044-3510, tel 410-997-2200, fax 410-992-3924, e-mail aipt@aipt.org, http://www.aipt.org – conducts 'high-quality experiential exchanges which enhance the ability of individual participants, employers and host organisations.' It helps around 250 US citizens in exchanges with 25 or so other countries every year (including destinations in Central Europe) and for 2,000 people from 70 countries to train with US employers.

The Central Bureau for Educational Visits and Exchanges, 10 Spring Gardens, London SW1A 2BN, tel 0171-389 4004, fax 0171-389 4426, Campus 2000 01:YNK330 – runs the Language Assistant Scheme which enables modern language students from Britain and over 30 other countries to spend a year working in a school or college where their target language is spoken. The Central Bureau also arranges numerous other exchange programmes (and see above).

Council on International Educational Exchange (CIEE), 205 East 42nd Street, New York, NY 10071-5706, USA, tel 212-822-2695, fax 212-822-2689, http://www.ciee.org/ – sponsors 2-4 week volunteer projects in the USA and abroad during the summer months. Choosing from over 600 projects worldwide, participants join an international team of 10-20 volunteers to work on an environmental or community service project alongside local residents.

GAP Activity Projects, Gap House, 44 Queen's Road, Reading, Berkshire RG1 4BB, tel 01734 594914, fax 01734-576634 – GAP arranges voluntary work placements in over 34 countries around the world including Central and Eastern Europe for young people in their 'gap' year between school and further education (aged 18-19 only). Volunteers pay a GAP fee on selection, £390 in 1997, and all travelling costs, but once at their placement, board and lodging are provided, and sometimes pocket money. Jobs include teaching English in Hungary, the Czech and Slovak Republics, and Bulgaria. Those interested should apply from September in the year before final examinations.

International Association for the Exchange of Students for Technical Experience (IAESTE UK), The Central Bureau, 10 Spring Gardens, London SW1A 2BN, tel 0171-389 4774, fax 0171-389 4426 – arranges an exchange scheme whereby penultimate year students from scientific and technical backgrounds can spend 8-12 weeks mainly in the summer vacation in many countries in the region. Students should apply to the programme in the autumn for placements beginning the following summer.

For schools and universities, the Central Bureau also publishes various guides to Russia and the Central and Eastern European countries which are available from the Publications Sales Department at their London address.

International Schools

International schools tend to be regarded as the best alternative by expatriates who are considering the long-term education of their children. This is often because they offer the qualifications better known to selection bodies for UK or US universities, and there may be less disruption in your children's education; or simply they are felt by some parents who themselves have an international lifestyle to be most appropriate for their offspring.

Standards can be high – or not so high – and you should certainly do some research and ask the right questions – and do this, in conjunction with your children, and involve them as far as possible in this decision. Lists for schools in these countries are available from the *European Council of International Schools (ECIS)*, 21 Lavant Street, Petersfield, Hants GU32 3EL; tel 01730-268244 or 263131; fax 01730-267914; e-mail ecis@ecis.org; internet: http://www.ecis.org. (The most recent updated ECIS lists can be found at this internet address). International schools also teach French and German curricula; and ECIS also lists such schools. There are at present international and American schools in most of the countries of Central and Eastern Europe, as well as Moscow, St. Petersburg, Vladivostok, Kiev, and other major CIS cities.

The Media and Communications

Books and Newspapers

Expatriates are often advised that a subscription to a newspaper or book club can be a good way to maintain a connection with home. This is true especially in the more 'remote' destinations where it can be hard to get hold of English-language books or videos etc. and it is quite easy, in fact, to receive the main British and American newspapers almost anywhere in them world.

The *Financial Times* has subscribers and subscription services in all of these countries and will send further details (Number One, Southwark Bridge, London SE1 9HL). Americans will find that the *International Herald Tribune*, 181 Avenue Charles de Gaulle, F-92521 Neuilly-sur-Seine, France, and the *Wall Street Journal (Europe)* are quite widely available in the larger cities, the latter with very good coverage of Central and Eastern European matters. *The Guardian Weekly* subscription rates are currently £30 for Central Europe for six months (£55 for one year). Write to *The Guardian Weekly*, 164 Deansgate, Manchester M60 2RR. *The Weekly Telegraph* is a similar digest of news culled from *The Daily Telegraph*: PO Box 14, Harold Hill, Romford, Essex RM3 8EQ.

Some expatriates may also wish to subscribe to UK book clubs with an overseas department. One extremely useful organisation in this respect is *The Good Book Guide Ltd.* which produces a monthly magazine. This publication contains independent reviews on a wide selection of books, videos, audios, CD-ROMs and also gifts which can be mailed anywhere in the world. For a complimentary copy of *The Good Book Guide Magazine* and information on subscriptions you can contact them on 0171-490 9901 or at 24 Seward Street, London EC1V 3PB. English-language bookshops are opening in many countries, and a recent venture in Moscow is the *Anglia British Bookshop* organised by *Escolar International Book Distribution Ltd*, 2/3 Khlebny Pereulok, 1212069 Moscow, Russia; fax 095-203-0673; e-mail dint@glasnet.ru; telephone number 095-203-5802.

Communications

Communications can be rudimentary, or up to the highest international standards, depending on what you are prepared to pay and where you are. Mobile phones are popular; the local phone network may be unreliable in some areas, with telephone directories hard to obtain and enquiry services non-existent; and certainly not English-speaking. This is less true of Central Europe where new systems have been installed; and postal communication with the rest of Europe now takes two or three days (in Russia allow two or three weeks, especially in the slower winter months).

Post

The *Royal Mail* has a useful *Keepsafe* service for those on shorter trips. They will hold all your post for up to two months while you are away; and deliver it on the day of your choice (cost at present up to £15 for two months). Opening a PO Box Number may be another useful step if you wish to keep your mail 'on hold' for up to a year (the cost is presently a little more than £50 if you collect from time to time; or more for this to be forwarded on). More practical will be to have your mail rerouted if you have your onward address; and leaflets on all these services can be found at local Royal Mail offices or depots telephone number in your phone book. This applies similarly in the United States.

As in the UK, urgent or registered letters and packages may be taken to a post office in any Central or Eastern European country. Post is delivered to your door or apartment building, or to be collected if it is a larger packet, and by paying a surcharge if the package weighs in excess of (normally) a 500g or 1kg limit. For those who have no fixed abode the poste restante service is useful, and will be located in the main post office – in all the major cities across the region (which can also organise a box number for you for a small charge, if you do have a local address).

To send a letter for collection like this, just write the word 'HOLD', the addressee's name, then the restante number and the place name and country name on the envelope: the addressee can then pick this up from the Central Post Office, bringing a passport or ID card as identification. Lightweight air mail letters or aerogramme are normally best for this kind of letter.

But the most reliable means of communication of all to Russia and Eastern Europe will be by fax.

Telephones

The new telephone services, both national and international, which have been set up in many countries, will be automatic and like those anywhere in the world. Local phones will be more unreliable; and inflation and general economic disorder have meant that, in some CIS countries, local calls which previously required a token from a public call box are now effectively free. Tokens are used in Russia, and these are available from kiosks and metro stations. There will be many such call boxes – and in the more developed countries there are phones using a local phonecard available from post offices, or one of the international cards which can be purchased anywhere. Hotels often have credit card phones as well. Codes for national and international dialling are often given in the telephone booths and can also be obtained in post offices. Person-to-person calls are sometimes made through the operator. One business-related innovation in some countries is an English-language telephone directory.

The codes for each of these countries and all their regions can be found in the standard UK and US telephone directories and only the regional or city code is included where a telephone or fax number is listed in this book. For the UK, dial the international code, then 44, and continue immediately with the UK number, omitting the first number of the UK area code, a zero. To telephone any country from Britain, dial 00 first, and then for example 7 for Russia, the system which is familiar around the world. This makes the code for Russia rather easy to remember, if you are a James Bond fan: 007.

To call another country from Russia, for example, you dial 8, then wait for the tone, then 10, and then the country code. Calling another regional number within the country, in most of the the CIS countries, you also dial 8, wait for the tone, and then dial the number, or call the operator who can put you through: the international operator number in Russia is 194 or 196, after you have dialled an 8, and they should be able to put you through, or may even offer to call you back. Ringing some regional numbers in Russia and its neighbours is like this as well, and you simply wait for the operator to call. Local directory enquiries (if you speak Russian) in Russia is 09.

When telephoning inside the country, dial the complete provincial code for the area you are calling, including the initial zero, after you have dialled an 8. Obviously, if you are ringing a number in Moscow from Moscow itself you would not need to include the city code – and using your phone book even before you go, making copies of these pages to take with you, is a good idea, for all the country and regional codes you need. Telephone and postal information also features in most of the city guides you can obtain from tourist offices; and is to be found on arrival in many hotels.

One tip, for any message which you want to get through urgently, and much better than a letter, is to send a fax. How to find one will be a problem – if you are not working from an office – but this is really an indispensible item for all those considering living and working in Eastern Europe. You may also do what you certainly cannot do in Britain or the USA and go into any local shop or office and make a polite request to use their fax machine for an urgent message, offering some suitable payment. There are 'fax shops' in some cities but this is a surprisingly successful way of doing it if you don't have your own.

Strangely, faxes in Russia and the CIS countries must also be registered with the authorities, usually the local telephone company. A laptop computer which you connect to the Internet is another useful means of instant international communication. For faxes and computers and other similar gadgets you should take a suitable telephone socket adaptor with you.

Radio and Television

Another item to pack is a small shortwave radio. Your hotel room or residence may have one, or it may not. The *BBC World Service* (Bush House, London WC2B 4PH, e-mail worldservice.letters@bbc.co.uk) recommends a short-wave radio which covers the frequency ranges 5950-6200, 7100-7600, 9400-9900, 11500-12100, 13600-13900, 15000-156000, 17700-17900, 21400-21800 kHz, to receive its programmes anywhere in the world. It also publishes a monthly listings magazine *BBC On Air* with comprehensive programme information, background information, and advice on how to listen. A subscription is £18 per year; you can telephone 0171-257 2211. Radio programmes are also relayed through many local stations; there is now a BBC worldwide television service available by satellite or cable.

Some local TV stations also carry the BBC 24-hour news service; and satellite services like CNN and Sky are also available in the main hotels, along with the usual German-language satellite stations.

Transport and Utilities

Transport

Coaches are the means of budget travel to many countries and there will be local short and long-distance bus services as well. For travel within these countries, and for most people getting there, flying will however be best, considering the great distances involved in travel through Russia and its neighbours. Are these safe? Airlines like *Transaero* and *Ukrainian International Airlines* or *Estonian Air* certainly are, as are all those who have adopted a western style of service and US-built or European planes. The national rail network is another option – but travel for the first time with a more experienced traveller if you can, to get a feel for how things are done. This is really a necessity for inexperienced travellers in Russia.

Do not expect cleanliness, even if Russian trains are often surprisingly comfortable and well-adapted for the long-distance trips they make. Routes already used by westerners like the one between Moscow and St. Petersburg, or the trans-Siberian and trans-Manchurian lines may, paradoxically, be the most dangerous so far as theft or petty crime is concerned. In other more out of the way places, people will be surprised to see you and the atmosphere will be more relaxed.

In all the capitals and many of the larger cities there will be a metro (now that Warsaw has finally completed its own metro line); and there will be buses and trams or trolleybuses as well (tickets to be obtained from the nearest kiosk, as in many European countries, or when you get on). All of this is cheap, as is the local custom in Eastern but not Central Europe of hailing a private car, much as you would a taxi, and offering the driver a dollar or two to take you out of his way. This is not recommended at night, or when you are alone. Neither are many local taxi services, even in Central Europe, where the ones to catch are the ones with telephone numbers on top; here mini-cab drivers often don't know the way and are much less reliable. In Russia, the more reliable taxis are the ones with a green light on the roof, which are often much harder to come by.

Never get into a cab with another passenger, who may or may not be the driver's criminal accomplice, and agree the price beforehand if you use a private car or unregistered taxi. Some car rental services locally may be similarly unreliable; it is advisable to arrange your pick-up from airport or hotel with a reputable car hire or limousine firm; and not to take the taxis which will be waiting outside with drivers who may approach you, and who should be refused with a polite 'no thank you'. Better than this, even if you are arriving for the first time, is to catch a bus, anywhere, and get out of the often dubious environs of the airport, railway or bus terminal. Having someone you know come and pick you up is best of all.

Cars

The road system is often rudimentary in Russia; but many more motorways are now being built even here, and in Central European countries like Hungary and Croatia, making road communications with Western Europe rather better in these latter places. There are more service stations in Central Europe than these destinations further east, although you can come across some quite modern ones in countries as far afield as Azerbaijan, offering the range of services to be found at any petrol station anywhere. One hazard will be the police, who may pull you over and spend much time inspecting your various documents and finding some reason for you to pay a fine. Importing cars involves a lot of paperwork, and is best avoided.

Another worry is highway theft which begins roughly where the former Soviet Union starts, but is not unknown in Hungary or Poland either. An 'International Driving Permit which you can obtain before departure will be valid in each of these CEE or CIS countries, as may your own British or European Union license too. If you do apply for a local one, during the time it takes for the new licence to be processed you will be given an official receipt for your old one and a photocopy, all of which should satisfy the traffic police.

Insurance

The basic legal requirement for car insurance is third party only; thus drivers are insured for claims made against them, but not for any accident which may befall driver or car.

Most credit card holders can also obtain a standard third party insurance; and if you rent or hire a car you will also need an International Insurance Certificate (or

'Green Card') here. These are available on request from all insurance companies, or is organised by the car hire agency; alternatively it can also be obtained at some borders. Theft insurance may also be a good idea (see *Insurance* in the previous chaoter for more on this). For those travelling by car to Central or Eastern Europe, *Derek Ketteridge & Associates*, 2nd Floor, 7A Middle Street, Brighton BN1 1AL; tel 01273-720222; fax 01273-722799, can arrange continental breakdown assistance insurance with the AA at net rates from £10.90 currently.

Utilities

It is essential to understand that although all public services are widely available in these countries, and that the service in question will always be provided in the end, when it actually arrives is far less certain. Moreover, unlike in the UK where several polite reminders for unpaid bills are issued before supplies are cut off, electricity, telephone and water bills must all be paid promptly.

Electricity

The domestic electricity supply in Russia and throughout the region is mostly 220v, 50Hz, as in many European countries, and less commonly 110v or 125v AC. Once all the plugs have been changed on UK electrical appliances to fit Russian two-pin sockets, your UK appliances should perform quite adequately, if a little more slowly than in the past. Adaptors are available in many high-street shops (or at the last-minute at the airport). Electricity is supplied through the overhead lines of an extensive grid system linking the hydroelectric and atomic power stations with cities, towns and villages throughout the former Soviet Union and its neighbours. It is essential to organise meter installation or reconnection through the local electricity company well in advance, as the waiting lists for both services can be very long.

Water

In principle, the water is perfectly safe to drink in almost all urban areas as government regulations require public water supplies to be treated and clean. However, for this same reason the water can have an unpleasant taste of chlorine; and many richer locals and most expatriates afraid of the tap water follow the worldwide fashion nowadays, and drink bottled water instead. This is cheap, good quality, sometimes medicinal and sold at practically every food shop and supermarket. There can be cholera and other epidemics in more remote districts of Former Soviet Union – which horrify the locals as much as westerners – but you are unlikely to come into contact with these, although a number of vaccinations are recommended – see under *Health* below.

Although these European countries have an adequate natural water supply, shortages do occur over the summer months as the water system is still not administered well enough to guarantee a constant unrestricted water supply in many areas. The problem mainly arises because the municipalities control the supply, and plans to lay national pipelines are continually frustrated by other issues, and the underinvestment which dogs almost every aspect of transport, communications and the utilities in Eastern Europe and Russia. Consequently, although there is plenty of rainfall there is not always plenty of water in the dryer months, which involves a corresponding shortage of water in many areas. This problem is exacerbated for obvious reasons in the desert conditions of some

Central Asian countries. Water filters can be bought before departure; and never drink the water on a train unless it has been boiled.

Gas

The use of gas is common in Russia and its neighbours, as it is in the UK, and there is usually a mains household supply. However, in country districts, bottled gas supplied in cylinders is also relatively cheap and commonly used for cooking and heating in many homes; as is coal and other fuel like firewood for wood stoves in more out of the way places and country homes. These can be easily refilled through the butane delivery services which operate in most areas or these bottles and coal can be purchased in local general purpose stores. As with electricity, gas bills for piped gas are sent monthly and are sometimes included in your apartment rent.

Health

The Health Service

In theory, the legacy of communism in most countries has been a national health service which – again theoretically – operates very much like the British one, open to everyone who makes social security payments or who receives a state pension, is unemployed or is under the age of 18, and so on. Facilities are sometimes good, although sometimes as bad as they are painted in the media, with poor services for psychiatric patients, orphans and the disabled, where some international aid agencies are helping.

One such is the *Red Cross*: 9 Grosvenor Crescent, London SW1X 7EJ; tel 0171-235 5454; fax 0171-823 1621). In 1997/8 it launched its 'emergency appeal to help over a million people living on the edge of survival in the former Soviet Union' where in some places – like some parts of Siberia – diseases such as TB have reemerged which are due to poverty, and poor health and housing facilities.

Doctors may treat a foreigner in distress for free. More often, there will be a charge, and sometimes the locals make their way through the system by informal payments like these as well. Never offer money in the first instance (even in the more distant corners of Russia and the CIS countries as it will be assumed, as a foreigner, that you have this anyway and in a public hospital you may cause grave offence. However gifts can be given afterwards to doctors, dentists and the like.

You should have your insurance certificate (or a copy) wth you. Countries like Poland or the Czech Republic, and larger cities across the region, have a health service that more closely resembles an impoverished version of our own. The British or US Embassy will have a list of suitable international clinics in most places; and it is important to have suitable health insurance to cover unexpected emergencies, and also photocopies of all the documentation. The reality in most countries is that free health treatment is only available in certain hospitals in certain areas whose waiting lists are long, and getting longer.

This applies particularly to those who need hospital treatment for terminal diseases; and coverage for many illnesses requiring more expensive treatment is still severely limited. The shortcomings of the system are well exposed by the recurrence from time to time of diseases like cholera which are unknown in Western Europe. Then there is the current epidemic of TB in Russia; and HIV/AIDS is another growing problem. Generally speaking, conditions in Central

Europe are more like those at home. Check on vaccinations with your doctor before departure, and a dental checkup is also a wise precaution (see the *Russia* section of this book for more about preparation and health).

The root of the problem lies in underfunding; and the often old-fashioned and bureaucratic way social security resources are administered and distributed in these countries. Not surprisingly, many of the richer locals are now taking out private health insurance, to replace a situation where knowing someone who knew someone was probably the best way of getting the best healthcare.

On the other hand, medical staff are often as highly trained as their colleagues in Western Europe or the United States. Many are succeeding in doing a difficult job with limited resources. Some treatments, like spas and hydrotherapy, are rather better known here than in Britain – and attract many tourists, to Hungary for example, and there is more emphasis on preventative rather than curative medicine than there often is in Britain. Hoidays for health are even being promoted in many places, like Hungary, Slovakia, Estonia, and Croatia, which can make a health cure one good reason for visiting them. These trips tend to be more popular with continental Europeans, like the French, Germans or Swiss, than with Britons or Americans.

Anyone living and working in in any of these countries who is classed as a resident and below retirement age must make a monthly contribution to the local national health service or social security system. This is usually deducted at source from your salary (see under *Taxation* below). Health is often a major concern of expatriates, who worry about what they have read about hospitals or pollution for example. The more enlightened employers make arrangements for healthcare cover for their expatriate staff, to give them some reassurance. In a recent survey, 67% of expats in Azerbaijan said that medical care was not acceptable there; declining to 60% in Kazakstan; 58% in Ukraine; and 40% in Russia and Uzbekistan (see *Managing Expatriates in the CIS* published by Price Waterhouse).

Some hospitals and clinics only treat private patients; there are American and international clinics in locations like Baku, Moscow and Kiev (but not in provincial towns and cities elsewhere in the former Soviet Union). It is as well to know which hospitals in your area provide private or public health treatment. See also the *Russia Survival Guide*, published by Russia Information Services, Montpelier, VT USA, which has a city-by-city listing for these and other services in Russia, including local hospitals. A list of these health centres and hospitals as well as English-speaking doctors should also be available from your embassy.

The kind of 'What's On' publications national tourist offices can send you directly in Britain or the United States – or even airline magazines – are also good sources of information; and usually more up-to-date and comprehensive than most guide books. So, for health information too, it is a good idea to get hold of some of these – and see the country chapters which follow for some useful contacts.

First of all, you should inform your doctor or GP in the USA or UK, who can advise on immunisations etc. If you are already intending to move to Central/Eastern Europe/CIS, you should read no further and call your doctor now!. In the UK, other suitable sources of information are *MASTA*, the Medical Advisory Service for Travellers Abroad (a premium rate line: tel 0891-224100); the *Foreign Office*, which has an advice to travellers line, on political but also health risks (tel 0171-238 4503/4); the *Department of Health* hotline on health and travel (which is free: tel 0800-555777); and the *National AIDS Helpline* with detailed and confidential advice on AIDS/HIV (tel 0800-567123).

The Department of Health also publishes a *Travel Safe* booklet with advice for travellers on avoiding AIDS and HIV. Other publications which can be useful include: *Traveller's Health*, ed. Richard Darwood (Oxford University Press); the

ABC of Healthy Travel, E.Walker, G.Williams, F.Raeside (British Medical Journal); and *Travel with Children*, Maureen Wheeler (Lonely Planet).

Reciprocal Health Care Agreements

If you are going to one of the countries listed below from the UK and are resident in the UK – and in some cases even if you are not a British national but live there – you should telephone or write to:

Department of Health International Relations 2C, Room 512,
Richmond House, 79 Whitehall, London SW1A 2NS; tel 0171-210 5318.

If you are going to live and work in one of these countries these arrangements or may not apply. Write to:

Contributions Agency (International Services), DSS,
Longbenton, Newcastle-upon-Tyne NE98 1YX; tel 0191-213 5000.

There are reciprocal health care agreements between Britain and the following countries. Listed are the documents needed, what is free, and what you pay charges for:

BULGARIA

You need: UK passport and NHS medical card
Free of charge: Hospital, other medical and dental treatment
You pay for: Medicines from a pharmacy

CZECH REPUBLIC

You need: UK passport
Free of charge: Hospital, other medical care
You pay for: Medicines from a pharmacy and dental treatment

HUNGARY

You need: UK passport
Free of charge: Treatment in hospital, polyclinc or doctor's surgery
You pay for: Dental and eye treatment, and a flat rate for medicines

POLAND

You need: NHS medical card
Free of charge: Hospital, some dental treatment, other medical treatment
You pay for: 30% of prescribed medicines, for the doctor to visit you

ROMANIA

You need: UK passport
Free of charge: Hospital, some dental treatment, other medical treatment
You pay for: Medicines from a pharmacy

RUSSIA

You need: UK passport
Free of charge: Treatment in State Hospitals
You pay for: Prescribed medicines

FORMER SOVIET UNION/CIS COUNTRIES

You need: UK passport
Free of charge: Hospital and other medical treatment, some dental treatment
You pay for: Prescribed medicines

FORMER YUGOSLAVIA AND SUCCESSOR STATES

You need: UK passport
Free of charge: Hospital and other medical treatment, some dental treatment
You pay for: Prescribed medicines

See the current *Health Advice for Travellers anywhere in the world* leaflet which comes with the E111 form from post offices in Britain for any changes on the above. Contact your doctor as far as possible in advance about immunisation; and in the same leaflet there is a *Worldwide Country-By-Country Disease and Immunisation Checklist* giving guidelines on specific health risks; which need, however, to be checked with your doctor.

Health Insurance

Travel insurance will be suitable for shorter stays. Residents should take out private health cover. One of the leading providers is *BUPA International*: tel 01273-208181; fax 01273-866583. *ExpaCare* (Dukes Court, Duke Street, Woking, Surrey GU21 5XB; tel 01483-717800; fax 01483-776620) offers full cover for expatriates; and has plans for the over 65's as well as younger age groups. 'If you are taking out private medical insurance it is important you understand what you are paying for and are certain you are sufficiently covered for your circumstances,' BUPA say. *Derek Ketteridge & Associates* (2nd Floor, 7A Middle Street, Brighton BN1 1AL; tel 01273-720222; fax 01273-722799) offers private healthcare schemes. Other products available from their Billericay office (tel 01277-630770; fax 01277-630578) include general long-stay insurance and non-UK residents insurance.

Wherever you work or retire, you don't have to go without BUPA.

When it comes to overseas health care, you'll find BUPA International goes to the ends of the earth to help.

To: BUPA International, Russell Mews, Brighton BN1 2NR, UK. Tel: +44(0)1273 208181
Fax: +44(0)1273 866583 www.bupa-intl.com advice@bupa-intl.com

Please send me information on BUPA International Lifeline ☐

Name   Address

Company   Nationality   Telephone

BUPA International Lifeline

LW

Local healthcare policies are also sometimes available: payment for medical treatment may be made in the form of vouchers provided by the insurance company rather than having to pay initially and claiming back the treatment cost from the insurance company afterwards. But although the premiums on local insurance policies may be much cheaper, there could also be drawbacks; the policy could be limited to specific local hospitals, for instance, or have other limitations. Read – or get someone to read for you – the small print very carefully. You should only go ahead when you are familiar with the details of the local scheme and how it works – and this will only be for long-term residents who are already familiar with the country, or companies making provision for their staff.

Social Security

You will make local social security payments if you are working and will need to check with your embassy or the local social security ministry Write, hopefully, to their 'International Department' or 'Information Department' to see what this entitles you to. They may be surpised enough to reply!. There may, in fact, be several social security systems, for members of the civil service or the armed forces, for instance, or for old age pensioners. But you will be an expatriate in a somewhat different sense in Russia and Eastern Europe than if you were an EU citizen working in another EU country; and you will be wise not to cut your ties with your own country and its social security system.

When some of the countries above join the EU, the two systems of national insurance will become 'interchangeable', meaning that if you return to Britain at any future time, you will not be held responsible for the missing UK social security payments or vice versa. Until then, this EU system does not apply – and is very unlikely to be introduced retrospectively – and you are advised to keep up your UK payments while working there if you can.

See the following chapter – and country chapters – for more about tax and social security.

What to Take

The E111 form many UK visitors take to European Union and European Economic Area countries does not yet apply here. But some of the advice it offers does. There is a 'disease and immunisation checklist' for countries worldwide; and advice on 'health risks around the world and how to avoid them;' on 'eating and drinking safely;' and medical kits. Certainly in Eastern Europe, medicines may not be so easy to come by and some paracetamol and aspirin, 'Lemsip' or equivalent, and cough sweets like 'Strepsils', sticking plasters and a bandage, antiseptic cream, vitamin tablets, clove oil (which relieves dental pain) or similar toothpaste – all in a small box marked with a cross to indicate their medical use if you can – some chocolate bars or other emergency food supply, along with other useful items like a swiss-army-style knife, shampoo, soap, plastic cups, and so on, have all accompanied the author in his occasional peregrinations in the region.

Try to cover all the angles. If you suffer, even occasionally, from asthma or hay fever, take a suitable inhaler (pollution is a problem in many places). If you are a diabetic, get an official-looking letter from your doctor explaining your syringe and needles, and their medical use. The E111 form itself (although entirely without any official validity) looks impressive enough to convince border guards in the more out-of-the-way locations of your general robust health and upstanding official status. These are easily obtainable (in Britain) in your local post office. Get an international vaccination certificate from your doctor as well: if there is an outbreak of cholera or some similar disease, travellers will need this kind of document to get out of the country. A copy of your medical insurance certificate and details of the insurers is also very useful if you come into contact with medical or other bureaucracy.

You will have informed the British or US Embassy of your presence in the country. Try to have a contact there, even if it is not someone you know, and keep this name and embassy address on you as well. The business card of the British or US ambassador would not get you very far in many countries of the world; but it will in Russia and Eastern Europe, and looks like a guarantee of your status and moral probity.

Finally, be prepared for bad weather conditions, which in winter in many of these countries means extreme cold, and in summer in some of them oppressive heat. Plastic overtrousers, warm underwear, and a woolly cap sound like a joke in Britain. In Russia they could keep you alive. The locals wear two pairs of trouser when the going gets tough, and several insulating layers of shirts and sweaters and so on under one or two coats. You could do worse than do the same. Take insulated boots that do not leak. Listen to the advice which the locals have about local conditions too. Their solutions may work for you

One rule of expatriate life in Russia is that foreigners look ridiculous wearing fur hats. A woollen cap might be more your scene, in a modest, brown or black colour: the multicoloured skiing outfits popular in the Germany or France haven't yet caught on in most parts of Russia. When you feel cold, go somewhere warm, into the metro, or look around a shop, or sit in a café, go anywhere indoors... In this, you are doing as the locals do; and the British disregard for cold and rain certainly won't work in Russia or Poland. Many North Americans and Canadians will know what to do.

In this section on health, it may seem otiose to mention money. But this is often the solution to many of life's problems; and a store of money, not the small change you keep in your pockets, but many more dollars hidden about your person, can be one way of meeting an unexpected emergency, medical or otherwise. When you are travelling, this habit is worth getting into; and carrying photocopies of important documents like medical insurance and passports etc. and the aforementioned and highly recommended ambassadorial business card. All these are ways of promoting health and personal security in Russia and her neighbours.

Money and Finance

The cost of living may be higher in Russia than at home; or less in Central and Eastern Europe. The money you need to earn to support your stay will depend on how you live and your lifestyle, whether you live in a way which is like that of your own country or more like that of the locals. This will depend on the person, and on your personal circumstances.

Imported goods tend to be expensive, and some countries have tied their currency to the German mark, making the food on supermarket shelves the same price as in Germany, expensive in other words. Local people tend to live more cheaply; and one of the choices you will have to make is how far you are prepared to adapt to local circumstances. Western companies tend to assume their employees will not; which is why generous provisions are made for expats living here, often on top of their usual salary. Is the pound or dollar down or up? The strength of the currency will be another important factor when you go; and make a big difference to your real take-home pay.

Travel and finance go together when you are living abroad – in the sense that a trip home, even by one of your friends or colleagues, will be a chance to stock up on some locally more expensive items. If you are going there for the first time, the best idea is to consider carefully what you will need, and then take what you can – even in these modern times when most of the goods you need will also be on sale when you get there, in exactly the same way as at home. But take as much of what you need with you as is practicable, especially more portable items. Unless money is no object, you will discover that many are more expensive in Russia and its neighbours.

Convertible Currencies

If the currency is convertible, you will be able to exchange some before departure. If not, you can't. In many countries, dollars or deutschmarks tend to be more acceptable than pounds sterling; and you will in most cases get a better rate of exchange on arrival. Take a credit card – like American Express, MasterCard or Visa – but not travellers' cheques, which are usually hard to exchange almost everywhere.

Bank Accounts

These can be opened quite easily. You should choose a local bank with international connections if you can; and look carefully at the charges. A problem in many cases will be that they need a large deposit for them to open an account for you. This depends on the bank. It would be wise in Eastern Europe to maintain your own bank account at home as well, however long you are staying, as this is the most secure place to keep the bulk of your savings. Also, financial services – like mortgage, insurance and property services – in nearly all these places have not quite caught up with their present state of sophistication in Britain or the United States.

During any interim period between arriving and receiving your residence permit, you are only likely to be allowed to open non-resident accounts with local banks. These are generally of three kinds:

Non-resident convertible accounts: These can be credited with foreign currency (which is then immediately converted into the local currency if it is convertible); or with local currency transferred from outside the country. All payments locally then can be made through this account quite easily. But you cannot receive payments or money transfers into this kind of account which originate from the country, only from abroad. Put simply, it is a kind of local currency account for foreigners – which will suit some regular business visitors needing an emergency supply of cash, although in many countries and capitals your credit card and a cashpoint machine will do just as well.

Non-resident foreign currency accounts: These are provided for non-residents who wish to hold accounts in foreign currencies (often deutschmarks or dollars). Provided that the money is not converted into the local currency it should not be subject to any transfer restrictions (but you should check on this). Credits to these accounts can only come from another non-resident account or from money earned in special circumstances set out in the taxation laws. You should endeavour to find out from a local bank (or much better before departure) about this kind of account.

Non-resident local currency accounts: This account is entirely non-convertible; it cannot deal in foreign currency of any kind. However, it will be the most useful on a day-to-day basis as it can be credited with money from any of the other accounts and also with income which originates locally. It means simply opening what is in effect a local current account.

Money Transfers

Your best bet for this will be *Western Union* as mentioned (UK tel: 0800-833833; USA tel: 800-325-6000) a quick and easy way of transferring cash abroad or back home in an emergency which offers a high standard of service, and is also well-known in the region. From some countries, you will find – even by Western Union or *Thomas Cook* – that there are limits on the amount of cash you can send out in one transaction, which the local office or bank you go to will enforce. There will be no such bar on money coming in. Take the Western Union enquiry number for the country with you when you go, and their leaflet or a list of their outlets there. Leave this with friends or family in Britain/USA as your emergency way of receiving money).

Bank transfers take longer. *Barclays*, *Lloyds*, the *Midland*, *NatWest* and the *TSB* bank will take from two to five, and in some cases up to 12 days to send money to and from these countries. In all cases too the charges can be considerable. *NatWest* also has an *urgent transfer* service where the transfer should arrive the following day.

Western Union takes about ten minutes; and the money can be picked up on production of suitable ID, and by giving the answer to a suitable 'test question' if the sender has requested this, which will identify the recipient. This can be done at any one of their outlets in the country concerned: you do not have to choose which one if you are sending money, only the person and the country concerned – and it will get there. Its country contact numbers in the UK and USA are 0800-833833 and 1-800-325-6000 respectively, as mentioned above, and also: Albania, 42-34979; Belarus,095-119-8250; Bulgaria, 2-9800806; Czech Republic, 2-2422-9524; Estonia, 095-119-8250; Georgia, 095-119-8250; Hungary, 01-267-4282; Kazakstan, 327-243-3593; Latvia, 095-119-8250; Lithuania, 22-232-613; Moldova, 095-118-8250; Poland, 2-2-31-7008; Russia, 095-119-8250; Slovakia, 7-832-789; Slovenia, 061-140-1223; and Ukraine, 095-119-8250/044-229-6095.

Procedures for Transferring Money

The main rule for non-residents who may be living there for less than six months in any one year is that any money you earn or make is classed as domestic and needs to be converted into non-resident form to bring it back to Britain or the USA. So, if you are doing business or making money a simple current account will not be enough. The permission of the national bank will be needed to transfer this money out of the country; and taking out a cash sum and then bringing it back is not a legal option. For larger sums, a bank transfer will be best if you can arrange this; so when you open any of the above accounts check on these charges in particular – which can be considerable – as well as that bank's usual exchange rates.

It is important that the correct procedures are followed when you transfer money accruing from property or other transactions back to the USA or UK or your country of origin; which usually means much queuing and form filling at the bank; as well as informing the local national bank (which your own bank should do for you automatically. This means also ensuring all taxes have been paid and checking on the clearance to transfer it back. There are usually limits on how much money originating in the country you can transfer back at any one time, which applies also to the moeny you take out of the country in cash.

In CIS/CEE, filling in currency declaration forms when you take cash into the country is also often a necessity. These declarations should be as accurate as you can make them, down to the last dollar or two. But it is not surprising that many foreign workers – given the bureaucracy involved – often return home from Russia and the CIS countries with a quantity of undeclared cash. This is not recommended. And remember that it is a strict legal requirement almost everywhere to carry out local transactions in local currency.

An instant cash transfer service like the one run by *Western Union* will often be more convenient for many of the more remote countries dealt with in this book, for both sending and receiving money in the quickest and most secure way.

Financial Advice

As mentioned earlier, it is not necessary – even if you are moving permanently – to give up all your accounts at home. In fact it will usually be wise to keep the majority of your assets in UK or US-based form, in pounds, or dollars, always making a clear distinction between this money (which you keep for security) and any other purchases or investments made locally, for business or to buy a house for example. Otherwise, you will need just enough for your daily expenses; and access to more in an emergency. When Russians and others are so keen to organise assets for themselves in other countries, to do the opposite and take all your money with you seems somehow to be missing the point.

The Central European countries are an exception to this general rule that money is more secure when it is in pounds and dollars, and better kept in an international bank, or back home. But generally local currency is what you spend, not what you save. Otherwise, when you live and work in Russia and its neighbours you will find dollars useful (in small denominations, and preferably not old or damaged notes) as these are easily exchanged in street corner kiosks as well as banks at all times of the day. Don't change all you dollars at once, either, in some of the more inflationary economies, as this – and the exchange situation – can swiftly mean you lose out.

Get insurance on your credit card, too, or find out if this already covered, and keep the right telephone number with you to call if you do lose it, or it is mislaid. It may be difficult to check on the credentials of local banks: if in doubt, for savings and larger sums of money, stick with one you know. Or ask your present bank or building society before you go, about there international services, and if they have any partners there, or banks they have regular dealings with. *Western Union* may also send you a list of their local agencies, which may be another source of these useful local contact names and addresses. In the kind of 'What's On' guides and tourist information for many destinations mentioned in the previous chapter you will find some more local banks, many of them also advertising their international services.

For investment advice and a wide variety of services including worldwide investment management and financial planning, contact Robin Lindsay-Stewart at *Brewin Dolphin Bell Lawrie Ltd.*, 5 Giltspur Street, London EC1A 9BD; tel 0171-246 1028; fax 0171-246 1093; e-mail rlindsay-stewart@bdbl.co.uk.

Wherever you may be, professional advice need not be far away

BREWIN DOLPHIN
BELL LAWRIE LIMITED

Stockbrokers and portfolio managers since the 18th Century

For further information contact **Robin Lindsay-Stewart**

5 Giltspur Street, London EC1A 9BD

Telephone (44) 171 248 4400 Facsimile (44) 171 246 1093

A member of the London Stock Exchange and regulated by The Securities and Futures Authority Limited
Registered in England no. 2135876 at 5 Giltspur Street, London EC1A 9BD

Resident Accounts

Once you are in possession of the residence permit and/or work permit, your local account will operate in exactly the same way as it does for local people. You may still keep your convertible local and foreign currency accounts if you wish, but will now be taxed on the interest earned on these. Also, before you go, and if you are intend to be resident in any of these countries, you should also make arrangements with your bank or building society at home not to pay tax on interest earned on accounts you have there. In Britain, non-UK residents are asked to fill in Inland Revenue Form R105, which is a declaration that you are not ordinarily resident in the UK and not therefore liable to pay UK tax on this. Do this in plenty of time, and keep a copy. Also give your tax office your forwarding address.

Usually transferring money home from a local current account is only a problem if this is a non-convertible currency. Check on the situation with the relevant embassy beforehand, as more and more currencies in Central Europe in particular are now of 'equal' status to pounds or dollars. In banks locally individual financial services have made more progress than elsewhere in the region; and short-term savings accounts like the ones offered by building societies in the UK may now be another option which means that your money is accessible, and you receive some interest on this as well. But almost everywhere, even when you become a resident, you may be better keeping your dollar or other foreign currency account; and using a local current account only for your local expenses and payments.

Opening Your Account

The normal local currency account above (which can be opened on the spot) is the one which most people will get when they go to live and work in these countries, alongside savings or other accounts at home. It can easily be credited with any foreign currency too; and will be as easy to open in most parts of Eastern Europe nowadays as anywhere else, although banks may be thinner on the ground in Azerbaijan, say, than they are in our own countries. Employers will often be able to help, and point you in the direction of the bank they use as perhaps the most convenient one for you.

Credit Cards

Visa, Mastercard and others usually have local partners; and these international' credit cards are now accepted in more and more shops, restaurants and hotels with an international clientele, increasingly and especially in the Baltic States and Central Europe. These are also used by the more affluent locals as well. There will usually be at least one exchange bureau or agency (like *Thomas Cook*) which can accept these as payment for local currency, if you need this in an emergency.

Banking Procedures

Bank statements tend to be sent out to customers every three months, but should be available on request at any time. Unlike the UK, though, charges are often made for day-to-day banking procedures, like credit card and cheque transactions.

Offshore Banking

This will be a suitable option for some more affluent expats and companies. Offshore banks offer tax-free interest on deposit accounts and investment portfolios through banking centres in tax havens such as Gibraltar and the Channel Islands. More and more high street banks and building societies – along with the investment banks located in the City of London or on Wall Street – are setting up offshore banking facilities. The list given below offers only a handful of the most widely-known which offer such services.

The minimum deposit required by each bank will vary; ranging from £500 to £10,000, with the norm being between £1,000 and £5,000. Usually, a minimum of £10,000 is needed for the year-long deposit accounts while the lower end of the minimum deposit range applies to 90-day deposits; instant access accounts are also available. Here are some useful offshore banking and tax minimisation service addresses:

Abbey National Offshore: 56 Strand Street, Douglas, Isle of Man IM99 1NH; tel 01624-662244; fax 01624-677643.
Abbey National (Gibraltar) Ltd: 237 Main Street, PO Box 824, Gibraltar; tel 76090; fax 72028.
Bradford and Bingley Ltd: 30 Ridgeway Street, Douglas, Isle of Man; tel 01624-661868; fax 01624-661962.
Credit-Suisse (Gibraltar) Ltd: PO Box 556, Neptune House, Marina Bay, Gibraltar; tel 78399; fax 76027.
Ex-Pat Tax Consultants Ltd: Churchfield House, North Drive, Hebburn, Tyne and Wear NE31 1ES; tel 0191-483 7805; fax 0191-428 0530.
Halifax International (Jersey) Ltd: PO Box 664, Halifax House, 31/33 New Street, St Helier, Jersey, Channel Islands JE4 8YW; tel 01534-59840; fax

01534-59280.

Halifax International (Isle of Man) Ltd: PO Box 30, 67 Strand Street, Douglas, Isle of Man IM99 1TA; tel 01624-612323; fax 01624-670086.

HSBC Group: Overseas Banking Unit, Midland Bank Plc, PO Box 648, Poultry and Princes Street, London EC2P 2BX; tel 0171-260 3955/6; fax 0171-260 7431.

Lloyds Bank Plc: Isle of Man Offshore Centre. PO Box 12, Peveril Square, Douglas, Isle of Man IM99 1SS; tel 01624-638104; fax 01624-638181. One of their services is the *Lloyds Bank Overseas Club*.

Moores Rowland Chartered Accountants: Clifford's Inn, Fetter Lane, London EC4A 1AS; tel 0171-831 2345; fax 0171-831 6123. With partners in 500 offices around the world providing home and host country tax compliance and tax minimisation services.

Rothschild's Old Court International Reserves multi-currency fund: tel 01481-713713 (an account offering money transfers to many countries for no charge).

Seatax Ltd: 100 East Leith Gate, Doncaster DN1 1JA; tel 01302-363673; fax 01302-738526. Charges £142 currently for use of their services over 12 months.

Wilfred T. Fry Limited: Crescent House, Crescent Road, Worthing, Sussex BN11 1RN; tel 01903-231545; fax 01903-200868. A comprehensive tax and compliance service. They may send a copy of their useful free guide *The British Expatriate*.

Summary

Consider how much money you need to keep in the country, both before you leave and when you officially become a resident, as once you have opened a domestic local currency account its 'convertibility' will be severely limited. The main thing is to follow all the correct procedures both when taking (or transferring) money into the country, and taking it out. Do not rely, either on your own behalf or anyone else's, on taking in or out large amounts of cash without first checking on the rules for this. Embassies and Consulates are often able to advise on currency and similar matters.

Useful Publications: *The British Expatriate*: see above; *Nexus Expatriate Magazine*, International House, 500 Purley Way, Croydon CR0 4NZ; tel 0181-760 5100; fax 0181-760 0469; and *New Markets Monthly*: STE Publishing Ltd, 45 Beech Street, London EC2Y 8AD; tel 0171-628 4442; fax 0171-628 4442. These all occasionally cover business, tax and banking matters in Former Soviet Union and Central and Eastern European countries.

Other more specialist banking, tax and business publications are published by the *Financial Times* (and tend to be expensive). These include: *Banking and Finance in Eastern and Central Europe, Banking in Russia* and its monthly *Offshore Financial Review*; tel 0171-896 2294.

Overseas Jobs Express: Premier House, Shoreham Airport, West Sussex BN43 5FF, tel 01273-440220/540 fax 01273-440229, http://www.ahoy.com/oje/ – has some living abroad, finance and tax articles, and a 'letters to the editor' section where these kinds of questions are often answered. On the Internet, you can send a blank e-mail to *OJE@zoom.com* for subscription information and answers to frequently asked questions (FAQs).

Taxation

Despite all you may have heard, this is no longer the 'Wild East', where taxes aren't paid and the system has broken down. It may be under strain – but it works! And there is little scope – or any good reason which outweighs the risks – to avoid paying tax in CEE/CIS.

This is not for most of us a place to get rich quick without too many rules and regulations to get in the way. In fact they do, and it seems no single source of information can encompass it all. The end of communism (post-1989 or 1991) has paved the way for the introduction of tax systems in all these countries which are surprisingly close in their operation to our own – with income, sales and property taxes and so on just like the ones we are familiar with at home. These are all new, and constantly being revised, so check on the current situation if you can. There are now variations within all the countries of the Commonwealth of Independent States where previously these rules and regulations were uniform, as there are in the rest of Central and Eastern Europe too. Any person who spends more than 183 days a year in these countries is normally considered to be a resident for tax purposes (in fact residency is itself really a tax definition).

Another refinement of this international 183-day rule is that anyone who is not resident there, i.e. who spends less than 183 days in the country each year, is still liable for the local taxes on income which originates there, e.g. from business activities. In every case, the recipient of the income will be taxed in Russia (or wherever they are earning this income) and will have to apply for relief when they pay income tax in their own country.

As for a person who is temporarily abroad, the extent of his or her liability to UK tax depends on several factors, the principal one being whether you are classed as resident in the UK for tax purposes or not (see above). In the simplest of cases, where a UK citizen works abroad full-time during an entire tax year (i.e. 6 April to 5 April), there will be no liability for UK tax, as long as that person does not spend more than 91 days in the UK on average in one tax year. An outline of residence and its effect on tax liability is given in the Inland Revenue's leaflet IR 20, *Residents' and Non-Residents' Liability to Tax in the United Kingdom*.

Where a person who is abroad remains resident in the UK for tax purposes, she or he may in some circumstances be liable to tax both in the UK and in the country they are visiting. If this happens, however, they can often claim relief under a Double Taxation Agreement made between the two countries from either one tax or the other. Details are given in the Inland Revenue's leaflet IR 58 *Going to Work Abroad*.

Expenses

A person who is abroad but remains liable to UK tax may also be able to claim certain expenses for travelling (and expats may also do this if they come under the Russian or other local system, and are classed as being resident there). Details of the rules can be obtained from any local office of the Inspector of Taxes (to find the address of your local office, look in the Telephone Directory under 'Inland Revenue'). Inland Revenue leaflets are available from any local office of the Inspector of Taxes.

Other general enquiries, claims and problems should be addressed to the *Inland Revenue Financial Intermediaries and Claims Office (FICO)*, Non-residents

Section, St John's House, Merton Road, Bootle, Merseyside L69 9BB. Enquiries about claims to exemption under a Double Taxation Agreement should be addressed to *FICO (Nottingham)*, Fitzroy House, Nottingham NG2 1BD.

The Tax System

The general system of personal taxation is based on salary and other sources of income, e.g. incentive payments and bonuses and housing allowances in excess of your actual expenses. There are often quite generous allowances for these in some countries, and taxes also which concern only businesses and profits from businesses. There will also be a Value Added Tax or purchase tax in each case. But residents will be mainly concerned with income tax, which may be anything from 10% at the lowest rate to 30% or 40% at the highest. As stated above, non-residents may also be taxed if they are regarded as having a permanent establishment in the country or are operating some kind of business there.

Income Tax

The maximum amount of income you can earn at the lowest 12% rate in Russia is currently 14 million roubles; in Azerbaijan this is 0% up to 720,000 manats, and 12% thereafter, rising to 40%. The top rate in Russia at present is 30%. In Kazakstan the lowest rate is 5% (up to 3,480 tenge) rising to 40%; in Ukraine income tax bands range from 0% up to 40%; and a similar pattern is repeated in the other CIS countries. The tax year is from 1 January to 31 December, with tax declarations to be made usually by 31 March, and sometimes shortly after your arrival, when you will need to register with the Tax Authority in the country concerned, usually before 30 days have elapsed. Married couples usually make separate tax returns, and only couples engaged in the same business activity will make a joint declaration.

Fortunately, Britain and the United States both have – or are negotiating – reciprocal agreements with many of these countries (including Russia) which avoids, as we have mentioned, the possibility of someone being taxed twice on the same income or interest. The exception for Britons is during the initial period of residency when, as the UK and local tax years run from April to April and from January to January respectively, UK nationals may end up being taxed by both the local and UK authorities in the overlapping months of their first year in their new country of residence. In this case, though, you are able to claim a refund of UK tax by applying to the Inland Revenue through your local tax office.

They will supply you with the elusively-titled SPA/Individual form, which offers relief at source for tax refunds concerning interest, royalties and pensions, or with the yet more obscurely-titled SPA/Individual/Credit form which provides repayment on dividend income for anyone who has suffered double taxation on moving to Russia and many CIS and Eastern/Central European countries. Once the form has been filled in, take it to the local tax authority office: they will stamp it and then you can return it to the British tax authorities as proof that you have paid local tax and are therefore no longer liable for British tax (a process which one imagines is easier on paper than it is in reality). It is a procedure which obviously should be carried out while you are in the country and not after your return to the UK. It is also important to keep good records of all your income etc. while in the country, to meet any problems should these arise.

For more information on the local tax system, contact its embassy or consulate, or the Economy Ministry (and as in almost all your research, these most direct and up-to-date details will be the best).

Tax Returns

You can even draw up your own tax return – with a little help from your friends – even in these CEE/CIS countries. Advice on how to do this may be available from the local tax authority.

Various deductions are available from income tax totals for those who are married and/or whose children, parents or grandparents live with them; invalids also receive a deduction. Additionally, if you have bought a house in the current tax year or if you are making payments on one, you may be able to deduct a percentage of that amount from your income tax total. Further information about tax or any changes in rates can be found in English-language leaflets available from some Central and Eastern European embassies.

There is sometimes some mystification of these issues but you should remember that it is much easier for a local person to understand these rules than it is for you: after all they live there, and really do know the country. Other employees pay tax in just the same way you do if you are working there – so a sympathetic colleague should also be able to offer some advice, or a local accountant or lawyer.

If you are working independently, you just need to find somebody like this who is reliable and who can help. Managers sending staff to the region should also seek advice from a locally based adviser or consultancy; or some of the organisations like *Moores Rowland, The Russia House* and *The Centre for International Briefing* mentioned earlier.

Working in Russia and Eastern Europe

Employment

Most of the general procedures for immigration, work and residence are covered in the preceding chapters and for each subsequent country chapter there is also a *Working in...* section about employment and doing business there. So for each country, there is a general review of these rules and regulations, as well as some work and business contacts to follow up. An organisation which can supply some more of these direct contacts for employment or business in all the CEE/CIS countries is *English Contacts Abroad*, PO Box 126, Oxford OX2 6UB, UK.

This information applies to work and doing business specifically in these countries. The following is a general overview of work and business in the CEE/CIS region as a whole.

General Background

It is important to make preparations for your departure – and especially applications for tourist, business or residence visas – as far as possible in advance (see earlier chapters) and in most cases at least two or three months before your departure. *Moores Rowland* provides a range of services for expatriates including executive briefings, pre-assignment planning, tax compliance, remuneration, tax, social security and other issues. Contact *Moores Rowland Chartered Accountants*: Clifford's Inn, Fetter Lane, London EC4 1AS, tel 0171-831 2345, fax 0171-831 6123.

The Russia House Ltd. organises visa procuration, travel, and exhibitions, trade meetings and seminars, with many other services, and has offices in London, Edinburgh, New York, Stockholm, Hong Kong, Brussels (from September 1998), Moscow, St. Petersburg and Tbilisi.. Contact: *The Russia House Ltd.*, 37 Kingly Court, Kingly Street, London W1R 5LE; tel 0171-439 1271; fax 0171-434 0813. See the chapter on *Preparation and Arrival* for more of these organisations which brief expatriates and business people before departure.

Procedures for immigration and visas may be subject to change, and you are advised to check on these well in advance with the embassy concerned. There may be restrictions on the import and export of local and international currency – and the embassy or consulate will advise on procedures for this. A company which offers a visa service discounted air fares and special hotel rates in the region is *Overseas Business Travel Ltd.*, 8 Minories, London EC3N 1BJ; tel 0171-702 2468; fax 0171-488 1199.

Employment Contacts

UK Newspapers and Representatives

Agencies in the UK which represent a wide variety of newspapers and other publications in this region for advertising purposes are: *Frank L. Crane Ltd.*, 5-15 Cromer Street, Gray's Inn Road, London WC1H 8LS, tel 0171-837 3330; *Mercury Publicity*, 16 John Street, London WC1N 2DL, tel 0171-831 6631; and *Powers International*, 515-523 Fulham Road, London SW6 1HD, tel 0171-385 8855.

There are English-language publications like *The Warsaw Voice* and *The Budapest Sun* in many countries, aimed at the local business and expatriate communities, and which may be suitable for placing a 'situation wanted' ad, and many of these also have representatives in Britain or the United States.

New Markets Monthly – for 'traders and investors in the newly emerging markets of Eastern Europe and Asia' – is a source of news about UK and US companies investing in the region, and general economic developments: *NMM*, STE Publishing, 45 Beech Street, Londin EC2Y 8AD; tel 0171-628 4442; fax 0171-628 4443; e-mail new.markets@btijnternet.com. A subscription is currently £55 within the UK and $160 overseas.

For more specific employment opportunities there are many sources of vacancies and ads – including the kind of vacancies you can 'create' yourself if you take a more creative approach to your jobseeking. See the *Directory of Jobs and Careers Abroad* (Vacation Work) for more on this; and all the contacts and references in this book – here and in the specific country chapters – can be useful and a potential source of job opportunities in a range of 'independent' areas of employment as well from tourism to voluntary work, English teaching and other fields. If you are looking for work independently, you will find an informal approach like this, which involves following up the contacts you have – or which you can help to create yourself – is at least as useful as the more formal approach of writing interminable letters to recruitment agencies and/or following up ads.

This is especially so in the context of the CEE and CIS countries dealt with here.

One very important source of direct job opportunities – and useful background information – for those considering living and working overseas is *Overseas Jobs Express*: Premier House, Shoreham Airport, West Sussex BN43 5FF; tel 01273-440220/540; fax 01273-440229; http://www.ahoy.com/oje/. *OJE* has a wide range of vacancies and the latest news on international work and jobseeking worldwide. In the UK, *Nexus Expatriate Magazine* also handles many foreign vacancies, including some in this region, and provides other valuable information for expatriates. This publication is available from *Expat Network Limited* at International House, 500 Purley Way, Croydon CR0 4NZ; tel 0181-760 5100; fax 0181-760 0469; e-mail expatnetwork@demon.co.uk; internet http://www.expatnetwork.co.uk.

The Internet: For many useful Russian and Eastern European employment contacts you can begin at the *OJE* website mentioned above or use the contacts listed in an important book for all those considering living and working in Russia, the *Russia Survival Guide*, published by *Russian Information Services, Inc.*, 89 Main Street, Suite 2, Montpelier VT 05602, USA; tel 802-223-4955; fax 802-223-6105; e-mail 73244.3372@compuserve.com. You can visit their website at: http://www.friends-partners.org/rispubs.

WE CAN REACH THE PEOPLE WHO WILL HELP YOUR BUSINESS GROW

GOOD MANAGEMENT - WHO NEEDS IT?

In a Global Market, recruiting the high calibre people who will help your business to develop and grow offers an increasing challenge.

At Antal International, we've adopted a unique approach that provides effective recruitment solutions throughout the world – and particularly in the new Central and Eastern European markets where we are firmly established as leading recruitment experts.

Our Matrix Portfolio Management (MPM) system enables us to work closely with clients and to achieve exceptional results by developing:

1 Knowledge of your organisation
2 Expertise in your industry sector
3 Comprehensive experience in the skill set and formal discipline sought
4 An integrated team based approach

MPM is supported by our three way methodology of Search (Headhunting), Selection (Advertising) and Antal Portfolio (Database) all delivered through an international network that keeps us in touch with local trends and developments.

The record of the Antal International approach speaks for itself – we have a success rate in our retained assignments of above 90%. If you'd like to know more, please call Aimee Watson **NOW** quoting refence VW3229 on **+44 (0)171 637 2001**.

ANTAL INTERNATIONAL LTD

2ND FLOOR · 90 TOTTENHAM COURT ROAD · LONDON W1P 0AN
TELEPHONE: +44 (0)171 637 2001 · FACSIMILE: +44 (0)171 637 0949
web site: www.antal-int.com

A member of the Antal International Group of Companies

UK • CZECH REP • FRANCE • GERMANY • HONG KONG • HUNGARY • ITALY
KAZAKHSTAN • POLAND • ROMANIA • RUSSIA • UKRAINE • USA

Your search engine may lead you in the right direction on the Internet if you use key words like the name of the country you are interested in, which all experienced Net users will be able to do. These are some of the many starting points on the Internet which can greatly help in your background research, and in taking a more creative approach to your jobseeking.

International and Local Press: In many ways the most direct contacts are offered by the international press – or better still the local newspapers in the local language which you may obtain (as a last resort perhaps) through the embassies of the country concerned. This is especially so if your focus is on a particular destination or country.

These foreign-language newspapers are also to be found on sale in newsagents, in places where there may be an expatriate community of Russians, Poles or Czechs etc. Embassies and cultural organisations also have their reading rooms; or you can arrange a subscription to a suitable newspaper through their UK or US advertising agents if you can track these down, and who may send you a copy on request of some of the publications they represent if you are interested in advertising in them.

Apart from *Overseas Jobs Express* for vacancies internationally, the major US newspapers carrying international recruitment advertising are: the *Chicago Tribune*, 435 North Michigan Avenue, Chicago, Ill 60611; the *Los Angeles Times*, Times Mirror Square, Los Angeles, California, CA 90053; and the *New York Times*, 229 West 43rd Street, New York, NY 10036. The *International Herald Tribune*, 181 Avenue Charles de Gaulle, 92521 Neuilly-sur-Seine, France, also contains some high-flying vacancies, as does the *Financial Times*, Number One, Southwark Bridge, London SE1 9HL; and also British newspapers like *The Times*, *The Daily Telegraph* and *The Guardian*.

One useful media contact is *Reuters Business Briefing*, an on-line service for subscribers giving access both to news and 2,000 business publications from around the world, including newspapers and trade journals. Information can be retrieved 'by word search or selection lists for companies, countries and topics': tel 0171-250 1122; e-mail paul.waddington@reuters.com Etweedie@firefly.co.uk. Also, a full list of general and specialist newspapers and magazines published in the UK is given in *British Rates and Data* (known as 'BRAD'). This is usually available in public reference libraries and is an invaluable source of research information on media-related topics.

Willings Press Guide gives much the same kind of worldwide information. The 'overseas' volume lists each country's press in straightforward alphabetical order, along with any relevant advertising agents. Check some of these general sources of information if you are researching the media and newspapers in these countries. Or take a more direct approach and ask someone who has been there which are the most important local language and English language publications. Then contact these publications direct, and request a copy.

Directories: To get more detailed information like this about companies with operations in the CEE/CIS countries, you will also find that the more direct the approach, the more successful you will be. The directories which exist have a habit of recording the situation one, two, or three years before, not how it is now. So contact these companies now if you can, or compare two or three sources of information, which is another way of raising the quality of these mailing-list-type contacts. Write to someone directly who you know, or knows someone who knows someone who knows.. These are the contacts which will often work best.

Consider also the need to send off hundreds of speculative letters of application, and if this is really necessary. Or will one more effective and focussed interview with the right person not be more productive in the long run? Take your own approach, the one which suits you, and you will give yourself the greatest chance of success. Prospective employers may appreciate this too, and feel you are someone to be relied on (a very important factor in this sometimes unstable region).

Valuing your own integrity is a part of jobseeking here. There may also be more creative and direct ways of going about making yourself known to these companies and recruiting organisations than a simple letter of enquiry or application, a more creative approach which will be more interesting, and will not so quickly exhaust your patience!

But these directories of information do exist, and can be useful. One is the *Directory of Corporate Affiliations* (National Register Publishing, New Providence, NJ), a listing of international companies, subsidiaries, and non-US holdings classified according to the sectors in which they operate, and a good source for companies in a particular area or sector of industry. For multinational companies, there is also *Worldwide Branch Locations of Multinational Companies* edited by David S. Hooper (Gale Research).

If you have £1,040 to spare you can buy the hardback and CD Rom versions of the *Major Companies of Central and Eastern Europe & the Commonwealth of Independent States* directory (*Graham & Whiteside*, Tuition House, 5-6 Francis Grove, London SW19 4DT; fax 0181-947 1163). You might more profitably spend time in your free local library though. A directory with profiles of major international companies which can be found in most business libraries is *Hoover's Handbook of World Business*, edited by Patrick J. Spavin and James R. Talbot. It has quite a comprehensive country-by-country guide, including Central and Eastern Europe.

The local telephone directories and 'yellow pages' offer perhaps the widest and most up-to-date range of contacts you can find, and which you know are there! Why not use these, in conjunction with information from a trade association or chamber of commerce for instance? If you are not used to research, you should at least try (and remember that research can be a creative process too, and is not just a question of going through dusty volumes day after day). Ask yourself the question, what kind of information can help you, and then be direct in your efforts to find it.

Embassies stock their own national directories (like libraries) but here an appointment is usually necessary for access, so try your local library first. This is really the best place to go, or pay a visit to the business or careers library of your local college or university. These are often very helpful, although sometimes today also becoming a paying service. There are some more specialist trade or business or cultural libraries too which are listed here.

Libraries: A large selection of international newspapers is to be found at the *City Business Library*, 1 Brewers Hall Garden, London EC2V 5BX; tel 0171-638 8215. Remember that even these specialist business libraries will not always have the publication you want though, so you should telephone in advance. In the USA, these major libraries include the *Library of Congress Information Office*, LM-103, Washington, DC, tel 202-287-5108 (open 8.30am-9.30pm Monday to Friday, 8.30am-5pm Saturday, 1pm-5pm Sunday) which provides a reference service on subjects including business, economics, and employment in Central and Eastern Europe; and the *Federal Trade Commission Library*, 6th Street and Pennsylvania Avenue, NW, Washington, DC 20580, tel 202-236-2395 (open 8.30am-5pm Monday to Friday) which also contains many international trade and commercial directories. The *Los Angeles Public Library*, 630 West 5th Street, Los Angeles, CA9007, tel 213-612-3320, has a large business and economics section, and an on-line computer search service. For researchers who cannot visit the *Westminster Reference Library* in London also has an 'Information for Business' service (tel 0171-976 1285).

Another source of research material may be your trade association or union. For example the union *BECTU*, for broadcast and entertainmant staff in Britain, has a regular vacancy list with some international vacancies. They publish directories of specialist staff in the areas they cover and can supply information about the international organisation of media unions – *MEI* – which has affiliate members throughout the CEE/CIS region. This is one example of a more creative approach to finding out about vacancies and potential job contacts. In this region in particular getting a job depends on research which may require some lateral thinking – and making some more direct contacts of your own.

Research Services: There are also several research services specialising in Central and Eastern Europe, of interest to jobseekers and business people alike, although it must be said that these tend to be expensive and are aimed more at companies and organisations than individuals. They tend to advertise in the trade and business press like *New Markets Monthly* or the special reports on CEE/CIS countries which appear from time to time in the *Financial Times* or *Wall Street Journal* for example. Back issues of these newspapers or magazines can be found of course in the periodicals department of your local library... *PHI Research* is one independent research company specialising in market, consumer and business research in the CIS: tel 0181-653 9909; e-mail 101612.2203@compuserve.com.

These research services will usually be efficient, but often not too cost efficient, and will suit some of companies and the larger organisations at which they are aimed. They can do research for you, but generally independent jobseekers and business people who want to find out more about working (or living) in the region will be better off doing their own. Best of all, speak – or know someone who speaks – the local language who can help you to translate or navigate your way around the information available in that language. If you are ploughing for hours through reams of research material, consider whether or not there is a more direct way of getting to the information or contacts you want, and try this. Think of local embassies, or tourist offices, the local British Council office, British and American Embassies, Chambers of Commerce, trade offices and ministries, the Internet, friends and personal contacts you have, or the research services and sources which are mentioned in the pages which follow, for specific countries, like *English Contacts Abroad* (PO Box 126, Oxford OX2 6RU, UK).

Recruitment Agencies

The *Management Consultancies Association* (11 West Halkin Street, London SW1X 8JL) is another trade association in Britain for management consultancies. In the UK, details of employment agency members of the national organisation, the *Federation of Recruitment and Employment Services Ltd.* can be obtained direct from their London address by post only. This is *FRES*, 36-38 Mortimer Street, London SW1X 8PH. The agencies listed here will usually recruit only qualified and experienced staff. More specialising in the region can be found in the pages of *Overseas Jobs Express* (see above).

In addition, the *CEPEC Recruitment Guide*, produced by *CEPEC Ltd.*, Lilly House, 13 Hanover Square, London W1R 9HD, tel 0171-629 2266, fax 0171-629

7066, lists over 400 recruitment agencies and search consultants in the UK, about half of which will undertake assignments abroad, including many in the CEE/CIS countries.

The recruitment agencies listed below all deal with Russia and/or the CEE/CIS countries and may accept applications for a broad range of overseas management, technical or professional positions. You will usually need to be qualified and experienced to try this approach to getting a job in Eastern Europe and Russia. Consultancies and recruitment agencies advertising in the national or trade press should also be contacted, even those on your local high street or in your local telephone or business directory perhaps; they can often can offer further guidance.

See also the guide to *The Former Soviet Union* published by *Expat Network Limited*, International House, 500 Purley Way, Croydon CR0 4NZ, tel 0181-760 5100, fax 0181-760 0469, e-mail expatnetwork@cityscape.co.uk, which contains information on Russia and its neighbours and some 'recruiters hiring for the Former Soviet Union States.'

Antal International Ltd.: 2nd Floor, 90 Tottenham Court Road, London W1P 0AN, tel 0171-637 2001, fax 0171-637 0949, e-mail info@antal-int.com – deals with middle to senior management placements in all disciplines, and has regional offices in Moscow, Warsaw, Krakow, Kiev, Prague, Budapest, Bucharest, Almaty, Paris, Milan, Hamburg, New York and Hong Kong. Future expansion is planned for Latin America and Australia. 'By the year 2000 we will be the number one recruiter in emerging and developing markets.' Their client base includes most global multinationals, as well as local companies.

Anthony Moss & Associates: 173/175 Drummond Street, London NW1 3JD – recruits international experts in banking, training, transportation, water, waste, agriculture, construction, oil and gas and manufacturing, at middle and senior management level in Europe.

ASA International: 63 George Street, Edinburgh EH2 2JG, tel 0131-226 6222, fax 0131-226 5110 – specialises in the recruitment of accountancy staff and financial management for overseas clients, both in the profession and in industry and commerce. Suitable applications are kept on file for matching with appropriate vacancies as and when they rise. Offices also in Aberdeen, Glasgow, London, Prague, and Warsaw.

Barton Executive Search/Barton Interim Management: Bere Barton, Bere Ferrers, Yelverton, Devon PL20 7JL, tel 01822-840220, fax 01822-841134 – is a research-driven senior executive consultancy which seeks to identify qualified candidates wherever they may be. Middle and senior management and board level assignments in all sectors of business and industry in Europe are dealt with. Minimum length of contract: three years (executive search), 3-6 months (interim management). CVs are held against client requirements.

Berenschot Euro Management: PO Box 8039, NL-3503 RA Utrect, The Netherlands, fax 291-6827 – is involved in managing and implementing large international projects, and European affairs and public procurement coonsulting and recruits professional consultants and experts from all disciplines, with an emphasis on administration reform, privatisation and regional development for the European Commission and other international agencies. Requirements are experience of project work in Central and Eastern Europe, the former Soviet Union, and/or the Mediterranean countries. Applicants should also have a knowledge of the process of European integration and the accession of those countries to the EU.

The activities of the recruitment consultant below are mainly in the field of finance. Other consultants with a wider scope to be found under the heading *Consultants and Agencies*.

Bower and Company: 36 Essenden Road, Sanderstead, Surrey CR2 0BU, tel 0181-657 3564, fax 0181-651 4754 – specialises in the use of IT in banking, and recruits staff for North America, Eastern Europe, the EU and Scandinavia.

Butler Service Group UK Ltd: Kings Mill, Kings Mill Lane, South Nutfield, Redhill, Surrey RH1 5NE, tel 01737-822000, fax 01737-823031 – is one of the world's leading providers of technical specialists and managers in all areas of industry. Appointments in most parts of the world, including Central and Eastern Europe. *Butler Service Group, Inc.* has 50 offices throughout North America (Corporate offices: 110 Summit Avenue, PO Box 460, Montvale, NJ 07645, USA). The majority of personnel are highly qualified in their field of expertise. UK enquiries to the Recruitment Department, Operations and Recruitment Manager.

CCL Recruitment International Ltd: 298 High Street, Dovercourt, Harwich, Essex C012 3PJ, tel 01255-506001, fax 01255 506002 – regularly advertises vacancies in Central and Eastern Europe, including technicians, engineers, and automotive and construction experts

Daulton Construction Personnel Ltd: 2 Greycoat Place, London SW1P 1SB, tel 0171-222 0817, 0171-233 0734 – also advertises construction and allied jobs in CEE and CIS.

GMZ: PO Box 5180, D-65726 Eschborn, Germany, fax 6196-797-302 – recruits worldwide on behalf of the German government and other donor countries in the development field, with openings for consultants in finance, small enterprise development, and management consultancy. Qualifications, several years' experience, as well as proven management ability are required. Many of these projects are in Eastern Europe.

Grafton Recruitment Ltd: 35-37 Queens Square, Belfast BT1 3FG, tel 01232-242824, fax 01232-242897, http://www.msldb.com/grafton, e-mail Recruitment@Grafton.com – with offices in Northern Ireland, Dublin, Prague, and Budapest – is Ireland's leading consultancy group. The *International Division* recruits experienced and qualified personnel mainly for the Czech Republic, Germany and Hungary, but also some other CEE destinations. Sectors handled include accountancy, catering, construction, electronics, IT, nursing, and sales and management; the 'necessary skills and experience' are required. A CV, passport photos, references and copies of qualifications/memberships should be forwarded to the relevant office. The other Irish and overseas addresses can be obtained from the Queens Square office.

Mottet & Associates: 25 rue Vlasendael, B-1070 Brussels, Belgium, tel 2-527-03-09, fax 2-527-16-99 – are management consultants for top and middle management positions in all types of industry and business in mainly Central and Western Europe. Suitable experience is required, and speakers of other languages are particularly welcome. *Mottet Selection* is their department for middle management; *MBA Transfer* is for MBA graduates.

Opta: Cockayne House, 126-128 Crockhamwell Road, Woodley RG5 3JH, tel 01734-695600, fax 01734-691412 – is primarily a management consultancy specialising in the telecommunications market. They also provide sub-contracted resources to companies across Europe (through *Opta Resources* at the above address) especially in France and Germany, but also further afield.

Pepper, Hamilton & Scheetz: 9 Haywards Place, London EC1R 0EE – is one of the most experienced firms in Russia and former Soviet Union with offices in this region, and a varied, interesting and challenging practice. At least four years' experience is required and fluent Russian is preferred.

Preng and Associates: Langham House, 29/30 Margaret Street, London W1N

7LB, tel 0171-580 1144, 0171-580 1444 – recruitment of specialists in the oil and gas industry for Former Soviet Union.

Scott Neale & Partners: Scott House, Basing View, Basingstoke, Hampshire RG21 4JG, fax 01256-460582 – places institutional development experts in areas such as asset sales, business appraisal and planning, marketing, healthcare management, and management development in Eastewrn Europe, CIS and Africa. Experience in public administration, manufacturing, and transportation is an advantage. You should specify your specialism and sector and write to the Chief Executive at the above address.

Sherry Sherratt Technical Recruitment Ltd: PO Box 4529, London SW18 3SX, tel 0181-875 1849, fax 0181-875 1894 – has occasional vacancies for qualified accountants (ACA, ACCA, CIMA, or MBA finance stream) with appropriate language skills to work in Central and Eastern Europe and Russia. Fluent German may be relevant for some vacancies.

Systematic Management Search (SMS): Bahnhofstrasse 69, CH-8001 Zürich, tel 01-211-27-50 – also with offices in Dusseldorf, Frankfurt and Berlin, specialises in headhunting top and senior executives on an international basis. They have associated partner companies in Paris, London and New York.

Sheffield International Ltd: 10-15 Quarry Street, London EC4N 1TJ – specialises in top-flight banking, financial and legal services, including investment analysts and economists throughout the world, including Eastern Europe and East Asia.

Stanlake Search: 61 Stanlake Road, London W12 7HG, tel 0181-749 4786, fax 0181-248 7436 – is an executive search agency specialising in IT with overseas assignments in the EU and Eastern Europe.

Transtec SA: Ave. de Tyras 75, B-1120 Brussels, Belgium, tel 2-266-49-50, fax +2-266-49-65, compuserve 100571,2403, e-mail TRANSTEC@TRANSTEC.be – recruits high-level consultants to governments and other international bodies in the areas of transport, tourism, urban and rural development, irrigation and export promotion. Only those with a minimum of 10 years' experience of high-level consultancy, advanced degrees and fluency in foreign languages can be considered.

Consultancies

Chartered accountancy firms nowadays also offer business advice and consultancy services throughout the CEE/CIS region, with offices in each of these countries which can be a source of much local background information and advice, and will also provide employment for some. Contact their head office in the first instance, and these firms also recruit on the annual 'milk-round' of recruitment seminars and fairs at British universities.

The major international accountancy and consultancy firms based in the UK are:

Arthur Andersen: 1 Surrey Street, London WC2R 2PS.
Coopers & Lybrand: 1 Embankment Place, London WC2N 6NN.
Deloitte & Touche, Hill House, Little New Street, London EC4A 3TR.
Ernst & Young: Becket House, 1 Lambeth Palace Road, London SE1 7EU..
KPMG: 1 Salisbury Square, London EC4Y 8BB.
Price Waterhouse: No.1 London Bridge, London SE1 3TR.

Some of these consultancies may merge their operations in future, so the above addresses may be subject to change. See also the very useful and comprehensive

Official ICAEW List of Members and Firms (Macmillan) which lists their many international offices and branches, along with some other UK-based international accountants and consultancies with operations in the countries of Central and Eastern Europe and Former Soviet Union, along with their local offices from Krakow to Krasnoyarsk.

Teaching

Britain:
The British Council's *English Language Information Unit – ELIU* – Medlock Street, Manchester M15 4PR, tel 0161-957700 – provides information on all aspects of English language teaching abroad. The ELIU also produces various publications, including a free information pack. This is the main UK source of information on English language teaching, and as it applies to the CEE/CIS countries. Also see under *Voluntary Work* below for some English language teaching opportunities, and under the separate country chapters of this book.

Apart from teaching and other posts within the British Council itself, the *BC* is also active as a recruiting agency for teaching and educational advisory posts in foreign governments and institutions. Most vacancies are for senior English language positions at all levels of education so the necessary requirements at this level of teaching in Russia and Eastern Europe are usually a degree or diploma in education, or a TEFL qualification at Diploma or PGCE level. Further details can be obtained from the *Overseas Educational Appointments Department*, The British Council, Medlock Street, Manchester M15 4PR, from whom the free booklet *Teaching Overseas* is available.

The many BC offices and resource centres in CEE/CIS countries and their noticeboards can be a useful source of vacancies and contacts for private tutors, and for jobs in local language schools and universities sometimes, where experience and qualifications – while helpful – will not always be required.

United States:
In the USA, the emphasis is on university degree courses in linguistics, although increasingly universities are offering intensive TESL training (the American acronym for Teaching English as a Second Language). For a guide to the academic courses (but not the more intensive ones, there is the *Directory of Professional Placement Programs in TESOL in the US* (TESOL Inc., 1600 Cameron St, Suite 300, Alexandria, Virginia 22314-2751).

Useful Addresses:
AFS Intercultural Programs: 313 E. 43rd Street, New York, NY 10017, tel 212-949-4242.

The Central Bureau for Educational Visits and Exchanges: 10 Spring Gardens, London SW1A 2BN, tel 0171-389 4004, fax 0171-389 4426, CAMPUS 2000 01:YNK 330 – arranges assistantships for undergraduates and graduates on an exchange basis. Applications should be made by December of the year preceding appointment. Appointments are for one academic year, and are available in approximately 30 countries worldwide.

Council on International Educational Exchange (CIEE): 52 Poland Street, London W1V 4JQ, tel 0171-478 2006, fax, 0171-734 7322, e-mail infouk@ciee.org – administers the US/UK Career Development Programme to promote transnational training for qualified individuals. The aim of the programme is to gain practical work experience in the USA or the UK. This programme is administered in the USA by *AIPT*, 10400 Little Patuxent Parkway, Suite 250, Columbia MD 21044-3510, tel 410-997-2200, fax 410-992-3924.

The European Council of International Schools (ECIS): 21 Lavant Street, Petersfield, Hants GU32 3EL, tel 01730-268244, fax 01730-267914, e-mail 100412.242@compuserve. com, http://www.ecis.org – is an organisation of over 420 independent international schools around the world from Ukraine to the United States. It has associate and affiliate members among other education-related organisations; and assists in staffing member schools and advertises vacancies on the ECIS World Wide Web site. ECIS publishes: the *ECIS International Schools Directory* (which is also accessible at their web-site), enabling global access to information about 800 or so independent and international schools; a newsletter; and the semi-annual *International Schools Journal* concerned specifically with education in international schools.

ECIS North American Office is at: 105 Tuxford Terrace, Basking Ridge, New Jersey 07920, tel 908-903-0552, fax 908-580-9381, e-mail malyecisna@aol.com.

English Contacts Abroad: PO Box 126, Oxford OX2 6UB – is an international networking service for English language teachers thinking of going abroad specialising in Central and Eastern Europe and the CIS countries; and will put you in touch with a teacher on the spot or supply lists of local schools currently recruiting teachers. An administration fee of £48 is charged; and an SAE should be enclosed with your enquiry. They may also provide useful information and advice about living and working in that country and the recruitment of teacher agents.

Georgetown University Internship Programs: PO Box 2298, Washington DC 20057-1011, tel 202-298-0200 – runs the *Academy for International Training (AIT)* 'Teaching English Conversation' internship program for recent college graduates who would like learn about and participate in the political and humanitarian dimensions of global events. It is a fee-charging program. Interns are responsible for training and travel costs to the point of entry; adequate housing, health care, foreign language training and a monthly stipend equivalent to that paid to a local teacher are all supplied. Countries which are covered include Poland, Hungary, Bulgaria, the Czech and Slovak Republics, and several others.

i to i international projects: Notre Dame SFC, Saint Mark's Avenue, Leeds LS2 9BL, tel 0113-245 3515 (for information pack), fax 0113-245 3350, e-mail 106144.174@compuserve.com, http://ourworld.compuserve.com/home pages/i-to-i – offers placements in St. Petersburg for people aged 17-25. Length varies from six weeks to three months. Board and accommodation provided. Volunteers must find their own travel and insurance costs, plus the placement fee presently of £390. All teaching assistants will need to take a twenty-hour TEFL course.

inlingua Teacher Service: Essex House, 27 Temple Street, Birmingham B2 5DB, fax 0121-456 3264 – each year recruits approximately 200 teachers of English as a Foreign Language to work in one of its 160 associated schools abroad. Candidates must have a degree and/or teaching certificate. Schools prefer applicants who have attended an *inlingua Introductory Method Course* as held in Birmingham throughout the year. For application forms and details of posts and courses in Russia and Eastern Europe contact the Recruitment Officer at the above address.

International House: 106 Piccadilly, London W1V 9FL, tel 0171-491 2598, fax 0171-409 0959, e-mail 100733.511@compuserve.com -- offers around 300 TEFL posts a year in around 93 affiliated schools in 25 countries from Argentina to Ukraine – and is the largest trainer of RSA/Cambridge Certificate (C/TEFLA) and Diploma (D/TEFLA) candidates in the world. It has around 300 jobs to offer each year. The minimum qualification for an appointment with 'International House' itself – which chooses the pick of the candidates it trains – is a C/TEFLA with a Pass Grade B.

International Placement Group (IPG): 72 New Bond Street, London W1, tel/fax 0171-739 2723, e-mail ipg@praha.demon.co.uk – See under *Working in the Czech Republic – Teaching*. Teachers also required for Poland, Russia, Hungary and Slovakia.

International Schools Service: PO Box 5910, Princeton, New Jersey 08543, tel 609-452-0990, fax 609-452-2690 – primarily seeks to place state certified teachers (for a placement fee) in English-medium international schools following an American curriculum. They hold recruitment meetings in February and June attended by approximately 100 schools worldwide.

Language Matters: 2 Rookery Road, Selly Oak, Birmingham B29 7DQ, tel/fax 0121-477 1988 – places qualified language teachers in posts in Poland and other European countries. Contracts are usually for 9 months with full local employment protection. A CV, photographs and references are required.

Nord-Anglia International: 10 Eden Place, Cheadle, Cheshire SK8 1AT, tel 0161-491 4191, fax 0161-491 4408 – recruits internationally – and for an increasing number of schools in CEE/CIS – and for its summer schools in the UK. RSA/UCLES Certificate or equivalent required.

Office of Overseas Schools: SA-29, Rm 245, Dept. of State, Washington, DC 20522-2902, tel 703-875-7800.

Saxoncourt Recruitment: 59 South Molton Street, London W1Y 1HH, fax 0171-499 9374 – is a specialist EFL recruitment service recruiting over 200 teachers annually for schools throughout the world, including Eastern Europe. Candidates must have either RSA/Cambridge or Trinity College London TEFL Cert. Applicants should send a CV and covering letter to the Recruitment Manager at the above address.

Services for Open Learning (SOL): N.D.P.C, Vicarage Street, Barnstaple, Devon EX32 7HB, tel 01271-327319, fax 01272-376650, e-mail sol@enterprise.met – is a charity set up to support the extraordinary needs of the countries of the former Eastern Europe in relation to the teaching and learning of English – its main income is from courses it runs at its centres in North Devon for students and teachers from Eastern Europe. It recruits 60-70 graduate teachers to work for at least an academic year in state schools and universities. Currently these are placed in Belarus, Czech Republic, Hungary, Romania and Slovakia with the greatest numbers in Hungary and Romania. Poland and Croatia may be destinations in future.

Teaching Abroad: 46 Beech View, Angmering, Sussex BN16 4DE, tel 01903-859911, fax 01903-785779, e-mail teaching-abroad@garlands.uk.com, http://www.garlands.uk.com/ta – requires paying teachers to work in Poland, Ukraine, and Russia. No TEFL or teaching qualifications are required. The prices you pay (ranging from around £500 to £2,000) include a home and all meals with a local family or in a comfortable hostel for teachers, and may include air fare.

United States Information Agency (USIA): English Programs Division, E/AL, Room 304, 301 4th Street, SW, Washington, DC 20547, tel 202-619-5869, fax 202-401-1250, e-mail english@usia.gov, http://www.usia.gov/education/engteaching/eal-ndx.htm – recruits American academics in the field of TEFL/TESL and Applied Lingustics for short-term assignments in CEE/CIS, to work on curriculum projects, teacher training, English for Specialised Purposes, training seminars, materials development and similar short-term projects. They may also supply a list of *Opportunities for Teaching English Abroad* with organisations recruiting US citizens for English language teaching positions abroad. Most teachers are hired directly by the centre in question. A list of centres is available from the above address.

Under the auspices of UISA, the *Fulbright Commission* administers the *Council for International Exchange of Scholars*: 3007 Tilden St NW, Suite 5M, Washington, DC 20008-3009. A PhD is normally required for high-level teaching vacancies in a variety of countries, particularly in Central and Eastern Europe.

WorldTeach: Harvard Institute for International Development, One Eliot Street, Cambridge, Massachusetts 02138-5705 – is a private non-profit organisation sending English-speaking volunteers abroad primarily to teach English. There are programmes in Eastern Europe and the CIS. A fee is paid to cover transportation and other costs; and teachers receive a stipend equivalent to local teaching rates.

Worldwide Education Service (WES): Canada House, 272 Field End Road, Eastcote, Middlesex HA4 9PE, tel 0181-866 4400, fax 0181-429 4838 – recruits mostly full-time teachers worldwide for international schools. WES maintains a register of qualified teachers. This service works at the nursery, primary and secondary levels of teaching, as well as tutorial organisations and English language schools. *WES* is a consultancy for the Bell language schools and is part of the *Bell Educational Trust* or its various affiliates.

All the organisations above provide brochures and information on their services. Recruitment is often in spring and summer for early September. If you want to apply direct to schools abroad, local telephone or business directories are a good starting point. Another is the local *British Council* office.

Other Contacts:
Teaching English Abroad: by Susan Griffith (Vacation Work) has indispensable information on training for TEFL, how to find work abroad, and lists of language schools and agencies in many CEE and CIS countries.

Tourism

The travel agencies, tour operators and information offices in the pages which follow are all potential sources of information, especially tour operators' and travel agents' manuals which many tourist offices produce. These have the up-to-date names and addresses of hotels, airlines, restaurants and other tourism services you need. You are recommended to contact these organisations and enquire about employment directly. Also see your high street travel agent and its brochures for some tour operators which feature holidays in your chosen destination; and you should consider making your application from four to six months in advance.

These jobs in tourism are generally not very well-paid and if you find your tourism or tourism-related job locally you will be working for an even lower local rate. In Russia and its neighbours some guides and reps are even expected to do this for board and lodging only.

But if you have wider tourism experience and can offer assistance in this area you may also be able to work as a consultant with some of the travel agencies in this region which are upgrading their services and operations. There are business and work opportunites for consultants like this working independently, or those offering incoming services to some of these travel agencies and tour operators in Russia/CIS.

Voluntary Agencies

The UK and US governments as well as many non-governmental organisations and charities also promote schemes which send volunteers to the developing and former communist countries where the need is often for expertise in restructuring or privatisation, or social projects in health or education. The work is usually on fixed-term contracts; and the ultimate goal will be to train local staff to administer and carry on the work; and to set up local structures which can be self-sustaining.

One important agency in Britain is the *Overseas Development Administration (ODA)*, 94 Victoria Street, London SW1E 5JL, tel 0171-917 0286, fax 0171-917 0523, which runs the British Government's programme of aid to developing countries. Their work is carried out in cooperation with the *EEP: East European Partnership*, Carlton House, 27 Carlton Drive, London SW15 2BS; tel 0181-780 2841; fax 0181-780 9592.

Charity and NGO vacancies occur on an ad hoc basis and are normally advertised in the national press, professional journals, and overseas. Particular skills are usually required, in 'professions such as law, sociology and accountacy, as well as more familiar areas like agriculture, engineering and economics,' the ODA says. You can write off for the *ODA Guide to Working Overseas for the Aid Programme* booklet for more details and a 'skills list'.

East European Partnership is a *VSO* initiative (see below) for around 100 volunteers at any one time in many Central and Eastern European countries working with local goverment and NGOs involving teachers, health-care workers, and business trainers. Send an for application form to *EEP* at the address above.

The *ODA* also keeps a register of people interested in working for the aid programme; and study awards are offered under the *APOS (Associate Professional Officers Scheme)* to those less qualified, giving academic training to masters degree level, followed by a period of practical training in many CEE/CIS countries. These schemes are often run in collaboration with the local British Council or British Embassy – which may also be good sources of information.

These *APOS* awards are presently in the agriculture, agricultural engineering, animal health/animal production, biodiversity preservation, biometrics, environment, engineering, physical planning, forestry, agro-forestry, fisheries, health and population, institutional development, natural resources economics, small enterprise development, and social development sectors.

Their ODA's *Recruitment and Personnel Management Branch (RPMB)* looks after recruitment matters, and preparation for moving abroad, and it also assists in the recruitment of specialists for the field programmes of the United Nations and its specialised agencies. A number of useful free booklets, such as *Action for the Environment, Action on Health and Population, Women in Development*, and *British Overseas Development* – a bimonthly magazine on development topics – are available on request from the *ODA Information Department*: Room V523, 94 Victoria Street, London SW1E 5JL, tel 0171-917 0503.

United Nations Volunteers (UNV): Palais des Nations, CH-1211 Geneva 10, Switzerland, tel 798-58-50 – recruits highly qualified and experienced volunteers from all UN countries work in over 70 countries for UN-sponsored development projects for a period of two years (and some shorter-term relief work). Travel to and from the country is provided for volunteers and dependants are authorised to accompany them. A modest monthly allowance is provided at either single or dependency rates, along with a settling in grant. Appropriate academic or trade qualifications in a particular profession are required, along with a minimum of 2 years' working experience in that field. UK applicants should contact *Voluntary Services Overseas* – see under *Non-Governmental organisations* below.

Crown Agents for Overseas Governments and Administration: St Nicholas House, St Nicholas Road, Sutton, Surrey SM1 1EL, tel 0181-643 3311, fax 0181-643 8232 – is a long-established and nowadays self-funding body providing a recruitment service to over 100 governments, public authorities, and international aid agencies and in most CEE and CIS countries. Overseas positions are either direct with a client government or on an aid-funded project managed by Crown Agents. Personnel-related activities are greatest in the emerging economies of Eastern Europe and former Soviet Union, with some in Africa.

Peace Corps: 1990 K Street NW, Washington DC 20526, tel 202-376-2550 – is the official agency for the US government which sends some 60,000 US citizens each year to work on 2-year assignments throughout Eastern Europe and the former Soviet Union.

Workcamps and Exchange Schemes:
Those wishing to work in a workcamp or summer camp in the Eastern European or former CIS countries are advised to check with an organisation with a branch in their own country first. These include *International Voluntary Service (IVS)* in the UK, and *SCI-USA* or *Volunteers for Peace (VFP)* in the USA (see below). Also see *East European Partnership* and the *Peace Corps* above which may have some similar schemes suitable for young people.

AIESEC (French acronym for *International Association for Students of Economics and Management*): 29-31 Cowper Street, Londom EC2A 4AP, tel 0171-336 7939, fax 0171-336 7971 – offers students and recent graduates within accountancy, business administration, computing, marketing, economics, and finance the opportunity to take placements in diverse working environments through its Work Abroad programmes. Placements last between six and seventy-two weeks in any one of its 87 member countries. AIESEC wishes to stress that very few placements will be available to those from Eastern European countries because of an imbalance in the numbers of outgoing and incoming students.

AIESEC US: 135 West 35th Street, 20th Floor, New York, NY 10020, tel 212-757-3774 – operates these schemes in the USA, for many Central and Eastern European countries. Again, the main precondition for an overseas placing is membership of an AIESEC chapter in an American university, and the need to ensure an equal number of work exchange positions for foreign students in the USA, which limits numbers.

Association for International Practical Training (AIPT): 10400 Little Patuxent Parkway, Suite 250, Columbia, MD 21044-3510, tel 410-997-2200, fax 410-992-3924, e-mail aipt@aipt.org, http://www.aipt.org – conducts 'high-quality experiential exchanges which enhance the ability of individual participants, employers and host organisations.' It helps around 250 US citizens in exchanges with 25 or so other countries every year, and 2,000 people from 70 countries to train with US employers. Around half of these exchange schemes are with other member countries of IAESTE, of which it is the American branch (like the *Central Bureau* in Britain – see below). AIPT's major scheme is the *Career Development Exchanges Program* for recent graduates, young professionals, and businesses in many career fields which offers opportunities in the Slovak Republic, Hungary, and some other CEE countries.

The Central Bureau for Educational Visits and Exchanges: 10 Spring Gardens, London SW1A 2BN, tel 0171-389 4004, fax 0171-389 4426, Campus 2000 01:YNK330 – runs the Language Assistant Scheme which enables modern language students from Britain and over 10 countries in Central/Eastern Europe to spend a year working in a school or college where their target language is spoken. Appointments as Junior Language Assistants are also available in some CEE countries nowadays. The Central Bureau arranges numerous other exchange programmes, and provides useful information on educational and school exchanges.

Concordia (Youth Service Volunteers) Ltd: 8 Brunswick Place, Hove, Sussex BN3 1ET, tel 01273-772086, fax 01273-327284 – in conjunction with similar foreign organisations, recruits for voluntary work in Eastern Europe. Applicants must be aged 18-30; and a registration fee is payable. Send SAE for details

Council on International Educational Exchange (CIEE): 205 East 42nd Street, New York, NY 10071-5706, USA, tel 212-822-2695, fax 212-822-2689, http://www.ciee.org/ – sponsors 2-4 week volunteer projects in over 600 locations worldwide. Participants join an international team of 10-20 volunteers to work on an environmental or community service project alongside local people. The cost of participating is $300-$800 plus travel to and from the project site. Room and board is provided. The Council recruits only US residents directly and receives international volunteers on projects in the USA through its partner organisations in other countries. For further country-by-country details write to the above address. There is also a UK address: 52 Poland Street, London W1V 4JQ, tel 0171-478 2000.

GAP Activity Projects: Gap House, 44 Queen's Road, Reading, Berkshire RG1 4BB, tel 01734 594914, fax 01734-576634 – arranges voluntary work placements in over 34 countries around the world including several in Central and Eastern Europe for young people in their 'gap' year between school and further education (aged 18-19 only). Volunteers pay GAP a fee on selection of around £400, and all travelling costs, but once at their placement, board and lodging are provided, and sometimes pocket money. Jobs include teaching English in Hungary, the Czech and Slovak Republics, and Bulgaria; social work; and assisting in hospitals. Those interested should apply as far as possible in advance.

International Association for the Exchange of Students for Technical Experience (IAESTE UK): The Central Bureau, 10 Spring Gardens, London SW1A 2BN, tel 0171-389 4774, fax 0171-389 4426 – arranges an exchange scheme where penultimate year students from scientific and technical backgrounds can spend 8-12 weeks mainly in the summer vacation in more than 60 countries worldwide gaining practical experience abroad. Students should apply to the programme in the autumn for placements beginning the following summer.

International Voluntary Service (IVS) Britain: Old Hall, East Bergholt, nr Colchester CO7 6TQ – runs a Workcamps Programme which and sends British volunteers to take part in projects in about 25 countries in Western and Eastern Europe, and some other places.

Non-Governmental Organisations

Here are some of the most important NGO's with operations in Central and Eastern Europe and the CIS countries:

British Executive Service Overseas (BESO): 164 Vauxhall Bridge Road, London SW1V 2RB, tel 0171-630 0644 – recruits retired volunteer business executives with professional, technical or specialised management skills to advise on projects overseas, including Eastern Europe. Short-term placements on an expenses only basis.

British Red Cross (BRC): 9 Grosvenor Crescent, London SW1X 7EJ, tel 0171-235 5454, fax 0171-245 6315 – works as part of the *International Red Cross and Red Crescent Movement*, protecting and assisting victims of conflicts and natural disasters, with neutrality and impartiality, in the UK and overseas. *BRC* volunteers not only provide a trained and skilled response to emergencies, but also care for people in crisis, by offering vital services in the local community. The *BRC* also maintains a register of suitably qualified doctors and nurses, administrators, mechanics, engineers, agriculturalists, programme managers, telecommunications specialist, development advisers and others with relevant professional experience who are willing to go abroad on short-term assignments to assist victims of disasters. Longer-term development projects are occasionally undertaken. Age group 25; airfares and allowances are provided.

There is a one-week residential course for briefing before taking up residence overseas.

CARE International UK: 36-38 Southampton Street, London WC2E 7AF, tel 0171-379 5247, fax 0171-379 0543 – is one of the world's largest relief and development charities, working in many countries in Eastern Europe. It employs health professionals with extensive experience in their field, preferably gained with an organisation similar to CARE.

Quaker International Social Projects (QISP): Religious Society of Friends, Friends House, Euston Road, London NW1 2BJ, tel 0171-387 3601 – sends volunteers abroad, through exchange agreements with other volunteer organisations in Bulgaria, the Czech Republic, Poland, Slovakia, and Ukraine. The minimum age for projects abroad is 18. Applicants aged 18-24 should have completed a project in the UK, or had similar volunteering experience, or should have lived abroad. Applicants over 24: no requirements. Special skills or qualifications are not necessary. Motivation, enthusiasm, and commitment to living and working in a group are. Volunteers work as a team of 8 to 15 people people who come from all walks of life and nationalities. Food and accommodation (usually basic) are provided free of charge. *QISP* charges a small registration fee (£22 unwaged, £33 student, £44 waged). Volunteers arrange to pay for travel to the project. To receive a programme (for the spring programme before January; for the summer programme before April) send a large (C5) stamped SAE and a cover letter stating age and, if applicable, volunteer experience.

Save the Children: 17 Grove Lane, London SE5 8RD, tel 0171-703 5400, fax 0171-703 2278 – is the UK's largest international voluntary agency, with offices in many CEE/CIS countries; it is concerned with child health and welfare – and long-term programmes for with health, nutrition, community development, and welfare. Recruitment is generally within each country (where there is some scope for volunteers). In addition, there are paid posts for qualified and experienced project coordinators, medical officers, nurses, midwives, tutors, health visitors, nutritionists, engineers, social workers, disability specialists, and others.

Tear Fund: 100 Church Road, Teddington, Middlesex TW11 8QE, tel 0181-943 7888, fax 0181-943 3594 – is an evangelical Christian relief and development agency which provides personnel and other assistance to churches and Christian groups. Skilled and experienced personnel are needed for community development programmes, mainly in the following skill areas: doctors, nurses, midwives, community health advisors, physiotherapists, agriculturalists, technical trainers, programme managers, community development advisors. Appointments are generally for four years. For further details contact the *Overseas Service Advisor*.

Voluntary Service Overseas (VSO): 317 Putney Bridge Road, London SW15 2PN, tel 0181-780 1331, fax 0181-780 1081, e-mail enquiries@vso.org.uk., http://www.oneworld.org/vso/ – enables men and women to make a long-term commitment – usually two years – to share their skills. Placements are offered in a whole range of skill areas including education, technical trades, small business development, health, agriculture, social work/community development and sport. Also see under *East European Partnership* above.

Qualifications

The question of the mutual recognition of professional qualifications between Britain (or the USA) and Russia/CIS and most of the other countries in this book is only just being addressed; and a misunderstanding of the qualifactions they have will sometimes sometimes be an obstacle to those seeking work there. This can work in two ways; and sometimes conditions are still so disorganised – or at least informal – that many otherwise unqualified Britons and Americans – many of whom will have much to offer, and others less so – will have no problem getting a job as, say, a secondary school or university teacher.

But again not in all countries. It depends really where you are. There are always more 'offical' ways to have your qualification recognised or validated – which may seem daunting, and will involve approaching the relevant ministry which administers this aspect of life – for teachers, the Ministry of Education, for lawyers the Ministry of Jusice, and so on. This can take months, or years.

But you should take copies of all your relevant certificates and diplomas when you visit these countries to look for work or take up employment, for possible translation into the local language. These will (probably) be enough to satisfy most employers.

Embassies in some rare cases will have information on qualifications as they apply to employment. Your local Training and Enterprise Council or *TEC* in Britain (these are currently called 'LECs' in Scotland) may be one place to go, for leaflets and advice on mutual recognition of qualifications, for employees and self-employed people. Find your nearest one in the local Yellow Pages. Appropriate professional bodies in either Britain or America, or in the country concerned, may also be contacted – through the equivalent UK or US professional association or trade union of which you may already be a member. Also, the *UK National Academic Recognition Centre (NARIC)* provides information on the comparability of overseas qualifications; it can be contacted at ECCTIS 2000 Ltd., Oriel House, Oriel Road, Cheltenham, Glos. GL50 1XP; tel 01242-260010; fax 01242-258600; e-mail 106736.2043@compuserve. Or you can contact the *British Chambers of Commerce* at their *Certification Unit*, BCC, Westwood House, Westwood Business Park, Coventry CV4 8HS; tel 01203-695688; fax 01203-695844.

Other Contacts

The *East European Trade Council*, Suite 10, Westminster Palace Gardens, Artillery Row, London SW1P 1RL, tel 0171-222 7622, is an advisory group attached to the Department of Trade and Industry promoting trade opportunities and offering business advice with an extensive library on Eastern Europe. Researchers will find many contacts here for recruitment as well as trade and business. *Nexus Expatriate Magazine* (see above) also runs regular features on specific areas such as telecommunications with extensive listings of international recruitment agencies in that field. Also see the international jobs newspaper *Overseas Jobs Express*.

The publications available in the UK from your local Jobcentre and their advisers – who can put you in touch with *Careers Europe* and their database of vacancies (called NATVACS) – also should not be overlooked; but more opportunities are available in the European Union than Central/Eastern Europe at present. The accession of Poland, the Czech Republic, Hungary, Slovenia and Estonia to the EU may mean more vacancies in these countries becoming available in this way in future.

The *Directory of Jobs and Careers Abroad* (Vacation Work) available from good travel and general bookshops is an invaluable source for anyone who feels that they need a hands-on guide on how to research the job market, or what career direction to take, with advice on CV's and the best ways to go about your job search, with sections on *Specific Careers* and *Worldwide Employment*, and including a short section on Central and Eastern Europe.

Other Opportunities

These include construction work, especially for craftspeople and skilled builders, as well as for consultants and construction companies, engineering and infrastructure projects – like roads and airports, and in all the areas of consultancy and running a business. Insurance companies, accountants and many others providing services to expatriates are discovering opportunities in many of these countries which often come from being the first international organisation to get there. But a knowledge of local conditions – which can only come from working with local people – will also be very important.

Banking and financial services will be very important in all of these countries too, and there are still some opportunities in these emerging markets for those who know about investment – and have the right local experience and knowledge.

Business and Industry Report

These opportunities in CEE/CIS are not just in English teaching or voluntary work. The reconstruction of the infrastructure is the background against which business – and the employment of most British or American expatriates – is done in all these countries. A business and industry report is included for each country giving the essential background to this. This process can be complex, but includes the expansion of British and international companies into these emerging markets and the development of locally based companies also interested in international trade, and sometimes needing foreign expertise and advice.

Other business people operate perfectly well in some CEE/CIS countries from a distance – which may be advisable for some small businesses operating further afield in some of the riskier places. This is how businesses are often set up there. Crime will not be such a problem; and this is still one which afflicts many small and medium-sized businesses operating in Former Soviet Union. Many manage to offer a service in these countries while basing their operations in Britain or the United States.

So, a job in one of these CEE/CIS countries may in reality involve many business trips – and this can shade into a kind of 'part-time' presence in the country – but not actually living and working there. This is part of a similar trend in business and employment worldwide in fact, where these boundaries are increasingly blurred.

Business Opportunities

Many business opportunities come from the process of transition itself; others come sometimes from the restrictions and inefficiencies in what still remains of the previous system (which enabled some of those who were in the know at the time to make their fortunes when the old regime came down). See the individual country chapters which follow. At the end of each chapter there is more about working in that country; and the *Business and Industry Report* highlights some of these local opportunities. It is difficult to generalise about so many economies which are making this transition to liberal democracy at a greater or lesser rate.

Some of these are caught in a kind of 'Soviet' era of authoritarian government, you will find, where decisions come from the top. Here, government to government, or business to business contacts in a formal sense are still very important. One such which has taken this rather retrograde step is Belarus. Another may be Serbia. These more conservative economies still tend to be very highly regulated with many anomalies in their legal systems, and grey areas between legal and illegal economic activity.

Others economies are becoming very unregulated – with a fast-track approach to privatisation. The aim has been to forget the past, and then to get on with the 'real' business of running a prosperous economy along Western European lines and which is as far away as possible from the Soviet model; and relies much less on the other Eastern European markets. An example of this is Hungary – which like many others also depends to a large extent on foreign investment, especially from Germany.

In fact, the more we look at this region, we see that it is really several regions which are interlinked and interlocked. The process of economic development has really been very difficult even in these more advanced economies, and very patchy even within the various countries. The opportunities in employment and trade are equally diverse and varied.

There was no common starting-point; and there have been many patterns of development; and as many business and job opportunities in this vast CEE/CIS region as there are different economies and patterns of employment. But there are some general themes or strands which can be discerned in all these economies:

Unemployment: This is low in a few countries but rising in most as these economies have been restructured.

Inflation: This has always rocketed after independence and/or the introduction of capitalism; and then come down almost as dramatically. In most countries, it has now been brought under control.

Salaries: Unemployment and low salaries are the price local people have paid to control inflation. For local workers wages are always much lower than in the 'West'.

Democratisation: Most of these countries are now democracies and have made great progress in a short time after years of relative economic and industrial isolation. The former communist parties are now social democratic parties; having accepted democracy and the basic outlines of the free market.

Social Protection: This has fallen behind the growth of the economy. Health and social security system reform is now a preoccupation of many governments.

Social Change: Communism stressed the equality of people; these were, generally speaking, egalitarian societies where privilege was a matter of status and influence, not money. The new consumerism seems to stress difference between people; and has aggravated some social tensions and ethnic divisions in society.

Wealth and Poverty: There are now great disparities in almost every country between the very rich and very poor in these new post-communist societies.

Inefficiency: The many inefficiencies which still exist are mainly of two kinds: structural ones created by the mismanagement of the previous centralised economy, and also a cultural deficit as the more efficient and productive ways of running organisations are still relatively unfamiliar.

Business and Employment in Russia and Eastern Europe

Whether you intend to work as an employee, employer or entrepreneur in Central or Eastern Europe, or Russia, or anywhere in the former Soviet Union or Commonwealth of Independent States, this is a good time to make your own 'transition' to this dynamic and rapidly changing region. In nearly every one of these economies – from the most progressive and liberal to the most traditional or conservative – there is a generally favourable climate for employment for international workers, and many opportunities for investors and international business people too.

The Baltic States

Estonia, Latvia and Lithuania

Introduction
Living and Working
Residence and Entry
Daily Life
Employment
Doing Business

Baltic Region

Introduction

This section comprises Estonia, Latvia and Lithuania: the 'Baltic States'. But this *Baltic Region* could be said to include some other countries as well. There is the Russian enclave of Kaliningrad between Lithuania and Poland for instance; Poland itself – with its Baltic coast and historical links with Lithuania; Germany too – a Baltic country which has left its crusader's castles and architecture all along this coast – and Denmark, and Sweden, all these used to be major powers in the region before the Russians came.

There are the close cultural connections between the Estonians and the Finns (another Baltic people) who speak a similar Estonian/Finnish language (very different from those of Latvia, or Lithuania, or Poland). And there were other Baltic peoples who are now extinct – speaking one of these 'Baltic' languages, too, similar to Latvian or Lithuanian, who were displaced by later invaders: the 'Baltic' Mazurians and Kashubians, along with other Slavonic tribes, who have also changed their names or lost their identity: the Volhinians, Podolians, Polesians and others who are now Lithuanians, or Ukrainians, or Belarussians...

These were and are some of the many Baltic states. All these regions overlap; indeed this is their distinctive feature: a much greater *lack* of identity or definition than is found among the peoples and nations of Western Europe, even today. The independence movements in each of these countries today have – to some extent – as their objective to overcome this lack of definition. All of which makes the Baltic States (the three main ones which are the subject of this section) really part of a much greater *Borderlands* region; between Russia and Eurasia on the one hand; and Europe/Central Europe on the other.

These countries were all part of this Soviet Empire. Their revolt against it created the modern notion of the Baltic States – and the idea these countries have of themselves today. Instead of conformity, now there is difference. Small scale ways of working are best. Perhaps individualism is better than teamwork. But it is the community here which counts, and not some generalised notion of society. Democracy is important in all these countries; but politicians talk less often about 'workers', or the 'people'...

This ideas can only be part of the truth (as all stereotypes must). There are darker themes or strands of Baltic history, as there are in Eastern Europe generally. But it is this post-Soviet and post-imperial concept we meet everywhere in Former Soviet Union – and all along these borderlands which the world is now aware of once again – which seems to define them most closely. These are nations, born in war or peace, which have all thrown off the shackles of bolshevism. In this they have been born again.

Geography and History

For more about their geographical position, see the *Borderlands* section which follows, and its *Introduction*. The three Baltic States of Estonia, Latvia and Lithuania are situated between Russia and the Baltic Sea. Their recent history was marked by Russian occupation during the 19th century; and again in 1940 and 1944/5 (the Germans were here in between). Each is now keen to assert its own national identity and to join the various European institutions, a little like the Central European countries. They are culturally very different, although they each still live in the looming shadow of their larger neighbour.

They are looking to a 'European' future; and these are – in this sense – the most European of the states formerly belonging to the Soviet Union. Russian is spoken by all except the very young; but the locals prefer to speak English or German to foreigners, or Finnish, or French, or anything. The Estonian language belongs (like Finnish) to the Finno-Ugric family of languages (and has even more case endings, 14, which may be some kind of linguistic record: nomative, accusative, genitive, and then what?). Estonian, we may point out here, also has a unique – in Europe – form of the verb; it corresponds to the impersonal idea represented in English by 'There is...' but has also the idea of a person. Whole stories can be told like this: 'There was (by me) a visit to the cinema; there was great rustling of crisp packets and eating of popcorn...;' and so on.

Latvian and Lithuanian belong to a more European family of languages: the Baltic group; and stand, therefore, in some relation to the Slavonic and Germanic families. So they should be easier to learn. Language is a live issue here, and is seen as an expression of national identity. Many Russian settlers are now having to master the local tongue to get a job or get a work permit – although they may have lived in these countries all their lives. In Estonia, they (or you) can get free lessons. When you speak a language like Estonian, you need no other way to affirm your national independence perhaps: so if the Russians learn Estonian – or Latvian, or Lithuanian – which as settlers coming here they generally did not – then the locals feel they are welcome to stay.

Other cultural influences have been Swedish, Polish, Danish and, especially, Hanseatic German: the architecture in all the coastal towns can be reminiscent of Germany or Holland. There are even a few hardy German-speakers along the coast; and we remember that Kaliningrad used to be Königsberg in East Prussia, which today has been throughly 'Sovietised' and remains an isolated outpost of Russia. In this enclave between Lithuania and Poland some of the Baltic Fleet is still based – or just abandoned here; and it can be visited most conveniently by boat, across the sea from Gdansk.

The Baltic States have a mixture of continental and maritime climates. The sea can freeze over here; but prevailing westerly winds mean that it usually does not below the Gulf of Finland; and it is a moderating influence on the climate. In Latvia – with Estonia in the north and Lithuania to the south – the mean average temperature is 6°C – the daytime average in January being 5° and in July 17°.

Some differences are religious as well as cultural. Estonia and Latvia are predominately Lutheran; Lithuania is mainly Catholic. There are also Protestant, Russian Orthodox and Evangelical Reform churches everywhere, and some still surviving synagogues. Their mutual history is bound up with that of Russia and Sweden, Poland, and even the Ottoman Empire (although the Turks never quite came so far north).

Geographically, the Baltic States are bounded by Finland, Sweden and Poland in the West, and Russia, Belarus and Ukraine in the east.

Estonia

Introduction

Estonia is an independent country on the way to EU membership, but one where Russia and its history have been important. Only in the 1920s and 30s did the country know a similar period of independence to the one it has achieved today. In the nineteenth century there was a policy here and throughout the Russian Empire which the local Estonian-speaking peasants resisted, of Russification. Towns grew in size; and a middle class emerged. This is when the Estonian dream of national independence from Russia was born.

Living in Estonia

History

This is one of Europe's most ancient peoples. Estonians have been here, it seems, from time immemorial, living between the Baltic and the Gulf of Finland – since the time of Stonehenge at least, and long before the Anglo-Saxons came to Britain. There have been many invasions: by the Vikings first of all; then in the thirteenth century the Danes came – 'Tallinn' meaning 'Danish Castle' – who were then driven out in the fourteenth century by the Teutonic Knights. These Baltic states were left under German Hanseatic control until the fifteenth century.

There were wars between Russians, Poles and Swedes for these Estonian and other Baltic lands. The Swedes won; and this is remembered today in Estonia as 'the good old Swedish time,' which left as its memorial the Lutheran religion. After a devastating Nordic War in the eighteenth century – which only a third of the Estonian population survived – they kept their local system of government and law, but were incorporated by degrees into the Russian Empire.

The country's first glimpse of independence came in 1918, after the Russian Revolution and the First World War. There was economic growth, and progress in education. This was both a national and, unusually for the time, a cosmopolitan or 'European' movement. The Second World War – and the Nazi-Soviet pact which divided up Poland, the Baltic States and Finland put an end to it, and threatened the country's national survival.

In 1941, the German occupation of Estonia replaced the Russian one, and was replaced again by the Russians in 1945. There were massacres and deportations of political prisoners and others, old people, women and children among them. During and after the war, the country lost a quarter of its population, some of which was replaced by immigration from all parts of the Soviet Union.

The economy was ruined; and Estonians also resented the pollution and heavy industry, the barbed wire and military bases which littered parts of the landscape. This feeling for their country and for nature is one very Estonian characteristic: and possibly for this reason the indoctrination which afflicted other parts of this vast empire stood less chance here.

There were other more independent-minded religious and cultural traditions in Estonia, which is why, perhaps, the main resistance in the 1980s in Former Soviet Union started here, and in the other Baltic States. After the war many had watched in helpless despair as their country was subjugated. Others resisted in forests and marshes, and were defeated by the Russians in the 1950s. Then there were dissident movements which appeared when the Helsinki Treaty was signed between the United States and the Soviet Union in 1972, which made some provisions for human rights. This was a more long-lasting kind of resistance, and during the 'perestroika' period there was a strategy of grabbing bits of sovereignty from Moscow 'step by step' as it was described, until the opportunity for full independence came. The coup by the old-style communists in Moscow had failed – and Estonia declared its independence at midnight on August 21 1991.

Or rather: 'the still existing pre-war Estonian Republic was reproclaimed,' as the Estonians themselves put it. The Czech Republic had its 'Velvet Revolution' but this one is remembered by Estonians as their 'singing revolution' – as their mass protests were often combined with a nationalistic tradition of song festivals which had begun in the nineteenth century.

Geographical Information

Estonia in the north, then Latvia, then Lithuania is the list of these Baltic States from north to south. The population is 1.5 million and nearly a third of these live in the capital Tallinn. Other big towns are Pärnu, Tartu and Narva, which straddles the border with Russia and has the greatest Russian population. It covers 17,462 square miles. The landscape is not unlike that of Finland, with forests, lakes and islands. There are few raw materials and Estonia relies like its neighbours to the south mostly on imported commodities to produce finished goods. Agriculture and increasingly tourism are important. Privatisation was quite a rapid process here; and the cost of living is high. The currency is tied to the deutschmark.

Climate

Estonia has a climate somewhere between temperate and continental with considerable temperature variations. Winter can last from November to the beginning of April and the sea can freeze over. Summers can be pleasant and warm, with the greatest rainfall in August.

The Language

Estonians in Tallinn can understand the Finnish programmes they can watch on TV. But there are some differences of grammar and pronunciation which make these separate languages, although members of the same Finno-Ugric family. The most popular second language today is English. This is still less widely spoken than the more unpopular Russian, but Estonians are learning fast.

The Currency

1 kroon (EEK) = 100 sents. Dollars and deutschmarks and (presumably) the Finnish currency are all easy to exchange. These *kroons* are 'crowns' by the way, in the Estonian spelling, which favours such double letters: Estonia in Estonian is 'Eesti' for example, and after the Russian occupation Talin changed its name to 'Tallinn'.

There are exchange services for dollars everywhere; and many banks, including an increasing number of joint ventures, which offer a wide range of international financial services like money transfers and so on. See the *General Overview* for more on this, and the *Western Union* money transfer contact numbers for the Baltic States under *Money Transfer* in the *Working in Russia and Eastern Europe* chapter.

Getting There

Estonian Air has a service direct from London Gatwick (and a fleet of Boeings) and also via Copenhagen. There is an economy and a business class, with facilities for group bookings, and fast-track services for business travellers: in other words this is a modern international airline which has little to do with the old Soviet ones. In the UK, call 01293-534735. In Estonia, tel 6-401-160. There are onward services to Kiev, Minsk, Moscow and Vilnius.

To Riga (with onward connections to Tallinn) you could also try *RIAIR – Riga Airlines* (see the *Latvia* chapter which follows). In the CIS and FSU countries, the best service is often available from the privately-owned independent airlines like these, *Ukraine International Airlines* being one, which generally have a more modern fleet of Boeings or Airbuses. Travellers can have less confidence in some of the other former Soviet carriers though. Like many other business services in Estonia – and all these CEE and FSU countries – the best ones are the ones which have started from scratch.

For *RIAIR* sales, marketing, ticketing and reservations in the UK call 01293-535727. *Air Baltic* (UK tel: 01871-828 4223) is the Latvian state airline and also has connections onwards to Tallinn, Vilnius and Helsinki. Other airline contacts are *British Airways* (UK tel: 0345-222111), *Austrian Airlines* (0171-434-7300), and *Lufthansa* – which has a large Eastern European network and offers other business and accommodation services (tel 0345-737747). *Lufthansa* has four flights to Tallinn a week. *Finnair* (tel 0171-408 1222) and *Transaero* (tel 0171-828 7613 – *CIS Travel Services*) are other options, also *Lithuanian Airlines* (UK tel: 0181-759 7323; fax 0181-745 7346) which operates daily flights to Vilnius from Heathrow and has onward connections to Tallinn. *SAS (Scandinavian Airlines)* also flies there: UK tel 0345-010789.

Travel Agencies

Booking with a local travel agency is often best. They know the country, and if your communications with them are good can make the right arrangements for you.

Baltic Travel Service: Subaciaus 2, 2001 Vilnius, Lithuania; tel 2-620-757; fax 2-222-196. Offers destination management, hotels and tours etc. in each of the Baltic States.
Estonian Holidays: has an incoming department. Contact them at: Viru väljak 4, EE-100 Tallinn; tel 6-301-930; fax 6-301-900 – near the *Virü* hotel. Also guides and interpreters.
Fregata Travel: 13 Regent Street, London SW1Y 4LR; tel 0171-451 7000; fax 0171-451 7017; 117A Withington Rd., Manchester M16 8EE; tel 0161-226 7227; fax 0161-226 0700. City breaks in all the Baltic States.
Interchange: 27 Stafford Road, Croydon CR0 4NG; tel 0181-681 3612; fax 0181-760 0031. For the CIS and FSU countries.

Liberty International (UK) Ltd: 11 Grosvenor Street, Chester CH1 2DD; tel 01244-351115; fax 01244-351116; e-mail liberty@chester.itsnet.co.uk. Full destination management services for each of the Baltic States.
Raeturist: 18 Raekoja Square, EE-0001 Tallinn; tel 2-444-333; fax 6-313-308. (A partner of *Latvia Tours* and *Lithuanian Tours*).
Reisibüroo Estravel: (see under *Useful Addresses* below).
S.I.B. Travel: (Latvian Agency for Foreign Tourism) 18 Dzirnavu St., Riga, LV-1010; tel 7-33-39-88; fax 7-83-02-07. Air transport, incoming services and accommodation for all Baltic States and the CIS countries.

Residence and Entry

EU citizens and US passport holders do not require a visa to visit the country for up to 90 days in any one year. Residence and work arrangements may be made in the country or before departure. For further information you should contact the *Estonian Embassy* in the UK or USA (see below) for their useful advice sheets. For travellers who do need one, a visa for one Baltic State allows travel to the other two. This does not apply to your onward travel to Russia, Belarus or Ukraine. The Consular Department will tell you if you need an entry visa.

Contact the Embassy in the morning – this is advice which is good for all the FSU and many other countries – with your enquiry about residence and entry. In London, they also have a helpful advice sheet *How to Find Work in Estonia*.

Work Permits:
These applications require a completed work permit application form, certificate(s) of education (original and copy), employers application/invitation, two photos, and a cheque, presently for £130, payable to the Estonian Embassy. Volunteer workers do not need to pay this. If you are working there you need a residence permit too.

Residence Permits:
To apply you need the completed application form (which the Embassy will send you), your invitation (from an individual or legal entity), passport (original and copy), birth certificate (copy), medical certificates (for TB, syphilis, HIV, and – remarkably – a 'certificate proving mental fitness' – perhaps a letter from your own mentally fit doctor to this effect), proof of income or funds, two passport-type photos, and the cheque for £130 (in the UK) made payable to the Estonian Embassy.

Applications in Estonia should be made to the *Department of Citizenship and Immigration (Kodakonsus ja Migratsiooniamet)*, Lai 38-40, EE-102 Tallinn; tel 2-88-43-33; 26-31-37-44. Foreigners may not work in Estonia who have not been granted these residence and work permits.

Customs

There are no restrictions on items for personal use. 18% VAT is charged on goods exceeding the established limits. You can bring an unlimited amount of currency and personal items into Estonia. If you have any doubtful items go through the red channel.

Courier Services

Inter-Logistic Worldwide Courier: Unit 7, Craufurd Business Park, Silverdale Road, Hayes, Middlesex; tel 0181-569-0616; fax 0181-569 0616; e-mail XK241@DIAL.PIPEX.COM. *DHL*, *EMS* and some other international courier services have offices in Tallinn.

Accommodation

If you travel with *Estonian Air* from London they can make reservations for hotels throughout Estonia: tel 01293-534735. There are several 'international-standard' hotels, the recommended business hotel being the *Hotel Palace*, with others like the *Hotel Viru* which have comfortable facilities but fewer western guests; and there are an increasing number of budget hostels nowadays, as Tallinn has somehow found itself on the international backpacking map, as well as private bed & breakfasts which one good place for private visitors and business people to stay. See *Tallinn This Week* (Narva mnt 11E, EE-0001 Tallinn; tel 6-40-80-26; fax 6-40-80-80). This useful city guide has information on accommodation, but also transport, entertainmemnt and a wide range of ther useful 'what's on' information. Or contact the *Estonian Tourist Board*, Mündi 2, EE-0001, Tallinn; tel 6-411-420; fax 6-411-432. You can visit their website at: http://www.estonia.org.

Utilities and Communications

Electricity

Electricity is the standard 220 volts AZ, 50Hz as throughout the Baltic States and Former Soviet Union: a standard continental-style adaptor can be used if you take electrical items.

Telephones and Post

The principle is the same for all those FSU and CIS countries which have installed new telephone services. There is the old system (as it was in Former Soviet Union and is generally in Russia today) which is gradually being replaced by the new one. So it is not unusual to have to try a number twice. Sometimes a '6' (new system) or a '2' (old one) will be the beginning of your Tallinn number. The country code from the UK is 00-372. There are two types of phone, six-digit 'old-fashioned' analogue ones, and the seven-digit newer digital kind, as in Latvia. Regional calls from within the country are made by dialling an eight, and then the regional code, i.e. this is 8 then 2 for Tallinn. This is how it should be, but calling numbers and finding the right code will sometimes be a matter of trial and error: 'if your fax or telephone connection squiggles to the dead end think of the Tallinn citizen who has been waiting to have a phone connected in his flat since 1950,' as one locally produced guidebook puts it.

The *Central Post Office* in Tallinn is opposite the *Viru Hotel* and has some international telephones next door (to the right of the main entrance) and various airmail and currency exchange services. The telephone centre is usually open until 7pm or so. Letters to the rest of Europe take three or four days. For a *Business Centre* for hard-pressed foreign business people see under *Doing Business* below. These facilities will usually have a telephone, fax, and e-mail service. In Estonia, you may ask politely – and offer to pay – in shops or travel agencies if you have an urgent fax to send, and they will probably be quite helpful.

Transport

Bus and Coach Services:
There is no direct coach service from London (but see under *Poland* for travel to Warsaw, and then there is the onward rail connection between Warsaw, Vilnius, Riga and Tallinn). At the coach station in Tallinn there is a board giving details of international services and an information desk. In the city there are also the brightly-coloured trams, buses and trolleybuses. Tickets can be bought from the driver or a kiosk and there is a monthly pass which covers all of these.

Car Rentals:
Contact *AVIS*: 0181-848 8733 in the UK; or *Hertz*: tel 6-388-923 in Estonia.

Driving:
Bring all your documents and an international driving licence. Allow extra journey time for crossing each of the Baltic borders and, if you are driving from Britain, to cross the German-Polish border. Petrol stations are quite common; seat-belts should be fastened. Another way of getting there by car is by ferry – see below.

In built-up areas the speed limit is 50kph and out of town 90kph. In an accident, do not admit your liability on the spot but always contact the police to report an accident and ask for a police notice. The police number is 02.

Ferry:
There are direct routes from Sweden, but most of the ferries come on the Helsinki to Tallinn route where there are several companies like *Tallink* (tel 6-409-808) and *Silja Line* in Helsinki (tel +358-0-180-41; fax +358-0-180-4402) operating several services every day. Estline operates a service to Tallinn from Stockholm.

Taxis:
The meter should be on; if it is broken, agree the price beforehand; do not use unregistered cars but preferably the taxis displaying their telephone numbers to be found quite easily at the taxi ranks. In Tallinn, tel 6-552-552 for 'taxis and vans'.

Daily Life

Health Service and Hospitals

The health service (like others in FSU) provided a free service for all. But now there are some charges. In Estonia, accident and emergency treatment is free; and a hospital doctor is likely to treat you for some minor ailments free of charge. Otherwise you should count on paying, and international health insurance is advised – see the *General Overview – Section I*. Take some basic medicines with you. There are many pharmacies (often open until 8pm or 9pm) and also some private medical facilities, and a public hospital and clinic in Tallinn. For an ambulance dial 03.

Banks

See under *Currency* above. *Eesti Forekspank* has several branches in Tallinn with currency exchange and transfer services etc.

Books

Maps and guide books for Estonia are available from local bookshops; also from the national tourist office, and in the UK from *Stanfords* (12-14 Long Acre, Covent Garden, London WCE 9PL; tel 0171-836 1321) which may send you its Eastern European catalogue); or the nearby *Zwemmer Bookshop* (28 Denmark Street, London WC2 8NJ; tel 0171-379 6253). Expatriate organisations recommend that you continue to subscribe to newspapers, and take books and videos etc. One extremely useful organisation to contact is the *Good Book Guide* – see under *Books and Newspapers* in the *Daily Life* chapter of the *General Overview*. *Homeros*, at Vene 20, Tallinn, has English and German-language books.

Newspapers

The Baltic Times: Balasta dambis 3, Riga, Latvia; tel 7-46-21-19; fax 7-46-33-87. For news about Estonia and Lithuania as well as Latvia. The most important English-language newspaper for the region.

You can find the *Financial Times*, *Wall Street Journal*, *The European*, the *International Herald Tribune* and other publications like *Time* and *Newsweek* in some of the hotels and kiosks in Tallinn.

Cultural Background

Religion:
This is a predominantly Protestant (Lutheran) country, with Russian Orthodox and some smaller Protestant Churches.

Song Festivals:
These began in 1869; and became important for the Estonians in their search for national identity. Patriotic songs (like 'My Native Land My Dearest Love') are sung, as they were on the *Song of Estonia Day* organised by the Popular Front in 1988 (see *History* above). It attracted 300,000 people, a truly mass protest. Jazz, rock and classical music are also part of Estonia's musical inheritance, and there are open-air concerts and clubs. Its best-known composer is *Arvo Pärt*, whose music is religious and spiritual in style, inspired by choral church music.

National Holidays

January 1; February 24 (Independence Day); Good Friday; May 1 (Labour Day); June 23 (Victory Day); June 24 (Midsummer Day); Christmas Day; and Boxing Day.

Useful Addresses

Estonian Embassy: 16 Hyde Park Gate, London SW7 5DG; tel 0171-589 3428; fax 0171-589 3430.

Estonian Embassy: 2131 Massachussets Avenue NW, Washington DC; tel 202-588-0101.
Estonian Consulate: Suite 2415, 630 Fifth Avenue, New York, NY; tel 212-247 1450; fax 2121-262-0893.
British Embassy: Kentmanni 20, EE-0001 Tallinn; tel 6-313-353 or 461/2.
US Embassy: Kentmanni 20, EE-0001 Tallinn; tel 2-312-021/4.
British Council: Vana Posti 7, Tallinn EE-0001; tel 6-314-010/2-441-550; fax 6-313-111.
American Express: Estravel, 15 Suur-Karja Street, EE-0001 Tallinn; tel 6-266-266; fax 6-266-262. Also in Tartu.
Estonian Tourist Board: Mündi 2, EE-0001 Tallinn; tel 6411-420; fax 6411-432.

Working in Estonia

Economy and Trade

The privatisation of industry has proceded furthest of all in this most northerly of the Baltic States, which regards itself, like Finland, as being part of Scandinavia (although geographically this is not quite accurate). Along with Finland – when it joins the European Union – it will also share an important land border with Russia. There are many commercial opportunities which make Estonia a logical choice for operations which have a Russian or CIS connection.

Employment

Advertising:
You could advertise your services in the *Baltic Times* (see above) or the Estonian weekly publication *Eesti Ekspress*, and there are English-language job advertisements in these publications. Also contact the Estonian Embassy which may provide further information.

Employment and Business:
Trade and development are also important sources of these opportunities for independent or self-employed workers, in import-export companies, consultancy, translation work, research into investment opportunities, English teaching, and many other fields. The best way is to provide a service which local people cannot offer – as you cannot compete with them directly in their local labour market – or one which has an international connection perhaps, and to make some contacts there in advance (see the *Directory of Jobs and Careers Abroad* – Vacation Work – for more on this more independent and creative dimension to job hunting). Contact British, US and international companies, or those where you can offer special expertise. Contact the decision-makers – and meet the people who can decide to do business with you, or offer you employment. Use the *Chamber of Commerce*, *DTI*, and other sources of information in this book to create a file of information and contacts. And use the Internet – if you can – as one part of your research and networking. These are some ways – which apply to both employment and business – to make international connections before you go to Estonia.

Throughout this book, these contacts and addresses are all given as a starting-point – for you to create your own network of contacts and information. In this way you can minimise the uncertainty which is an inevitable part of jobseeking or doing business in another country, and increase your chances of success.

English Teaching:
The *British Council* in Tallinn (see above) has some English language school and local school and university contacts and is a useful resource centre where occasional private teaching opportunities are advertised. There are many new private language schools springing up. The *Estonian Embassy* in the UK and USA may also have details of these; and the *Teachers' Training Centre* which is a part of the *Ministry of Culture and Education* offering posts in secondary schools in collaboration with local State School Boards:
TEA: Liivalaia 28, Tallinn EE-0001; tel 2-449-253.
Tallinn Language School: Endla 22, Tallinn EE-0001; tel 2-452-377.
Language Learning Service: Tonismagi 3, Tallinn EE-0001; tel 6-408-777.

The International School of Tallinn, Tolli 1 (Corner Pikk 69), EE-0001 Tallinn tel 64-11-404 – provides quality education and recreational opportunities for the children of the diplomatic corps and foreign business communities. Founded in 1992. Instruction in an international curriculum in English.

English Contacts Abroad provides a research and direct contacts service for EFL teachers in all CEE countries: PO Box 126, Oxford OX2 6UB, UK. Write in the first instance for a questionnaire -- or with any tips or contacts of your own. There is an administration fee of £48.

Teacher Agents: A way for EFL teachers and others to bring their group (usually of secondary school or university-level students) to the UK to learn English: write in the first instance to *Speak English Schools*, PO Box 126, Oxford OX2 6RU, UK.

University Teachers:
The *Central European University* (Civic Education Project, Taboritska 23, 130 87 Praha 5, Czech Republic; tel/fax +42-2-272-498; e-mail; cepprg@ecn.gn.apc.erg) sends western-trained academics to the other CEE countries including Albania, Bulgaria, Czech Republic, Estonia, Hungary, Latvia, Lithuania, Poland, Romania, Russia, Slovakia and Ukraine.

Tourism:
There are some hotel, travel agency, and other opportunities – although you will not be able to work for the low wages the locals are used to. Better to find an opportunity in consultancy or a business connected with tourism.

As the economy develops, so more and more young Estonians will take the opportunity to visit the UK, to learn English for example. There will be many other opportunities like this, for example independent travel is already taking off, but Estonia does not yet have any travel agencies dedicated to this. See under *Tourism* in the *Lithuania* chapter for some other options for those with a qualification in tourism.

Doing business and looking for work in these FSU countries are very often two sides of the same coin; and contacts in one may lead to opportunities in the other.

Voluntary Work:
There are some places for English-speaking au pairs nowadays. And see the general note about workcamps in Former Soviet Union under *Voluntary Work* in the *Lithuania* chapter.

The Tax System

Estonia has the 183-day residence rule found elsewhere; many items – for example private school fees and relocation expenses – will be tax-free; and the system is progressive as it is in Western Europe and throughout the Baltic and Eastern European countries as well.

Doing Business

The currency is now convertible. It is tied in value to the German mark; and there is a double taxation and a trade and investment agreement with Britain. Estonia is in the lead, so far as its economic development is concerned, of all these Baltic States – and will be the first to join the EU, probably in 2002. There are many opportunities for investors and an environment for doing business which is not unlike that of neighbouring Finland. If this is your first trip to the Former Soviet Union, Estonia may seem like an undeveloped country but if you have visited some others it will feel like a rich one (although this prosperity has not come to everyone).

Privatisation is one of the means to this end of greater prosperity. Contact the *Estonian Privatization Agency* (Rävala pst 6, EE-0100 Tallinn; tel 6-305-619; fax 6-305-620) for current projects which include the *Port of Tallinn, Estonian Energy Sector, Estonian Railways*, and *Estonian Telecom*. Privatisation comes first and the restructuring comes afterwards in the case of Estonia, which does not have enough resources to put into the various improvements which are needed itself. The Stock Exchange opened in 1997; and already 70% of the economy is in private hands, with more to follow.

Estonians are laid-back and inward-looking sometimes, a little like their Finnish cousins. But a business trip still means bringing gifts (as you might in Russia). But this is giving way to a more relaxed way of doing things; there are some local banks offering international services too, like the *Hansapank* – 'We sell pure, granulated gold' – whose Tondi branch is on Pärnu mnt. 106, Tallinn; tel 6-502-092/5.

Tallinn Business Center: 631-0500; fax 631-0501. Central location, 'western-style multi-functional facility' (or as we might more prosaically say an office block). *EBRD, Ernst & Young*, and other international organisations are there. Contact General Manager Arno Kannike for details of their facilities for business people.

Business and Industry Report

A handicap for both businesses and workers there will be the bureacracy (as in the other Baltic States). But the Estonians really don't like this either; and you will not find the same level of unnecessary form-filling, or fear, which is at the bottom of most bureaucratic behaviour perhaps. Official Estonian organisations really do wish to communicate something about themselves and their country, for example, the embassies in particular; and Estonia would head an informal league table in this respect as 'the most helpful Eastern European country.'

This openness is a big advantage for business people without much experience of Eastern Europe and the Former Soviet Union. So is a kind of Scandinavian interest in the English-speaking world (although the economic influence of Germany is strongest of all in the Baltic States). It is unlikely that many Britons will speak Estonian – or Finnish – but this will be an enormous advantage here.

Other than this, Russian is still used – by Russians and some Estonians – although it raises other sensitive issues.

It is a suitable country for those with interests in the former Soviet Union to set up an operation or head office. International communications are good, and although they have their own outlook on the world, Estonians also understand Russia; and usually speak its language. Its membership of the EU in 2002 or thereafter will also give it a great advantage in this respect, as a country half-way between Russia and the West.

Sources of Information:

The 'trade publication' for businesses and investors interested in all the new markets of Eastern Europe is *New Markets Monthly* (45 Beech Street, London EC2Y 8AD; tel 0171-628 4442; fax 0171-628 4443; e-mail new.markets@btinternet.com). The *British Embassy Commercial Section* provides services for business travellers and others interested in Estonia (c/o *British Embassy* address above). They help to organise briefings, advice on how to approach the market, visits to companies, and so on, all across Central and Eastern Europe where the British government is now making an effort to capitalise on some of its cultural and commercial assets. The *DTI (Department of Trade and Industry)* also runs – along wth the embassies and the *Foreign and Commonwealth Office* – various campaigns and trade missions to raise the profile of British business in the region,

There is a Baltic States *Helpdesk*. They can supply some general publications and specific information for exporters (tel 0171-215 5265, or 0171-215 5000 for the switchboard). The *DTI* (and also British and US embassies) maintains a database – and can probably send you a list – of UK companies interested in these markets. They also have a library in London which is useful for background research (see *Latvia* and *Lithuania* which follow; also see the previous *General Overview* for other research contacts. Another useful source of business contacts and information in Britain is *Sources of Information – Finance and Advice for Trade and Investment in Central and Eastern Europe and the Former Soviet Union* (DTI Export Publications; tel 0171-510 0171; fax 0171-510 0197).

The *East European Trade Council* (tel 0171-222 7622; fax 0171-222 5359) has its own business library; and can offer advice on business and trade in Former Soviet Union. *Dun & Bradstreet* publish a directory of *Major Companies of Central & Eastern Europe & the Commonwealth of Independent States* (tel 0181-947 1163) – which is the good news. The bad news is it costs (for hardback and CD Rom) £1,040.

Latvia

Introduction

Latvia covers 25,000 square miles and has a population totalling 2.6 million. It borders Estonia to the north, Lithuania to the south, the Russian Federation to the east, and Belarus to the south-east. The capital is *Riga* with 850,000 inhabitants. Other towns are *Liepaja* on the coast, *Daugavpils* in the south-east, *Rezekne* in the east, *Valmiera* to the north, *Jurmala* – by the sea near Riga – and nearby *Jelgava*, the main towns of their respective districts (*rajona*). The coastal plain is flat but inland the landscape becomes hilly, with forests and many rivers and lakes.

Pollution is a problem along the Baltic coast, but there are also wildlife areas. Key industries include the manufacture of railway rolling stock and light machinery, fertilisers, chemicals, and electronics. At present, more than one hundred joint ventures have been established between Latvian and UK companies. Salaries are low – on average £120 a month – which might be an advantage for investors and business people – but a drawback for some of those who may be considering living and working there.

Living in Latvia

History

Many Latvians and others in the region see their future as having more democracy, more nationalism, and less to do with Russia. This is how these Baltic States see themselves today, as more modern European nations than the other former members of the USSR, and with what they hope will be a more stable identity.

Their history is bound up with that of their neighbours. The Teutonic Knights fought their way across the original Baltic region of Prussia, displacing or converting the indigenous Balts who spoke a language similar to Latvian or Lithuanian. These really were crusaders, similar to the ones who went to Palestine or conquered Jerusalem. If anything they were more fanatical. Prussia, where northern Poland is today, became associated with these Germans and not the original Baltic peoples who they had displaced. East Prussia was the region which has become Latvia and Lithuania today.

The capital Riga (in Latvian with a horizontal bar across the 'i') was founded in the 13th century by these missionary knights, who founded Königsberg; and set an example of German expansion to the east for others to follow. A date for visitors to Latvia to jot down will be the celebrations here, in 2001, to mark the 800th anniversary of the foundation of Riga.

The town became a thriving centre for trade and commerce and was admitted in 1282 to the Hanseatic League, an association of these powerful merchant towns across northern Germany. In the centuries which followed, Latvia was subjected to a succession of foreign rulers like these, whose main qualification it seems was that they were not Latvian. This included invasions by the Poles and Swedes, and various other powers which ebbed and flowed across these borderlands between East and West until the eighteenth century, when Russia became a great power. By 1795, the whole of modern Latvia was under Russian control (like neighbouring Lithuania) and was called by them 'western Russia'.

These were the years of intolerant and – for the various ethnic minorities within the Russian Empire – intolerable Tsarist rule which led in one direction to the Russian Revolution in 1917; and in another to various nationalist movements, and the proclamation of Latvia's independence in 1918. There were some gains, in terms of the development of local institutions and a middle class. 1920 saw the signing of a non-aggression pact with the Soviet Union but in 1940 – and again in 1945 – the Russians invaded all three Baltic States and inflicted their Soviet system – with its own version of ethnic cleansing – on each of them.

One in ten of the locals was killed, or deported. Some Russians also moved in and settled down in these new, unindependent 'Socialist Republics'. There was a wave of immigration which the locals resented and then revolted against. The first Congress of its democratic and nationalist Popular Front was held in 1988 (anticipating bloodier revolutions to come). This party won the Supreme Soviet elections within the then Soviet Union in 1990 – another act of collective defiance. For Russia, there was the ignominy of retreat and withdrawal, after the failed coup of 1991.

On August 21 1991, Latvia officially declared its independence. For over two hundred years they had lived under various autocratic forms of rule, but had never lost this desire for national self-determination.

Geographical Information

'The past, however painful, has given way to a unique process of rebirth in which all of Latvia rejoices in the new spirit of optimism and determination to create a better future' – as the Latvians themselves put it, with just a hint of the spirit of socialism. The *Latvian Tourist Board* (otherwise known as *Vialatvia*: 4 Pils Locums, LV-1050 Riga; tel/fax 2-22-99-45) publishes many guides, maps and brochures for all the cities, towns and regions of Latvia, where it has many tourist offices. It should be contacted at the address above. The brochures *Latvia has a rich past and a challenging future*, *Latvia, Heartland of the Baltics*, and its map of *Latvija* which has a list of these regional tourist offices will be useful for visitors.

If you have the Internet, their website can be visited at *http://www.ltboard.apollo.lv*. If not, see the map published by *New Markets Monthly* and *Lufthansa* of the *New Markets of Eastern Europe and Asia* for a different view of its geographical situation, on the rim of the former Soviet Empire.

Climate

There is a temperate climate, but with considerable temperature variations. Snowfalls are common in winter which can last from November to the beginning of April and be very cold; although autumn is relatively mild in these parts. August is quite rainy and the ports of Riga, Liepaja and Ventspils are ice free during the winter.

The Language

Latvian is one member of the Baltic family of languages, along with Lithuanian. So was Prus before the Teutonic Knights came. It has several dialects. In Latvian, 'excuse me' is *piedodiet*; 'how are you' is *ka klajas*; 'thank you' is *paldies*; and 'please', *ludzu*. Russian is still the main second language and for many people who live there it is their first. German is also spoken. English is used for international communications and is the main language which young people are learning.

The Currency

1 Lat (LVL) = 100 santims. Dollars are easier to exchange here than pounds sterling. There are 24-hour exchange services (for example at the Central Station in Riga). Banks like *Rigas Komerc Banka* (head office: 6 Smilsu Street, Riga, LV-1803; fax 7-32-34-49; e-mail http://www.rkb.lv) offer a wide range of financial services from foreign exchange to bank transfers to Lat and foreign currency accounts.

Getting There

Planes
Riair has services from London Gatwick to Riga (with onward connection to Moscow operated by *Transaero*) five times a week at present. For sales, marketing, ticketing and reservations in the UK tel 01293-535727 (or contact them on 7-20-73-25/77-25 at Riga Airport). *Air Baltic* (UK tel: 01871-828 4223) is the Latvian state airline and also flies to Riga from London with connections onwards to Tallinn, Vilnius and Helsinki. Other useful contacts are: *British Airways* (UK tel: 0345-222111 – or tel 7-20-70-96/7 at Riga Airport); *Austrian Airlines* (0171-434-7300 in London); *Lufthansa* (UK tel: 0345 737747) which flies there from Frankfurt; *Finnair* (London tel 0171-408 1222); and *Transaero* (London tel 0171-828 7613 – CIS Travel Services); and also *Lithuanian Airlines* (tel 0181-759 7323; fax 0181-745 7346) which operates daily flights to Vilnius from Heathrow; and is allied with *Estonian Air* (UK tel: 01293-534735) with its various services to Estonia.

Trains:
Travel agents, or the *International Rail Centre* in Victoria Station, can organise your rail ticket to Lithuania (tel 0990-848848; fax 0171-922 9874).

Travel Agencies

Association of Latvian Travel Agents: 10 Basteja Blvd., Riga LV-1050; tel/fax 7-21-00-65.

Baltic Travel Service: Subaciaus 2, 2001 Vilnius, Lithuania; tel 2-620-757; fax 2-222-196. Destination management, hotels and tours etc. in each of the Baltic States.

Interchange: 27 Stafford Road, Croydon CR0 4NG; tel 0181-681 3612; fax 0181-760 0031. For the CIS and FSU countries.

Latvia Tours: (also *American Express* office) Kalku St. 8, Riga, LV-1050 Latvia; tel 7-21-63-06; fax 7-82-00-20; e-mail It@mail.bkc.lv. 'Your reliable travel partner in Latvia.

Liberty International (UK) Ltd: 11 Grosvenor Street, Chester CH1 2DD; tel 01244-351115; fax 01244-351116; e-mail liberty@chester.itsnet.co.uk. Full destination management services in each of the Baltic States.

S.I.B. Travel: (Latvian Agency for Foreign Tourism) 18 Dzirnavu St., Riga, LV-1010; tel 7-33-39-88; fax 7-83-02-07. Air transport, incoming services and accommodation for Baltic States and CIS countries.
Via Riga: tel 7-06-11-71; fax 7-06-11-72.

Residence and Entry

EU citizens and US passport holders do not require a visa to visit the country or for transit, up to 90 days in any one year. Residence and work arrangements may be made in the country or before departure. For further information on employment and work placements in Latvia, contact the *Ministry of Welfare*, Department of Employment, K. Valdemara iela 38, Riga. But for immigration, residence and similar matters, you should contact your home country *Latvian Embassy* for their useful advice sheets. And for travellers who do need a visa (i.e. not Czech, Danish, Estonian, British, America, Hungarian, Irish, Lithuanian or Polish people) a visa for one Baltic State allows travel to the other two. This does not apply to travel onwards to Russia, Belarus or Ukraine.

Contact their Consular Department in the morning if you can. In the USA, for example, the consular offices are open Monday to Friday from 10am to 12am, so make an early start if you plan to visit the embassy.

If you are staying longer than 90 days, you need a visa. 'If the individual would like to stay in Latvia for more than 90 days in certain cases a special visa of up to one year validity can be issued or temporary residence permit must be requested through Latvia's *Department of Citizenship and Immigration* (Raina bulvaris 5 in Riga; tel 7-21-91-33).' For a residence permit, you will need your original passport, passport photo, and fee (from $15 for single entry to $90 for a 'rush' multiple entry visa and the multiple entry visas require an official invitation). 'Pre-paid envelope for return of documents – pre-paid Federal Express or Express mail – is recommended and money orders should be made out to 'Embassy of Latvia'; no personal cheques are accepted.

Temporary Residence Permits:
This should take no longer than 10 days. See the Embassy and Consular address for Britain and the United States below. For a residence permit in Latvia, you may be better advised to make your application on the spot, where these permits can be issued by the local police. Tales from the region concern employers who do not know the procedures and 'documents which absolutely do not exist except in the minds of burcaucrats' so you may consider first of all making an appointment at the *Department of Immigration and Citizenship* or the *Ministry of Welfare* (addresses above). To obtain a temporary residence permit from outside the country, apply to the Embassy first.

Residence for Study or Business:
If entering to study, you need a letter from that institution. For temporary residence for business you need a 'document certified by the Enterprise Registry of Latvia, a notarised copy of its registration certificate in Latvia, its statutes, and any other similar information which may be requested, which means if you do it this way you need the help of the Latvian company you are doing business with, which must be properly registered.

Work Permits:

These are issued for people needed by the State or local government as 'foreign experts/specialists', by companies who have a contract with foreign companies and needing foreign staff, and for those who have received an invitation from an employer legally registered in the Republic of Latvia. Extending your visa or permit will be the most difficult exercise of all. Contact the *Dept. of Citizenship and Immigration* on tel 7-21-91-33.

Foreigners may not work in Latvia who have not been granted these residence and work permits.

Customs

There are no restrictions on items for personal use, and goods – for non-commercial purposes – up to 300 Lats, and for individual items with a value of less than 15 Lats. Visitors should declare everything else and keep their slips for their departure. Bring evidence that you have enough money to live, or your bank or credit card statement, or something similar which is evidence of your financial standing. For pets you are bringing in you will be asked to show a certificate issued by the *State Border Veterinary Control Agency* (tel 7-32-74-72; fax 7-32-74-73).

Courier Services

Inter-Logistic Worldwide Courier: Unit 7, Craufurd Business Park, Silverdale Road, Hayes, Middlesex; tel 0181-569-0616; fax 0181-569 0616; e-mail XK241@DIAL.PIPEX.COM. *DHL* (tel 7-01-87-38), *UPS* (tel 7-21-21-85), and the other international courier services have offices in Riga. The UK number for *DHL* is 0345-100-300; for *UPS* tel 0345-877-877; and for *Parcel Force* general enquiries tel 0800-22-44-66.

A leading freight forwarding company with operations throughout Eastern Europe is *Eurogate International Forwarding Co. Ltd.* (tel 0171-459 2900; fax 0171-588 9058).

Accommodation

The *Radisson* chain has come to Riga; and there are several 'international-standard' hotels; as well as bed & breakfast, self-catering and budget accommodation, and some property agents for apartments. The British or US Embassies may include lists of these in the information they give you about Latvia. Many hotels are members of the *Latvian Hotel Association*: 55 Elizabetes Str., Riga, LV-1050; tel 7-21-28-45; fax 7-128-35-95. Also see *Riga in Your Pocket* (P.O. Box 615, LV-1050; tel 7-2205-80; tel/fax 7-22-34-16; and *Riga This Week* (tel 79-21-25-40; tel/fax 7-28-63-21). Each of these useful city guides has information on accommodation, but also transport, entertainment and a wide range of ther useful 'what's on' contacts.

Utilities and Communications

Electricity

Electricity is the standard 220 volts AZ, 50Hz as throughout the Baltic countries, so a standard continental-style adaptor can be used.

Telephones and Post

The country code from the UK is 00-371. There are two types of phone, six-digit 'old-fashioned' analogue ones; and the seven-digit newer digital kind. Regional calls from within the country are made by dialling a zero before the code, i.e. this is 07 for Riga from within the country; but to call from Britain you dial simply 00-371-7. A supplier of cellular telephones is *Perkons un deli Ltd.* (85 Brivibas st., Riga, LV 1001; tel 7-27-86-72; fax 7-82-03-86).

The *Central Post Office* in Riga is at 21 Brivibas bulv. The telephone centre is along the street at number 33 (open until 8pm – 7pm on Sundays). Letters to Western Europe take three or four days. There is a *Business Centre* (for hard-pressed foreign business people) with telephone, fax, e-mail service etc. (55 Elizabetes, hotel 'Latvia'; tel 7-22-22-11). To consult the Internet, go to *Bilteks Ltd.* (20 Jekaba Street). In Latvia you can also ask politely – and offer to pay – in almost any shop or organisation if you have an urgent fax to send. They will probably be quite helpful.

Emergency numbers are 01 (fire); 02 (police); 03 (ambulance). The transition from the old analogue system to the new one means that telephone numbers and codes can and do change – in all the Baltic States; and there may be two or more numbers for the same organisation. *Lattelkom* has a special *helpline* for this (tel 079) and the operator may speak English. There is a 24-hour information service for 'foreign companies' and organisations' fax numbers' (tel 7-01-87-39); and a private directory service for business telephone numbers; tel 077; 073; or 36-77-77 in Riga.

In Riga and the main towns nowadays, the new green-red-and-white telephone booths take telephone cards costing two, five and ten Lats available from kiosks or shops.

Transport

Bus and Coach Services:
There is no direct coach service from London: but see under *Poland* for travel to Warsaw; then there is an onward rail connection, or a bus service between Warsaw, Vilnius, Riga and Tallinn. There is a *Eurolines* office in Riga, though, which may contradict the above: contact Eurolines in London, tel 0990-143219; or in Riga at tel/fax 7-21-11-58. At the bus station in central Riga there is also a board giving details of international services and an information desk (bus information: tel 7-21-36-11).

In the capital Riga there are trolleybuses, buses and trams, but no metro: you need separate tickets for the buses. The monthly pass covers each of these; and is currently 12.80 Ls per month.

Car Rental:
Contact *AVIS*: 0181-848 8733 in the UK; or *Hertz*: tel 2-726-940 (Lithuania); 7-207-980 (Latvia); 6-388-923 (Estonia).

Driving:
Bring all your documents and an international driving licence. Allow extra journey time for crossing one of the Baltic borders (and if you are driving from Britain, to cross the German-Polish border). *Statoil* or *Shell* petrol stations are quite common; seat-belts should be fastened (even if the locals don't always do this). In built-up areas the limit is 50kph; and out of town 90kph – quite low – and there are speed traps nowadays. In an accident, do not admit your liability on the

spot; always contact the police and ask for a police notice (tel 02). The number for you to report an accident is 37-70-00.

Ferry:
There are few ferry boats directly to Riga; one route in summer is with *Travemünde* in Germany and on to Slite on the east coast of Sweden; another route is via Tallinn where there are regular ferry lines operating some large and small ferries from Helsinki. *Estline* operates a service there from Stockholm.

Taxis:
Tel 070/077/073 or 7-33-40-41. The meter should be on; if it is broken, agree the price beforehand; do not use unregistered and – preferably – not the private taxis but the state-owned orange-and-black ones. For transfers etc. contact the *Riga Limousine Centre*: tel 7-36-23-50; fax 7-36-20-10.

Train: *Latvian Railways (LD)*: tel 7-23-31-13.

Daily Life

Health Service and Hospitals

There are no international hospitals here, but the *Ars* hospital in Riga has an emergency home service (tel 20-10-03/5). The *Stradinsh Clinical Hospital* is at 13 Pilsonu iela; tel 61-1201/12. Health insurance is advised (see *General Overview* under *Health Insurance*) and take some medicines you need.

Education

There are over a thousand state schools and 24 private schools; 17 universities or colleges; and ten private ones. Latvian is the main medium of education (although in the 1995 academic year still only 60% of students were being educated in Latvian). Other nationalities, like Russians, Ukrainians, Tatars, and others, tend to go to the Russian-language schools. There are five Polish schools, and one Jewish one; with other classes held in Estonian, Lithuanian, Belarusian, Ukrainian and Romany.

Banks

See under *Currency* above.

Books

Maps and guide books are available from local bookshops or from the *Latvian Bookshop*: 72 Queensborough Terrace, London; tel 0171-229 1652; also from *Stanfords*: 12-14 Long Acre, Covent Garden, London WCE 9PL; tel 0171-836 1321 – they may send you their Eastern European catalogue – or the nearby *Zwemmer Bookshop*: 28 Denmark Street, London WC2 8NJ; tel 0171-379 6253.

Newspapers

The Baltic Times: Balasta dambis 3, Riga; tel 7-46-21-19; fax 7-46-33-87. This is the biggest local English-language weekly.

You can find the *Financial Times*, *Wall Street Journal* and other major newspapers in the main hotels.

Television

There are five TV channels, including the state-run LTV-1 and LTV-2. CNN and all the satellite channels are here.

Radio

BBC World Service is also on 100.5 FM. *Super FM* is the Top 40 music station; *Latvijas radio 1* (Latvian State Radio 1) has a programme in English at 8pm each day (107.7 FM).

Cultural Background

Religion:
This is a predominantly Protestant (Lutheran) country, with relatively more Roman Catholics located in the east, with Russian Orthodox and quite a range of smaller Protestant churches, and six remaining synagogues.
Entertainment and Social Life:
See the invaluable English-language publications *Riga In Your Pocket* and *Riga This Week* cited above for everything from hotels to concerts, restaurants and nightlife.
Food:
Local food specialities include the inevitable cabbage soup, ravioli (filled with bacon and onions) which in Poland is or are *pirogi* and here is *piragi*, and apparently 'grey peas with fried meat.' A Riga speciality is Black Balsam, a mysterious concoction drunk with coffee or mixed with vodka, and whose recipe is a closely guarded secret.

Useful Addresses

Latvian Embassy: 45 Nottingham Place, London 1M 3FE, tel 0171-312 0040; fax 0171-312 0042. Has a *Latvia, Information for Travellers* advice sheet and other useful information.
Latvian Embassy: 4325 17th Street, NW, 20011 Washington DC, tel 202-726-8213-4; fax 202-726-6785. Consular office open from 10am to 12 noon.
British Embassy: Alunana iela 5, LV-1010 Riga; tel 7-33-81-26.
US Embassy: Raina bulvaris 7, 1050 LV-Riga; tel 7-21-00-05.
National Tourist Board of Latvia: Pils Laukums 4, Riga 1050; tel 7-22-99-45.
British Council: (Resource Centre) Vilniaus 39/6, 2600 Vilnius; tel 2-616-607/222-615; fax 2-221-602.

Working in Latvia

Economy and Trade

The privatisation of industry has proceded further here than in Lithuania – management consultancy, legal work and other services for industry and trade being growth areas. The aim is for the government to control only essential infrastructure, like roads and airports. Large state – and former state – enterprises include the *Latvian Shipping Company*, *Ventspoils Nafta* (the state oil company, with an oil terminal in Ventspils) and *Latvijas Gaza*. Manufacturing and trade are important, as the country has few raw materials. Agriculture and forestry play their part and fuel – still imported from Russia – accounts for a large percentage of its imports. Political stability is an important asset.

British companies with operations there include *Royal Ordnance*, *Glaxo*, *Rover*, *AVRO*, *Ove Arup*, *BP* and *Shell*, and many smaller ones. The *Latvian Development Agency* can supply useful information on the economy and investment opportunities: Perses 2, Riga. The *British-Latvian Chamber of Commerce* (Marlborough House, 68 High Street, Weybridge KT13 8BL, tel 01932-831150; 01832-831160) has a database of contacts within Latvia and works closely with the *Latvian Development Agency*. Business information is available from: *Latvian Chamber of Commerce*, Brivibas bulvaris 21, Riga LV-1442; tel 728-3424; fax 728-2524 or 782-0458. It can also supply information on foreign companies investing in Latvia.

English Teaching:
The *British Council* in Riga should be your first port of call for information (see under *Useful Addresses* above). *English Contacts Abroad* provides a research and direct contacts service for EFL teachers in all CEE countries (PO Box 126, Oxford OX2 6UB, UK). Write in the first instance for a questionnaire – or with any tips or contacts of your own. There is an administration fee of £48.

Teacher Agents: A way for EFL teachers and others to bring their group (usually of secondary school or university-level students) to the UK to learn English; write in the first instance to *Speak English Schools*, PO Box 126, Oxford OX2 6RU, UK.

University Teachers:
The *Central European University*: Civic Education Project, Taboritska 23, 130 87 Praha 5, Czech Republic, tel/fax +42-2-272-498, e-mail cepprg@ecn.gn.apc.erg – sends western-trained academics to the other CEE countries including Albania, Bulgaria, Czech Republic, Estonia, Hungary, Latvia, Lithuania, Poland, Romania, Russia, Slovakia and Ukraine.

Tourism:
The professionals will consult the annual *Latvia Agent's Manual* published by the *Latvian Tourist Board* (otherwise known as *Vialatvia*: 4 Pils Locums, LV-1050 Riga; tel/fax 2-22-99-45/). Here are all the hotel, travel agency, and other addresses you will need. See under tourism in the following chapter for an idea of some of the options open to those with a qualification in tourism. If you have the Internet (as mentioned above) the Tourist Board site can also be visited on *http://www.ltboard.apollo.lv*.

Voluntary Work:
International Exchange Centre: 2 Republic Square, Riga LV-1010; tel 327-476 – requires camp counsellors for summer camps in Latvia and Lithuania from June to August. Accommodation and a small allowance is provided. The refundable registration fee is $50.

Joint-Stock Company Minta: Perkuno al. 4. 3000 Kaunas, Lithuania; tel 3707-202-560 – recruits volunteers for international work camps in Latvia as well as Lithuania; teachers are paid 'by arrangement' for summer camps; and there are places, too, for English-speaking au pairs.

See the general note about workcamps in Former Soviet Union under *Voluntary Work* in *Lithuania* which follows.

Doing Business

Life is changing fast in this Baltic country which is adopting more western ways, and the pace of change is somewhere between that of Lithuania and Estonia which befits its geographical position between the two. There are as yet no international banks operating in Latvia; but many local ones offering international services. Again, *Riga in Your Pocket* or *The Baltic Times* can be your guides: the latter has some detailed business and economy coverage as well.

Business and Industry Report

So far as doing business is concerned, there is also a new, more liberal outlook – especially among younger people. Your first port of call in the UK should be the *British Latvian Chamber of Commerce*: Marlborough House, 68 High Street, Weybridge KT13 8BL; tel 01932-831150; fax 01932-831160. Membership for companies is £250 (£100 for Latvian companies. The *British Embassy Commercial Section* provides services for business travellers and others (c/o *British Embassy* – address above). They help to organise briefings, advice on how to approach the market, visits to companies and trade missions all across Central and Eastern Europe, where the government is now making a consistent effort to capitalise on some of Britain's cultural and commercial assets, after lagging behind somewhat at the beginning of the 1990s.

Many important opportunities were lost then, in Latvia and in other CEE markets; but the *DTI (Department of Trade and Industry)* has at least run some useful campaigns to raise the profile of British business in the region; it has a Baltic States *Helpdesk* and some general publications for exporters (tel 0171-215 5265 or 0171-215 5000 for the switchboard). The *Latvian Development Agency*, 2 Perses Street, Riga 1442, tel 728-3425, has published a report on *Development Potential* which summarises areas where Latvia needs inward investment.

Useful Addresses

American Chamber of Commerce: Jauniela 24, Riga; tel 7-21-52-05; fax 7-82-00-90.
British Chamber of Commerce: Dome Square 6, Riga; tel 7-22-32-23; fax 7-22-50-26.
EBRD: (European Bank for Reconstruction and Development) Kalku 15, Riga; tel 7-22-50-68; fax 7-83-03-01.
EU-Phare Programme: Smilsu 1, Riga; tel/fax 7-82-03-20.
IMF: Smilsu 1, Riga; tel 7-21-23-84; fax 7-82-02-96.
UNDP: (United Nations Development Programme) Skolas 24, Riga; tel 7-24-26-55; fax 7-24-26-59.
USIS: (United States Information Service): Smilsu 7, Riga; tel 7-21-65-65; fax 7-82-00-77.

Lithuania

Introduction

Lithuania is the largest of the Baltic States, with a population of 3.7 million. 600,000 live in Vilnius, the capital. Other cities are Klaipeda, Palanga and Kaunas. It borders on Latvia to the north, Poland and the Russian enclave of Kaliningrad in the south-west, and Belarus to the south-east. The landscape is one of of plains and low hills with many lakes, most of which are in the east. There is a great dependence on agriculture, with the food industry dominated by the production of milk, meat and fish. Textiles and knitwear, electrical, electronic, and optical goods are also produced; there is light rather than heavy industry and the economy relies heavily on imported raw materials.

Living in Lithuania

History

Established in the 13th century, Lithuania became – with its partner Poland – one of the most powerful medieval states in Central Europe. In 1569, a united Lithuanian-Polish Commonwealth was established, lasting until the defeat of Napoleon and its partition. Lithuanians tend to emphasise their separateness from Poland before then, while Poles remember this union as beginning in 1385 when King Jogaila married the Polish and Catholic Jadwiga and converted from the local brand of paganism.

This was one of the last parts of continental Europe to convert to Christianity in fact. The medieval English writer Chaucer knew of it, and one of his characters in the 'Canterbury Tales' was a crusader there. This means he fought alongside the Teutonic Knights, who were themselves defeated decisively by this combined Polish and Lithuanian alliance in 1410. Poles are still remembered in the south of the country as occupiers, not allies, and they regret the loss of their northern outpost Vilnius, which they called Wilno.

But this Polish-Lithuanian Commonwealth was weak; and invasions by the Turks, the Swedes, and then the Russians (for the first time in 1772) weakened it further. Lithuania became part of Russia, reemerging as an independent state only in 1918. After its illegal occupation by the Soviet Union in 1940 and 1945, it became an independent country once again on March 11 1990.

Lithuanians have been scarred by these experiences. The figure given for Lithuanians and Poles from these border regions who were deported to Siberia or died, is 10%. It is arguable how far the Allies assented to this Soviet version of ethnic cleansing which followed the war. The aim was to simplify this mosaic of nationalities, and to deport intellectuals and potential troublemakers, and anyone who might disagree with the current regime. Many Poles fled west and occupied land given up by the retreating Germans. Some Russians moved west too, into newly occupied Lithuania and its neighbours and into the Kalinigrad region which

Stalin annexed. Today, Lithuanians think of this Russian enclave as an occupied part of Lithuania.

These are all events which are reminiscent of more recent wars in Bosnia and Croatia, and other similar episodes which preceded them. By this time, Lithuania's large Jewish population had also been massacred or sent to the death camps by the Nazis, some by Lithuanian collaborators who took this chance to liberate their country from the Russians.

Lithuanians, Latvians and Estonians all now subscribe to a broader kind of nationalism based on liberalism and democracy; and this is how most of the peoples in this region have come to see themselves, as making this transition to the modern world, or to Europe, or the West, as they see it. But there are some more ancient discontinuities which underly this change.

Geographical Information

The *Lithuanian Tourist Board* (see below) publishes guides like the *South-East Lithuania Area Guide* for all the different regions of the country.

The Language

Lithuanian is the other member of the Baltic family of languages along with Latvian, and some dialects of these. In Lithuanian, 'hello' is *labas*; 'goodbye' is *sudiev*, or *viso gero*; 'thank you' is *aciu*; and 'you're welcome', *prasome*. In Lithuanian, Lithuania is *Lietuva*. German and also Polish are spoken while English is used for international commerce and by those who work in tourism.

The Currency

1 Litas = 100 centas. Dollars are still easier to exchange here than pounds.

Getting There

Lithuanian Airlines: tel 0181-759 7323; fax 0181-745 7346 – or tel 2-753-212/752-588, fax 2-354-852 in Lithuania – operates daily flights to Vilnius from Heathrow; it cooperates with *Estonian Air* (UK tel: 01293-534735); *Air Baltic* (UK tel: 01871-828 4223) which flies to Riga from London has connections onwards to Tallinn, Vilnius and Helsinki. Other useful contacts are: *British Airways* (UK tel: 0345-222111); *Austrian Airlines* (tel 2-662-000 in Vilnius or 0171-434-7300 in London); *Lufthansa* (UK tel: 0345-737747; or 2-636-049 in Vilnius) which has an extensive Eastern European network; *Finnair* (London tel 0171-408 1222; 2-619-338 in Vilnius); and *Transaero* (London tel 0171-828 7613), which may have flights there in future. *Air Baltic* in Vilnius is tel 2-236-000. *SAS* (*Scandinavian Airlines*) is a partner of Lufthansa nowadays; and has flights to eleven cities in Poland, Russia, Estonia, Latvia and Lithuania: tel 0345-010789 in the UK.

Another contact for flight and airline enquiries is *Vilnius Airport*: tel 2-669-481 for 'international services'; or there is a fax enquiry service which can tell you more about its operations: fax 2-260-000.

Travel Agencies

Baltic Travel Service: Subaciaus 2, 2001 Vilnius, tel 2-620-757; fax 2-222-196 -- were granted the first commercial licence issued by the Lithuanian government (license number 000001) and have branch offices in most major cities. It is an agent for many airlines and other travel services. (On the employment front it is also recruiting some staff as well – see under *Employment* below).

Interchange: 27 Stafford Road, Croydon CR0 4NG; tel 0181-681 3612; fax 0181-760 0031. For the CIS and Former Soviet Union countries.

Lithuanian Tours Ltd: Simyniskiu St. 18, 2005 Vilnius; tel 724-163/723-931; fax 721-815; e-mail contact@Lithuaniantours.com.

SVEBAS Travel Agency: J. Tumo-Vaizganto str. 9/1. Vilnius 2001; tel 2-226-620; fax 2-226-551 – or tel 6-253-825, fax 6-291-175 in Klaipeda.

Residence and Entry Regulations

Contact the Lithuanian Embassy in the UK or USA. UK and US passport holders do not require a visa to visit for up to 90 days. If you do need a visa, a visa for one Baltic State allows travel to the other two (but not to Russia, Belarus or Ukraine). They will send you a leaflet about this if you are not British or American.

For a residence permit, you will need your original passport, photos, and fee; and this can take one or two months to come through; so you may be better off making your application on the spot, where these permits are issued by the local police. You will also need the help of your prospective employer, and a letter from them showing you have a job – or other proof of funds – to get your work residence permit, as well as proof of accommodation. It is best to make an appointment at the *Migration Department of the Ministry of the Interior*, the Embassy in London advises. This address is: *Migracijos departamentas*, Saltoniskiu g. 19, 2600 Vilnius; tel 2-72-30-69.

Customs

There are no restrictions on items for personal use; visitors should also declare all of these and keep their slips for their departure. Nowadays, to get in, you will need at least $15 on you for every day of your stay which is what the government deems you will need to live; or your bank or credit card statement or something similar will suffice.

Courier Services

Inter-Logistic Worldwide Courier: Unit 7, Craufurd Business Park, Silverdale Road, Hayes, Middlesex; tel 0181-569-0616; fax 0181-569 0616; e-mail XK241@DIAL.PIPEX.COM. In Vilnius, you can call *DHL* (tel 725-144; fax 725-285) or *UPS* (tel 610-883; fax 226-111).

Daily Life

Accommodation

Lithuanian Hotels Association: Vytenio 9/25, Vilnius; tel 2-23-27-11; fax 2-23-27-60.

Utilities and Communications

Electricity is the standard 220 volts AZ, 50Hz as throughout the Baltic countries,

so a standard continental-style adaptor can be used.
The country code from the UK is 00-37. Letters to Western Europe take three or four days. Regional calls from within the country are made by dialling a zero before the code, i.e. this is 02 for Vilnius from within the country; but to call from Britain you dial simply 00-37-2.

Transport

Car Rental: Contact *AVIS*: tel, 2-733-226; or 0181-848 8733 in the UK; or *Hertz*: tel 2-726-940.

Driving: Bring all your documents and an international driving licence, we are advised, available from 'your local Dept. of Motor Vehicles.' Allow extra journey time for crossing one of the Baltic borders (and if you are driving from Britain, to cross the German-Polish border). In built-up areas the limit is 60kph, and out of town 90kph – and there are speed traps nowadays. In an accident, always contact the police (tel 02) and ask for a police notice. Steering wheel locks and red breakdown warning triangles are also good things to bring with you if you are driving there.

Ferries: These link Klaipeda with Germany, Sweden and Denmark.

Cultural Background

Religion:
Primarily Roman Catholic, with Protestant, Russian Orthodox, Jewish and other minorities.

Social Life, Entertainment and Food:
See the invaluable English language bi-monthly publication *Vilnius In Your Pocket* (P.O. Box 52, 2000 Vilnius; tel 2-222-976; fax 2-222-982) for everything from hotels to concerts, restaurants and nightlife.

Useful Addresses

British Embassy: PO Box 863, Antakalnio 2, 2055 Vilnius; tel 2-222-070/1; fax 2-727-579; or tel 2-222-070 (Commercial Section).
US Embassy: Akmenu 6, 2600, Vilnius; tel 2-223-031.
Lithuanian Embassy: 84 Gloucester Place, London W1H 3HN, tel 0171-486 6401.
Lithuanian Embassy: 2622 16th Street, NW, 20009 Washington DC, tel 202-234-5680 or 234-2639.
Lithuanian State Tourism Department: Gedimino pr. 30/1, 2695 Vilnius; tel 2-226-706.
British Council: (Resource Centre) Vilniaus 39/6, 2600 Vilnius; tel 2-616-607/222-615; fax 2-221-602.
American Express Lithuania: Lithuanian Tours, Seimynskiu Str. 18, 2005 Vilnius; tel 3702-724156.
AmEx recommends that clients call before travelling to verify services. 'Due to local regulations/business practises, not every office provides every service.'

Working in Lithuania

See the introduction to this chapter for a general economic overview; and the sources of information in the *Business and Industry Report* below. The wholesale privatisation of industry has resulted in opportunities in re-equipping and management consultancy. The air traffic control system at *Vilnius Airport* was installed with help from the French-owned *Thomson* company for instance. *Lithuanian Airlines* (see above) has a fleet of made-in-America Boeing 737s. Recently the American steel works company *Penninox* has invested in the free economic zone (FEZ) of Klaipeda where it has started building a foundry. The *Lithuanian Investment Agency* can supply other information on privatisation and investment opportunities: Sv. Jono St. 3, 2001 Vilnius; tel 2-623-870; fax 2-220-160.

Teaching:
The British Council in Vilnius advises that information concerning the employment of English language teachers is provided by Mrs. A. Svilpiene, Ministry of Science and Education, A. Volano str. 2/7, 2691 Vilnius, tel 2-617-649. *English Contacts Abroad* provides a research and direct contacts service for EFL teachers in all CEE countries (PO Box 126, Oxford OX2 6UB, UK). Write in the first instance for a questionnaire – or with any tips or contacts of your own. There is an administration fee of £48.

Teacher Agents: English teachers there may also bring their group (usually of secondary school or university-level students) to the UK to learn English and earn a small commission; write in the first instance to *Speak English Schools*, PO Box 126, Oxford OX2 6RU, UK.

The *Central European University*: Civic Education Project, Taboritska 23, 130 87 Praha 5, Czech Republic, tel/fax +42-2-272-498, e-mail cepprg@ecn.gn.apc.erg – sends western-trained academics to the other CEE countries including Albania, Bulgaria, Czech Republic, Estonia, Hungary, Latvia, Lithuania, Poland, Romania, Russia, Slovakia and Ukraine.

Tourism:
Travel agencies need staff – like *Baltic Travel Service* Subaciaus 2, 2001 Vilnius; tel 2-620-757; fax 2-222-196 – 'for research into existing market conditions in outlying Lithuanian cities, securing finance, editing and clarifying English language correspondence...' and so on. For a speculative application, in the Baltic States and across Central and Eastern Europe, if you have these kinds of consultancy skills, writing to a travel agency may be no bad idea. Names and addresses of agencies and tour operators etc. are usually available from the national tourist offices.

Voluntary Work:
International Exchange Centre: see *Latvia*.
Joint-Stock Company Minta: see *Latvia*.

A general note for readers which does not necessarily concern the above is to beware of some of these workcamps in the CIS and other countries. They really can be workcamps, with one correspondent saying that this made it possible for her to understand why the Soviet system collapsed, and others complaining about the food and working environment. These are for those of a more adventurous disposition perhaps. We are pleased to hear reports to the contrary – or anything about living and working in these countries for future editions – but voluntary workers in the Baltic States and the Commonwealth of Independent States should in the meantime be cautious.

The Tax System

Lithuania has the 183-day residence rule found elsewhere; and many expenses expatriates receive – for example for school fees – are also liable to be taxed. Business-type expenses, a car, accommodation allowances and so on, are exempt from income tax; and the system is progressive, ranging from 0% at the lowest rate to 40% for the top tax band.

Russia, Belarus and Ukraine

Introduction
Travel
Residence and Entry
Daily Life
Employment
Doing Business

Russia

Introduction

In terms of employment, immigration, new contacts and new markets, practical advice about safety and daily life as well as the general background to living and doing business here, information is included in the chapters which follow on *Travel, Residence and Entry, Daily Life, Employment* and *Business* which will be most helpful to readers. We begin here with a general overview: an introduction to its history, geography and culture.

Russia and the Soviet Union

The beginning of 'modern' Russian history used to be regarded as 1917 when the Soviet Union began. Now it is not. The more recent democratic revolution which ended it was in 1991 and this brought the Russian Federation into being. There was an earlier abortive revolution in 1905 by communists and others (and the century has ended with this Soviet period now in parentheses, and the beginnings of democracy).

The Russian Federation used to be just one of the constituent parts of the Soviet Union. It was this Russian Federation Parliament – the 'White House' – which in 1991, when the similar regional parliaments in Vilnius and Riga had also declared their *de facto* independence from the Soviet Union – which was defended by the democrats, including Boris Yeltsin, against the coup which Gorbachev's enemies and formerly trusted lieutenants had launched.

They fought off the tanks which surrounded the building, and persuaded the coup leaders to surrender. At this time – which was the turning point of modern Russian history – the future of the Russian Federation/Soviet Union hung in the balance. The democrats won, and Gorbachev was converted to democracy too late. From now on, the social democrat Yeltsin was in charge, reversing the Bolshevik coup of 1917 and installing the democratic liberalism whch still – just – prevails in Russia today. Maybe the system which Gorbachev had inherited could only support the kind of changes he had made by itself changing. This is what happened when the Soviet Union ceased to exist.

The Commonwealth of Independent States

The CIS was created in December 1991, when the Russian leaders met their newly independent opposite numbers from Ukraine and Belarus, and created a new union for the former Soviet empire, and the USSR became the CIS, a little like the post-imperial British Commonwealth. So this is no longer the Soviet Union, it is the former Soviet Union, or Former Soviet Union as we can say, or FSU. Then, the leaders of the five new Central Asian republics decided to join this new Commonwealth.

Their reasons were mainly economic and practical: these were separate countries but with economies which were still still almost inextricably linked. The former Soviet countries needed to work together – they decided – during their separate transitions to democracy and the free market. This is the current status quo – making this the most important political and economic grouping in the region. What would happen if there were a coup in Russia? It is very unlikely that the ex-communists would return, but in the present climate these economic reforms would continue, under a dictatorship which would be not unlike that of the ex-President Pinochet of Chile.

Reform in Russia

Yeltsin and Gorbachev were not the first Russian leaders to propose reform and modernisation. This is a *leitmotif* of all Russian history in fact. Even 1917 does not seem quite the radical break with the past that it once did – for both the supporters and opponents of communism. These changes also dramatise a larger conflict, which is a sempiternal feature of Russian life, between the left and the right, or liberalism and autocracy, the Whites and the Reds... In a society which has always been much more polarised than the propaganda suggested, this division persisted throughout this long and traumatic twentieth-century period.

Peter the Great (1672-1725) was the first of its autocratic leaders to try reform; he tried to bridge the gap between domestic inefficiency and his ambitions to make Russia a great imperial power by introducing more 'modern' technology and innovations which came from the 'West', to create in Russia an empire and a nation like the ones he saw emerging in Western Europe. It was an emerging European and Asian empire then. Now it is an emerging market.

Early History

In 1300, the Prinicipality of Moscow covered an area of only 8,000 square miles. During the next 50 years it grew more than fifty-fold. By 1600, immediately prior to the conquest of Siberia, it was as large as the rest of Europe. By the time of its conquest of Siberia, the Russian Empire reached something like its modern extent, with more expansion to come in the nineteenth century.

More than any other European leaders the rulers of Russia equated political power with territorial growth, and the absolute rule of the landowner – a rigid system not in tune with the international order of the time, which was based more on a compromise between the various sections of society, and on a larger international scale a compromise between different countries. Russia was an absolutist empire, where the word of the Tsar was literally law. Only military confrontation with the rest of Europe made its rulers realise the backwardness of their country.

The Nineteenth Century

In Russia, a reading of the literature is as suitable an introduction as any to its history – in particular Tolstoy's *War and Peace*. The world of the nineteenth century was agitated by questions of national identity and reform. One point of comparison for visitors from Britain will be the similarity between this growing land empire and the largest empire in the world at the time – rivals not just for local but international power – the Russian and the British Empires. Reading up about Russia means finding out something about the Crimean War, or Russian expansion into Central Asia, its nineteenth-century novels, or the Charge of the Light Brigade...

East and West

East and West are relative terms, meaning different things to different people – just as the ideas of Western, Central and Eastern Europe themselves can come to seem to have a relative and not an absolute meaning. It all depends on where you are and how you look at it. What do we mean by these terms 'East' and 'West' which are so often disputed between these countries in Eastern Europe, and especially in relation to Russia?

Even the existence of a area which we can call Eastern Europe is a subject of much dispute. Its politics, economics and history are at times obscure – and have become much more so today with the end of communism. This created a simpler dividing line across Europe which now – in our consideration of where Central Europe begins and Eastern Europe ends – is no longer very helpful. This is true of what these terms East and West mean in Russia as well.

This fundamental structure can also explain the strongly held opinions – and sometimes the preconceptions – which many Britons and Americans have about the region. An opposition between the two is one of the ways we consider the Russian identity today – how many Russians see their country too – as being 'not quite European' and belonging more to the East. There is an ambiguity in the modern Russian identity in fact – and in the countries all across this Central and Eastern European region. Is it a Eurasian or a European country? This is one question which is being answered today in modern Russian politics, in its foreign policy, and in daily life as well.

This is a much more fundamental difference than the one which used to be to do with 'Eastern' and 'Western' Europe, with the division of the continent into two opposed camps, and the Iron Curtain in between. All those going there need to know – and perhaps no more than this – that East and West are not about geography, or history, or politics. They are really ideas.

The Russian Idea of the State

The idea of a state which can be separated from those in power – as democrats and liberals in the West tend to see its role – and where it can be benign, where a constitution guarantees individual human rights and aspirations has never really taken root in Russia. Russians tend to support a strong leader who gets things done, and see their own lives as being unconnected to politics and their happiness divorced from it, if not from the church and spirituality. These are conditions which may be rather favourable to writers and intellectuals – of which it has had more than its fair share – but are not very conducive to the development of a civil society.

Many Russians even see now, in Boris Yeltsin, the man who brought them democracy, someone who has donned the mantle of a Tsar, and brought a new kind of dicatorship which is associated in the minds of some with capitalism. This is how the political situation in Russia feels today; and there is a rather uneasy tension between autocracy and democracy which seems likely to be confirmed as the status quo. It seems unlikely, however, against this larger cultural background, that Russia would ever aspire to becoming a fully 'westernised' or liberal.

Geography

There is also a dividing line between East and West geographicaly, the Ural Mountains which divide Europe and Asia. As we move east, the climate becomes generally less hospitable and more continental. We think of Russia or Belarus, or even Ukraine as being more like the North, but Moscow or Novosibirsk are no further north than Edinburgh. Many parts of the country are actually further south than Britain, but the climate is certainly more extreme.

Few will be considering heading east for the weather, though, except perhaps the Black Sea coast where the climate is more moderate. Another difference from Western Europe is the population density which also decreases the further east we go. Who lives in Siberia today? The answer, in many places, is almost no-one.

Taken as a whole, the Russian Federation is one of the least populated countries in the world. On the map, it stretches from its borders with Finland, the Baltic States, Belarus and Ukraine in the west across the Ural Mountains and through Central Asia and Siberia to the port of Vladivostok in the east and the peninsula of Kamchatka. It is about twice the size of the United States in land area (nearly 7 million square miles) and has an average population density of 8.7 per square kilometre.

Cities and Population

The capital Moscow has 9 million inhabitants. Other major cities are St. Petersburg, Arkhangelsk, Nizhniy Novgorod, Volgograd, Vorkuta, Ekaterinburg, Omsk, Novosibirsk, Irkutsk, Yakutsk, Khabarovsk, and Vladivostok. There is a patchwork of different republics which are all regarded as being part of Russia, Adygheya, Astrakhan, Bashkortostan, Buryatia, Chechnya, Chukotka, Chuvashia, Dagestan, Gorno-Altai, Ingushetia, Kabardino-Balkaria, Kalmykia, Karachayevo-Cherkess, Karelia, Khakassia, Komi, Mari El, Mordovia, Northern Ossetia, Sakha (Yakutia), Tatarstan, Tuva, and Udmurtia. The whole country is divided up into larger regional units like the North, North-West and Centre in European Russia and Western and Eastern Siberia.

Language and Religion

Russian is universally spoken, with some English, French and German, and many local languages, notably Turkish and its Central Asian variants. This is quite a widely spoken second language all across the Russian Federation and CIS, not unlike Spanish in the United States.

The religion is mainly Russian Orthodox, with Muslim, Buddhist, Catholic, Protestant and Jewish minorities.

Travel

It is customary to begin reports like this with the consideration of safety. However, no journey can be successful if we consider only the dangers. This is a vast region – but communications are getting better. Where we would be accustomed to travelling by car, Russians tend to go by long-distance train, and there is more than just the famous Trans-Siberian line but also a whole network of railways all across the Former Soviet Union – which may not be not clean but apart from this are quite comfortable, and truly one of the transport wonders of the world. There are great opportunities to get around the country in this way – which independent travellers are beginning to discover – and usually in safety.

Getting there may not be so easy. It depends how you want to go: Moscow and St. Petersburg, when you get out of the airport and through the customs formalities, are quite straightforward destinations; and it is becoming quite cheap to fly to Moscow today. There are also other 'gateways' into the country which the more enterprising of its neighbours in Central and Eastern Europe are trying to promote, seeing themselves as bridges for trade between East and West.

So, a flight with *Finnair* can take you via Helsinki, and be as logical as flying direct to your Russian destination – and a train from here, as Lenin discovered, would take you to the Finland Station in St. Petersburg. *Austrian Air* fly direct from Vienna. *Lufthansa* has routes usually through Germany in its very extensive Eastern European network; and so on. Safety (and also convenience) means that in most cases – for most business travellers – it is better to arrive direct so far as other destinations in Russia are concerned, from outside the country, and not via Moscow or St. Petersburg or another Russian airport. Hence the importance of Helsinki, Vienna or Frankfurt. You are better flying via another European country, and should not get an onward internal flight if this can be avoided.

Lufthansa, Transaero, Air France, British Airways, KLM and many other airlines fly to a range of destinations in the Russian Federation today, direct from British, American and Western European airports, and even rail and coach connections to Russia can be quite good from most Western European cities nowadays. Via Poland is a good 'budget' route from London – unless you are going through Scandinavia or the Baltic States – with an onward (late night is best) train from Warsaw Gdansk station and a connection you get then across Belarus and through Minsk to Moscow. No transit visa for Belarus will probably be needed if you are going on to Russia through Belarus, but if you travel via some other countries, like Ukraine, it probably will be.

If you are travelling via Warsaw, or Prague – or another CEE gateway like this – first-time travellers may now be aware that they can also make their visa arrangements for Russia in these third countries, quite easily if you make the effort to go to the appropriate embassy in good time. This may even be cheaper even allowing for the supplement you need to pay for an express visa application than doing it at home, although you will be leaving this rather to the last minute, and the best way to make all these arrangements is as far as possible in advance. So there is no harm in contacting your home country embassy before you go, even if your way into Russia is a more circuitous one and via a third country.

You can book a coach from London – see *Eurolines* or *Fregata Travel* below –

even to Minsk and Moscow nowadays. Russian airlines are changing as well, with the privately-owned and international services of *Transaearo* competing with the other western companies. It carried more than two million passengers in 1997 and operates five weekly Boeing 737 flights from London-Gatwick to Moscow via Riga. It currently operates a fleet of 16 aircraft, three DC10-30s, seven Boeing 737s, five 757s and one IL-86. New aircraft will join the fleet in 2001.

The airline is also planning to develop its *Transaero Express* operation into a fully fledged regional airline, using key Russian cities as feeder hubs for its expanding international and domestic route network. The airline says these new routes are needed by communities which lost unprofitable regional air links following the collapse of the Soviet Union. Connections are also to other parts of Russia and the CIS, London, Paris, Frankfurt, Los Angeles and Hong Kong. Today it is Russia's second-largest airline. For bookings in Britain call 0171-636 2545 or 0171-436 6763.

Ukraine International Airlines is your best route into that country (see the *Ukraine* chapter which follows; and *Belavia* is the national airline of Belarus (call *CIS Travel Services* on 0171-393 1201 for their all-inclusive packages to Minsk). And see the previous *Baltic States* section for more on air travel there. *Aeroflot*, too, is busy upgrading its services, with the largest network in Former Soviet Union, which can still get you almost anywhere in Russia and its neighbours.

Standards here are going up. Western visitors who have not been there before may not notice these changes – in transport and many other areas of life – but they are considerable. There were many restrictions on travel in the former Soviet Union, but this was also a 'golden age' of adventurous travel for some, which came to an end a year or two after the Soviet Union did, when flights all across the country were just a few dollars, and conditions really were difficult, hotels extraordinarily dilapidated, and the adventurous really could travel almost anywhere on a budget.

Now all this has gone, but knowing some of this history can help us to travel in Russia today. We can see the importance of the right local contacts, and the then even-more-hard-to-obtain visa. Only a few Russians could travel abroad; but the USSR itself was vast, and many Russians you meet today will have their own travellers' tales of life in Armenia, or Georgia, or Azerbaijan, all places which may be now more difficult for them to get to. In the United States it can be like this too; but life in Britain is on a smaller scale, and this feeling of vastness and remoteness, of a country stretching on for ever, may be one of the first impressions visitors have when they travel to Russia.

There used to be one government-owned travel and tourism agency in Russia, *Intourist*. Now even this has been privatised, or split up into its various parts; and thousands of others have sprung up all across the country, all eager to do business with western visitors. *The Russia House* is one very important and long-established agency which can handle all your visa, travel and accommodation requirements, for private individuals, businesses and business travellers.

Travel Agencies

Academservice: 117393 Moscow, ul. Arkhitektora Vlasova 49, Moscow 117393; tel 095-120-9005; tel 095-120-9006; fax 095-128-9684/8096; e-mail notes@academ.munic.msk.su. A wide range of incoming services across Russia and CIS countries.

Colin M. Barnet and Associates: 14 Elm Grove, Eccleston Park, Prescot, Merseyside L34 2AX; tel 0151-426 4045; fax 0151-426 0100. Advice on airfares, visa support, and a wide range of business services especially to St. Petersburg.

Comintour: Griboedov canal 5, office 319, 191186 St. Petersburg; tel 812-210-7545; tel/fax 812-210-7615 or 314-8451; e-mail cominto@mail.wplus.net. Hotels, excursions, tours, events, business travel.

Fregata Travel: 13 Regent Street, London SW1Y 4LR; fax 0171-451 7017; or 117A Withington Road, Manchester M16 8EE; tel 0161-226 7227; fax 0161-226 0700. See below.

IMISP: PO Box 10, St. Petersburg 193060, Russia; tel 812-271-1968; fax 812-271-0717; e-mail imisp@mail.wplus.net; http://www.wplus/net/pp/imisp. Study and business tours to St. Petersburg and Russia. For foreign students, executives and officials who wish to learn how to do business in Russia.

Interchange: 27 Stafford Road, Croydon CR0 4NG; tel 0181-681 3612; fax 0181-760 0031. For the all the CIS and FSU countries.

Intourist: 13 Mokhovaya street, Moscow 101000; tel 095-292-22-60; fax 095-292-20-34. Has a useful 'Travel Agent's Manual' with various details and contact addresses for Intourist and its many branches and services, which it may send you on request.

Intourist Warszawa: ul. Nowogrodzka 10, 00-509 Warsaw; tel/fax 22-629-02-02 or 625-08-52 or 622-32-06. For travel, hotel reservation etc. all over CEE/CIS and throughout Russia and its regions.

Intourtrans: 15/13 Petrovka str., Moscow 103031; tel 095-929-8890; fax 095-921-1996. Trips around Russia and CIS countries, hotels, and onward connections.

Liberty International (UK) Ltd: 11 Grosvenor Street, Chester CH1 2DD; tel 01244-361115; fax 01244-351116; e-mail liberyty@chester.itsnet.co.uk. For full destination management services, including conference and meeting organisation, hotel reservations, guide and tour services, study tours and special interest groups.

Overseas Business Travel Ltd: 8 Minories, London EC3N 1BJ; tel 0171-702 2468; fax 0171-488 1199. *Moscow*: 125047 Moscow, Majakovskaya Square, 2 Tverskaya Jamskaya No. 6; tel 095-250-22-31; fax 095-250-22-64. Office also in Kazakstan. Business travel, flights, hotels, transfers, 'full office facilities'.

The Russia House: 37 Kingly Court, Kingly Street, London W1R 5LF; tel 0171-439 1271; fax 0171-434 0813. A range of services from visa procuration to exhibition and trade meeting organisation, courier servies etc. 'The largest and best equipped to deal with Russia.' Offices in London, Edinburgh, New York, Stockholm, Hong Kong, Brussels (from September 1998), Moscow, St. Petersburg and Tbilisi..

S.I.B. Travel: 18 Dzirnavu St., Riga, LV-1010 Latvia; tel 7-33-39-88; fax 7-83-02-07. Air transport, incoming services and accommodation for all Baltic States, the CIS countries and Russia.

Siti Travel and Tourism: 193060 St. Petersburg, Smolny; tel/fax 812-232-0942. Full range of incoming and business travel services.

Sputnik-Altai Tourist Co: 87 Sotsialisticheskii Prospekt, Barnalil 656099; tel 3852-36-71-89; fax 3852-36-72-75. Tourism services in the Altai Mountains, excursions, visa support etc.

Transaero Tours: London tel 0171-636 2545. Moscow tel 095-946-1013 (tourist services); 095-945-5320 (booking air tickets); fax 095-945-5183. This is an independent agency acting as UK sales agents for Transaero Airlines. Their office intends to expand its activities working closely with sister offices in Moscow, Frankfurt and Tel Aviv arranging flights, visas, hotels, car hire, transfers, business services and tailor-made packages throughout Russia and neighbouring countries.

Airlines

There are many scheduled services from Britain and Western Europe, as well as the United States, making this no more complicated than travel to any other country, if you have organised your visa application successfully. Here are some with routes to Moscow and St. Petersburg and elsewhere in Russia: *Transaero* (UK tel: 0171-636 2545), *Aeroflot* (UK tel: 0171-355 2233 or 0171-491 1764 – or their agents *IMS Travel* tel 0171-224 4678), *LOT Polish Airlines* (UK tel: 0171-580 5037), *British Airways* (UK tel: 0345-222111), *Austrian Airlines* (UK tel: 0171-434 7350), *Lufthansa* (UK tel: 0345-737747), *Delta Airlines* (from the United States tel: 2-26-94-77; fax 2-26-71-41), *KLM* (UK tel: 0990-750900), *Czech Airlines* (UK tel: 0171-255 1898), *SAS* (*Scandinavian Airlines* – UK tel: 0345-010789). *British Midland*, *Finnair* and many others also have scheduled services.

Charters

At the time of writing, few charters are available, although some may wish to charter a plane themselves in the more remote areas: contact *Transaero* above. But Moscow is now relatively inexpensive to get to by air thanks to a price-cutting war at the moment which has so far not extended to other Russian destinations. City breaks, cruises and other tours and holidays are available through many travel agents, notably *Fregata Travel* which has a *City Breaks and Holidays* brochure for Moscow and St. Petersburg (13 Regent Street, London SW1Y 4LR; fax 0171-451 7017; or 117A Withington Road, Manchester M16 8EE; tel 0161-226 7227; fax 0161-226 0700), *Norvista*, the travel agency run by *Finnair* – tel 0171-408 1222 (reservations) – and through some of the other agencies mentioned above. Also see the brochures of some major tour operators which are beginning to feature Russian and CIS destinations, at your local travel agency, or specialist independent travel agencies in Britain and around the world like *STA Travel* or *Campus Travel*. There are also those advertising in newspapers and magazines offering special interest tours – for example of the Russian waterways or the 'Golden Ring' around Moscow.

Transport and Communications

Coach

The international coach company *Eurolines* is part of the same group as the Central and Eastern European specialist *Fregata Travel* nowadays (see above) and may be contacted direct in the UK on 0990-143219. It features coach destinations throughout CEE, as well as many in Russia. Or try contacting *White Eagle* in London, which has a comfortable route to Warsaw, from where you could get an onward connection by train or coach, with video and hostess service (it takes about 24 hours to get to the Polish border from London by coach); or *ATAS* coach lines (tel 0181-9935000 – UK and 22-6254682 in Poland itself. Another 'budget' route from London is via the Czech Republic and onwards. One coach operator to Prague from London is *KCE – Kingscourt Express*: 15 Balham High Road, London SW12 9AJ; tel 0181-673 7500. You check in at least 30 minutes beforehand for this kind of service; and make preparations like bringing food and a change of clothing.

Railways

Routes into Russia are through Poland, Finland and the Baltic States (often via Belarus, where a transit visa will usually be required in addition to your Russian visa – you should check on this). The interesting *Europe by Train* by Katy Wood (Ebury Press, London) which is updated annually says that 'as a foreign tourist you will only be given a choice of the best types of train accommodation.' Some might disagree; but it is true that Russia is a country which is perhaps best visited by train; and the European timetable published by Thomas Cook will suggest some ways of getting there. In Russia itself, the timetable information in railway stations itself – which you should make a note of if you can is the most reliable source of information about routes we know... Your trip will often be reasonably comfortable and relatively cheap. Often this will be the only way to get there for many of the more out-of-the-way places too, where many business people and consultants nowadays may end up living and working.

Travel by train in Russia is not for the faint-hearted though. See the *General Overview – Section I* of this book for some tips on this.

Removals and Freight

For a list of UK-based international removals and freight companies, many of which specialise in Central Europe, please see *Removals*, in the *General Overview – Section I* at the beginning of this book.

Onward Connections

Your onward travel, flight, hotel and other transfers in Russia can all be arranged by *Fregata Travel*, or travel bureaux like *Intourist* and *The Russia House* (see above) or the many private travel agencies which are based there and advertise their services for international visitors, of which we have listed only some. A personal recommendation is probably as good a way as any of choosing one of these. There are bus and coach services between major cities as well, which may not be comfortablke but will probably get there.

Hertz Europe, Europa House, 804 Bath Road, Cranford, Middlesex TW5 9US, tel 0181-759 2499, can provide details of their car hire services in Russia. Their partners in Moscow and St. Petersburg are: *Richmont Transportation Services*, 4 Cherniakhovsky Street, 125319 Moscow; tel 095-151-5426; fax 095-956-1621; and *Morex Ltd.*, Nekrasova 40-1, 191014 St. Petersburg; tel 812-272-5045; fax 812-275-3800.

Import Procedures

Contact the Russian Embassy for these (see *Useful Addresses* below). Personal items are duty free and pets need their appropriate vaccination certificate.

Customs

You need to fill in the currency declaration forms for foreign currency entering or leaving the country. There are no restrictions on items for personal use, and visitors should also take care keep these declarations for their departure, otherwise duty will probably be payable on these kinds of goods.

Courier and Delivery Services

A leading freight forwarding company with operations throughout Eastern Europe is *Eurogate International Forwarding Co. Ltd*: tel 0171-459 2900; fax 0171-588 9058. *DHL* and many other international courier services have offices in Moscow and St. Petersburg. The UK number for *DHL* is 0345-100-300; for *UPS* tel 0345-877-877; and for *Parcel Force* general enquiries tel 0800-22-44-66. Two courier services are:
Inter-Logistic Worldwide Courier: Unit 7, Craufurd Business Park, Silverdale Road, Hayes, Middlesex; tel 0181-569-0616; fax 0181-569 0616; e-mail XK241@DIAL.PIPEX.COM.
The Russia House: 37 Kingly Court, Kingly Street, London W1R 5LF; tel 0171-439 1271; fax 0171-434 0813 – has a regular courier service from London to Moscow.

Useful Addresses

British Embassy: Sofiyskaya Naberezhnaya 14, Moscow 109072; tel 503-956-7200; fax 503-956-7420 (main embassy); 503-956-7440 (visas).
British Consulate-General: Pl. Proletarsky Diktatury 5, Smolnisky Rayon, St. Petersburg 193124; tel 812-325-6036; or 871-144-5136 (satellite); fax 812-325-6037.
Russian Embassy 13 Kensington Palace Gardens, London W8 4QX; tel 0171-229 3628/9/0; fax 0171-727 8624/50.
Russian Embassy, visa department: 5 Kensington Palace Gardens, London W8 4QX; tel 0171-229 8027; fax 0171-229 3215.
United States Embassy: Novinsky Bulvar 19/23, Moscow; tel 95-252-2451/9 or 252-1898 (after hours); fax 095-956-4621.
US Consulate-General: ul. Furshtatskaya 15, St. Petersburg 191028; tel 812-275-1701 or 850-4170 or 274-8692 (after hours); fax 812-110-7022.
Russian Embassy: 2650 Wisconsin Avenue NW, Washington, DC 20007; tel 202-298-570; fax 202-298-5735.

Residence and Entry

Entering and leaving Russia you will need a valid visa. Contact the Russian Embassy or Consulate where you are for a visa application form; and they will need your original passport, three photos (signed on the back), the visa fee and the letter of invitation from your sponsor or sponsoring porganisation; this is your contact who is inviting you, or your travel agency, officially registered hotel etc. depending on what kind of visa you are applying for, for private individuals, tourism or business – see the *General Overview* for more on this. The general idea is that you must be visiting Russia for a reason, which you may have to explain to the officials who issue your visa, although a document of invitation is usually sufficient. This is not just some hangover from the previous era, but how all visas work, anywhere in the world. They are an official permission to enter the country (and when they run out, and you are still there, you are no longer invited, and may have great difficulty renewing it). Russian visitors to the United States or Britain need to do this too, and may find our own bureaucracy matches theirs.

Business visas require an invitation from an officially registered organisation, registered with the *Ministry of Foreign Affairs* or their local representative office. An official letter or invitation from any other state organisation will do. For private visits to friends or relatives an invitation letter issued by the visa department of the *Ministry of the Interior* is required as well as a letter from your friends and their cooperation to get this permission in the first place. Transit visas need your visa or your invitation or your itinerary and/or air ticket for your country of destination. This is all best done in person at the Embassy. A self-addressed and prepaid envelope is required for postal applications. Contacting travel agencies like *Intourist* or *The Russia House* who know the visa situation may be advisable.

All foreign travellers to Russia must also register their passports with the Passport and Visa Service (otherwise known as the *UVIR*) when they arrive. British and US as well as Russian Embassies can also tell you the local address for this and supply you with the current regulations for visas and residence. This registration should be within three days of arrival (and if you stay in a large hotel it will probably happen automatically). There is a system in other words for them to register your presence with the *UVIR*. It is a good idea to take along your letter or letters of invitation there as well, and any other documentation you which you do not need necessarily to present but which may come in useful.

Foreigners working in Russia must also register their work permit or accreditation with the *Federal Migration Service* and its *Department of External Relations*.

If you have lost your visa – which you need on departure – you should report it to the nearest police station, and get a signed and stamped police report (*spravka*). Then get three more photos, confirmation of your original letter of invitation from the person/organisation which issued it and report this to the British Embassy or Consulate (who will give you a 'letter of support' if you take along the police report and your passport). Then you submit all this to the central or local *UVIR* office together with your passport and an application for a visa; a fee of around 30 roubles will be required for this. If you lose your passport, there seems to be no place in this procedure for you to get any further until you have a replacement passport; so contact your nearest British/US Embassy or Consulate straight away and seek their advice.

Visa Support Services

Many of the travel agencies mentioned in the *Travel* chapter offer visa suppport services. Make your application at least fourteen days in advance. This process is the subject of some controversy between Britain and Russia at the moment – Russians do not feel their own visa applications are always handled correctly – but there is nothing inherently complicated about it and you should be able to do it yourself without booking a package tour with a travel agent. But this is obviously the simplest way.

An express service will be available for last-minute applications, but much more expensively. You can even negotiate a price for this sometimes, if your visa is very expensive and you complain about this – as you can for many of the CIS countries in fact – especially if you have a name or contact of someone working in the embassy who can help you which you can mention – a much more reasonable procedure here than it would be in some other countries – and that all important business card for someone in the Embassy. You can produce this with a flourish, and this will usually produce results, a clue to how business is done and official organisations are dealt with when you are in the country. All this may expedite your application.

Travel Advice

The *Foreign and Commomnwealth Office* offers the following travel advice.

Carry ID at all times.

We advise against travel to the Chechen Republic, Ingushetia, North Ossetia east of the capital Vladikavkaz and to the western areas of Dagestan bordering on the Chechen Republic.

Cross-border traffic with Georgia and Azerbaijan is subject to restrictions.

Incidents of mugging, sometimes violent, theft and pickpocketing occur in all cities, especially St. Petersburg and Moscow. Be vigilant and dress down. Be particularly wary in Moscow of groups of young children/vagrants. Keep expensive jewellery, watches and cameras out of sight. Use officially marked taxis which you should not share with strangers. When travelling by train store valuables in the compartment under the bed/seat. Do not leave the compartment empty. Ensure the door is quite secure from the inside by tying it closed with wire or strong cord. Do not accept food or drink from strangers as it may be drugged.

Russian criminal gangs operate in major cities and this can occasionally result in violence between rival gangs. This violence is not directed against foreigners, but in February 1996 a shooting incident resulted in the death of a British businessman.

It is not known whether aircraft maintenance procedures are always properly observed. Where possible fly directly to your destination on a scheduled internatoional flight originating outside Russia.

Daily Life

General Background

You will be perceived as a westerner; or as a European or American. Normal codes of courtesy which apply anywhere also obtain and Russian hospitality is welcoming, and an enjoyable part of living there. It is really your duty to accept hospitality in the workplace or in the context of business, though, and to reciprocate by bringing gifts and presents.

You will also need some business cards which in the local etiquette are best if they are bilingual, with your details in English on one side and the same thing in the cyrillic alphabet on the other. These look nice; and can be prepared before you go. Even if you print off some business cards at the airport this is a good idea before departure as everyone arriving in Russia to do business or for any other reason should have a small store of these – they are your portable guarantee of status and respectability which most Russian people will recognise and appreciate, and expect to receive: a small scale and cheap way to show 'Russian-style' largesse.

Also you should take some other small and lightweight mementos of yourself and your visit, and rather larger presents for closer friends or colleagues. These gifts will be expected if you are going to meet Russian people (and travel agents dealing with Russia usually acquire quite a store of Russian memorabilia and lace tablecloths brought by visiting Russian guests for example) – and there are even firms who will manufacture these presents for you, like pens with your name on or whatever, which seems to be taking things too far. Something which has a personal meaning to you will be best – and in a world where feelings and 'sentimentality' are important the absence of feeling in such a gift may be what your Russian colleagues remember about it most. This is not just a duty – in the Russian way of looking at things – but also a sign of your own personal and sincere regard for your friends.

These bilingual cards are a clue to how these two languages go together when you are living and working in Russia, and how life is led there by foreigners. Expats and business people may quite easily live and work in an English-speaking environment and letters or faxes may be sent to most Russian companies and organisations in English, for example, especially in trade and tourism, in the reasonably confident expectation of a reply. It is seen here too as the international language of trade and commerce, although with German coming a close second.

Language is less of a problem when you fax. But if you want to get a letter to Russia, write the address on it in the cyrillic alphabet if you can, and in the 'reverse' order which is normal in Russia and its neighbours, which do this the other way around – with country name first and personal name last. And then write underneath this – in English capital letters – the city name and country name – RUSSIA – for your local postman or lady at home.

A useful precaution, which will minimise tha chances of the letter being stolen, is to make it as unobtrusive and 'normal' looking as possible; which usually means an aerogramme or small plain envelope. Most will get there safely; and if you want to send post home, to Britain or the United States, we recommend the reverse procedure to the one described above – again an unobtrusive aerogramme or similar envelope is best – which can be easily obtained from post offices there – but with the name and address in the English style, and above this printed in large letters the city and country names in the cyrillic alphabet.

So learn this. And if you are going to live and survive in Russia for even a short time – for example to decipher the word 'toilet' or 'exit' – you are going to have to learn this alphabet. There is really no alternative. If you know the Russian alphabet it will also be easy to read the Ukrainian one, and indeed the similar alphabets of Serbia or Bulgaria for instance.

The Alphabet

All the language courses – books or books-with-cassettes – have this list of letters (see the *General Overview* for some of these). Some, like the 'l', are like ancient Greek, a lambda. Or they are easily learnt: A, E, O, K, M and T are like English. E is pronounced 'ye'; or if it has two dots over it it is 'yo'. A is more like an British long 'ah' as in 'rather', than the British short 'a' sound. 'T' does not have the slightly harsh-sounding aspiration which Britons and Americans give it; it is softer (as are the plosive 'p' and 'k' sounds for instance). B, H, P, C, Y and X are easy – at least on an English keyboard! – and stand for the sounds 'v', 'n', 'r' – a rolled 'r' which may come most easily to Scottish people – 's', and a 'ch' or 'x' sound – like 'loch' when Scottish speakers say this. Then there are the sixteen letters for 'b', 'g', 'd', 'zh' (as in 'pleasure'), 'i' (as in 'in'), 'l', 'p', 'f', 'ts', 'ch' (as in 'church'), 'sh' (as in 'shaft'), 'sh-ch' (as in 'cash-cheque'), 'e', 'oo' (as in America 'duke') and 'ya' (shorter than the German 'ja'). These you will all have to learn.

The Language

Then there are all the sounds of Russian, not too many, which makes it a not-too-difficult language to learn. Also, the cyrillic alphabet fits it much better than our roman letters fit English; so this is more a less a phonetic one. This makes it easy to read signs and words, and also to write, or at least print, with just a litttle practice.

And when you have practised copying these, learn the written form, which again is different, like handwriting in English compared to the printed letters. This will be useful too. What seems like a 'g' on an envelope is really a 'd' in the written Russian script, for example, standing for 'dom', or house, an important part of Russian addresses. These cursive forms should all be practised, as should the vowels – which are quite a simple combination of mainly front and back vowels, rather like Italian – and then practise the few consonants which are different from English, like the longer 'sh-sh' sound at the end of the Russian word for beetroot soup, which is 'borshsh'.

The Language Deficit

A language which is easy to learn is not being learnt, at least in Britain. This maximises the opportunities in the world of work and your daily life for you to take advantage of this so-called 'language deficit'; and be one of the quite small minority of English speakers who also speak Russian.

Surprisingly, at present the number of students in Britain studying Russian at university has fallen to its 1980 Brezhnev-era level. The image of the country is a major problem apparently. In 1996, there were only 91 students in the United Kingdom entering university to do a single honours degree in Russian. Russia is seen by students as 'dull, boring or dangerous' according to one academic. But those who do study the language say the rewards are great – in terms of visiting the country and meeting its people, as well as in many areas of employment where Russian speakers are needed. A consequence of this language deficit is that many of these jobs are being snapped up – even in Britain – by Russians.

Companies should also act to prepare their staff, with at least some grounding in the language as part of their preparation. There are many language courses catering for western business people or residents which can be found on the spot as well.

Language Courses

OMIS Ltd: P.O. Box 551, 197198 St. Petersburg, Russia; tel/fax 812-233-1785.
International Education Centre (IEC) Ltd: c/o 11 Ebenezer Place, Sussex Street, Norwich NR3 3DQ; tel 01603-631951; fax 01603-763378.
Institute of Foreign Languages: Bolshoi Trehgorny pereulok 11, Moscow 123022; tel 095-205-7202/7611/255-6915; fax 095-205-7202/255-6915.

Very many Russians you meet will also wish to practise their English, and see you as their opportunity to do this. This can be a way of exchanging conversation or lessons to improve your own knowledge of Russian as well.

Culture Shock

For more on some the issues surrounding culture shock, see *The Directory of Jobs and Careers Abroad* published by Vacation Work, and the chapter on 'Preparation and Follow Up'. Less well-known is that some of these issues may also confront your Russian colleagues, who may not have such a wide experience of international travel, or meeting westerners before.

This is controversial ground; and detracts somewhat from the idea which many Russians have of their country as being as an international and outgoing kind of place – or a modern and technologically advanced one – but there are many poreconceptions – and perhaps fears – which are attached to foreigners. In the West, cosmopolitanism has this weak but mainly positive meaning that you have been everywhere and done that, something like the character in O. Henry's short story *A Cosmopolite in a Café*. But this is not always so in Russia.

New Russians

There have been many changes in the last ten years. One is a hangover from the 1980s – like the 'yuppies' who came and went in Britain and the United States. Out of this very unideological generation which came to prominence in the 1970s and 80s – who paid lip-service to the prevailing ideology and but never believed in it – who were schooled in some way in this habit of thought but were more interested in getting things done, came these 'new Russians'. They were more interested in getting on in life, than any preconceived ideas or social orthodoxies. They were disillusioned but also somehow more forward-looking people – who nowadays are felt to be a rather decadent and valueless generation.

Freedom from the state and also prosperity – or more nakedly, money and power – are the goals of some of these Russian *nouveaux riches* – and many young people who are into western pop music and all the vacuous trends spread by satellite TV – Russia's 'generation X' in fact. Then there are those in their thirties of forties who are buying or building their *dachas* out of town. This building boom has seen prices skyrocket out of the reach of most Britons or Americans, who may find themselves living in more modest accommodation in Moscow or St. Petersburg; and the wealth enjoyed by a very few gives them a lifestyle which it will be hard for most expats who are not themselves very rich to emulate.

Most Russians deplore these new yuppie-style values which seem more like a transitional stage, as Russian society meets head-on this confused rush of consumerist ideas without discriminating too much between them, much as we do in our own countries of course. So do the people living in the villages where the new Russians build their country homes.

Old Russians

These country and provincial people are the old Russians; poor but with enough to get by; saving where they can; still paying a low or subsidised rent; but having to adapt to this sudden shift in values – and to the increase in prices of food, clothing, rent, and all the essentials of life which most just about have enough of to get by. Some really are old; but this really means all those who have been left behind by these social changes, often working in the public sector where salaries are low, even in Moscow but they are really very low in the provinces where life is very different from the big cities.

Interesting consequences are, for example, a rise in rural gangsterism – as the old Russians burn down the houses of the new Russians – and a generalised resentment which is felt by all those who perceive these new injustices but have no resources to do anything about them; or have the feeling that they cannot. Hence the surprising popularity of the old and once again legalised communist party perhaps.

The New Poor

Some of these 'old' Russians have teetered over the edge into a more absolute kind of poverty. 'The transition to a market economy and collapse of government welfare systems, unemployment and hyperinflation are among the factors which have plunged hundreds of thousands in the region into poverty,' says the *International Red Cross*. This is one organisation which is working to remedy some of these social problems – and there are many others listed under *Voluntary Work* in the *General Overview* section – working in Russia, and even poorer neighbouring countries like Belarus and Ukraine. Contact the *International Red Cross* at its UK headquarters (9 Grosvenor Crescent, London SW1X 7EJ) if you wish to work as a skilled and trained volunteer or make a contribution to its current emergency appeals for Russia, Ukraine, Belarus and Moldova.

Getting Around

Cars: All vehicles coming into the country are subject to customs control and the driver must present valid proof of registration and international liability insurance which you can purchase at any border crossing. You will need an *International Driving Licence* or equivalent. Also check on the duty which may be payable. The road assistance number is 981; and the national police number is 997.

Buses: There are trams and buses running until midnight or later in Moscow (and other big cities) and now some night buses too. Tickets and coupons may be bought in metro stations and all news-stands and kiosks, also from drivers in buses and trams. Buying this from a tram driver may be more expensive though.

Car Rental: Car rental companies include *Avis, Europcar*, and *Hertz*. *Green Line* is a local limousine service in Moscow: tel 095-954-9094/0067. The local *Hertz* number is 095-284-4391 or 578-7532.

Utilities and Communications

Post and Telephones

Telephones: Phones requiring a card are becoming more common, as are credit card phones. Other phones you can use are available in post offices, paying for your call after use. Calling from Russia you dial an '8', wait for the tone, then '10', and the number you are calling. To call a regional number from Russia, dial '8', then wait for the tone, then dial the number preceded by its regional code. The principle is the same for nearly all these FSU and CIS countries, some of which have installed new telephone services. Everywhere there is the old mechanical network which is being replaced by digital ones, with different regional and international codes; which all means that including these regional codes is important when you note telephone numbers in Russia, as these may not all be the same.

The new systems which are coming in are of digital and also satellite phones – which are most reliable in far-flung locations, but are often useful in the big cities as well. In the cities, most call boxes require special tokens (usually on sale nearby) and there are business 'service centres' in the major hotels. The country code from the UK is easily remembered by fans of James Bond: 007. This is followed by the regional code – e.g. 095 for Moscow – followed by the local number. From the USA this international code for Russia is 011-7.

The number for operator-assisted international calls is 8, then 194 or 196 in Moscow for example. 09 is the number for directory enquiries or general enquiries about the city. 07 helps you to dial an inter-city or regional number, the operator in other words. 927-0009 is a paid directory enquiry and address service which you can use from your hotel. Emergency numbers are: 01 (fire); 02 (police); 03 (ambulance); and 04 (gas leaks and accidents).

Post: Letters to Western Europe and the United States can take a week or two, or much longer from outlying regions.

Electricity: Electricity is 220 volts AZ, 50Hz in Russia. A standard continental-style adaptor or plug can be used.

American Express Offices

Amerian Express Travel Service: 21 A. Sadovaya-Kudrinskaya, 103110 Moscow; tel 095-956-9000 or 956-9004; fax 007-956-9005.
American Express Travel Service: 1/7 Mikhailkovskaya Street, Grand Hotel Europe, St. Petersburg 191073; tel 812-329-6070; fax 812-329-6071.

Western Union

Their 'emergency' number is 095-119-8250.

Issues Facing Expatriates

See the *General Overview* section of this book for more about issues ranging from preparation to setting up home in Russia and its neighbours. One professional organisation which may be contacted is *Moores Rowland* which provides a range of services for expatriates including executive briefings, pre-assignment planning, tax compliance, remuneration, tax, social security and other issues. Contact: *Moores Rowland Chartered Accountants*: Clifford's Inn, Fetter Lane, London EC4 1AS; tel 0171-831-2345; fax 0171-831 6123.

The Russia House Ltd. organises visa procuration, travel, and exhibitions, trade meetings and seminars, with many other services; and offices in London, Edinburgh, New York, Stockholm, Hong Kong, Brussels (from September 1998), Moscow, St. Petersburg and Tbilisi. Contact: *The Russia House Ltd.*, 37 Kingly Court, Kingly Street, London W1R 5LE; tel 0171-439 1271; fax 0171-434 0813.

The Centre for International Briefing: Farnham Castle, Farnham, Surrey GU9 0AG, tel 01252-721194, fax 01252-719277, e-mail cibfarnham @dial.pipex.com – provides fully residential scheduled and customised briefings for all countries in the world to prepare executives and their families to live and work in this challenging location. Customised business overview briefings are also available for frequent business travellers and home-based international managers. Each programme provides in-depth information on country background including politics, economics and social issues. Current advice on the business and working environment, as well as the practical aspects of living in the destination country is provided by recently returned expatriates and those with current business interests in the specific region or country, including security and health issues where appropriate.

Or contact *Worldmark*: the 'specialist joint venture company founded to facilitate trips to FSU and Eastern Europe' (see below); or some of the travel agencies also offering preparation and business travel services mentioned in the preceding *Travel* chapter.

Books

Taking a good book is high on the list of recommendations which expatriates already living in Russia make. One way to keep in touch with the world of books and publishing is to take out a subscription to the *Literary Review* magazine. From the UK, books and publications like this can be ordered through the *Good Book Club* – see *General Overview* – *Section I*. This is a long-established book club popular with expatriates. The Internet now features several similar firms who will be glad to airfreight their books to any address in Russia, and indeed anywhere in the world, one of the first global businesses which is really taking off on the Internet. This important resource should not be overlooked as a way to keep in touch with family and friends at home as well – and its array of services is as accesible in Krasnoyarsk as it is in Colchester.

Expatriates, English teachers and others will also benefit from a new venture in Moscow which has been set up by *Escolar International Book Distribution Ltd.* who may be contacted at the following address. This is the *Anglia British Bookshop*: Khlebny pereulok 2/3, 121069 Moscow; tel 095-203-5802; fax 095-203-0673; metro *Arbatskaya*.

Health Care and Hospitals

This is another concern for all those thinking of going to Russia, especially expatriates with families. One serious drawback of the medical treatment provided by the Russian health system is that it does not always include payment for drugs or more expensive operations and hospital treatment. There can be long waiting lists and at present the system caters particularly poorly for out-patient and after-care treatment and facilities – although preventative medicine and various other specialist services have often been developed to a high standard there.

You can make do with the Russian health service; but most international employees and workers will use the various western or international medical facilities like these:

American Medical Center (Moscow): tel 095-956-3366; fax 095-956-2303.
European Medical Centre (Moscow): tel 095-956-7999.
British Embassy Clinic: tel 095-956-7270; fax 095-956-7446.
MediClub Canadian Clinic: tel 095-931-5018; fax 095-932-8653.
American Medical Center (St. Petersburg): tel 812-326-1730; fax 812-326 1731.
Novaya Bolnitsa Medical Association: ul Zavodskaya 29, Ekaterinburg 620109; tel 3432-42-50-62; fax 3432-46-39-30.

A list of English-speaking doctors is available from the British or US Embassy (where their respective citizens should always register on arrival – or at the nearest Consulate). This will, however, often involve using private facilities.

Other Health Issues

An important part of this is preparation: having a full medical check-up and dental check-up before departure, visiting the optician, arranging vaccinations and contacting your doctor about all these matters. Also see under *Health Insurance* in the following chapter, which is recommended for all those moving to take up employment or live in Russia.

Personal Safety

Last but not least on this list of expatriate concerns is crime and personal safety (although few of those writing *Live and Work in Russia and Eastern Europe* about their own experiences have reported any personal experience of crime). See some of the *Personal Experiences* in *Appendix III* of this for more of these reports and personal impressions of life in the Former Soviet Union.

The publicity is negative, but car crime and offences like burglary may be more common in Britain than they are in Russia. It should be emphasised that this is generally a very law-abiding society with much less of the public antisocial behaviour than you might find even in Britain or the United States. One reason why crime is so widely reported is that this is still a relatively new or unfamiliar phenomenon. It also expresses some deeper anxieties about social change, as it does in many other countries around the world today.

The most serious difficulty crime raises for visitors to Russia is in setting up a small business, which is difficult when there are so many protection rackets and organised criminals around. Here there really are organised criminals and gangsters, who will only be interested in you if you attract attention to yourself. One tip if you are doing business there is not open an office, if you do not really have to.

The managing director of *Worldmark* – who can send you their free *Business Guide to Travel in the Former Soviet Union and Eastern Europe* and can be contacted on tel 0171-799 2307 – offers some of the following tips for 'safe and efficient travel'. Generally he advises using your common sense and taking all the necessary practical steps to prepare, like 'investigating visa procedures before you go.'

'Buy hard, lockable suitcases for long trips where you have a lot of luggage to take,' he says. 'Arranging a business meet at the airport' and having 'ready cash for when you arrive' are also very important. 'Also, do not catch taxis in the street. Finally, you should be 'streetwise and behave as you would in any other unfamiliar location, especially at night, dressing down and not flaunting wealth by wearing large watches,' for example.

'Much of the success of a trip to the FSU will depend on how much you prepare in advance. Deciding to go one day and then leaving the next is just not possible. Once actually there, follow procedures and employ common sense and you should have no problems.'

Employment

Getting a Job

There are many new opportunities for international workers in Russia – in everything from consulting to voluntary work. It is also a challenge: to live in a country whose history and way of life may be different from the experience of most Western Europeans or North Americans. Expatriate workers can be roughly divided into those sent there by large companies, and are therefore paid at international rates, and those who work for local organisations, and are paid at the local rate (see the *General Overview*). There are some areas of work – such as English teaching – which fall between these two categories.

The *Appendices* to this book have the personal experiences of some of those living and working in Eastern Europe and Former Soviet Union today, giving an idea of the variety and levels of employment which can be found. Job hunting will be the main concern of those who have had to relocate for some other reason; and have to find a way to support themselves. This is not too difficult for anyone with some grasp of teaching, or the language, or who can present themselves well, when there are so many vacancies for English teachers and so great a need for private lessons.

For others the picture is not so bleak as might be imagined either, with many specialist recruitment agencies and useful ways into work like the *Overseas Jobs Express* newspaper (also see the *General Overview*). For list of these agencies, and international companies there you can contact the Embassy as well as Chambers of Commerce and all the other *Useful Contacts* mentioned in the *Business* chapter which follws.

So go, if you have to, and if you have to get a job out there you will probably be able to do so on arrival. Also, do your research before you go, so you have the greatest access to these opportunities and contacts when you arrive. A main avenue to explore is English teaching – so contact the *British Council* and its many offices and other outposts in Russia (again see the *General Overview*). Also, find out more about private language schools in the region and some names and addresses. Sometimes this information may be easier to come across in Britain or America than it will be in your new circumstances in Russia, so do your best to find this out before you go.

Others will be those working for joint ventures or international companies. Many nowadays are setting up operations in Russia. Others may be medical staff, others still volunteer teachers. Salarywise, the range is from these volunteers who are usually working for low local salaries, or nothing at all, up to highly paid consultants, executives and business people, two groups of expats who may move in very different worlds.

But the growth in future in the jobs available to expatriates in Russia will be in what are known as 'medium-risk' jobs – in teaching, training, secretarial, retail, technical, and managerial positions – as the Russian economy develops and becomes more like those of the more developed countries of Western Europe. This is already happening but in a very patchy way at present, with many more types of jobs relating to this second phase of medium-risk development in

Moscow or St. Petersburg than elsewhere.

These two cities are where the UK and US expatriate populations are concentrated today. Then there are the still relatively less advanced regions – although here consultants in a wide variety of areas relating to agriculture, oil and gas exploration and mining etc. are already working, and making their own contribution to the local economy; and introducing new ways of working and operating a business more along western or international lines.

Everywhere the infrastructure is dilapidated: roads, railways, airports; telecommunications... But this is also an opportunity as these facilities all need to be updated and renewed. Construction workers are also needed, these are all areas of local skills shortage. Manufacturing facilities and distribution systems are all being set up or revamped, often in collaboration with local firms – but sometimes independently now by western or international companies setting up their own businesses there.

There will also be opportunities in local companies – for those who speak Russian. Local firms themselves are rapidly becoming more international, and may need foreign staff. Some like Gazprom or Lukoil which are the largest companies in Russia – if not exactly household names outside the country – have become major players on the world stage. These firms tend to be the banks and oil companies; but also increasing in importance are the service industries like food distribution and retailing.

Recruitment Contacts

These are listed in the *General Overview* section. One extremely useful organisation for staff with the right qualifications and experience which is currently recruiting staff on its own account for its operations there is *Antal International Ltd*: 2nd Floor, 90 Tottenham Court Road, London W1P 0AN; tel 0171-637 2001. There are offices in Moscow, Warsaw, Krakow, Kiev, Prague, Budapest, Bucharest and other locations. Recruitment is in all areas, and all their own staff specialise in these regions as well. Future expansion will be to St. Petersburg (also into Asia). 'The fall of the Berlin Wall will undoubtedly be one of the most enduring images of the late twentieth century, signifying as it does the opening up of Central and Eastern Europe and with it new markets and new possibilities for organisations everywhere. The *Antal International* mission is to build a fully integrated global management recruitment business which will serve the needs of these rapidly emerging economies.'

Also see publications like *Overseas Jobs Express* (mentioned above). The Commercial Section of the *British Embassy* in Moscow and the Consulate in St. Petersburg are important contacts for lists of British companies with operations here; and see also the organisations mentioned in the following *Business* chapter like the *Russo-British Chamber of Commerce*. These can all be useful sources of information and may also supply details of companies operating in Russia. *Nexus Expatriate Magazine* (International House, 500 Purley Way, Croydon, Surrey CR0 4NZ; tel 0181-760 5100; fax 0181-760 0469; e-mail expatnetwork@cityscpae.co.uk) has a *Jobsearch* recruitment section including some vacancies in Russia; and publishes lists of contact addressess etc., as well as occasional features on living and working in Russia/CIS/CEE.

Finally, they also publish a very useful *Former Soviet Union* contact directory, including recruiters and useful sections on specific opportunities, insurance, legal practice and other matters.

Teaching English

A general estimate is that even today 90% of Russian business people don't speak any English. This figure is much higher throughout the general population. Adverts for English language courses abound in Russian newspapers as older people try to catch up. In the past, French or German was often taught as a main second language, or the other Eastern European ones. But today it is English.

The amount it is spoken, however, will vary enormously depending on your location, with more English spoken in Moscow and St. Petersburg than in most of the rest of the country. The level of English ability will also vary with the different professions: for example, much more English is spoken as a rule in the chemical and engineering or computer industries, and in this kind of working environment, than it is among more ordinary people. Simply, it is part of the job, and this is also where the need is greatest for trained English teachers to help the Russian economy get back on its feet, those with a qualification in these more technical areas perhaps to teach specialised courses.

In science and engineering, a lot of the textbooks are only available in English. This 'globalisation' of the language is a worldwide trend which is being felt in Russia too. Young people are generally more proficient than their parents, as in many other countries.

In Moscow or St. Petersburg, a hard-working foreign teacher who takes on some private lessons could make as much as $1,000 a month, although most earn less. We should also know that a modest bedsit in Moscow starts at $300 a month, even for the locals; and that foreigners often pay considerably more than this, up to $5000 a month for a refurbished apartment. In other words, rents are astronomical and salaries are low.

The *British Council* is the first contact you should approach in any of the CEE/CIS countries for English language teaching work – which will often be advertised on its noticeboards – and on occasion for some ancillary jobs – like driving for example – for English language speakers. These are also places to advertise your private lessons. In Russia, they have resource centres at: *The Library of Foreign Literature*, Ulitsa Nikoloyamskaya 1, Moscow 109189; tel 234-0201; fax 975-2561; *Nizhny Novgorod Institute for Development of Education*, Ulitsa Vanyeva 203, Nizhny Novgorod 603122; tel 8312-67-76-54; the *British Council*, Naberezhnaya Reki Fontanki 46, St. Petersburg 191025; tel 812-325-6074; fax 812-325-6073; *British Information Centre*, Ul. Gogolya 15a, Ekaterinburg 620151; tel 3432-56-92-05; fax 3432-56-92-07; with some other resource centres planned or opening. The mailing address and contact for the *BC* Moscow is c/o Mailing Section, 10 Spring Gardens, London SW1A 2BN; tel 095-917-3499; fax 095-975-2561. They may also send their photocopied *TEFL in Russia – A Brief Guide* and university and private language school contacts in Russia.

The *Central European University*: Civic Education Project, Taboritska 23, 130 87 Praha 5, Czech Republic, tel/fax +42-2-272-498, e-mail cepprg@ecn.gn.apc.erg – is based in Prague but sends western-trained academics to the other CEE countries to assist in a wide range of programmes, also in Russia and Ukraine.

English First (EF) is 'the world's largest group of private language schools recruiting teachers for many countries. It is expanding its operations in Central and Eastern Europe, including Russia. Contact: *EF English First*: Kensington Cloisters, 5 Kensington Church Street, London W8 4LD; tel 0171-795 6645; fax

0171-795 6625. Their salaries in Russia are 'based on local cost of living, currently in Mocow $650 a month and $450 in St. Petersburg, with rates for Vladivostok and Nizhny Novgorod yet to be set.' Travel and insurance are organised too. They say 'working in Russia can be a very different experience from working in Europe or North America. You will have to cope with difficult and stressful situations every day... Local costs and standards of living are lower but a 'western' lifestyle can be expensive'.

International Placement Group: 72 New Bond Street, London W1Y 9DD, tel/fax 0171-739-2725, e-mail ipg.@praha.demon.co.uk – is a teacher recruitment agency with a head office in London and specialising in the countries of Central and Eastern Europe including Russia, placing teachers in these countries and offering programmes in the UK as well.

Teacher Agents: This is a way for EFL teachers and others to bring their group (usually of secondary school or university-level students) to Britain to learn English, and to earn some commission or have their travel and accommodation expenses paid. This is often for one, two, or three-week courses in the summer, but can be all year-round; and for other visits for business people, and cultural and activity tours for adults and children as well as all over Britain. One organisation offering courses like this all year round for many students from Russia and other countries is *Speak English*: PO Box 126, Oxford OX2 6RU, UK. Write to the Director for details.

Tourism

Salaries are even less; but there are opportunities here because this is another English-speaking world, or one where more English-speakers with local experience are needed. The best way will be to offer your services as something more than just an English-language guide or receptionist, and be more like a consultant to some travel agencies there if you have suitable experience and expertise in this area.

Travel agencies outside the country send holidaymakers to Russia as well – more and more of these in fact. These can be contacted via the various contacts throughout this *Russia* section or more directly. Use all the hotel, restaurant and travel agency contacts in this general tourism and hospitality area which you can 'create' with the material available from travel agents and tourist offices. Your search for employment here – and in every area of work in fact – should be 'creative' and depend on your own research into up-to-date contacts, very useful in tourism as in many other fields.

Voluntary Work

For other employment contacts and advice see under *Employment* in the *General Overview – Section I* where there are more English teaching and Voluntary Work contacts.

International Ecological Camp, 665718 Bratski-18, Irkutsk Region, PO Box 52, Russia – organises workcamps and voluntary projects in Siberia. About 80 workcamp volunteers are involved, each one lasting for 2-3 weeks. Volunteers who speak fluent Russian are also required to lead the workcamps, and some English teachers. Registration fees are payable.

Taxation and Insurance

Finance

Anyone considering retiring to Russia or any of its neighbours – and anyone going to live and work there – should take specialist financial advice regarding their own situation. Most people in a position to retire overseas have an amount of capital to invest, or will have once they sell their UK home. This may be in Britain, or the United States, or in off-shore accounts (see the short section on this in the *General Overview* section). It is essential to take good advice on how and where this may best be done.

Usually, there is no reason why you should not continue with bank accounts or investments already established – and many good reasons to do this – and in most cases interest will be paid on deposits paid without deduction of tax where one is non-resident. Your bank or building society can tell you more about the declaration you need to fill in and the many other international services banks offer nowadays.

General Taxation

In Britain some impartial advice can be obtained from the UK Inland Revenue. It is quite reasonable to contact them in the first instance (your local tax office in other words) and maintain your good relations with them. However, if you do move permanently to Russia there will be no way for you not to pay tax in that country and every reason to go by the book, as penalties and fines for non-payment of tax are quite high. Ask the *Inland Revenue* about the double taxation agreement between Britain and Russia (which in future is 'open to revision' apparently).

One of the more controversial issues in politics in Russia at the time of writing is the introduction of a new and universal tax code (not unlike our own). The Russians are introducing a new system for registering and taxing imported cars, for instance, as well as ironing out some other anomalies and cracking down on tax evasion and illegal smuggling activities and so on. VAT and the tax on company profits are going down and tax collection is supposed to be improving. So in this current circumstance these rules will be subject to change; and it is essential to seek advice – from the UK, US or Russian Embassy. But the general outline of taxation will remain the same.

This means a tax year from January 1 to December 31; with the 183 day in any one year residence rule in operation elsewhere in the world. Before this limit, you are only taxed on your earned income coming from Russia. After this, you are regarded in exactly the same way and will be in the same position as a Russian citizen and your best source of advice will probably be a local English-speaking accountant or lawyer familiar with the vagaries of the system.

On the plus side – on paper at least – the system is quite like our own; with a sliding scale of income tax bands currently from up to 12,000 Roubles (12%) to 48,000 Roubles and over (35%) with an annual personal allowance of 1,000 Roubles (and the same for each dependant – this was the situation in 1997). Many of relocation and business expenses for expatriates will also be tax deductible.

Personal Taxes

When you arrive as an employee in Russia, you have to register with the Tax Authority within 30 days, when you should also take along a preliminary tax return. (You should further have been to your local visa registration office within 72 hours of your arrival). After you have made your intiial declaration – with an estimate of your earnings – your tax is payable quarterly – the important dates being May 15, August 15 and November 15; and then March 1 of the following year, by which time your final declaration and payment should have been made. Not to do so means risking a heavy fine. If your arrive in the country near the end of the year and anticipate earning less than the minimum tax threshold you do not have to make a tax delaration for that year. For more advice on financial planning and tax matters for individuals and companies in Russia, you can contact the consultants *Price Waterhouse – Russia* (Nikolayamskaya 13, Moscow 109240; tel 095-967-6000; fax 095-967-6001) who may supply further information on all tax, business, employment and residence matters.

The upshot of all this, though, is that you will probably pay more or less the same amount of tax on your income in Moscow as you would in Manchester.

Corporate Taxes

See the *Business* chapter which follows.

Employment and Tax

A large number of American and British teachers and others often work illegally, unable to deal with the paperwork involved in the seemingly endless struggle to obtain a work permit. No-one seems to mind, but this is probably not advisable. Some don't declare their income and effectively join the 'grey' economy. This is probably a mistake, too, and may put you at the mercy of an unscrupulous employer, or an unwieldy and unsympathetic legal system.

Others at the 'higher' end of the spectrum will have these various tax and other regulations dealt with for them. UK or US-based managers will be making these arrangements; which means they will need information on Russia (and its neighbours) which may be difficult to come by. Some of the agencies mentioned in the *Travel* chapter also offer resettlement and expatriate services like this. One useful publication in this respect is *Managing Expatriates in the CIS* published by Price Waterhouse (Southwark Towers, 32 London Bridge Street, London SE1 9SY – and see their Moscow address above).

Health Insurance

The multi-trip worldwide policies mentioned in the *General Overview – Section I* will suit most readers of this book. Europe in these travel insurance terms is usually considered to include Moscow and St. Petersburg, by the way, and to extend as far as the Urals, but check on this. 'European' cover might be equally good for European Russia therefore. But for those who really do become residents, it will be a good idea to take out a more long-term policy. You are entitled, of course, to the same free healthcare as a Russian citizen but you may be better off with a policy which will pay for one of the private international clinics or hospitals in an emergency. Contact *ExpaCare* or *BUPA*. Also see *Healthcare and Hospitals* above.

ExpaCare (Dukes Court, Duke Street, Woking, Surrey GU21 5XB; tel 01483-717800; fax 01483-776620) is one company which offers full cover under its international health plan. Standard Care covers in-patient care plus local ambulance service, nursing at home, repatriation and local burial and emergency evacuation, with Special Care increasing the benefits to full in-patient and out-patient care plus routine dental treatment.

Derek Ketteridge & Associates (2nd Floor, 7A Middle Street, Brighton BN1 1AL; tel 01273-720222; fax 01273-722799) offers private healthcare schemes. Other products available from their Billericay office (tel 01277-630770; fax 01277-630578) include general long-stay insurance and non-UK residents insurance.

One of the leading providers of healthcare insurance for expatriates around the world is *BUPA International*: tel 01273-208181; fax 01273-866583. 'If you are taking out private medical insurance it is important you understand what you are paying for and are certain you are sufficiently covered for your circumstances,' they advise.

Business

Doing Business in Russia

Market Summary

Russia is a fully independent state, but also is a member of the Commonwealth of Independent States (CIS) with which it has strong links. Essentially, the old organisation which linked all of these regions of the Former Soviet Union is slowly adapting to this new political reality of a plurality of nation states.

Where there were monocultures before, and large-scale planning and heavy industry, there is a slow but momentous change to private enterprise and smaller-scale businesses. There has been a shift away, too, from manufacturing to the service sector which is where much of the growth has been. Manufacturing in Russia often means 'make and mend' and adapting and upgrading some of the existing equipment and machinery (there has been new investment too); and services will often mean 'starting from scratch;' and setting up systems where none previously existed.

There has been the introduction of a whole range of 'mid-range' economic activity in these areas of commerce and the service industries which previously did not exist, and were indeed outlawed. This sector is where the greatest focus of foreign economic activity will be in future – and may be of greatest interest to most expatriates and business peoplee visiting Russia. There is also foreign investment in the important extractive or 'primary' industries (including agriculture) where the process of exploiting a great natural wealth has often been hampered by inefficient practices which have one main cause: lack of investment.

Another aspect of industry and employment in Russia is the 'information deficit' which has meant that the true extent of these natural resources – like the oil in Siberia or the Caspian Sea – was only known to a few specialists, and not even to the international oil companies and investors for example.

Brokers in Russia, in oil, mining, or the other primary areas were able to take advantage of this information gap not just to bring the producers and suppliers and potential purchasers together but also to open up these new possibilities for investment to western companies. This is what happened in the late eighties and early 1990s. Often the crucial information was simply that these resources existed; and then the first investor or trading partner on the scene could take advantage of this great opportunity, a pioneering approach which is also coming to an end.

On a much broader scale, it seems like the economic transformation which came to Britain in the 1980s: large-scale privatisation and the restructuring or closure of some larger enterprises in mining and manufacturing (and bringing most of this back into the private sector). With greater importance now being attached to financial services and the stock market, there really are similarities in these changes which have come to economies around the world, and not just in the ex-communist countries.

Russia, too, was launched on its own 'yuppie' era and changes in the service sector meant there were now places for the yuppies to go shopping. Whole new areas of economic activity had sprung up, like mass tourism, which meant that many richer Russians could visit the West for the first time or send their children to study abroad. Foreign travel is another of the status symbols of the new Russia.

Many of the old working practices were in themselves quite efficient (and very efficient when it came to dealing with unexpected situations, like late deliveries and broken down machinery). Staff were and are often highly trained and competent. What was missing was investment – the money to buy new plant and invest in new technology – and all the superstructure of finace, distribution and business systems which the administrators ignored, or were ignorant of. Perhaps it was communism itself which was ignorant of this 'cultural' superstructure, the intangible factors of information, knowledge and training which in fact make an economy run.

The best practice in Russia today means involving managers and employees as much as possible in decision-making, and devolving power down, finding a context in which managers feel confident enough to take their own decisions and giving them some responsibility and 'independence'. This requires some greater dynamism – in the context of the inertia of the previous system – but may not involve wholesale changes. In many Russian companies today there are gains which have already made and strengths which can be built on.

Currency

1 Rouble (Rub) = 100 kopeks. The *rouble* has recently had three zeros knocked off its face value – as happened in some other CEE countries – meaning there are old and new rouble notes at present, with the former slowly being phased out. This is meant to be a sign of the stability of the currency; and Russian roubles must be used in all your transactions in Russia. US dollars are very useful to take with you, though, and should be declared, along with your other money and any items you are importing at customs. When you exchange money, always keep the receipt – something which is useful but not essential to have on departure, especially if you are spending quite a lot. Credit cards can be used in hotels, shops and restaurants in most major cities nowadays, but in the more far-flung provinces and regions there is still a 'cash' economy.

Background to Doing Business

Russia has a huge range of natural resources where private ownership is becoming more common, and rich farming land. Oil and gas are major export earners, as well as coal and minerals including gold and diamonds, nickel, copper, and iron ore. The economic situation in Russia has improved, but the infrastructure of road and telephone communications remains poor. There is an extensive rail network, and air-routes which connect the main cities to the more distant centres.

Many international firms have developed joint ventures with Russian partners, or are involved in setting up their own operations in the country. Business and work relations are often developed through personal contacts and trust and not in more formal ways. Deficiencies in the legal system mean that investment is often still a risk, however.

Those arriving in these CIS (Commonwealth of Independent States) or former Soviet countries for the first time – in this region sometimes known as 'FSU' or Former Soviet Union – will need the services of a guide; and professional help from companies such as *Worldmark* (Alliance House, 12 Caxton Street, London SW1H 0QS; tel 0171-799 2307) or *The Russia House Ltd* (37 Kingly Court, Kingly Street, London W1R 5LE; tel 0171-439 1271; fax 0171-434 0813).

Current Trends

Industrial production has been cut back, but this has not led to very high unemployment, as people have moved into the largely unrecorded private sector. The British, US and Western European expatriate and business presence has been growing, especially in Moscow and St. Petersburg, which have become much more like other international cities in recent years. Moscow in particular is one of the most expensive places to live in the world.

Now the focus has changed, to some other regions where these companies are developing important economic interests – often based on one single industry related to mining or agriculture. This is so of the oil-producing parts of Siberia for instance – or Azerbaijan – in areas like food processing and trade. There are many products like these in which the former Soviet Union and the current Russian Federation is rich, like diamonds, or furs, or cotton.

Doing Business

The parallel is with the emerging markets of Latin America, where the pattern of business and economic development has reached a similar stage.

Important will be your personal relations; and contacts face-to-face are really much more effective than any business transactions which are conducted at a distance, at least to start off with. Indispensible, for anyone who wishes to do business or trade with Russia, is at least one personal visit.

Hospitality

It takes no special preparation or training to understand and appreciate Russian hospitality and culture. But an awareness is required of these different values, experiences and expectations.

Social Life and Social Attitudes

The conditions for social life were very different until very recently in Former Soviet Union. These social conditions are all changing, though.
How much should you try to adapt? The pace of social change means you should probably not try to do this too much; and stick with the ways of meeting, dealing and socialising with your colleagues which you also feel comfortable with. Your own way may be as right as any other.

In Russia, there is still a great emphasis on receiving special permissions, on form-filling, and on meeting the various demands of bureaucracy. A certain fear is still attached to this, of what might go wrong in a bureaucratic system rather than the positive view of what can go right. Status – and the local perception of your status – is aso very important in Russia nowadays.

Business Ethics

After 1991, one of the great problems was one of ownership. Nobody knew who owned what. Another was the legal framework which Russia had inherited from communism. The welter of bureaucratic regulations – which originally was intended to outlaw private enterprise itself – was bound to create distortions which would encourage crime; and this was all a disincentive to investment or to going public where your business activity was concerned.

Associated with the idea of business for many was this numinous notion of illicit activity, which continues today. This also encouraged the 'grey' economy and a general atmosphere of conspiracy which surrounds the worst aspects of business life all across the former Soviet Union.

There is no need either to participate in or encourage this. It can be dangerous to do so, and in any case the local people will be experts where you are only an amateur. So on the first suggestion of mafia or illegal activity, it is always better to make your more black-and-white ethical position clear and unambiguous. Be alert, as the Foreign Office says, to suspicious behaviour. In any circumstances it would always be better to do this.

Best of all, if you are doing business here, is to be working for a large organisation whose credentials and general probity are well-known. Small business people will be the main targets of organised crime as visitors will encounter it, not so much the big ones who can afford to protect their investments and their reputation. Surprisingly perhaps, there is this moral aspect to doing business in Former Soviet Union – unless getting rich quick and getting out fast is your main aim – an ethical dimension which in our more settled economies is not so apparent, and is sometimes taken for granted.

Here it is not like that, and we can see – in its absence – how a stable framework of law, and simply a familiarity with the concepts of private enterprise, is essential to any free market economy, and how this is all underpinned by shared values and attitudes. Perhaps many western business people in the past have got the wrong end of the stick and been attracted by the 'Wild East' image of Russia and its neighbours. This is not an approach which will work now.

Many local people have helped to build a society based on law – in the aftermath of a kind of institutionalised lawlessness – not just the outside advisers and experts who came in post-1991. This is the greater tendency in Russian society today – despite all the negative headlines – in the emerging middle class, and among the ordinary people who also supported the change to democracy. It is the wish of the vast majority of ordinary Russians to have as normal a life as possible, away from some of the confusions and distortions of the past.

There is also a good climate for international companies and their workers to come and work here, to do business or invest, which will help in the long run to confirm some of these trends towards stability.

Taxation and Business Advice

Business Taxes

Taxation for a privately-owned company – it would be called sole trader status in Britain – is considered to be similar to tax for the individual; and the same tax rates and thresholds etc. apply if you are self-employed. A tax declaration must be made separately for the business – and it may be better for English teachers and others working on a self-employed basis in Russia to manage their tax affairs in this way. A Russian friend or adviser familiar with the ins and outs of the system may be the right person to help you organise your affairs like this – and you need to have enough local knowledge – or an experienced business adviser – to get through the bureaucracy.

On a larger scale, the main approved vehicle for foreign investment – which the government insists on in some cases – is a 'joint venture'. This means you have to set up your business with a local enterprise or partner. The idea is based on cooperation between local and western firms, or a distrust of independent foreign investment and foreign companies, depending on how you look at it. This has been the first way in every ex-communist country – along with the introduction of workers' cooperatives – of trying to promote free trade and freer markets. In the first place the aim was to attract foreign investment; and in the second to keep this under local control – not always compatible aims but certainly progressive ones at the end of the nineteen-eighties. This is what a 'joint venture' means in Russia and its neighbours today: it is the current fashion, or a phase in their economic development.

For more advice on financial planning and tax matters for individuals and companies in Russia you can contact the consultants *Price Waterhouse – Russia* (Nikolayamskaya 13, Moscow 109240; tel 095-967-6000; fax 095-967-6001) or any other of the many international consultancy firms based there. These may all supply further information on tax, business, employment and residence matters.

Useful Contacts

Here are some other starting-points if you are visiting Russia to do business (and also see the preceding chapters for some other direct sources of information about Russia and its neighbours). Useful contacts for anyone visiting Russia to do business will also be other business people who have direct experience of living and working there. The British or US Embassies will have lists of businesses there which can be one starting-point. One way is via the Internet. Another is through:

English Contacts Abroad: PO Box 126, Oxford OX2 6UB, UK. An independent advice and research organisation which also welcomes contacts with UK and US-based business people with experience or advice they may wish to offer others considering working and doing business in Russia and its neighbours. Direct contacts may be requested for English Teaching, Voluntary Work, Working Independently, Job and Recruitment Agencies, Recruitment and Travel Press, Entry and Residence, Travel and Accommodation, Doing Business, Rules and Regulations, Preparation and Follow Up, Language and Translation Services etc.

EGO Translating Company: tel 812-987-5757; fax 110-4788; e-mail director@cgotrans.spb.su. Address: Russia, St. Petersburg, Apraxin Dvor, build. 1, entrance 69, 3/F.

EGO Translating Company specialises in written translation, in sectors including construction, financial, customs, banking, accounting, economic, scientific medical and technical documents, promotion and advertising materials, fiction and journalism, and others – as well as interpreting and guiding and some other business services; they are able to deal with large-scale projects, and produce accurate and high-quality translations into Russian.

OMIS Ltd: PO Box 551, 10A Vvedenskaya Ul., St. Petersburg 197198, Russia; visiting address 4th floor, 18/2 Metallistov Prospect; tel 233-1785/224-0668/528-7685; fax 233-1785/224-0668; e-mail centre@omis.spb.ru.

OMIS is an education centre specialising in courses for administrative staff, and a consultancy service for establishing cooperation between Russian and foreign companies. Also, recruitment of personnel for Russian and foreign companies, jobsearch and an information centre among other services.

The British Embassy Trade Office, Ekatarinburg: tel 432-56-49-31; fax 432-59-29-01; e-mail uk.ekate@vmail.sprint.com.

The Bulletin of the Russo-British Chamber of Commerce: 42 Southwark Street, London SE1 1UN; tel 0171-403 1706; fax 0171-403 1245; e-mail 106074.23@compuserve.com; http://www.russian-com.co.uk/russian-com/rbcc.htm. This is the journal of the *Russo-British Chamber of Commerce* which will also have lists of useful contacts, news of forthcoming trade exhibitions, customs clearance, legal and other useful contacts.

The *East European Trade Council* (tel 0171-222 7622; fax 0171-222 5359) has a useful business library and can offer advice on business and trade throughout the Former Soviet Union.

The *US Department of Commerce* also has a business information service 'for the Newly Independent States': Room 7413, US Department of Commerce, Washington, DC 20230; tel 202-482 4655; fax 202-482-2293.

Another contact for business people is the British Government's *Know How Fund* which sponsors projects in FSU: Know How Fund, Foreign and Commonwealth Office, Old Admiralty Building, Whitehall, London SW1A 2AF; tel 0171-210 0065.

In Britain, the *London Chamber of Commerce* is one of many local Chambers of Commerce which can also supply useful information on Russia, and many other countries. In Russia, local Chambers of Commerce should also be contacted. The best business links are often also with municipal administrations.

The federal republics – like Dagestan or Ingushetia – also have their own state governments or administrations which should be contacted if you are considering doing business there, and not the central goverment in Moscow. Tourism offices and brochures which many now produce will be one way to get in touch with these Russian republics.

Belarus

Introduction

It has few natural resources in comparison with the other CIS countries, and is recovering economically after some lean years. Manufacturing is focused on industrial production, in particular of agricultural machinery which is one export, along with chemicals; and oil and other raw materials are generally imported from Russia. Belarus is roughly the size of Britain, the larger part of it lowland, and the capital is Minsk.

Living in Belarus

Residence and Entry Regulations

Applications for entry visas may be made in person or sent by post/courier, although these will not be accepted by fax. Write in the first instance for an application form and their 'Information about Visas to the Republic of Belarus' leaflet. You will need a valid passport, one recent passport-sized photograph, a formal invitation from an individual or corporate body, or a letter of support, and the appropriate visa fee. These are most expensive for a multiple entry business visa (for one year) which costs £200, and cheapest for transit visas and a group tourist visa: £10. There are no less than eighteen categories of these, all explained clearly in the documentation they will provide, including student visas, permanent residence visas and employment visas. 'Welcome to Belarus and have a pleasant trip,' they also say.

Useful Information

There is a post office at each Intourist hotel, and in major towns and cities, open from 9am to 6pm and closed at weekends. The time os GMT +2 (+3 from March to September). Electricity: 220V, 50Hz. Currency: the Belarusian Rubel.

Working in Belarus

Market reforms are continuing, although the Belarusian regime of President Lukashenko is one of the most authoritarian in Former Soviet Union. In essence, the nationalists have been defeated, or are weak, and the prevailing idea is of some form of union, or reunion with Russia.

Useful Addresses

Belavia (Belarusian Airlines): tel 0171-828 7613 (UK) or 250-231 (regular flights) 251-634 (charter flights) in Minsk.

Belintourist (Belarusian Joint-Stock Company for Foreign Tourism): 19v Masherov Ave., Minsk, 220078, Belarus; tel (375-172) 269 840; fax 231 143.

Consular Section of the Embassy of the Republic of Belarus: 6 Kensington Court, London W8 5DL; tel 0171-937 3288; fax 0171-361 0005.

British Embassy: 26 Sakharova Str., 220034 Minsk; tel 017-236-8687/236-8916.

CIS Travel Services: 7 Buckingham Gate, London SW1E 6JP; tel 0171-393 1201; fax 0171-630 8302. They offer packages to Minsk, transfers, hotels etc.

International Monetary Fund: Ul. Stamkevicha 1A, 220010 Minsk; tel 017-220-2533; fax 017-226-9936.

World Bank: Prospect Partizansky 6A, 5th floor; tel 017-226-0644.

Chamber of Commerce and Industry of the Republic of Belarus: Masherava 14, 220600 Minsk; tel 172-269-937; fax 172-269-936.

Ukraine

Introduction

Ukraine discovered its independence only in the seventeeenth century, when Polish rule created a cultural and political counter-movement, the first stirrings of a Ukrainian (or Cossack) nationalism. This revolt was led by Hetman Bogdan Khmelnytsky. With his Cossacks and the Crimean Tatars he led a rebellion in 1648 against Polish rule and founded a Cossack state.

A newly independent Ukraine was an unstable political entity which is remembered in Ukrainian history today simply as the 'Ruin'. The outcome was not the independence which Khmelnytsky had sought, but a reluctant unification with Russia in 1654.

The eastern part of the country fell more under Russian influence, and the west remained more Ukrainian. The latter became known as 'red Ruthenia'. White Ruthenia kept its name, and is today known as Belarus, or White Russia. To the south, this region became known as 'the Ukraine'. This was just a region of Russia in the nineteenth century, and into our own when, with its unexpected independence in 1991, the Ukraine became Ukraine, an independent nation once again. The correct etiquette here is not, as with The Netherlands, to keep the definite pronoun – non-existent in the Russian language anyway – but to call it Ukraine, which means the independent country as opposed to the province of Russia.

It is vaguely familiar from nineteenth-century Russian literature as a distant and exotic place, with its marauding Cossacks and endless plains, a landscape where Chekhov set some of his stories. Exoticism is also a keynote of the 'Great Gates of Kiev' by Mussorgsky (from his *Pictures at an Exhibition*). This was always an out-of-the-way place so far as the Russians were concerned, and one aspect of the national identity remains European. But Ukrainians also have this feeling of being on the outskirts of the former Soviet Union.

Living in Ukraine

Most Ukrainians have to, of course, and may wonder why foreigners do the same, when there are great problems in areas like accommodation, transport, medical facilities, and making enough to get by. So there are two economies: the one which most of the locals know, and a more expensive lifestyle (which would appear more or less 'normal' in Britain or the United States but here seems like expensive luxury). In this respect, the pattern of expatriation is roughly the same as that of Russia, or Central Asia, with a wave of business people first of all, occupying the big hotels and living separate lives from the locals, and then others who will get to know the local way of life more closely.

Geography

There is the Black Sea to the south and Russia and Belarus to the north. To the north and west are Poland, Slovakia and Romania, and Moldova in between, and eastwards again we find Russia, and then the Caucasus. 'Ukraine' comes from a Slavonic word 'krai' meaning a 'border' or 'borderland'. Its treeless steppes – there are two kinds of steppe, treeless and treed apparently – has been the traditional route for invaders from Central Asia down the ages. The population is nearly 53 million in an area of 233,090 square miles, making it larger than France, and giving Ukraine almost the same population as the UK.

History

All European countries have had this mixture of invasions and independence (in varying proportions) and express their own different versions of their national identity as well. Here, there is one national idea which is also Russian – harking back to the common ethnic and linguistic roots of these countries – and another which is more Ukrainian in character.

In Ukrainian, or Ruthenian, or Russian history, we should not forget the Vikings, who came here in the ninth and tenth centuries, another wave of settlement from the north. The first Russian prince, Vladimir (or Volodymyr) was one of these invading Vikings, who was invited in and settled down. He is claimed also by Ukrainians and Belarusians as their forerunner and first Christian monarch, the founder of these three countries which speak Russian or a related language.

Then there were the Tatar invasions of the thirteenth century. The Tatars attacked Kiev (or Kyiv) as well as Moscow, and conquered an area as large as the old Soviet Union. But the key to the Ukrainian identity and 'great soul' is not to be found in these often disputed ethnic origins (going back to the Armenians, or the Scythians, or beyond) but in a history in which nationalism has always been seen to lead to oppression and suffering.

There is a near consensus today that Ukraine should be an independent country, but a wariness of the consequences – after its recent tragic history – if these claims ever became too strident. There is also a corresponding more free-spirited version of the Ukrainian identity which stresses independence and a more modern outlook which is also in the ascendant, and a tension between these Ukrainian and Russian strands of history which became intertwined in the old Soviet Union, and which is simply a part of Ukrainian life.

Their still existing traditions of folklore and music may be little known outside the country, but for Ukrainians are very important. Also, independence has brought many problems, in the economy but also in other areas of life. Today it is most often in the news because of the Chernobyl nuclear reactor, which the government has unwisely made a bargaining chip in its negotions for US and international aid. It lacks sufficient alternative sources of energy, and the money to import fuel. Other social problems are poverty and organised crime. Some other tensions are expressed more obliquely, going back to the famine and in effect the genocide of Ukrainians during the twenties and thirties, the murky period of Ukrainian nationalism during the Second World War, and the great social disruption experienced by many Ukrainians throughout this century.

Residence and Entry

Getting There

Travelling in Ukraine is not a good idea for first-time visitors to the former Soviet Union – at least without making your arrangements in advance – or residence there for those without experience of travel in the region. It may not be a place to post your staff to for the first time, but other more adventurous souls may survive and prosper there. Good preparation will be important – with perhaps some advice from others who have already lived in the region. This will be the best way for you to get your bearings. For more about doing business and the working environment, see *Working in Ukraine* below. Also see the *Business* chapter in the following *Russia* chapters.

For advice about residence and entry you are recommended to contact 'Britain's largest and most experienced travel specialist to Ukraine': *Bob Sopel Ukrainian Travel*, 27 Henshaw Street, Oldham, nr. Manchester OL1 1NH; tel 0161-652 5050; fax 0161-633 0825. They can arrange flights, accommodation and visas, and also offer useful and up-to-date advice on visa and residence requirements. So can the *Ukrainian Embassy* – see their address below. *Ukraine International Airlines* (UIA) is an Irish (and Swiss and Austrian) joint venture and has a travel bureau which can also arrange accommodation for business people. There are connections to 12 European cities and a western style and standard of service making it the best carrier to the country (*UIA* – 14 Prospekt Peremogy, 252135 Kyiv-135; tel 44-221-8380 or 224-4528 or 216-6730; fax 44-216-8225 or 216-7994 or 229-6404). Reservations in the UK are tel 01293-553767; and in the USA tel 1-800-876-0114.

Get the bus from Boryspil Airport during the day, or have a hire car waiting – contact the travel agencies below. Taxis can be unreliable – costing a few dollars within the city and $25 or more to or from the airport – but hailing private cars in much the same way as you hail a cab, and offering the driver a dollar or two to go out of his or her way, is a normal (and sometimes the only) way of getting around.

Travel Agencies

Arktur: 4 Esplanadnaya Str., Kyiv; tel 44-220-70-24; tel/fax 44-227-01-55.
  Flexible and comprehensive services providing complete support facilities for visiting business people and tourists – in groups or single – with the availability of tailor-made packages for all tastes and occasions. A 'business information service' is one of those offered.
Dialog-Kiev: 16-22 B. Khmelnytsky St., Stes. 407, 403-6, 420, Kiev 252030; tel 44-225-4384; tel/fax 44-224-7079; fax 44-224-0470. All services including individual and group tours, hotels, guiding etc.
Eugenia Travel: 24 Evrelskaya str., Odessa 270045; tel 482-21-85-83; tel/fax 482-22-05-54 or 12 Suvorov str., Odessa 270026; tel/fax 482-22-40-47; 415 S. Orange Ave., Brea, CA 92621, USA. A professional private travel company for individual or group tourists, business people or clients with special interests. It specialises in all shore services for foreign cruise lines at Odessa and is experienced in other programmes, including visa support, accommodation and other travel and tour services.
Private Company 'Mandry': 44/9 Rynok SZquare, 290000 Lviv; tel/fax 322-271-661. They operate a regular bus line Lviv-London-Rochdale. Incoming and outbound tourism, fairs and exhibitions, hotel, air, bus and train reservations etc.
Vinnitsatourist: Pushkin Street 4, Vinnitsa; tel 0432-32-59-59; fax 0432-52-03-27.
  The largest in the province, with a tourist hotel, restaurant, summer resorts and transport facilities. Hotel accommodation, railway tickets, a conference hall, telephone and fax facilities etc. are some of the services they offer foreign visitors and business people, in Vinnitsa and throughout Ukraine.

Hotels

Hotel Bratislava: 1 Andriya Malyshko Str., Kiev 252192; tel 44-559-6920 (24 hours) or 559-7570 (reservations); fax 44-559-7788. A metro ride from the centre, and suitable for those of more modest means. The large business hotel (with casino and shady-looking characters in suits) is called the *Dnipro*. The *Hotel Ukraina* is also central, and has its more comfortable refurbished rooms on the upper floors.

The Language

Ukrainian; but Russian is mainly spoken in the east and usually in Kyiv. A peculiarity of Ukrainian pronunciation (compared to Russian) is that /g/ is sometimes pronounced /h/; and names which are written with an 'i' when transliterated from Russian tend to have a 'y'. Hence perhaps Kyiv, which is what Ukrainians themselves call their capital city. The alphabet used is very much the same; and when we know L'vov nowadays is called L'viv, we have found most of the main changes in the names post-1991. No offence is taken almost everywhere if you do speak Russian – and English is increasingly spoken by young people, and in the worlds of tourism and business.

The Currency

The currency is the *hryvnia*, which has replaced the hyper-inflationary *karbovanets* or 'coupon', which replaced the old rouble. Dollars or deutschmarks are still the most useful foreign currencies – with pounds likely to excite only suspicion at your local exchange booth. You need to have some small denomination dollar notes (in good condition) with you as you go about your business in Ukraine. Here, as elsewhere where currencies are as yet non-convertible, the hryvnia may not be imported or exported.

Customs

You need to fill in the currency declaration forms for foreign currency entering or leaving the country. There are no restrictions on items for personal use, and visitors should also declare all these, and keep the slips for their departure.

Education

This is quite a bright picture for expatriate families, with a local education system which is under pressure but still with usually high standards. There is also the *Kyiv International School* (vul. Nekrasovskaya 4; tel/fax 44-216-4313), as well as a new *British International School* (vul. Marshala Timoshenko 18; tel 44-412-9831/227-1551/244-7207).

International Removals and Freight

Inter-Logistic Worldwide Courier: Unit 7, Craufurd Business Park, Silverdale Road, Hayes, Middlesex; tel 0181-569-0616; fax 0181-569 0616; e-mail XK241@DIAL.PIPEX.COM.

Kaiser: ('your CIS partner') 102 Wien, Gesellschaft 15; tel 7820-6055/0; fax 720-6057. Truck and air freight service, charter flights, customs service, warehouse storage etc.

Cultural Background

Religion: The Ukrainian Orthodox Church is divided into 'Russian' and 'Ukrainian' factions. There are other Christian and Muslim minorities as well; and in western Ukraine a Uniate church owes its allegiance to Rome. The previous quite large Jewish community has been depleted recently by emigration.

Useful Publications:
East West Forum (EWF): Postfach 144, Klostergasse 9, A-1180 Wien; tel 47-03-850; fax 47-03-849. Eastern Europe business magazine.
Kiev Pocket Guide: *Air Ukraine* publication distributed by airlines; or call 44-223-6731; tel/fax 44-223-4844.
Panorama: Ukraine International Airlines magazine. UK advertising representative *Spafax Inflight Media*: tel 0171-706 4488; fax 0171-706-4812.
Welcome to Ukraine/International Tourism magazine: 5 A. Akhmatova St., Kyiv, 253068. Advertising dept: tel 44-228-0250; tel/fax 44-228-2557.

Useful Addresses

British Embassy: 9 Desyatynna Str., Kyiv 252025; tel 44-462-0011; fax 44-462-0013.
Ukrainian Embassy: 78 Kensington Park Road, London W11 2PL; tel 0171-727 6312; fax 0171-792 1708.
US Embassy: 10 Yuri Kotsyubinsky Str. 252053 Kyiv 53; tel 44-244-7349; fax 244-2400.
Ukrainian Embassy: 3350 M Street, NW, Washington, DC 20007; tel 202-333-0606; fax 202-333-0817.
Ministry of Foreign Affairs: vul. Mykhaylivska pl. 1, Kyiv; tel 44-212-833; fax 44-226-3169.
Chamber of Commerce and Industry: vul. Velyka Zhytomyrska 33, 254655 Kyiv; tel 44-212-2911/3290/2840; fax 44-212-3353.

National Holidays

New Year (January 1), Christmas (January 7), Easter, International Women's Day (March 8), Labour Day (May 1), Victory in WWII Day (May 9), Kiev Days (last weekend of May), Holy Trinity Day (June 2), Constitution Day (June 28), Independence Day (August 21), October Revolution Day (November 7,8).

Working in Ukraine

Business and Industry Report

Ukraine's economy spiralled into chaos following the collapse of the Soviet Union. Inflation reached 10,000% in 1993 before being brought down to more manageable levels today by the technocrats who are running the *Ministry of the Economy*, who are often assisted by outside experts.

Up until now, with its relative paucity of natural or primary resources, the Ukrainian economy has not taken off like that of Russia. The Ukrainians always remained – and still remain – the poor relations of the Russians. In part, this was because of this too-sudden transition to private enterprise, but more practically because there was simply not enough of a boom. Only an inflow of foreign investment or the release of funds which were previously 'hidden' could have overcome this inertia, and this unfortunately did not happen to quite the same extent.

Perhaps foreign investment is going to bring the Ukrainian economy into a more dynamic phase. But progress has been slow. The government is engaged in a delicate balancing act, trying to change the economic fundamentals, to bring in aid from outside, and in the meantime making sure there is enough money to pay for essential public services. The emphasis is on privatisation, and for investors willing to take a risk there will be a correspondingly high return. This is a country of 53 million people, one of the largest in Europe, where the potential for manufacturing and commerce is great. In Ukraine, the future at least promises to be brighter.

Central and Eastern Europe

Czech Republic
Slovakia
Hungary
Poland
Albania
Bosnia-Herzegovina
Bulgaria
Croatia
FYR Macedonia
Moldova
Romania
Slovenia
Yugoslavia
(Serbia, Montenegro)

Central and Eastern Europe

Central Europe

Introduction

The main Central European countries covered in this book are the Czech Republic, Slovakia, Hungary and Poland. Of these, only Slovakia is not preparing for the transitional period of EU entry which will make these others the first to join the EU, and in addition Estonia and Slovenia have been accepted for membership.

This is one way to see them all, in fact, as future members of the European Union. In the past, it was the Austro-Hungarian Empire – along with Germany and 'Middle Europe' – which defined this part of the world. The Alps were considered to be in Central Europe – in the south of the region – along with Austria and Switzerland. So was Berlin, before Germany was divided into East and West; and it is once again the capital of a united country, as it was long before, of Prussia.

Today Austria and Germany consider themselves to be gateways into this larger Central and Eastern European region, and have the strongest cultural links with their eastern neighbours. *Austrian Airlines* and *Lufthansa* both have important Central and Eastern European networks as well, which means that many expatriates and travellers will arrive in the region via Frankfurt, or Vienna.

Some other CEE countries, like Estonia, Poland and the Czech Republic, also see themselves like this, as a kind of bridge between East and West. This is one of the ways that the region is defined today, in the aftermath of communism and the Warsaw Pact, as a kind of borderland between Eastern and Western Europe. Today, this is in the positive and cosmopolitan sense of a meeting of cultures and international trade, but in the past these countries all had much more to do with invasions and conflict, another Central and Eastern European tradition.

Czech Republic

Introduction

The Republic of Czechoslovakia was created in October 1918 out of the former Austro-Hungarian possessions of Bohemia, Moravia and Slovakia. In 1938, the country was taken over by Nazi Germany following the Munich Agreement – without provoking the British and French to war. After World War II, the communists seized power, supported by the Russians; and remained in charge until the bloodless 'Velvet Revolution' of November 1989. In 1992, it was decided after a referendum that the Czechs and Slovaks should go their separate ways; and the country split into independent Czech and Slovak Republics on 1 January 1993 (see the *Slovakia* chapter which follows).

The history is much the same as that of the rest of Central Europe: traditions of independence which grew in the nineteenth century; a 'bourgeois' revolution in 1848 followed by a clampdown by the occupying power. Independence in the 1920s and 30s – after the First World War – was followed – after the Second World War – by domination by the Soviet Union. There were the democratic reforms beginning in 1989, and the Soviet troops departed – leaving an independent country confirmed in its 'Central' European identity and looking with some confidence to the future. Like all these others, the Czech Lands are keen to enjoy the economic and poltical benefits of liberal democracy, if sometimes ambivalent in other ways about joining the West.

This is the Czech Republic today. Membership of the various European and international institutions is important to all these Central European countries, especially the European Union (EU). The Czech Republic has been accepted as one of the first wave of these CEE entrants into the former EEC, along with the other countries in the pages which follow – minus Slovakia and plus Estonia and Slovenia. It has joined NATO, the OECD, and all the other international bodies – and forged many new cultural and economic contacts with its neighbours, especially with Germany.

The 'Prague Spring' of 1968 was obliquely the theme of a book, 'The Incredible Lightness of Being', by one of its best-known writers Milan Kundera. This was a brief taste of democracy but the West – in the Cold War conditions which then prevailed – could bring no support or military back-up. The Soviet crackdown which followed created the conditions for even more discontent in Central Europe, helping to inspire the Solidarity trade union movement in Poland, and the other dissident and democratic movements in the region during the 1980s. This is something about the Czech Republic which almost everyone knows, that in this indirect way it helped bring about the collapse of the Soviet Union.

Another writer and playwright is now much better-known as the President of the Czech Republic, Vaclav Havel.

Living in the Czech Republic

People

A correspondent to *Live and Work in Russia and Eastern Europe* suggests that 'behind our official masks, we are a warm, hospitable and very generous people.' Some support capitalism and 'getting rich quick'. Others decry it, and worry about the future. Perhaps the Czechs are a people who do not know who they are – or where they are going – with a tradition of scepticism and introspection like this which can be traced back to the time of the Reformation and beyond. 'We are not passionate or religious like the Hungarians and the Poles, we are phlegmatic and funny,' our correspondent also writes. We may remember that the greatest Czech writer of them all – the German-speaking and Jewish Franz Kafka – was also phlegmatic, and funny, and tragic as well.

Geographical Information

The Czech Republic covers 31,000 square miles; the population is 10,300,000; and there are German, Slovak, Hungarian, Ukrainian and Polish minorities. Bohemia in the west is mountainous and there are hills and a rich agricultural plain in Moravia in the east. One third of its territory is covered with forests, which are popular places for hiking or climbing. South Bohemia is picturesque, with castles and palaces, and medieval towns. The climate is colder in winter and warmer in summer than Britain, but not unlike the north-west coast of the United States, the average in January being 0°C and in July 20°C. Prague, the capital, is an historic city on the banks of the River Vltava. Other major towns are Brno, Ostrava, and Plzen. The official language is Czech; but German and English are also spoken.

Cities and Regions

PRAGUE

The citizens of Prague have suffered more than most over the last four centuries. Controlled by the Austrian Hapsburgs, occupied by Hitler's Nazis in 1939, and repossessed by the Russians in 1948, it has somehow managed to retain its air of independence. In the last ten years, the greyness, as well as some of the pollution, has begun to lift, revealing a city which managed to stay intact throughout the Second World War and its aftermath. You can see the *Hradcany* (castle district) with its cathedral, castle, monastery, and thousands of red roofs below. There are modern shops, and ranks of apartment blocks stretching to the dusty hills in the distance. Unlike Vienna or Budapest, Prague has also retained many of its Gothic buildings (built by Charles IV) which give the city much of its distinctive character.

Music is a strength; and it has three opera houses, the smallest and most attractive being the *Estates*, where Mozart premiered 'Don Giovanni'. The *National* is on the banks of the *River Vltava*; the *State Opera House* used to be just for German speakers before the war. Jazz clubs have always been here; and the terraced restaurants and cafés combine to create an atmosphere like many other Central European cities, and yet not quite the same. Its proximity to Vienna and Budapest make it part of most Central European tourist itineraries, and it is firmly on the Central European city-break map with major UK tour operators like *Cresta Holidays* now offering holidays there.

BRNO

This is the Czech Republic's second city, with 400,000 inhabitants. It is in South Moravia, which has 2.5 million people, and its own long history, sometimes linked with Silesia to the north. Textiles became important in the eighteenth century. With castles, churches, and an old and new town, it would be an attractive place to live and work, with several language schools for example, for those considering a working destination away from Prague.

For detailed information about Brno and trade fairs, travel agencies, investment and business etc. contact the *City of Brno Economic Development Department* (Zelny trh 13, 601 67 Brno) or *Brno Trade Fairs and Exhibition Co. Ltd.* (Vystaviste 1, CZ-674-00 Brno; tel 5-41152970; fax 5-41153062) which may also forward your enquiry on to the city administration. The *Economic Development Department* produces some useful maps and guides like *Brno, Welcome... Bienvenue...* with all the up-to-date information and contacts you need. These may also be available from Czech tourist offices.

Getting There

Charters and Coaches:
Auto Plan Holidays Ltd. (Stowe Court, Stowe Street, Lichfield WS13 6AQ; tel 01543-257777; fax 01543-419217) advises that 'purchasing flights and accommodation separately is the least expensive way of organising a city break, the reason being that tour operators have to build in fat commission levels to travel agents.' So they are happy to book just accommodation, or flights (with *CSA*) or a combination of the two (also to Budapest and Krakow in this Central Europe region). Contact them for their useful brochure on any of these destinations, either to make a preparatory visit, or for your more long-term flight and accommodation arrangements. 'Prague by Rail' is another option which they organise (by Eurostar, via Cologne, which is another good route into the country). At the time of writing, few charters are available; but Prague is getting less expensive to get to by air. City breaks and cultural and general interest holidays are available through many travel agents, one of which is *Fregata Travel*, which has a *City Breaks and Holidays* brochure for Krakow, Warsaw, Prague, Budapest, Moscow, St. Petersburg, Sofia, Zagreb, Dubrovnik, Riga and Tallinn (13 Regent Street, London SW1Y 4LR; fax 0171-451 7017; or 117A Withington Road, Manchester M16 8EE; tel 0161-226 7227; fax 0161-226 0700). It offers Czech spas; brewery tours and opera visits there; and a wide variety of other Central European experiences.

Eurolines is part of the same group; and may be contacted direct in the UK on 0990-143219. It features coach destinations throughout CEE, in Austria (Vienna), Bosnia, Bulgaria, Croatia and Slovenia, Hungary, Poland, Romania, Russia, Serbia and the Slovak Republic, as well as many city destinations in the Czech Republic as well (it takes just over 24 hours to get to Prague by coach). An independent and now quite long-established coach operator to the Czech Republic from London is *KCE – Kingscourt Express* (15 Balham High Road, London SW12 9AJ; tel 0181-673 7500). There are stops at Plzen and Dover, and every three hours. You check in around 30 minutes beforehand for this kind of service.

Airlines include *Delta Airlines* from the United States (2-26-94-77; fax 2-26-71-41), *British Airways* (UK tel: 0345-222111), *Austrian Airlines* (UK tel: 0171-434 7350), *Lufthansa* (UK tel: 0345 737747), *KLM* (UK tel: 0990-750900), *British Midland*, and also the national airline *CSA* or *Czech Airlines*: tel 0171-255 1898 – two flights a day from London Stanstead. Many others also go to Prague and other Czech destinations. Also see the brochures of some of the major general tour operators for their latest packages, some of which will feature the Czech Republic. Or contact those offering cultural or 'special interest' tours for this kind of trip, like *Page & Moy* (136-140 London Road, Leicester LE2 1EN; 0116-250-7979). There may be cheaper charter flights here in future, especially to Prague.

Onward Connections:
Your onward travel, flight, hotel and other transfers, as well a guiding service (which some business visitors may require) can all be arranged by *Fregata Travel* – see above. *Thomas Cook* in Prague is on Václaské nám 47; tel 2-263106; fax 2-265695.

Hotels and Travel Agencies

For Prague the *Hotel Reservation Centre* has an 'accommodation line' which is 'ideal for the independent traveller' and a wide choice of smaller family-run and B&B-style accommodation as well as hotels. They offer 'clean, basic and centrally located' accommodation in these cities. *Accommodation Line Ltd*: 1st Floor, 46 Maddox Street, London W1R 9PB; tel 0171-409 1343; fax 0171-409 2606; http://www.accomm.demoin.co.uk.

Danube Travel has 'all-in-one' city breaks to Prague, Vienna, Warsaw, Krakow and Gdansk (6 Conduit Street, London W1R 9TG; tel 0171-493 0263; fax 0171-493 6963), *Intra Travel* (44 Maple Street, London W1P 5GD; tel 0171-323 3305; fax 0171-637 1425), *OdessAmerica* (170 Old Country Road, suite 608, Mineola, New York, 11501 USA; e-mail oac@odessamerica.com; website www.odessamerica.com – for river cruises in the CEE region), and the *Czech Tourist Centre* (178 Finchley Road, Hampstead, London NW3 6BP; tel 0171-794 3263; fax 0171-794 3265), are all travel agencies or tour operators specialising in the Czech Republic.

Travel agents, or the *International Rail Centre* in Victoria Station, can organise your rail ticket to the Czech Republic -- or Slovakia and beyond (tel 0990-848848; fax 0171-922 9874); and there are also monthly *Freedom, Inter-Rail* and *Rail Europ Senior Passes*. Czech Railways (*CD*) operates two classes; and the *Rychlik* or *Expresni* trains are fastest, stopping only at major towns. Also contact:

Fregata Travel: 13 Regent Street, London SW1Y 4LR; fax 0171-451 7017; or
  117A Withington Road, Manchester M16 8EE; tel 0161-226 7227; fax 0161-226 0700. See above.
Liberty International (UK) Ltd: 11 Grosvenor Street, Chester CH1 2DD; tel
  01244-361115; fax 01244-351116; e-mail liberyty@chester.itsnet.co.uk. For full destination management services, including conference and meeting organisation, hotel reservations, guide and tour services, study tours and special interest groups. Offices in Riga, Tallinn, Vilnius, St. Petersburg, Kaliningrad, Sofia, Bucharest, Budapest and Warsaw as well as Prague.

Residence and Entry Regulations

See under *Immigration* in *Working in the Czech Republic* below.

Embassies, Consulates and Tourist Offices

Embassy of the Czech Republic (Visa Section): 28 Kensington Palace Gardens, London W8 4QY; tel 0171-243 1115 (ring between 2pm and 4pm to make an

appointment). This is also the main Embassy number; or fax 0171-727 9654.
Embassy of the Czech Republic: 3900 Spring of Freedom St, NW, Washington DC 20008; tel 202-274-9100; fax 202-363-6308; e-mail 72360.544 @compuservce.com. http://www.czech.cz/washington.
British Embassy: Thunovská 14, 118 00 Prague 1; tel 2-2451-0439; fax 2-539-927.
US Embassy: Trziste 15, 118 01 Prague 1; tel 2-2451-0847; fax 2-2451-1001.
Czech Tourist Authority: 95 Great Portland Street, London W1N 5RA; tel 0171-291 9920; or tel 0171-794 3263.
Czech Centre/Tourist Authority: 1109-1111 Madison Avenue, New York, NY 100028; tel 212-5358814/5; fax 212-772-0586.

American Express: (Czech Republic), Vaclavske Namesti 56, 1100 Prague; tel 2421-9992.
British Council: (Prague), Národni 10, 125 01 Prague 1; tel 2491-2179 to 83; fax 2491-3839.
British Embassy Commercial Section: Jungmannova 30, 110 00 Prague 1; tel 2-2421-2876/2909 or 2423-0998; fax 2-2423-0997. Their library is open until 4.30pm.

Accommodation

All types of accommodation, from luxury hotels to private rooms and apartments, are available. Your best way to find this is through the local English-language press – see below. The *Aktuel Travel Agency* is involved with incoming services throughout the Czech Republic (Postbox 11, 128 00 Praha 28; tel 2-29-68-86/9000-8629; fax 2-29-88-02/72-72-89) including 2-5 star hotels in Prague, Bohemia and Moravia, and recommends the *Hotel Apollo* in Prague.

The Language

Czech is the official language, with German widely spoken, also some English and French.

Language Schools

Státni jazyková skola (State Language School) teaches many languages in Brno, including Czech and offers lessons to British residents. (*Státni jazyková skola*, Vranovská 65, 614 00 Brno; tel 5-45211236; fax 5-45211236. In Prague, tel 0327-3702 or 2491-2242.
Brno English Centre, VUT Kravi hora 13, 602 00 Brno; tel/fax 5-4121-2262; tel 5-4124-3982; e-mail www.brnoenglishcentre.cz – a langauge school and also a translation agency.

Media and Communications

Post: The post offices are easy to find. Airmail to the UK takes from three to five days. There is also a fast (and expensive) express service.
Telephones: These are generally reliable, but busy lines and broken phones are a problem. Cardphones are generally in good working order. From the UK, the code for Prague is is 00-42-2.

Public Holidays

January 1; Easter Monday; May Day (May 1); Liberation Day (May 8); Day of the Apostles St. Cyril and St. Methodius (in July); Anniversary of the Martyrdom of Jan Hus (July 6); Independence Day (October 28); Christmas Eve; Christmas Day; and Boxing Day.

Working in the Czech Republic

Business and Employment

There has been a return to prosperity and stability in the new Czech Rupublic, which is less hampered by a dependence on heavy engineering than its Slovak neighbour. Unemployment is very low by international standards, around 3% at the time of writing. Germany is now its main trading partner.

For those who wish to look for work there, there are now opportunities in English-teaching and voluntary work. Workers who are posted there from abroad include lawyers, bankers, economists, diplomats and journalists; and there are many other areas from retailing to consultancy which are open to international workers in the Czech Republic today.

Czechs regard themselves as an entrepreneurial people; and they have had a softer landing than some others in Central and Eastern Europe when left to cope with the rigours of the free market. There is less good news from this emerging market today, though. As prosperity grows, it brings with it its own problems. Growth is now not so high; and the trade deficit is running at more than 8% of GDP in 1998, as their semi-fixed exchange rate is making exports expensive and imports cheap. This exchange rate is the economic indicator to watch as devaluation would provide a much-needed boost to the economy – before this becomes impossible in the run-up to 2002.

Immigration

British and US passport holders do not require a visa to enter the Czech Republic and may remain for up to 30 days before they need to apply for a residence permit. Work permits are arranged by the employer at local Employment Offices, and a photocopy of your passport and qualifications / diplomas are required. Long-term Czech residence applications must include this permit and should be made to the Czech Embassy abroad. Those working or looking for work in the Czech Republic must register within three local days at the local police station, where they may obtain an Identity Card for Foreigners. There are various rules and regulations for some different areas of employment, for example for English teachers, who should submit a completed application form with a letter or certificate issued by the school or university; oand there are regional Employment Offices (as stated above) where all employers must apply if they wish to employ a foreign national. Voluntary workers need a certificate from the relevant organisation, but do not have their visa stamped 'work permit'; these visas for voluntary workers are issued free of charge. Enquiries about work and residence permits should be made to a Czech Consulate or Embassy abroad; and you will receive a detailed factsheet or letter from the Embassies in both London and Washington.

Employment

Finding a job is as much about imagination and finding the right contacts, as following some imagined 'correct procedure', so use some of this as well as the many organisations and contacts listed here, and which can also be found in your own country – your own local Chamber of Commerce or business advice centre for example. The background to employment and business in the Czech Republic is its privatisation programme and economic recovery – see under *Business and Industry Report* below.

Specific Contacts

Opportunities are at almost every level of the jobs market; there are 'high risk' and more long-term opportunites, especially for those who can speak German or Czech. The Czech Republic is also now 'getting ready for Europe' and busy bringing its rules and regulations into line with the European Union, which means that there will be many opportunities here for UK and other EU workers in all areas over the next decade.

Teaching:
Enthusiasm for learning English – and interest in life in Britain and the United States – is great almost everywhere in the region. Salaries may sometimes be low; but the way of life in Prague or Budapest may compensate for the traditional privations endured by EFL teachers the world over.

For a list of *English Language Schools* in Prague and elsewhere, you may contact the *British Council* (address under *Useful Addresses* above) which will send you – probably – a photocopy of the local Yellow Pages. The *BC* library is also the traditional meeting point for EFL teachers looking for work, with a noticeboard advertising some current school, university and private teaching possibilities – and also see under 'Jazykové Skoly' in the Prague or Brno Yellow Pages if you can find a copy of these yourself.

There is also some demand for teachers in other subjects, from primary school level up to universities. Salaries here are usually only adequate to cover local living expenses, but it may be possible to teach private classes as well. They also may help with finding accommodation. The following organisations can be contacted for work:

The *Academic Information Agency (AIA)*, Dum zahranicnich styku, MSMT CR, Senovázné Námesti 26, 111 21 Prague 1, tel 2-24 22 96 98 – recruits qualified staff for primary and secondary schools. Applicants are sent a questionnaire which is then circulated among schools who contact teachers directly when they are needed. Qualifications are necessary. Contracts are usually for one year and usually include free accommodation.

Anglictina Expres, Vodickova 39, Pasaz Svetozor, (Galerie), Praha 1, 110 00, tel 2-26 15 26 – was the first private language school to be licensed, in 1990. Requires teachers for classes in Prague, Brno, Jabonlec, Liberec, Hradec, Kralove, Olomouc, Sokolov and Ostrava. Caters for all levels of students, in particular business English.

Bell Language Schools recruit British teachers with a degree, RSA/Cambridge Cert.TEFL or Dip.TEFL and several years' teaching experience. Contracts can range from a few weeks to several years depending on requirements. Enquiries can be made to the *Bell Educational Trust*, 1 Red Cross Lane, Cambridge CB2 2QX.

Brno English Centre, VUT Kravi hora 13, 602 00 Brno; tel/fax 5-4121-2262; tel 5-4124-3982; e-mail www.brnoenglishcentre.cz – is a language school and translation agency employing annually 'one or two' experienced and qualified teachers.

The *Central European University*, Civic Education Project, Taboritska 23, 130 87 Praha 5, Czech Republic, tel/fax 2-272-498, e-mail cepprg@ecn.gn.apc.erg – is based in Prague, and sends western-trained academics to the other CEE countries as well to assist in a a wide range of programmes in Albania, Bulgaria, Estonia, Hungary, Latvia, Lithuania, Poland, Romania, Russia, Slovakia and Ukraine.

English First (EF) is 'the world's largest group of private language schools' recruiting teachers for many countries. It is expanding its operations in Central and Eastern Europe. Contact *EF English First*: Kensington Cloisters, 5 Kensington Church Street, London W8 4LD; tel 0171-795 6645; fax 0171-795 6625.

International Placement Group: 72 New Bond Street, London W1Y 9DD; tel/fax 0171-739-2725; e-mail ipg.@praha.demon.co.uk – is a Czech-based teacher recruitment agency specialising in the countries of Central and Eastern Europe like Poland, the Czech Republic, Russia, Hungary and Slovakia, placing teachers in these countries and offering programmes in the UK as well.

Státni jazyková skola (State Language School) teaches many languages in Brno, including Czech and English; and also requires trained German teachers. 'We have a constant lack of speakers of British English,' they report, so they may be pleased to hear from these.

Státni jazyková skola (State Language School), Vranovská 65, 614 00 Brno; tel 5-45211236; fax 5-45211236.

Teaching in the Czech Republic: The *International Placement Group* also has its main office in Prague ('most of our operations are from here'): *IPG*, 9 Jezkova, 130 00 Praha 3; tel 2-279-568; fax 2-748-067. It recruits EFL teachers for CEE and sends CEE students abroad to study English; as well as summer recruitment drives in the USA. Director Roman Kacin offers the following advice:

'Check out your local library or bookstore for background information and books about these countries; the typical academic year begins in the fall – although many schools also recruit for early January and for summer sessions beginning in June or July; and the hiring process begins up to six months ahead of time, so if you wish to begin teaching in September send us your application as soon as possible the previous spring.'

You can get teaching jobs from Britain or the USA, but it may be far easier to do this when you are physically present, and able to start immediately. The standard contract will be for about twenty 45-minute sessions each week; class sizes can range from one-to-one lessons to quite large ones, 25 or more in some schools, more in universities. Some private schools (or other schools or universities) might help with housing but very few will add transport costs. Dressing appropriately and neatly and acting professionally – which first and foremost means being on time and having good communications with your employer and students – is very important in what is often a very stressful and demanding job – and only sometimes a rewarding one!

In this region, acting in a courteous, quiet and respectful manner will be an important asset as well. In some schools, making out your lesson plans might be the activity they seem most interested in; others – more practically – will be mainly asking about your availability; and you will probably have to fill out a timetable or schedule for this every week. In many CEE countries nowadays,

Britons and Americans don't need visas to get in, but you should look carefully into this in each case. It may take up to a month to complete all the paperwork – but most good employers can help with this. A copy of your birth certificate, CV or resumé, and your qualifications or diplomas, will also be very useful.

Salarywise, £200 to £300 is the maximum you can expect in all these Central and Eastern European countries (before deductions) each week. Remember that finding accommodation can be a 'nightmare' (according to Mr Kacin). Good public transport and a wide variety of historical and cultural attractions are pluses, which means there is at least plenty to do and see, and the means to get there – and also see the 'Personal Experiences' in the *Appendices* at the end of this book for some true-to-life accounts of teaching English in all these countries.

Bring your own least heavy and most useful teaching materials like books and cassettes – like 'Ship or Sheep' or some similar course for pronunciation – and 'Streamline Departures' – the teacher's book, with cassette – which can help anyone teach beginners. Take some sticky 'blu-tack' as well if you can (you won't find it there so easily, and for teachers this tends to be a very useful thing to have). Taking some English-language books you like is a good idea anyway, and these may be useful for teaching more advanced students too. One of the unwritten rules of EFL-teaching is also, never lend your books to students! The British Council library in many countries is often a good source of materials (but sometimes only open to local English language teachers, but you can ask about this).

English Contacts Abroad provides a research and direct contacts service for EFL teachers in all the CEE and CIS countries: PO Box 126, Oxford OX2 6UB, UK. Write in the first instance for a questionnaire – or with any tips or contacts of your own. There is an administration fee of £48.

Teacher Agents: This is a way for EFL teachers and others to bring their group (usually of secondary school or university-level students) to the UK to learn English; and to earn some commission or have their travel expenses paid. This is often for one, two, or three week-courses in the summer; but can be all the year round. One school offering courses like this in Oxford is *Speak English*: PO Box 126, Oxford OX2 6RU, UK. Write to the Director for details.

Voluntary Work:
There is a great demand for voluntary workers, particularly for environmental projects. Prospective volunteers should take note of the escalating cost of living when considering their allowance. Free accommodation is a minimal requirement. Below are some of the organisations who send volunteers to the Czech Republic:
Education for Democracy USA, PO Box 40514, Mobile, Alabama 36640-0514, and *Education for Democracy UK*, 3 Arnellan House, 144-146 Slough Lane, London NW9 8XJ – aim to provide primary and supplementary conversational English teaching. Volunteers are asked to supply their own instruction materials.
INEX, Senovázne námesti 24, 116 47 Prague, tel 2-24 10 23 90 – needs volunteers to take part in international workcamps contributing to the environment and historical conservation in July and August. Volunteers pay for their own travel and insurance.

For further information on workcamps and voluntary work in the Czech Republic, see *Summer Jobs Abroad* and *Work Your Way Around the World* (Vacation Work). There are some more voluntary and teaching contact organisations in Britain and the United States listed in the introductory section of this book.

Recruitment Agency:
Antal International Ltd: 2nd Floor, 90 Tottenham Court Road, London W1P 0AN; tel 0171-637 2001. Offices also in Russia, Poland, Czech Republic, Hungary, Ukraine, Romania, Kazakstan, France, Italy, Germany, the USA and Hong Kong.
Also see *The Directory of Jobs and Careers Abroad* (Vacation Work) for some general international and CEE recruiters, and publications like *Overseas Jobs Express* (mentioned in this book's *General Overview*). The Commercial Department of the British Embassy, Prague, can also supply list of *British Companies in the Czech Republic*.

Trade Fair:
For training, recruitment, human resources managers and others *Baker McKenzie* laywers (with an office in Prague) helped to organise the *Attracting and Retaining Key Staff in Central and Eastern Europe* conference in London (with international and Slovak participants as well) and will be able to provide much of the legal background to employment, living and working in the Czech Republic: tel 0171-839 8391; fax 0171-839 3777; e-mail postmaster@visibis1.demon.co.uk.

Business and Industry Report

Currency: 1 Koruna (Kc) = 100 hellers

The Czech Republic is one of the leaders in terms of commerce, privatisation and democratisation in this region, with unemployment much lower than British or US levels at present. Banking has been restructured, the retailers have come – like *Marks & Spencer* and *Tesco* – and great progress has been made in financial services, for individuals and on the stock market – as well as in distribution, marketing, communications, and the media. Consumers are busy buying all the items from cars to foreign holidays which they do in Britain or thre United States, and Czechs are manufacturing some of these things in the Czech Republic today. Its most famous product – along with the beer – is the *Skoda*, once very unreliable and with an image to match, but nowadays owned by Volkswagen, with some German technology on the inside. It was even redesigned recently by the fashion designer Paul Costelloe, and has won an award for popularity with British owners.

Registration rules for creating limited and joint stock companies are fairly straightforward in the Czech Republic. Investors can take a 100% equity share in companies, except those in some areas of heavy industry, defence, and so on. Foreign-owned companies are subject to the same taxation rules as local companies, though some exemptions are available in certain cases. Contact the *Commercial Counsellor* at the Czech Embassy for these and similar details.

SITPRO is the *Simpler Trade Procedures Board*, with an office in London and a *Trade Efficiency Helpdesk* giving information on procedures, payment and documentation for exporters: tel 0171-215 0800; fax 0171-215 0824. It produces many different factsheets to help UK exporters with their queries, from general export rules to country factsheets – including the Czech Republic. Contact: *SITPRO*, 151 Buckingham Palace Road, London SW1W 9SS; tel 0171-215 0825; fax 0171-215 0824; e-mail sitpro.org.uk.

Open for Business, Central Europe is the name of the *DTI* catalogue of events and publications which will be useful for all exporters and investors in the Czech

Republic, and the Central European region (also including Slovenia). This joint DTI/FCO export initiative can be contacted on tel: 0171-215 8661; fax 0171-215 4743; http://www.dti.gov.uk/ots/centeuro. It concentrates on five main sectors: agribusiness; automotive components; consumer and retailing; electronics/IT; and healthcare; and continues during 1998.

Embassies on the spot tend to participate in these various *DTI* trade initiatives. More, no doubt, will follow.

Other Contacts and Services:
The *British Embassy Commercial Section* provides general briefings for business travellers and a *Market Information Service* (MIES); it 'answers to specific questions' and gives commercial information relating to many sectors of the economy and has a list of 'British Companies in the Czech Republic, also a *Programme Arranging Service* if you need something like this – a 'programme of appointments, travel directions' and so on:

British Embassy Commercial Section: Jungmannova 30, 110 00 Prague 1; tel 2-2421-2876/2909 or 2423-0998; fax 2-2423-0997. Their library is open unti 4.30pm.

Slovakia

Introduction

The Republic of Slovakia covers 17,000 square miles. The population is 5,300,000 and the capital Bratislava has 440,000 inhabitants. The other major city is Kosice, with 240,000 inhabitants. The northern area is hilly, and southern and eastern parts of the country are low-lying and agricultural. The River Danube connects Hungary with Vienna to the west and the Black Sea to the east. There are cold winters and mild summers. There are some mineral and gas resources, and also a large chemical industry. Agriculture is particularly important for exports: two of these are beer and timber; and Slovakia is making efforts to develop its tourism, in particular winter sports which, like hiking and hunting, are also popular with the locals.

Its main international vocation since independence in 1993 is – like its Central European neighbours – the membership of organisations such as the EU and Nato, which can confirm its independent status and help with economic development. It is developing new trading links with EU countries, especially Germany; and these also continue with traditional trading partners like Poland, Ukraine, and Hungary. Privatisation is the watchword of the Slovakian economy too; and experts are needed in the financial services field. It is also aiming to develop its traditional craft-based industries and to be less dependent on heavy industry.

This has been its main handicap to date: too many old-fashioned and ailing heavy industries, much as in Britain before the nineteen-eighties; and a bureaucracy which resembles that of its neighbours to the east as much as the more dynamic economies of Central Europe. EU membership – and a more liberal and democratic outlook – will come later. In the meantime, there are still many opportunities in trade and development, tourism, and English-teaching and voluntary work, for many international workers and businesspeople who generally find Slovakia a congenial place to live and work.

Living in Slovakia

The State

Became officially independent following the 1992 referendum in 1993.

The Language

Is officially Slovak; but Hungarian is also widely spoken.

The Currency

Is the crown, or *Koruna* (Sk). One of these is currently worth 2p. Dollars are easier to exchange there than pounds. *Cirrus* and *Mastercard* are received in more places than *Visa* here.

Getting There

Only smaller airlines fly into Bratislava (although the number of international passengers is now growing). But more come via nearby Vienna, from where there is a bus/coach service to the nearby Slovak capital, taking about 90 minutes. Or you can come from Prague, or get to the Tatra (or Tatras) region on your skiing or touring holiday more cheaply and easily through Poland. See *General Information – What you do not know about Slovakia* published by the *Slovak Agency for Tourism* (cited below) for many facts about Slovakia including local airline offices, embassies, traffic rules and customs etc. Recently, *Swissair* has become the first international airline to fly into Slovakia; and there will no doubt be others. Other useful contacts are: *British Airways* (UK tel: 0345-222111), *Austrian Airlines* (UK tel: 0171-434 7350) and *Lufthansa* (UK tel: 0345 737747).

Travel Agencies:
SATUR is the successor to the state-owned *Cedok* travel agency: Mileticova 1, 824 72 Bratislava; tel 7-542-2828; fax 7-566-1426; e-mail: satur-acr@ba.sknet.sk.
S-Tours Ltd: (Destination Management Company) 814 99 Bratislava, Laurinská 2, P.O. BOX 172; tel 7-5331-802 or 5330-648; tel/fax 7-5332-534 or 5335-517. Offices in Nitra and Prague.

Coaches:
Eurolines (UK tel 0990-143219) features coach destinations throughout CEE, and the Slovak Republic as well. An independent and now quite long-established coach operator to the Czech Republic from London is *KCE – Kingscourt Express* (15 Balham High Road, London SW12 9AJ; tel 0181-673 7500). There are stops at Plzen and Dover, and every three hours. You should check in around 30 minutes beforehand.

Trains:
Travel agents, or the *International Rail Centre* in Victoria Station, can organise your rail ticket to Slovakia (tel 0990-848848; fax 0171-922 9874). Also see under *Transport* below.

Accommodation

Contact *S-Tours* (see above) which can arrange hotel accommodation as well as city and many other tours in Bratislava and throughout the region. They also organise transport and transfers, airline and railway tickets, meetings, guiding services, restaurants and nights out; and have this Confucian motto: 'If you enjoy your job, you will never work a day in your life!'

Residence and Entry Regulations

Contact the Slovak Embassy in the UK or USA. You will need your original passport, photos, and fee for a residence permit (or visa), which can take one or two months to come through. These are issued by the local police.

'The Embassy of the Slovak Republic is only sending all documents to the Slovak Republic and has no influence as to the length of the procedure,' is what you will find in the small print. You may also need the help of your prospective employer to make these arrangements as you need a letter from them shpowing you have a 'fixed income' or other proof of funds, as well as proof of accommodation. EU and North American passport holders do not require a visa to enter the Slovak Republic. But foreigners may work there only after they have been granted these residence and work permits.

Applications should be submitted to the Embassy in the country of origin; and accompanied by a provisional work permit from the local labour office in Slovakia; a letter from the employer; a doctor's certificate; the 'Crime and Criminal Proceedings Register from the Slovak Republic'; and five photographs. These documents must be in Slovak or with an authorised Slovak translation. The procedure takes up to 60 days, according to other literature. The fee at present in the UK is £1 (to have your Criminal Record submission processed), plus a £96 'submission fee', £5 for each page of which the translation needs to be verified, and £13 for the entry visa.

Utilities and Communications

Electricity is 220 volts AZ, 50Hz and a standard continental-style adaptor or plug can be used.

The country code from the UK is no longer 42 (as it was for Czechoslovakia) but is now 421, this additional '1' now representing the country's independence. For Bratislava the code is still 7 (from within the country this is 07). 158 is the police number; 120 (or 0120) for directory enquiries.

Letters to Western Europe can take a week or more; an express service is also available in post offices.

EuroTel Bratislava is the largest local cellular phone company; owned by *Slovak Telecommunications* – which runs the national phone system – and the American telecoms company *Atlantic West*. There is an ambitious modernisation programme in progress which will bring the whole of the telephone system up to international standards and many more public and private phones are being installed.

Television:
The New York-based heir to the *Estée Lauder* cosmetics company owns the only private television channel, *TV Marzika*; and wants to buy one of the two state-run *RRTV* channels, which is also currently being privatised. (For videos the local system is PAL).

Transport

The Czechs and Slovaks are collaborating on improving their road systems; with an agreement in 1996 between their respective (and formerly linked) firms *Metrostav* and *Doprastav* who are busy constructing roads, motorways and tunnels: 450km of motorway and 28 more tunnels should be in place in Slovakia by 2005 under an ambitious road construction plan; with one aim being to integrate the road and rail system more fully (which we know in Britain means that railway stations will close).

Slovak Railways (*ZSR* – 813 61 Bratislava, Klemensova 8; tel 7-548-7000; fax 7-548-7044) operates some scenic routes; with fast *rychlik* trains and slower stopping *osobni* and *vlak*. Beautiful for tourists, but sometimes frustrating for the locals who await faster connections with the Adriatic and Baltic, as well as Western Europe and the international railway system. This will come in a programme to be implemented over the next decade. A metro is also planned for Bratislava.

A national airline – *Slovenske Aerolinie* (also to be known as *Slovak Airlines*) is only now at the time of writing being established. The major private operator is *Tatra Air* – linking Slovakia and Zurich along with its partner *Swissair*.

Driving:
Speed limits are low and the alcohol limit is zero so do not drink and drive. Certainly do not drink, drive, and speed – or you will be liable not only to an on-the-spot fine but also perhaps a prison sentence if you meet an unsympathetic traffic policeman.

Health Service and Hospitals

The health service (like others in Central Europe) provides a free service for all citizens in theory; but in practice is under strain. See the *General Overview* to this book under *Health and Hospitals* for the treatment you may receive free in Slovakia – and what you have to pay for. In practise, a sympathetic doctor is likely to treat a friendly foreign visitor for free for a variety of ailments in all these Central European countries. There are reciprocal health care agreements with Britain. Take some standard medicines with you as well, not because theese are not available but because it will be more convenient; and get Europe-wide or local health insurance (also see the *General Overview*). There are presently no international hospitals here.

Banks

Vseobecná uverová banka, a.s: Námestie SNP 19, 818 56 Bratislava; tel 515-8184; fax 531-7036/7250. With 210 branches throughout the country; and representative offices in Moscow, Prague and London.
Tatra Banka, a.s: Vajanského nábr. 5, 810 06 Bratislava.

Useful Addresses

Slovak Embassy: 25 Kensington Palace Gardens, London W8 4QY; tel 0171-243 0803. There is an 0891 number dealing with general visa information – 0891-600 360 – or cheaper will be to write to the Visa Department for a transcript!
Slovak Embassy: Suite 250, 2201 Wisconsin Avenue, NW, Washington DC 20007; tel 202-965-5160-1.
British Embassy: Grösslingova 35, 811 09 Bratislava; tel 7-364-420.
US Embassy: Hviezdoslavovo námestie 4, 811 02 Bratislava; tel 7-5330-861; fax 7-5330-098.
British Council: Panská 17; Bratislava; tel 7-5331-793.
Society of Friendship with the American People: Grosslingova 6; Bratislava; tel 7-323-956.
Slovakia Travel Service: Suite 3601, 10 East 40th Street, New York, NY 10016; tel 212-213-3865 or 212-213-3862.
Slovak Agency for Tourism: P.O Box 76, Kutlikova 17, 850 05 Bratislava; tel 7-832150/4846; fax 7-834846 / P.O.Box 497, 974 01 Banská Bystrica; tel/fax 88-746626. They can supply brochures like *Panorama of Slovakia, Slovensko in the Summer, Slovensko in Winter*, and *General Information – What you do not know about Slovakia*.
American Express Office: Tatratour, Frantiskanske Nam 3, 81101 Bratislava; tel 42-7-5211219/5335852. There are five offices in Slovakia, and AmEx

recommends that clients call before travelling to verify services. 'Due to local regulations/business practises, not every office provides every service...'

National and Religious Holidays

January 1 also commemorates the establishment of the Slovak Republic; January 6 (Epiphany and/or Christmas); Good Friday; Easter Monday; May 1 – Labour Day; on July 5 there is St. Cyril and Methodis Day; August 29 – Slovak National Uprising; September 1 – Slovak Constitution Day; September 15 – the 'Seven-Pain Virgin Mary's' Day; November 1 – All Saints Day; Christmas Eve; and then Christmas Day.

Working in Slovakia

Teaching Contacts

The *Slovak Academic Information Agency* recruits qualified staff for primary and secondary schools. Applicants are sent a questionnaire which is then circulated among schools who contact teachers directly when they are needed. The address for the Slovak Republic is: Na Vrsku 2, 81100 Bratislava; tel 7-533-5221.

Language schools which employ native English-language speakers include: *The English Club*, Pri Suchom mlyne 36, 81104 Bratislava, tel 7-372-411 (they will send you useful infoirmation about working for them); *Eurolingua*, Drienoná 16, 82101 Bratislava, tel 7-233-137; *ILC*, Sokolská 1, Brno, tel 5-412-40-493; and *Aspekt*, Piaristická 8, 94901 Nitra, tel 87-32-218.

The *Central European University* (Civic Education Project, Taboritska 23, 130 87 Praha 5, Czech Republic; tel/fax +42-2-272-498; e-mail; cepprg@ecn.gn.apc.erg) sends western-trained academics to CEE countries including Albania, Bulgaria, Czech Republic, Estonia, Hungary, Latvia, Lithuania, Poland, Romania, Russia, Slovakia and Ukraine.

The *Albion Language School* (Skuteckého 32, 974 01 Banská Bystrica; tel/fax 88-743-434) occasionally employs qualified UK and US teachers; and provides language courses for adults and children as well as specialist course for companies. They also send people to the UK to learn English.

English Contacts Abroad provides a research and direct contacts service for EFL teachers in all CEE countries (PO Box 126, Oxford OX2 6UB, UK). Write in the first instance for a questionnaire – or with any tips or contacts of your own. There is an administration fee of £48.

Teacher Agents: A way for EFL teachers and others to bring their group (usually of secondary school or university-level students) to the UK to learn English; write in the first instance to *Speak English Schools*: PO Box 126, Oxford OX2 6RU, UK.

Tourism Contacts

Slovak Ministry of Economy Tourist Department: Mierová 19; 827 15 Bratislava; tel 7-574 2322; fax 7-574-3321.

Tatra Regional Tourist Board: Nám. sv. Egidia 94, P.O.BOX 36, 058 01 Poprad; tel/fax 92-721-186.

The *Slovak Tourist Board* is involved in market research and its evaluation, tourism product creation and promotion, co-ordinating tourism activities and trade fairs, and so on, in the context of 'the economic prosperity of Slovakia and the need to protect the environment and the standard of living of the population,' and should be contacted by tour operators and travel agencies interested in Slovakia.

The country has suffered from the loss of some of its previous markets though – like many neighbouring countries which formerly relied on Russian and other CEE visitors – but is now rediscovering its appeal to international visitors. Three of UNESCO's world heritage sites are in Slovakia: the *Spis Castle* (the largest medieval castle in Europe), *Banská Stiavnica* (from the 13th to 18th century the most important mining centre for precious metals in the Austrian Empire) and *Vlkolinec* (historic settlements in Central Slovakia).

The *Tatra Mountains* are still – on this side of the border with Poland – relatively 'undiscovered', with a similar potential for tourism to that of the better-known Zakopane across the border. In Slovakia, there are the usual facilities for tourism and recreation, from spas to eco-tourism to winter sports like skiing. This is a Central European country to discover, where the way of life is still in many ways different from our own.

For the *Slovak Agency for Tourism* address, see under *Useful Addresses* above.

Business and Industry Report

Currency: 1 Koruna (Sk) = 100 hellers

EU membership is still the target, despite the relegation of Slovakia to the second wave of EU entrants, and an entry date that has yet to be determined. The Slovak government officially 'regretted' this decision of the EU; but declared its determination 'to do its utmost in the time available to meet the conditions for European membership.'

Among the larger investments have been some by *Volkswagen* (making cars in Bratislava), Norway's *Slovalco* aluminium company, and Britain's own *Tesco Stores*. Its traditional steelmakers and chemical companies are now also investing in joint ventures in automobile manufacture and looking to diversify into other manufacturing and service sectors. Other heavy industries are oil and gas refining, and nuclear power production (which is being expanded). There is controversy over a huge hydroelectric scheme east of Bratislava on the Danube, just before it enters Hungary. The Slovaks have told the Hungarians this will help to protect them against floods – but the Hungarians have yet to be convinced.

Sources of Information:

The *DTI* has a desk for Slovakia and the Czech Republic (tel 0171-215 8194; or 215-5000 for the switchboard) and also some general publications for exporters; and maintains a database of UK companies with interests and operations there. Also see *Sources of Information – Finance and Advice for Trade and Investment in Central and Eastern Europe and the Former Soviet Union* (DTI Export Publications: tel 0171-510 0171; fax 0171-510 0197). Or contact the DTI's resource and information centre (Kingsgate House, 66-74 Victoria Street, London SW1E 6SW, open from 9am to 8pm weekdays and until 5.30pm on Saturdays; tel 0171-215 5444/5445; fax 0171-215 4231; http://www.dti.gov.uk/ots/emic; e-mail EMIC@ash001.ots.dti.gov.uk). They will tell you what kind of information about Slovakia they have.

Another contact is the *Slovak National Agency for Foreign Investment and Development* (otherwise known as *Snazir* – Sládkovicova 175, 811 06 Bratislava; tel 7-533-5175; fax 7-533-5022).

Hungary

Introduction

Hungary's recent history is not dissimilar to that of the rest of the region: domination by the Soviet Union followed by democratic reforms beginning in 1989. The last Soviet troops left Hungary in June 1991. A particular feature of the Hungarian economy apparently was the early adoption – in the nineteen-sixties – of some free market reforms. The Hungarian uprising of 1956 against the Russians was also one early sign of dissent in these occupied countries. Today, negotiations with the EU have progressed well, and entry into the European Union is expected some time in 2002. This date will depend on factors like the success or otherwise of the euro, and the completion of these negotiations.

Already, integration with the world economy has gone much further than in some of its neighbours. Foreign investment is high, especially from Germany. Hungary is already a member of the Organisation for Economic Cooperation and Development (OECD) and is adopting many EU regulations which will benefit jobseekers and businesspeople from there in future (and be correspondingly disadvantageous to some Americans and others from outside Europe).

This cosmopolitanism is not welcomed by all Hungarians, though, and there is opposition to American troops and bases in some sections of society, much as there was to the Russians before.

Living in Hungary

Political and Economic Structure

Agriculture is still a major activity, accounting for 6% of Gross Domestic Product (GDP). Food products are currently 20% of exports. Industrial production started to grow again in 1992, following a severe contraction in 1989-1991. Inflation has been brought under control; and Hungary is also part of the Deutschmark (soon to be the Euro) zone, so prices are often expressed in that currency. Opportunities here are in English teaching, and in construction and investment projects (see *Working in Hungary* below), as well as for experts in industrial restructuring and finance, and also for some farmers from the IUK who have taken advantage of the cheaper land prices there. Pharmaceuticals, computers, telecommunications and mining are also important industries.

Government

It became, after 1848, a 'limited constitutional monarchy'; and pluralism was restored in 1989-90, with the amendment of the constitution taking place on October 23, the anniversary of the 1956 revolution. This involves a tripartite structure of head of state, parliament and government. The National Assemby is elected every four years.

Politics

The Hungarian Socialist Party (*MSZP*) was established in 1989 out of the former state communist party, the *MSZMP*. The Alliance of Free Democrats (*SZDSZ*) came out of the democratic opposition, in existence since the early 1980s. So did the Hungarian Democratic Forum (*MDF*). The Independent Smallholders Party (*FKGP*) was established in 1930 to represent the interests of the Hunagrian peasantry. The Christian Democrats (*KDNP*) were dissolved in 1949 and relaunched in 1989. There is also *FIDESZ* (the Federation of Young Democrats) formed originally as a kind of democratic alternative to the Young Comminists; and there are some other fringe parties.

History

The first Christian monarch was King Stephen, or István, who reigned from 1000-1038. He was an enlightened king who believed, unsually for his time, in pluralism as well as a central monarchy and state. His concept was of a 'nation', not a 'people'; and he wrote in the 'Instructions' which he thoughtfully handed on to his successor that guests and newcomers in Hungary 'should gain as much esteem as they can worthily take the place (at table) reserved for royal dignitaries ... and just as guests come from different regions and provinces, so they bring with them different languages and habits, different examples and weapons; and these adorn the country, and the lustre of the court, scaring foreigners away from superciliousness.'

So King Stephen was in favour of immigration, at least as far as the defence of his own court was concerned. And he wrote that 'a unilingual country with just one custom is a feeble and fallible one.' His successors in Central Europe have not always followed these wise precepts, but Hungarians even today are very welcoming in their attitudes to strangers, if at times a little phlegmatic compared to Britons or Americans. Some may find them a little downbeat. There is of course a Great Hungarian Soul, forged in the thousand years of tribulations that separate King Stephen's time from our own. This one, allegedly, is a little different from those of its Slavic neighbours: it is, we are are told, 'laughing and crying at the same time.'

Hungary's history has also been like this, with success and failure, victory and defeat following each other in swift succession. Stephen created a centralised state and court, and united the various clans who had arrived in the region at about the same time as the Viking invasions of Britain (898 AD). Like many of those wishing to legitimise their authority at this time – when the 'international community' meant one of the international religious denominations, based in Rome, or Constantinople, or Mecca – he had to get his seal of international approval from somewhere; and he chose the Pope, and the 'western' or Catholic sphere of influence.

Geographical Information

It occupies an area of 36,000 square miles. The population of 10,245,000 is largely made up of Hungarian-speaking Magyars (92%) with small German and Gypsy minorities. The language belongs, like Finnish, to the Finno-Ugric family. German is also widely spoken. Most of the country is flat; there are several ranges of hills, chiefly in the north and west; and the country forms part of the catchment area of the River Danube on whose banks the capital Budapest has grown up. There are thousands of lakes, of which the largest and best-known is Lake

Balaton, which is almost an inland sea and is a traditional centre for tourism mainly from Germany and Russia.

Budapest (the most popular destination for British visitors) has 1,930,000 inhabitants. Other cities are Gyor, Pécs, Szeged, Debrecen and Miskolc. Summers can be very hot, with the temperature frequently reaching 30°C, while during winter the average is around 0°C. Springtime, also, can be cold.

Cities and Regions

Six major topographical regions are to be found. The *Alföld* (Hungarian Great Plain) is situated in the central and eastern parts of the country. To the west there is the *Kisalföld* (Western Lowlands), another plain made up of alluvial deposits from the meandering Danube. More ancient are the Transdanubian Hills, the Central Mountain range of Transdanubia, the Sub-Alps and the Northern Hills.

Budapest is a lively and cosmopolitan city which is divided into two halves by the River Danube. Buda and Pest were unified in 1873 and today are linked by nine bridges, the most famous of which is the *Elizabeth Bridge*, which was the only one which was not bombed during the Second World War. The Buda side extends up into the hills, and Pest is flatter (and presumably more alluvial).

Budapest is the centre of road and rail communications and – as befits the capital – of the cultural life of the country which is rich and varied. The *Royal Castle* and Castle District are picturesque when viewed from the riverside. *Margaret Park* is on an island in the river near the Gothic parliament building; and is dotted with parks, sports grounds, swimming pools and a spa hotel. There are many other spas and Turkish baths going back to Ottoman and even Roman times. These are not just a tourist attraction but part of the social and cultural life of the city, a popular place for the locals to relax and unwind.

Getting There

Travel agencies specialising in Hungary include: *Budapest Breaks (Project 67 Ltd.)*, 10 Hatton Garden, London EC1N 8AH; tel 0171-831 7626; fax 0171-404 5588; e-mail BPBREAKS@AOL.COM); *Danube Travel*, (with city breaks also to Prague, Vienna, Warsaw, Krakow and Gdansk), 6 Conduit Street, London W1R 9TG; tel 0171-493 0263; fax 0171-493 6963; *Intra Travel*, 44 Maple Street, London W1P 5GD; tel 0171-323 3305; fax 0171-637 1425; *Hunguest Hotels*: 1126 Budapest, Orbánhegyi ut 49 (head office) and *Hunguest Travel Ltd.* 1074 Budapest, Dohány u. 27 (incoming section); tel 1-322-5845/1637; fax 1-322-5846; *OdessAmerica*, 170 Old Countrey Road, suite 608, Mineola, New York, 11501 USA; e-mail oac@odessamerica.com; website www.odessamerica.com – for cruises down the Danube. In Hungary, contact *Skyline Ticket Kft* (tel 1-112-4001) for cheap air tickets; or *Vista Air Travel Agency*, Károly krt. 21; tel 1-267-8754/269-6032/3.

Budapest Tourist: 1051 Budapest, Roosevelt tér 5; tel 118-15-10; fax 118-16-58. They welcome 'groups from all over the world' and individual travellers, offering tours, guides, interpreters, accommodation, folklore dinners, tickets for cultural events, transfers, and for firms organise meetings, conferences, programmes and excursions.

Attila Travel: Suite 311, 36A Kilburn High Road, London NW6 5UA; tel 0171-372 0470. Contact them for information about their regular coach service to Budapest, also providing accommodation and outbound services for education etc. Bp fax: 1209-0923.

Danubius Travels: 1052 Budapest, Szervita tér 8, Hungary; tel 1-266-6859 or 1-117-3115; fax 1-117-0210; e-mail danubtra@hungary.net. Services include hotel reservation, package tours, spa tourism, business travel, convention tourism, outgoing tourism, outbound tour operator and travel agent activities and cruising.

Hungarian Hotels Sales Office Inc: 6033 West Century Blvd., Suite 670, Los Angeles, LA 90045; tel 800-448-4321 or 310-649-5960; telex 510-600-4622; fax 310-649-5852.

Residence and Entry Regulations

British and EU citizens do not require a visa to enter Hungary; and may remain generally for 90 days (for UK citizens this is 6 months). Work and residence permits should be arranged in advance by the Hungarian employer with the local authorities in Hungary. Foreigners wishing to stay for more than a year must obtain a residence permit from the police force in the town of residence within six months. In the case of Budapest this is BRFK Igazgatásrendészeti Fooszály Külföldieket Ellenorzo Osztály, 6th District Varosligeti fasor. Addresses must be registered within 30 days of arrival. The form requesting a residence permit, two passport photos, a letter from the employer (in Hungarian) and medical certificate will be required. Another form needs to be completed in duplicate to register your address, including the signature of the landlord/landlady, a copy of the contract and details of rent paid. Certain high-level teachers and researchers, as well as executives and technical consultants sent to perform essential work for foreign companies with subsidiaries in Hungary, are exempted from work permit requirements. If you haven't obtained your work permit in advance, you may be expected to take some medical tests.

Embassies, Consulates and Tourist Offices

Hungarian Embassy (Consular Section): 35 Eaton Place, London SW1X 8BY; tel 0171-235 4048.
Hungarian Embassy: 3910 Shoemaker St, NW, Washington DC 20008; tel 202-362-6730.
British Embassy: Harmincad Utca 6, 1051 Budapest; tel 1-266-2888 or 1-226-1430.
US Embassy: Unit 1320, Szabadság tér 12, 1054 Budapest; tel 1-112-6450.
Hungarian Tourist Board: PO Box 4336, London SW18 4XE; tel/fax 0181-871 4009. May be contacted through the Embassy: tel 0171-823 1055; fax 0171-823 1459.
Hungarian Tourist Board: 150 East 58th Street, New York, NY 10155; tel 212-586-5230.
Tourinform: 1052 Budapest, Süto utca 2; tel 1-117-9800; fax 1-117-9578 (or write to PO Box 185, 1364 Budapest). They can supply leaflets, brochures, lists of local tourist offices etc.
Internet: www.hungarytourism.hu.

Accommodation

All types of accommodation can be found (and your way through to this is through the local English-language press, see below). For many other accommodation service contacts you can telephone *Tourinform* on 1-117-9800.

Removals

See the *General Overview* section of this book. And also:
Interdean International Movers: Budapest 1211, Szállitok utca 4; tel 1-276-7500/425-0277; fax 1-277-2877.

Import Procedures

Personal belongings may be brought in, and goods up to 8000 HUF on first entry, duty-free, and 500 HUF on each subsequent entry. Otherwise you have to import them, with a duty of 15% payable on many items; and a customs handling fee additionally of 2%. There is yet another tax on top of this, a general turnover tax, calculated on the entire amount on which the duty is paid, plus duty and customs handling fee etc., of 25%. Below 800 HUF (or 500 HUF subsequently) an oral declaration of the goods you have is sufficient (in other words, you go through the 'nothing-to-declare' channel); otherwise you must fill in the form and make a written declaration (and go through the 'something-to-declare' red corridor.

10,000 HUF may be brought in without a permit (but not banknotes with a denomination of greater than 1,000 HUF). Goods up to 20,000 HUF may be taken out (but not coffee, tea, cocoa, citrus and tropical fruits, drinks of imported origin, spices, synthetic and natural sausage casing, husked rice, as well as medicines, baby care products, coal, and other household fuels. You will have to leave that souvenir ember at home. You can get a tax refund for most of the souvenirs you buy as well.

The Language

Hungarian is the official language, with German widely spoken, also some English and French.

Language Schools

Interclub Hungarian Language School: 1111 Budapest, Bertalan L. utca 17; tel/fax 1-165-2535; fax 1-165-6695. Small groups, business, and one-to-one classes.
Hungarian Language School: 1067 Budapest, Eötvös utca 25/A; tel 1-312-5899.

Telephones

The new blue phones are the best, accepting 5, 10 and 20 forint coins (old kind). Cardphones are generally in good working order. 'Do not expect to have a phone installed,' the Budapest British Council office advises us though, rather pessimistically, 'as this takes a very long time.' Hence the proliferation of 'service centre' companies throughout the CEE for business people, who can provide you with an office, a fax and a phone. From the UK, the number for Budapest is 00-36-1. Directory enquiries are divided into different categories: 117-0170 (public institutions); 117-0000 (private numbers); 117-0188 (by address); 117-3033 (provincial enquiries); 117-0110 (operator); and last but not least 118-6977 (international directory enquiries).

For long-distance calls in Hungary the code is 06; 01 can be rung to place a call through the central exchange; and the code from Hungary for an international call is 00, followed by the country code. Emergency numbers are: 07 or 118-0800 (police, English spoken); and 04 or 112-3430 (ambulance, English spoken).

Driving

'You will quickly discover there is no such thing as a fast lane.' In towns the speed limit is 50 kph, minor roads 80 kph, 110 kph main roads, and 120 kph motorways. Dip your headlights, and have them on anywhere outside Budapest all the time. Seatbelts must be worn by front-seat passengers. Carry your driving licence and car registration papers. Car theft is a problem; alarms and/or locks are advisable. Drink no alcohol before you set off. And you have to get local plates within six months of entering the country (unless you drive out and back in again). You need those emergency triangles; and take a photocopy of your passport with you on the road as well. Car insurance is complex, but your UK or US green card insurance will cover you for six months; and you need the local kind thereafter.

The equivalent of the RAC or AA in Hungary is (or are) known as 'Yellow Angels'; and the *Hungarian Auto Club* operates an 'International Aid Service Centre' in Budapest which can tow you away if necessary: tel 1-212-3952.

Public Transport

In Budapest, this is very good, with an efficient and easy-to-navigate system exactly as in Western European cities. It is run by *BKV* (the Budapest Transportation Company). Three undergound lines, a yellow, red and blue one, connect most parts of the city. There are quite a few night buses (distinguished by a capital "E' after the number on the front). Buy your tickets before travel, at bus or tram terminals, or tobacconists (*dohánybolt*), or *Trafik* shops. These are HUF 35 presently; and valid for one continuous journey. Punch them either on board or at metro entrances. A month-long travelcard is available from the larger metro stations nine-to-five. They run from the first of the month and are valid until the fifth of the following month. There are inspectors (with red armbands) patrolling to check that you have validated your ticket; who may or may not be sympathetic to your ticketless tale of woe.

Taxis: The ones waiting outside hotels or at airports will charge double the fare. The registered taxis have a yellow number-plate; and some reliable companies are: *Tele 5 Taxis* (tel 155-5555); *Ftaxi* (tel 122-2222); and *City Taxi* (tel 211-1111). (Thanks to the *British Council* Budapest for much of the above information: they may supply you with their updated *Teachers' Handbook* about foreigners living in Budapest).

Schools and Education

The starting point for education in Hungary's long history was the arrival of the Benedictine monks in the time of King Stephen (see above). They built the first monastery, and the first school. The far-sighted Stephen also passed a law to make one in every ten villages build a school for themselves.

Banks

These are open from 10.30am until only 3pm on Mondays to Thursdays, and on Fridays close early at 1pm. For more information contact *Tourinform* on 1-117-9800.

Healthcare

Emergency treatment is free. No vaccinations are needed to enter the country; and travel or health insurance is advisable (see the *General Overview* of this book for more on *Health Insurance*).

Culture

'Absolute geometry, torsion balance, the carburettor, transformer, lightbulbs with tungsten filaments and krypton charge, radioactive tracing, the nuclear power plant, thermonuclear fusion, the cooling tower, the electric engine, supersonic flight...' the list goes on of these contributions which, we are are informed, Hungary has made to universal culture. This also seems like a legacy of communism in many Central and Eastern European countries, which always put the accent on modernity and science. The useful factsheets on Hungary produced by the Ministry of Foreign Affairs (and which can be supplied by the Embassy) are the source of the above. This extract is from No. 5.

Religion:
70% Roman Catholic and 20% Protestant, with some Orthodox and other minorities. There is no official state religion.

Entertainment:
Budapest has its bars and night-clubs, casinos and a famous Opera House, discoteques, many international restaurants, and all forms of music from classical, to gypsy, to pop and rock. The region around Lake Balaton also has a lively nightlife in the summer months.

Food and Drink:
Characteristic flavours of the local dishes are of course paprika but also onions, tomatoes, and red, green and yellow peppers. The most famous dish is *goulash* (to be made in a kettle over an open fire in the poriginal version). Noodles and pasta are part of the diet; rice and meat wrapped in sour cabbage leaves is nice; and there are fish soups and other fish dishes, washed down with some of the locally produced red or white wine of which Hungarians are rightly proud. Pastries and cakes show their Austro-Hungarian ancestry. In Budapest, you can find the central covered market – where there are many of these things, and local craft items like lace and embroidered tablecloths. This market is frequented by tourists as well as residents.

Shopping:
7am to 7pm are the hours when shops are open (with early closing at 1pm on Saturdays). Some open later; and there are now many shopping streets in Budapest which are open on Sundays.

Social Attitudes:
Most Hungarians enjoy modern music and culture; and few in the cities preserve their old traditions. Handshaking is customary; as is the use of Christian names when you get to know someone, and for business or work colleagues.

Useful Addresses

British Council: Budapest VI., Benczur utca 26, 1068 Hungary; tel 1-321-4039 (office) or 1-342-0918 (teaching centre); fax 1-342-5728/269-6594; internet

bharris@britcoun.hu.
American Express: 1052 Budapest, Deák Ferenc u. 10; tel 1-266-8680 (travel service); 1-267-2022 (card service); fax 1-267-2029 (closes at 5.30pm; or 6.30pm in summer; 2pm on Saturdays).

Public Holidays

Hungary has no less than three national days, of which one is the 'official' one. March 15 marks the outbreak of the 1848-9 revolution ('from which modern parliamentarianism in Hungary can be dated'); October 23 is the anniversary of the 1956 uprising against the Russians and of the proclamation of the Hungarian Republic in 1989. But August 20 is the 'official' national day. It is the feast of St. Stephen, who was Hungary's first king.

Working in Hungary

Employment

There is a large American expatriate community in Budapest; and services are springing up for these and others who live there ranging from Irish pubs to discoteques to listings magazines to social and arts events – and all the things which Americans abroad do. Some knowledge of German – and making an effort to learn at least the basics of Hungarian – will help with many aspects of your jobhunting or business activities in Hungary, as well as in everyday life. Budapest is still the number one destination, for tourism as for residence, but other tourism-related opportunities are springing up elsewhere. English is quite widely spoken by those working in tourism or the business community; and by an increasing number of young people. But here the main second languages are still German and Russian (the latter no longer widely taught).

Hungary, like its neighbours Poland and the Czech Republic, is now busy 'getting ready for Europe'. Land and property prices have already gone up, with some UK investors buying up great tracts of the countryside as an investment, and leaving them fallow, to the consternation of the locals. Some UK farmers have even moved here. Trade and employment will be further liberalised in future and in theory it will be as easy for Britons to get a job in Budapest as in Bradford from 2002 onwards (and Americans will lose out). There will be many opportunities here for UK workers in all areas over the next decade as a consequence of this tightening of the rules regarding the employment of non-EU nationals which will shortly be with us.

Newspapers:
Powers International in London can place advertisements in the national dailies *Magyar Hirlap* and *Nepszabadsag* and represents these for advertising purposes in the UK. *The Budapest Sun* (1122 Budapest, Városmajor utca 13; fax 1-214-0388; e-mail letters.editor@bpsun.hu) is 'Hungary's Complete English-Language Newspaper, with news about entertainment, style, property, services and jobs. The *FT* can also be delivered to you in Budapest: contact their Subscription Department, Europe on +49-69-156850; fax +49-69-596-4483).

Recruitment Agency:
Antal International Ltd: 2nd Floor, 90 Tottenham Court Road, London W1P 0AN;

tel 0171-637 2001. Offices in Russia, Poland, Czech Republic, Ukraine, Hungary, Romania, Kazakstan, France, Italy, Germany, USA and Hong Kong.

Also see *The Directory of Jobs and Careers Abroad* for some general international recruiters, and publications like *Overseas Jobs Express* (mentioned this book's *General Overview*).

Teaching:
Most people who go to teach English report that students are eager to learn; and find it an excellent place to work. This is not always well-paid, though, and you should bear in mind that the cost of living is high.

The *Central European University*, Civic Education Project, Taboritska 23, 130 87 Praha 5, Czech Republic, tel/fax +42-2-272-498, e-mail, cepprg @ecn.gn.apc.erg – sends western-trained academics to Hungary to assist in a a broad range of programmes.

E.T.A. – English Teachers' Association of Hungary, Dozsa György ut 104.II.15, 1068 Budapest, tel 1-132-8688 – will try to put prospective teachers in contact with primary and secondary schools. A TEFL qualification is desirable. Contracts last for at least one school year.

International Placement Group, 72 New Bond Street, London W1y 9DD; tel/fax 0171-739-2725; e-mail ipg.@praha.demon.co.uk – is a teacher recruitment agency specialising in the countries of Central and Eastern Europe like Poland, the Czech Republic, Russia, Hungary and Slovakia, placing teachers in these countries and offering programmes in the UK.

Teaching conditions are very much the same as in the *Czech Republic* (see under *Teaching* there). *English Contacts Abroad* also provides a research and direct contacts service for EFL teachers in all CEE countries (PO Box 126, Oxford OX2 6UB, UK). Write in the first instance for a questionnaire – or with any tips or contacts of your own. There is an administration fee of £48. In addition, Hungarian embassies can provide information on job prospects and work permits for language teachers.

Teacher Agents: This is a way for EFL teachers and others to bring their group (usually of secondary school or university-level students) to the UK to learn English; and to earn some commission or have their travel expenses paid. This is often for one, two, or three-week courses in the summer; but can be all the year round. One school offering courses like this in Oxford is *Speak English*: PO Box 126, Oxford OX2 6RU, UK. Write to the Director for details.

Trade Fair:
The *Hungarian Tourist Board*: organises *Hungary Welcomes Britain, Hungaria Incoming Workshop* and other tourism trade fairs. For more information, contact the *Hungarian National Tourist Office* in your home country (UK tel: 0171-823 1055).

Voluntary Work:
Biokultura Egyesület (The Hungarian Association of Organic Growers), Rezeda u. 2, 1024 Budapest, tel/fax 1-285-2723 or 285-6540 – is a non-profit organisation founded as a club in 1983, which seeks to promote sustainable forms of agriculture and ecological awareness. Volunteers are required for work on organic farms for up to six months, and on placements of 1-2 weeks between April and October, in exchange for food and lodging, with free time included and the opportunity to learn about organic farming methods.

Business and Industry Report

Currency: 1 Forint (Ft) = 100 fillér

Agriculture is still a major activity, accounting for 6% of Gross Domestic Product (GDP); and food products are currently 20% of exports. Industrial production started to grow again in 1992, following a severe contraction in 1989-1991. Inflation has been brought under control; and Hungary is part of the Deutschmark zone, so prices are often expressed in this currency. Opportunities are in in construction and investment projects, as well as for experts in industrial restructuring and finance. Pharmaceuticals, computers, telecommunications and mining are important industries; and there is tourism (see below).

Registration rules for creating limited and joint stock companies are fairly straighforward. Investors can take a 100% equity share in companies, except those in the protected areas of heavy industry, transport, defence and so on. Foreign owned companies are subject to the same taxation rules as local companies, though exemptions are available in certain priority areas. In Hungary, the priority has been privatisation, and a wide range of products as well as many consultancy services are actively being sought. Other than tourism and leisure, there are large-scale airport and motorway construction projects under way, with other opportunities still in specialist consumer goods and food products, electronics and other 'green field' site ventures, pharmaceuticals, car manufacture, and on a larger scale in coal-fired power generation. Germany is by far the largest foreign investor, with around 100 companies operating here and 36.7% of inward investment. The United States has 19% and 34 companies, with Britain in seventh place with only 3% of investment.

Business Services:
'Instant offices in Central Europe.' *Regus* supplies fully serviced business centres worldwide, and has opened offices in Prague, Budapest, Vienna and Warsaw. Warsaw: tel 22-657-0000; Budapest: 1-267-9144; Prague: 2-2185 1055; Vienna: 1-599-990.

Business Contacts:
The *British Embassy Commercial Section* provides general briefings for business travellers (Harmincad Utca 6, Budapest 1051; tel 1-266-2888; fax 1-266-0907). Or contact the *Embassy of Hungary Commercial Section* (46 Eaton Place, London SW1X 8BY; tel 0171-235 8767; fax 0171-235 4319) for commercial information relating to tourism and many other sectors of the economy. The *DTI* along with the Foreign and Commonwealth Office has a database of UK companies in Hungary; and may send prospective investors and exporters other useful trade-orientated information.

Poland

Introduction

Poland occupies an area of 780,000 square miles, equivalent to nearly 90% of that of Germany. Thirty-five per cent of the population of 38,418,000 still lives in the countryside, a figure which will come down when the country joins the European Union. There are the lakes and islands of Mazuria, wild forests to the east and along the border with Belarus, and the River Vistula which flows through the country to the Baltic Coast in the north. The climate is continental: there is a long winter when average temperatures are usually below 0°C and a mild summer when the average is 18°C or more.

Poland's borders have shifted westwards during its recent past. So, geographically as well as ideologically, it has moved to the west. The capital Warsaw, once in the centre of the country, is now in the east. In earlier centuries, Poland included much of neighbouring Lithuania and Ukraine as well, before this larger country was shared out by the Russians, Prussians and Austro-Hungarians at the end of the eighteenth century.

There is another east-west division today as well, with the greater economic growth nearer to the German border and the greatest poverty in the east. Krakow (or Cracow) is the historic and cultural capital, and today is a destination for many international tourists, who may also visit Vienna, Budapest or Prague on their Central European guided tour. The nearby Tatra (or Tatras) Mountains are popular with hikers and skiers, and drinkers of the local 'mountain tea'. Here are also many visitors from Britain and the rest of Europe. Other cities are Szczecin, Poznan, Wroclaw, Katowice, Lodz, Lublin, and Gdansk.

The religion is 95% Roman Catholic, with Orthodox, Jewish and Muslim minorities. There are still one or two Tatar villages near its eastern border, a reminder of the invasions which came to Poland from the east, which also helped to form its language and culture. Other monuments to its formerly large Jewish population will be found in Warsaw and elsewhere. The Holocaust and the Second World War was the darkest period of Polish history.

Today, Poles have turned their backs on their recent communist past, which is interpreted mainly as a period of unwelcome Russian domination. Britons and Americans fought alongside Poles in the war, but we should remember that the West sold out to the Russians too – this is what Churchill did at Yalta when trying to balance the rival claims of the various Eastern European countries to liberal democratic status, and preferred independence and democracy for Greece. This is how the post-war map of Europe was drawn up, and spheres of influence decided. He handed a document to this effect to Stalin.

Post-1989, Poland is once again where Poles would say it has always been, in Central Europe. In fact, the country is one of the eastern pillars of NATO and, economically, and in its transition to membership of the European Union, sees itself as a bridge between East and West.

Poles know both worlds, with their understanding of 'western' Catholicism on the one hand, and their cultural links with Russia and its neighbours on the other, and a long history as an independent and powerful state (set against periods of domination by stronger and intolerant neighbours to the east and west). There is a certain fear (or distrust) which Poles have of Germans and Russians even today, which can give some idea of their place in between these two larger neighbours during most of this century.

This ambivalence is one aspect of a rather complex psychology in which a nationalistic pride is tempered by an understanding of the consequences this can have – that pride can lead to a fall. Like everywhere else, too, you will find the Poles have their own great soul, which is perhaps more understated than the Russian version, more inward-looking or less melodramatic... This Polish spirituality is less often expressed in terms of the heights and depths of human emotion, and is usually without the Russian idea of an overbearing national greatness. In this more modest understanding which Poles have of themselves, human existence is not an ineffable tragedy, but a tragi-comedy of light and shade. Poles tend to be less fatalistic, in other words, than Russians.

Perhaps the landscape has something to do with it, in these borderlands which stretch from Estonia in the north, and through Poland and its neighbours, to the Black Sea in the south, criss-crossed by rivers, mountains and forests, but mainly flat and unending. These are all really overlapping regions in Central and Eastern Europe; Poland is also a Baltic state, and simultaneously in Central Europe and this less defined area between East and West. What is it like to live here? If we can imagine the immense solitude of a great forest – or the steppe, or the mountain valleys – and recall that each of these countries has a relatively low population – we can see a little of how this idea of a Great Soul has little to do with society, and much more to do with this sense of being connected to nature.

In this region, spirituality and nationalism tend to go together. But unlike many of the other Central/Eastern European peoples, Poles today tend to have no great desire to restore their former national greatness, or to expand beyond their present frontiers. No advantage can be gained from this and, unlike some of their neighbours, Polish people already have this sense of themselves as a nation, the element which, when it is missing, can lead to war. The Serbs, Croats, Abkhasians, or Chechens all knew they were a people but were seeking this more elusive and romantic notion of themselves as a nation too.

In Poland, it is not like that; and there is little of this sense of resentment towards neighbouring countries. This seems to be the main reason for the wars which afflicted some other of the outlying regions of the former Soviet Union post-1991, and why they didn't happen here. This is what happened all over Central and Eastern Europe in fact. For many of these peoples – free for almost the first time – this sense of nationhood could most easily be found – and a definition for this found – in their rivalry with their neighbours.

But even if most Poles have little reason to trust those who so recently – and tragically – invaded and occupied their country, there is little of this more deep-seated insecurity – which seems to result from tensions within the national identity – over their status as a nation. This makes Poles much more like the Czechs, and not like the Hungarians, and much more like Western Europeans, and makes for a more stable society and a better long-term outlook. Their desire today is simply for their country to take its place alongside the other European nations as an equal partner.

Of course, there will always be some nostalgia for the days when Poland really was one of the great European powers. Once famed for their martial prowess, the Poles today are becoming more pragmatic as well as idealistic.

One thing Polish people do when they travel abroad is cooperate and look out for each other. On the other hand, especially when it comes to politics, it only takes two or three to disagree – and Poles can be as quarrelsome as any of their

Central European neighbours. This is how they see themselves anyway. But another important value in Poland – and all these formerly communist countries – is the idea of consensus and working together.

Living in Poland

Political, Economic and Geographical Structure

Historically, Poland has had frequent boundary changes; for a time it was divided between Prussia, Russia, and the Austro-Hungarian Empire. Present-day Poland incorporates part of what was Germany; and has lost territory in Belarus, Ukraine, and Lithuania (with which, for a time, it formed one kingdom). Forty-five years of Russian domination came to an end in 1989, and one of the things it is most famous for (along with Polish vodka) is Solidarity, the independent trade union which helped to bring this to an end.

The crowds shouted 'Down with communism' more recently, in the 1997 parliamentary (or *sejm*) elections, when the Solidarity-led alliance defeated the *SLD* – or Democratic Left Alliance – the social democratic party which has inherited the communists' mantle. Poland now has a democratic right and democratic left, with a few fringe parties as well. The third political force is the pro-business *UW*, or Freedom Union; the *PSL* (Peasant Party) is the previous partner of the socialists in the government which lost out in this election. The right-wing *ROP* – the 'Movement for a Reconstruction of Poland' – currently commands about 5% of popular support. Both Solidarity and the Democratic Left (or Social Democratic Party) are modern and forward-looking political movements. Solidarity has more conservative attitudes on issues such as abortion, and the Church.

In economic and cultural terms, Poland now looks to the west; and has been transformed since its darkest days of ten or fifteen years ago, when the image of pensioners queuing in the snow for bread was basically true. In the 1980s, and early 1990s, this country suffered a much greater economic dislocation than Hungary or the Czech Republic. Now industrial production has recovered; many industries have been privatised; and many foreign firms have now invested here.

Today, almost every consumer item which can be found in Britain is on sale in its new supermarkets including, reportedly, Polish mozarella. Some parts of the country, like Gdansk and Silesia, are heaviliy industrialised, but it also has vast tracts of largely unspoilt natural landscapes, including the last relic of primeval forest in Europe, the Bialowieza National Park, home to the rare European bison.

Entry and Residence

British passport holders may enter and remain in Poland for up to six months without a visa. For US passport holders this is 90 days. Applications for work and residence permits should be made from outside the country (*Consulate-General of the Republic of Poland in London*, 73 New Cavendish Street, London W1M 8LS; tel 0171-580 0476; fax 0171-323 2320 – also see *Useful Addresses* below). There are various rules and regulations, for example for English teachers, who should submit a valid passport, and completed application form with two passport-sized photographs and a certificate issued by the head of that university; or the *Regional Employment Officer – Wojewodzki Urzad Pracy –* where all employers must apply if they wish to employ a foreign national, in any area of employment. This 'visa'

(really your work permit) will cost you or your employer £113 in Britain at present, a not inconsiderable sum. In America, this is $170; and applications should be made in the same way to the Consulate. They emphasise that 'work visas cannot be obtained in Poland.'
Voluntary workers need a certificate from the relevant organisation, but do not have their visa stamped 'work permit'. These visas are issued free of charge.

Useful Addresses

British Embassy: Aleja Roz No 1, 00-556 Warsaw; tel 22-628-1001.
 Director of Trade Promotion: tel 22-625-3030.
US Embassy: Aleje Ujazdowskie 29-31, 00-540 Warsaw; tel 22-628-3041.
Polish Consulate (London): see above.
Consular Division of the Polish Embassy: 2224 Wyoming Avenue, NW, Washington DC; tel 202-234-2501; fax 202-328-2152. Consulates also in New York, Los Angeles, and Chicago.
Polish National Tourist Office: First Floor, Remo House, 310-312 Regent Street, London W1R 5AJ; tel 0171-5808811; e-mail pnto@dial.pipex.com; http://w3.poland.net/travelpage.
Polish National Tourist Office: Suite 1711, 275 Madison Avenue, New York, NY, 10016; tel 212-338-9412.
British Council: (Warsaw) fax 22-219955.

In Warsaw, there is a British Council resource centre – and several other across the country – which kindly participated in our survey of international workers in Poland, as well as an *Alliance Française*, and all the other cultural organisations, clubs for expatriates and so on which you might expect in any major city.

Getting There

Charters and Coaches:
At the time of writing, few charters are available, and Warsaw is relatively expensive to get to by air. City breaks, skiing and other holidays are now available through some travel agents, notably *Fregata Travel* which has a *City Breaks and Holidays* brochure for Krakow, Warsaw, Prague, Budapest, Moscow, St. Petersburg, Sofia, Zagreb, Dubrovnik, Riga and Tallinn (13 Regent Street, London SW1Y 4LR; fax 0171-451 7017; or 117A Withington Road, Manchester M16 8EE; tel 0161-226 7227; fax 0161-226 0700). It offers a special train itinerary across Poland, Czech spas, brewery tours and opera, and a wide variety of other Central and Eastern European experiences.
 Eurolines is part of the same group; and may be contacted in the UK on 0990-143219 – or you can make your booking through *Fregata Travel*. It features coach destinations throughout CEE, in Austria (Vienna), Bosnia, Bulgaria, Croatia and Slovenia, the Czech Republic, Hungary, Romania, Russia, Serbia and the Slovak Republic, as well as many city destinations in Poland. Or try contacting *White Eagle* in London, which has a comfortable route to Warsaw with video and hostess service (it takes about 24 hours to get to Poland by coach); or *ATAS* coach lines (tel 0181-9935000 – UK and 22-6254682 in Poland). There may be cheaper charter flights here in future, especially to Krakow (or Cracow) and Warsaw.

Onward Connections:
Your onward travel, flight, hotel and other transfers, as well as excellent guiding services, can all be arranged by *Fregata Travel* (see above) or travel bureaus like

Best Western Plaza Hotels (00-973 Warszawa, ul. Niemcewicza 17; tel 2-659-38-95; fax 2-658-15-07) which specialise in hotels, but also conferences, exhibitions and business travel. Also contact the national tourist offices in the UK, USA and elsewhere for a wide range of useful English language leaflets and guides. Ecotourism is a popular theme of some of these. And see the English-language magazine guides like *Welcome to Cracow* or *Welcome to Warsaw* for a wide variety of business, residence and travel contacts.

Scheduled Services:
Then there are the scheduled air services. The national airline is *LOT Polish Airlines*: 313 Regent Street, London W1R 7PE; tel 0171-580 5037 (for reservations). *British Airways* (UK tel: 0345-222111), *Austrian Airlines* (UK tel: 0171-434 7350), *Lufthansa* (UK tel: 0345-737747), *Finnair* (tel 0171-408 1222 in London; 22-695-0811 in Warsaw), *KLM* (UK tel: 0990-750900), *British Midland* and many others also go there.

Travel Agencies:
ALES Ltd: al. Jerozolimskie 184, 02-486 Warsaw; tel 22-668-1960; fax 22-668-1960. For hotel booking, congress and conference arrangement, air tickets, railway tickets and business travel services.
BEST-HARCTUR Ltd: 00-973 Warszawa, 17 JU Niemcewicza str; tel 22-22-47-14/28-94; fax 2-658-1507. Domestic and foreign tourism, outgoing and incoming, for groups and individuals, holidays, adventure tourism, special events, incentive travel, travel and transport services, insurance, congress organisation etc. with a network of hotels and branch offices in Bielsko-Biala, Krakow, Radom, Kielce, Czestochowa, Lodz, Warszawa, Lublin, Poznan and Gdansk.
Fregata Travel: 13 Regent Street, London SW1Y 4LR; fax 0171-451 7017; or 117A Withington Road, Manchester M16 8EE; tel 0161-226 7227; fax 0161-226 0700. See above.
Liberty International (UK) Ltd: 11 Grosvenor Street, Chester CH1 2DD; tel 01244-361115; fax 01244-351116; e-mail liberyty@chester.itsnet.co.uk. For full destination management services, including conference and meeting organisation, hotel reservations, guide and tour services, study tours and special interest groups. Offices in Riga, Tallinn, Vilnius, St. Petersburg, Kaliningrad, Sofia, Bucharest, Prague and Budapest as well as Warsaw.
Polish Travel Bureau Co. Inc: 16 Bracka Str., 00-128 Warsaw; tel 22-827-2275; fax 22-827-1445; e-mail piotr.izdebski@pbp.com.pl. Outbound travel agency organising tourism from Poland.

Hotels:
Inter-Continental and *Radisson* have five-star establishments in Moscow, Prague, Riga, Tashkent, Szczecin, Warsaw and Zagreb (tel 0181-847 2277). Also contact *Best Western Plaza Hotels* (00-973 Warszawa, ul. Niemcewicza 17; tel 2-659-38-95; fax 2-658-15-07).

See the trade guide *Hotels in Poland* published by *Intourist Warszawa* (ul. Nowogrodzka 10, 00-509 Warsawa; tel/fax 22-629-02-02/625-08-52/622-32-06/622-32-11) who can arrange suitable hotel accommodation for you almost anywhere in the country; and offer a visa handling, accommodation, transfer, guiding, onward travel, sightseeing and group tourism service to many other Central and Eastern European destinations, as well as Poland. Also see under *Communications and Transport* below.

Information:
There are many guidebooks to Poland. The *Polish National Tourist Office* (in London and New York) is very helpful; and will provide maps and a wide range of brochures free of charge. The *Warsaw Voice* is the invaluable English-language newspaper for residents and business visitors, available in kiosks or almost everywhere expatriates go. It is represented for advertising purposes in Britain by *Frank L. Crane Ltd.*, 5/15 Cromer Street, Gray's Inn Road, London WC1H 8LS; or they can be contacted direct at their advertising department in Poland: *WV Marketing*, 64 Ksiecia Janusza St., 01-452 Warsaw; tel 22-36-63-77; fax 22-37-19-95. All visitors, before they go, should try to get hold of a copy.

Currency

The *zloty* (Zl) is divided into 100 *groszy*. Not so long ago it had four zeros removed from its notional value making 10,000 old zlotys worth one new one. It is now fully convertible.

Geography

It borders on Germany, the Czech and Slovak Republics, Ukraine, Belarus, Lithuania, and part of Russia, with the Baltic Sea to the North. Poland is divided into 49 administrative provinces, and the capital, Warsaw, is located on the aforementioned Vistula River.

Climate

Continental everywhere, but moderate and changeable, especially in spring. Summers and autumns are comfortable and not too hot; it is cold in winter, from December onwards when you will need your warmest clothing. Americans may recognise the climate as being like that of New England (or may not) and the autumn can be as beautiful here as New England or Canada.

Daily Life

Accommodation

Nearly all the expats we interviewed said they felt at home in Poland (see some of the *Personal Experiences* at the end of this book) but accommodation – as in the other CEE countries – is often said to be cramped. These living conditions are sometimes not as bad as they are painted though. If you have lived in a small council flat in Britain you will get the idea, and in one of the impersonal but comfortable apartment blocks, you will at least have an entryphone.

Cold winters mean taking things like heating and hot water more seriously than in Britain; if you keep your windows closed the cold cannot get in. All these services in apartment blocks are generally reliable, and communally run. For foreigners – as for the locals – finding even modest accommodation these days in Warsaw and Krakow is becoming more difficult and expensive. Poland is no longer a very cheap country to live in, although local salaries still often do not reflect this.

The rich are busy purchasing desirable residences out of town; the richest of all buy palaces and do them up, like the aspiring politician Radek Sikorski who bought a manor house at Chobielin in north-west Poland – after living in England for a time – and wrote a book about it: *The Polish House* (Weidenfeld & Nicholson). Prices are going up. You are advised to seek advice at the British Embassy or Consulate about reputable agencies and lawyers who can handle the paperwork. Many of the incoming travel agencies can also arrange private house or flat rental (see above) as well as hotel accommodation. This ranges from $20 a night (the very cheapest) to $400 in business class hotels, or indeed in palaces where visitors too can stay, like the *Kadyny Palace Hotel* mentioned below.

These country houses are one of the less-well known tourism resources in Poland. But there is plenty of budget accommodation too: contact the *Polish Association of Youth Hostels* (*PTSM* – ul. Chocimska 28, 00-791 Warszawa; tel 22-49-81-28/42-51; fax 22-49-83-54) or *PTTK* (ul. Senatrorska 11, 00-075 Warszawa; tel 22-826-2251; fax 22-826-2505) for some useful names and addresses.

Utilities

Electricity: 220V, 50Hz. Americans and Britons will need an adaptor/converter for their appliances. Tap water is safe for drinking.

Removals and Freight

For a list of UK-based international removals and freight companies, and many specialising in Central Europe, please see *Removals*, in the *General Overview* at the beginning of this book.

Import Procedures

Contact the Polish Embassy for these – see *Useful Addresses* above.
Personal items are duty free, and pets need their appropriate vaccination certificate issued at least ten days' earlier. All are allowed in, except parrots. If you bring more than $2,000 you have to declare it at customs. Your parrot, of course, may declare itself.

The Language

Is spoken by 99% of the population, so Poles have no problem communicating with each other, only foreigners who don't speak Polish... Try to learn some before you go. German, French, and Russian are also quite widely understood, as well as English.

Transport and Communications

CNN, the BBC and Sky, are all available. There is freedom of the press. The British Council is one place where you can find British newspapers; along with the Embassy and Consulates and some shops and kiosks.

Telephones: Public telephones are in metro stations and post offices; the modern ones requiring a card are becoming more common. Other call boxes require special tokens called *zetony* which are usually on sale nearby. There are business 'service centres' in the major hotels; and Poland's state-owned telephone company *Telekomunikacja Polska* also operates a number of service centres in

Warsaw with international phone and fax connections (ul. Nowogrodzka 45; tel 22-628-4620 – open 24 hours). The address for the forwarding of telex and fax messages is ul. Nowy Swiat 68, tel 22-826-5130 (open Monday to Friday, and Saturday mornings).

Public faxes are also available in some post offices. To dial a number in Poland from the UK, prefix it with 00 and then 48. Within the country a nought is added before the first digit of the number with the regional code (e.g. to call Warsaw dial 0-22). Calls are cheaper in the evenings (as in many places). To dial a country like Britain or America from inside Poland, dial a zero, wait for the tone, then another zero, then the country code etc. For cellular phone rentals, contact: *CENTERTEL*, ul. Jasna 24, 00-054 Warszawa; tel 22-826-9400/1; fax 22-826-8699.

Useful numbers are: 999 (ambulance); 998 (fire); 997 (police); 912 (intercity directory enquiries); 911/913 (local directory enquiries); and 981 (road assistance).

Getting Around

Cars: All vehicles coming into the country are subject to customs control and the driver must present valid proof of registration and international liability insurance (which you can purchase at border crossings) and all these documents should be in order (check with the Embassy). You will need an *International Driving Licence* or equivalent.

The road assistance number is 981; the national police number is 997.

Car Rentals: *Hertz* car rentals have offices nationwide. Contact your local office for details, or tel 22-621-1360, fax 22-629-3875 (Warsaw). *Avis, Eurodollar, Budget, Europcar* and *Fly & Drive* are other firms who can organise car hire in Poland, and give you some of their local addresses to contact.

Taxis: In Warsaw, try 919; 9624; 9622; or 9626; or in Krakow 67-67-67. These are listed in the Yellow Pages, and are always metered.

Trains: Trains arrive from Berlin in the west and carry on to all points east, south and north. The Central Railway Station in Warsaw is in the city centre near the coach station. There are regular buses there from the airport too. Good value at present is the *Polrailpass* which gives unlimited travel on the *PKP* railway network for $50 for eight days (second class) up to $130 for one month of first class travel. There is also a *Junior Polrailpass* for those under 26 – and these can be purchased at *Wasteels* offices (like the one in Victoria Street, London) or offices of the *Orbis* travel agency in Germany and Vienna. Be careful if you are travelling at night though.

Buses: There are international coach arrivals in Warsaw from the UK, Norway, Germany, the Czech Republic, and Turkey among other places, and it is quite easy to get to these other destinations from here. A useful board at the entrance has all this international coach information, and the telephone numbers of the companies. Or contact the national coach company *PEKAES* (Al. Jerozlimskie 114; Warsaw; tel 22-22-4811; fax 22-23-63-94/5/6). There are trams and buses running until midnight in the city, and now some night buses too. Tickets may be bought from kiosks or from the driver. Nationally, *PKS* is the longest-established bus and coach service; and *Polski Express* its new private-sector competitor. For reservations and information contact Polski Express (tel 22-630-2967) or the *Orbis* office at Warsaw airport (tel 22-650-4421).

Health and Hospitals

For emergency medical services call 999. There is a list of hospitals and health centres in Warsaw in the *Welcome to Warsaw* guide and *The Warsaw Voice* (see above).

Shopping

Shops are open generally from 8am until quite late, 8pm or 9pm, with some taking a break in the afternoon until around 5pm. On Saturdays they are usually open only until 1pm or 2pm. Some small shops are open on Sunday mornings. *NAMA* is a national chain of department stores. Handicrafts include hand-made folk items, embroidered tablecloths, hand-knitted woollen pullovers and carved or inlaid wood.

Public Holidays

These are: January 1 (New Year's Day); January 6 (Epiphany); Easter Monday; May 1 (Labour Day); May 30 (Republic Day); June 22 (National Holiday); the Feast of the Assumpion (August); December 25 (Christmas Day); December 26 (Boxing Day).

Working in Poland

Business and Employment

English is quite widely spoken in the business community. The etiquette involves having a business card, etc. There is a range of local agents and consultants (and some lawyers) who may be of assistance; but it is better to approach business contacts directly yourself.There are also the UK-based organisations and the *Chamber of Commerce* mentioned below. The background to investment and business in Poland is its privatisation programme and rapid economic recovery; see under *Economy*.

There are occasional special reports on the country in both the *Financial Times* and *New Markets Monthly*. (The *FT* can also be delivered to you in Warsaw: contact the Subscription Department, Europe on +49-69-156850.

Specific Contacts

Work opportunities in Poland are similar to those in Hungary and the Czech Republic, with openings for consultants and 'experts', and in English teaching and voluntary work. Speaking Polish and other language skills will be necessary for jobs at other levels, like secretarial work. Pay scales are low; and the cost of living is rising, so these are important factors to be borne in mind. It is advisable to obtain up-to-date information on exchange rates and the cost of living. Some international companies will pay an additional allowance to their expatriate workers.

Teaching:
Enthusiasm for learning English – and in life in Britain or the United States – is quite high. Demand for English teachers is such that almost anyone who can speak the language will find work. The main limitation is the salary; and

appropriate qualifications will be an advantage here, as most private language schools are familiar with the RSA/Cambridge and other qualifications. More of an advantage may be a university degree. There is also scope for private tuition. Some useful contacts are given below:

American English School, Ul. Kryniczna 12-14, Warsaw 03-934, tel 2-617-1112 – is looking for friendly and energetic English-speakers interested in teaching. Experience and qualifications are not prerequisites. A long-term commitment is desired. There are branches in Radom and Wolomin.

English First (EF) is 'the world's largest group of private language schools' recruiting teachers for many countries, including Poland. Contact: *EF English First*, Kensington Cloisters, 5 Kensington Church Street, London W8 4LD; tel 0171-795 6645; fax 0171-795 6625.

'Euro-Wiedza' Osprodek Ksztalcenia, ul. Gen.R.Abrahama 10, 03-982 Warsaw, tel 0-22-671-18-59, fax 671-18-59 – requires a TEFL certificate and one year's teaching experience or an MA in Education, and recruits teachers from Britain or the USA. Contact the Director in Warsaw.

Glenrex Educational Services Ltd, Iver House, Middlegreen Estate, Middlegreen Road, Slough, Berks. SL3 6DF.

International Placement Group, 72 New Bond Street, London W1Y 9DD, tel/fax 0171-739-2725, e-mail ipg.@praha.demon.co.uk – is a teacher recruitment agency specialising in many countries in Central and Eastern Europe, including Poland, and placing teachers in these countries as well as offering programmes in the UK.

Poliglota, ul. Kielasnicza 6, Wroclaw, tel 343-7879.

Program-Bell, ul. Fredry 7, 61-701 Poznan, tel 061-536-972 – requires English teachers and volunteers to teach and organise activities on summer camps.

The Polish Ministry of Education recruits some English-speaking academics to help train teachers of English at foreign language training colleges, and in some elementary and secondary schools. Free accommodation and a basic salary are provided. Copies of diplomas and CV's should be sent to the Deputy Director, Department of Foreign Relations, Al. 1 Armii Wojska Polskiego 25, 00-918 Warsaw, Poland. The *Anglo-Polish Universities Association (APASS)*, 93 Victoria Road, Leeds LS6 1DR, tel 0113-275-8121, is another useful contact, and recruits volunteers and paid teachers. For volunteers clear spoken English, but not necessarily teaching experience, is required. Also see the *Czech Republic* chapter and *Teaching* in the *General Overview* for more on working conditions and the way of life for EFL teachers in the region.

Teacher Agents: This is a way for EFL teachers and others to bring their group (usually of secondary school or university-level students) to the UK to learn English; and to earn some commission or have their travel expenses paid. This is often for one, two, or three-week courses in the summer but can be all the year round. One organisation offering courses like this is *Speak English*: PO Box 126, Oxford OX2 6RU, UK. Write to the Director for details.

Voluntary Work:
For further information on workcamps and voluntary work in Poland, see *Summer Jobs Abroad* and *Work Your Way Around the World* (Vacation Work).

Recruitment Agency:
Antal International Ltd: 2nd Floor, 90 Tottenham Court Road, London W1P 0AN; tel 0171-637 2001. Offices in Russia, Poland, Czech Republic, Ukraine, Hungary, Romania, Kazakstan, France, Italy, Germany, the USA and Hong Kong, and they are expanding their operations in the region.

Economy

Currency: Zloty (Zl) = 100 groszy

Poland was the first of these CEE countries to regain the level of production it had in 1989. Mind you, the country had suffered a severe recession throughout the 1980s – when martial law was imposed – meaning this was already low. There is some real progress here today in this country which associated in Western Europe with a kind of genteel poverty but today, in Central and Eastern Europe is a powerhouse economy, and one of the beacons of free trade, free speech and capitalism. This is Poland today. It is the size of Italy, with the population of Spain, and the is largest in the region. It has also become in many ways the most advanced in terms of this economic development.

Banking has been restructured, the retailers have come – like *Marks & Spencer* and their French and German equivalents – and great progress has been made in financial services for individuals and on the stock market, as well as in distribution, marketing and the media, and many other areas where there are opportunities in employment or business.

When it joins the EU for a transitional period, in 2002 or so, agriculture will suffer so far as the indigenous smallholders and peasant farmers are concerned – but international investors may care to snap up some of the land which is on sale now, while prices are still low. Soon it will be worth much more, and farmed in different ways. Property is in the same category – if you can find a suitable second home or apartment, or refurbish one, or do it up yourself. As far as investment is concerned, you can buy to rent – perhaps to other foreigners (one area of a growing private rental market where prices can be surprisingly high). A palace in the country is the price of a three-bedroomed semi in the UK, so there is still plenty of scope for this kind of higher level investment – and all kinds of publicly owned properties and facilities being privatised too – if you are prepared to take the time and money to renovate your property. There are many opportunities here for private individuals and for buisiness.

Registration rules for creating limited and joint stock companies are fairly straighforward. Investors can take a 100% equity share in companies, except those in the protected areas of heavy industry, transport, defence and so on. Foreign owned companies are subject to the same taxation rules as local companies, though 3-6 year exemptions are available in certain priority sectors, like construction, aviation, automotives, ports etc. For help starting a business, and this kind of macro-economic background briefing, contact the *Polish Agency for Foreign Investment* (PIAZ, Al. Roz 2, 00-556 Warsaw; tel 22-621-6261; fax 22-621-8427).

So far as investment is concerned, the Austrian-based *RZB* bank has outlets throughout Central and Eastern Europe (in Bratislava, Budapest, Moscow, Prague, Sofia, Warsaw and Zagreb, with representative offices also in Moscow and Kiev) offering commercial and investment banking services. Their London branch number is 0171-929 2288 (http://www.rzb.co.at/rzb). Investment banking and business advice are other employment opportunities as well. A range of books, from *The Illustrated Catalogue of Polish Products* to *International Transport and Forwarding in Poland*, is also available from the 'business book club' of the magazine *Polish Business* (238-246 King Street, London W6 0RF; tel 0181-748 6537; fax 0181-748 2778) and this magazine has a regular listing of business contacts and other useful services. The trade organisation *SITPRO* produces many different factsheets to help UK exporters with their queries, from general export rules to country factsheets (28 in total) including Poland. Contact: *SITPRO*, 151 Buckingham Palace Road, London SW1W 9SS; tel 0171-215 0825; fax 0171-215 0824; e-mail sitpro.org.uk.

Most Britons – and many Americans – have gone to live and work in Poland. Of all the countries in this Central European region it is perhaps the most amenable and welcoming. It is recommended for first-time visitors to CEE too. You may get there by coach, or train, or car, or plane. See some of the *Personal Experiences* which follow in *Appendix I* for more about living and working in Poland and the other countries of Central and Eastern Europe.

Central and Eastern Europe

The South-East

Introduction

In 1989, the countries of the Balkans (with the exception of Greece) experienced the crisis of popular revolt against communist governments; and a resurgence of nationalism. Where did these revolts lead? According to the recently elected President of Bulgaria, 'The Serbs fought for their liberty; the Bulgarians for their survival.' In Albania, there was a fight against an even more repressive form of communist power, which became a kind of anarchy.

Yugoslavia was a national identity in which only a few of its inhabitants believed. This South Slav nationalism was born in the nineteenth century in the context of the Austro-Hungarian Empire. In the countries which had liberated themselves from the Ottoman Empire before the First World War the sense of nationhood had different historical causes.

A odd feature of the history of the period is this almost mirror-like relation between Yugoslavia and the Soviet Union. Yugoslavia was outside the Soviet sphere of infuence – unlike its neighbours Hungary, Bulgaria and Romania. It was a neutral and non-aligned state, but with a disproportionately large army, and also broke up into its constituent nations, although it was outside the arena of this larger decline. But why? In Yugoslavia, 'we were fooled by what was only an illusion of freedom,' according to one observer quoted at the time.

Was this an illusion? There was a specificity to each situation, and a larger context of events spiralling out of control. What the two scenarios had in common was this idea – of which the West was not quite so aware – that communism was an empty show, a spectacle without substance, that it was merely propaganda, or words without belief... It was this failure – on the symbolic level at first – and which was somehow latent everywhere in Eastern Europe – which was expressed in all these revolutions at more or less the same time.

In Romania and Bulgaria, this was mainly a revolt against regimes which were kept in power by the former Soviet Union (which itself at the time was an empire in crisis). But these had adopted in the past a slightly more independent stance than some others in Eastern Europe. In Yugoslavia, there was an implosion which looks like the future rising up to meet the past. This crisis of belief was felt in two specific ways in the Balkans: in the complex inter-ethnic strife which gripped Yugoslavia; and the concentric revolutions against outsiders in the Soviet-backed regimes in Romania and Bulgaria.

An American writer, Robert D. Kaplan (in his *Balkan Ghosts – A Journey Through History* – St. Martin's Press, New York) unravels many of these diverse threads of Balkan history; and follows an earlier commentary and journey through the region: *War in Eastern Europe* by John Reid. This is recommended to all those trying to get a historical perspective on these complex events, which continue and are unfolding even today.

Albania

Introduction

The Illyrians once lived all along the shores of what is now Croatia; and came to the Balkans before even the Greeks. The Roman Emperor Diocletian was one. In the aftermath of the Roman Empire they were forced south, into the mountains. Today Albania is known as the 'Land of Eagles', or *Shqiperia* in Albanian.

Living in Albania

Language and Population

The language – 'Shqip' – has distinct northern and southern dialects, and links with the ancient Etruscan spoken in northern Italy. There are just 3.3 million Albanian citizens today.

Government and Politics

These people live in the chaos surrounding the collapse of the government led by Dr Sali Berisha, and in the wake of corruption and pyramid-selling schemes: the introduction to capitalism most people did not want after fifty years of oppression under the communists.

The social democratic (and formerly communist) party which has come to power is trying to bring order to the country – with little success in the south which is ruled at present by local militias as much as the central government. Many parts of the north are still loyal to the ex-president. This is a situation which needs to be alleviated before travel to the country becomes safe. There are also the so-called 'national salvation committees' which have tried to bring some order to this confusion, and an unstable situation in neighbouring Kosovo (a province of Serbia/Yugoslavia which has a majority Albanian population).

Albania is still best known for its previous hard-line communist regime – inspired by Stalin and its own equally wise leader Enver Hoxha – which found the former Soviet Union and even China, after 1978, too liberal. It had its own xenophobic ideology, like the North Koreans and Kim Il Sung, or like Nicolae Ceaucescu in Romania. We can call each of these systems something like 'national-communist' regimes – the first of which was founded by Stalin. The 'cult of personality' of its leader is of central importance to each of them; and the distrust of outsiders which was a part of communism became a kind of ethnic chauvinism. Each of the countries featured in this book is recovering from a version (extreme or otherwise) of this strange course which Marxism took when these dictatorial rulers insisted that communism was a present reality, and not a future dream, and allied themselves with nationalist sentiment in an effort to maintain their hold on power.

Each of the countries of South-Eastern Europe – between the Mediterranean and the Black Sea – has known something like this. In Albania, there was the most brutal repression of all.

Democracy is coming slowly. But this is still a strange society to find in Europe today, where family and clan allegiances are still more important than the state, and where the extremes of communism and capitalism have met in new, and sometimes unusual syntheses. Consider the incident in late 1997, after the victory of the Socialists, when a debate in parliament (over a proposal to raise VAT) ended with one Socialist MP shooting a Democratic Party and Berisha-supporting opponent. (But this did lead to the raising of his parliamentary immunity, and his prosecution).

The key to the Democratic Party's success during the revolt of 1990-91 was their strict control (organised by the MP who was shot, Azem Hajdari) of the security apparatus set up by Enver Hoxha. The forces which oppose this are best described as anarchistic and/or neo-communist. To many ordinary people, it seemed that the same repressive forces were still in charge when the democrats took over, leading many to prefer local leaders who were known to them – especially with the poor communications between different parts of this mountainous country – and when capitalism had failed to improve their lot overnight as some had expected.

The *Socialist Party* leader, Fatos Nano, was for a time a political prisoner under the previous *Democratic Party* government (which lends him some anti-communist credibility). The Democrats claim that television is back in the hands of the former communists – and so it goes on. Resentment between these two camps – with the absurd sideshow of the monarchists – still runs very deep.

Geography and History

As we have mentioned, dilapidated communications generally – in this country where private ownership of cars still a rarity – have also contributed to this breakdown of law and order; and the poverty which remains throughout the country today. The simplest consumer items are hard to get; and Albania is reckoned to be the poorest country in Europe. All of which means that the people tend to distrust the powers that be in Tirana. Their recent history has meant that most Albanians have lived in isolation from the outside world, but many dream of a new life abroad.

The geographical position is an unfortunate one. This country was always too small to free itself from one imperial yoke after another, without seeking an unfortunate alliance with someone else. So, the Austro-Hungarians replaced the Turks – against whom there were many Albanian revolts, notably by the un-Albanian-sounding George Scanderberg (or Skanderberg) in the fifteenth century. And then there were the Serbs, the Greeks, and the Bulgarians, who all tried to invade and subjugate it during the First Balkan War (1912). The province of Kossovo (or Kosovo) to the north, was ceded to Serbia – and still has a predominantly Albanian population, although it remains a reluctant part of 'Yugoslavia'.

On the other hand, the Greeks claim that many of the southern Albanians are really ethnic Greeks. There is also a sizeable Albanian minority (20%) in neighbouring Macedonia. This is a religious and ethnic fault-line – like that in Bosnia – which could cause great instability in the region in future. Any conflict here would mobilise each of the various nationalist forces in the Balkans; and a far-sighted settlement in the region would take into account the current weakness but also the legitimate aspirations of the Albanians and the great potential for instability which exists between Albania and its neighbours.

It is in the interests of some, perhaps, that this should remain a poor and divided nation.

Communism

During the Second World War, Albania had to fight against Italian and then German Nazi occupation. Then there was also the possibility of invasion by Greece to consider. Its former King Zog (whose son today cuts a rather absurd figure on the political stage) sold his compatriots down the river (to the Italians) and then fled the country.

In such extreme conditions, an extreme political philosophy was born. Enver Hoxha was a partisan (like Tito) who fought not only the Germans, but also the non-communist Albanian resistance. Albania and Yugoslavia went their separate ways at the end of the war (after the reoccupation of Kossovo – or Kosovo – by Tito and his Serb supporters and the massacre of many alleged Albanian 'collaborators'). At a meeting in Moscow in 1944 between Churchill and Stalin, where post-war control of the Balkans was discussed, Albania was not even on the agenda.

Today, the ghost of communism still haunts Albania; there are pavements full of traders and second-hand stalls in squares where statues of Hoxja and Stalin used to stand; which feels like an void which has yet to be filled. There seems to be nothing new to replace the old. But there are the ubiquitous bicycles, which represent one kind of hard-working normality; and the Mercedes cars – still incongruous when one appears on the streets of Tirana – which represent a new kind of dream. In Albania today there are many such jarring contrasts.

In the countryside there are thousands of bunkers – like the ones in North Korea – which were meant to be the way the people would defend themselves from invasion, and which also illustrate the paranoia of its former rulers. People live in some of them.

Poverty was here before, but basically it was disguised, or more generalised. At least the essentials of life were there – and even if they weren't no-one was going to complain. Nowadays it is more like everyone for themselves. There is satellite TV here too – Italian game shows are most popular TV programmes – and in this last bastion of the most extreme form of communism, capitalism also seems to wear its most inhuman face. The greatest goal for many is to emigrate.

The *Foreign and Commonwealth Office (FCO) Travel Advice Unit* says that this is still a lawless country; and advises against all travel there. See BBC Ceefax p.470 onwards, or the Internet under the address http://www.fco.gov.uk/, or call 0171-238 4503/4504 for their latest recommendations.

The Climate

There are hot summers and extremely cold winters. If you go, spring and autumn are the best time to visit.

The Language

Italian and Greek are also spoken, and some English, also see above.

The Currency

This is the *lek*, divided into 1200 *qindarka*. It may not be imported or exported. US dollars are the most useful currency. A few hotels and restaurants – amnd the main banks – take credit cards. Otherwise dollars are exchanged unoffically outside the bank on Skanderberg Square.

Getting There

The route via Corfu is one way in (see under *Tourism* below); or you bcan try going via Athens. Airlines with routes into Tirana are *Austrian Airlines, Lufthansa, Malev Hungarian Airlines, Olympic Airlines* and *Swissair*. When ferry services start again between Corfu and Saranda, the local travel agencies in this Greek island popular with British holidaymakers will be the people to contact. Some Britons live in Greece, and one or two of the more hardy may consider moving on to this more rugged coast... Tour operators include *Exodus* and *Explore Worldwide*. *Regent Holidays* (15 St. John Street, Bristol BS1 2HR; tel 0117-921 1711; fax 0117-925 4866; e-mail 106041.1470@compuserve.com) is an agency which offers 'individual arrangements, a one-week group tour and a longer one combining northern Greece and Albania.'

Visas

'These are now issued on arrival in Albania without prior authorisation' for EU and US nationals. Contacting travel agencies like *Regent Travel* who know the visa situation may be the best idea – but is not always necessary. Via the Albanian Embassy a completed visa application form, passport, photo, visa fee etc. then need to get to the *Ministry of Foreign Affairs* in Tirana. In the light of the *FCO* advice above, residence is not recommended.

Customs

You need to fill in the currency declaration forms for foreign currency when entering or leaving Albania. There are no restrictions on items for personal use (but quite a few smugglers) and visitors should declare all the items they bring in of any value, and keep the slips for their departure.

Utilities and Communications

Electricity is 220 volts AZ, 50Hz as throughout this region.

Communications in much of the country by telephone are poor; as is transport. Communications with the outside world are difficult as well at present when some airlines have suspended their flights to Tirana. The country code is 355, the Tirana code 42.

Health

Take your medicines with you; and get worldwide emergency evacuation health cover (see the *General Overview* at the beginning of this book). Vaccinations for Hepatitis A, polio and typhoid are advised, and you should consult your doctor well in advance of departure.

Accommodation

There are some three-star hotels in Tirana; one of them is called the *Hotel California*. The biggest is the *Hotel Europapark* (Bulevardi Deshmoret e Kombit, Tirana; tel 42-32-011; fax 42-35-030). Another option is the private B&B or guest house accommodation which is becoming available in some places. *Lufthansa, Austrian Airlines* and some others can arrange hotel accommodation for you, here and elsewhere in the region.

Getting Around

The roads and buses are in a poor condition, So are trains. The preferred method of transport for westerners and the richer locals are the four-wheel drive vehicles and hire cars. Generally, 'international' facilities are relatively undeveloped. For example, at the time of writing there are no Hertz car hire offices, no American Express offices, and no international banks. Street lighting in Tirana is poor; so a torch is one item to pack.

Cultural Background

Guide Books:
The *Blue Guide to Albania* or *Albania – A guide and illustrated journal* (Bradt Publications).

Social Life and Entertainment:
There are quite a few bars and restaurants in Tirana and on the coast. Local wine and cognac, as well as imported beer, Italian pizzas and pasta, as well as Turkish or Italian-style coffee are all available where the tourists go, or used to go. This is mainly along the 'Riviera of Flowers' from *Saranda* northwards. Social life means entertaining at home, and is largely connected with their hotels and embassies as far as expats and visitors are concerned. There are relatively few other Britons and Americans here (and quite a few more Italians and Germans) nearly all working for the international organisations and development agencies.

Shopping:
Local craft items can be found. There are recordings of Albanian music in the kiosks, some foreign-currency supermarkets, and seasonal markets for vegetables, lamb, cheese, eggs, and other local produce. Visitors tend to be expected to pay more than the locals.

Useful Contacts

Albanian Embassy: 38 Grosvenor Gardens, London SW1 0EB; tel 0171-730 5709; fax 0171-730 5747.
Albania Society of Great Britain: Vine Cottage, Church Hanborough, Witney, Oxfordshire OX8 8AA.
Regent Holidays: See above.
Sunny Home Travel Agency in Saranda: tel 34-79-88.

Working in Albania

Economy and Trade

See above for a general overview; and a few sources of information in the *Business and Industry Report* below. Prospects have been blighted by political instability and the failure of the 'get-rich-quick' pyramid-selling schemes. Albania's development will also be tied to its relations with its neighbours. This is hampered by poor communications, its geographical location, the emigration of many of its people and, as the Albanians see it, the indifference of richer countries to its plight.

Employment

Tourism: This offers some scope at the specialist or 'adventure' end of the market, combined with trips to northern Greece and – especially – Corfu. When the political situation improves, ferry services are likely to start again between Corfu and Saranda; travel agencies in this Greek island popular with British holidaymakers are the people to contact for some local expertise. The picturesque Albanian village of *Qeparo* on the coast is the location for a project funded by the EU to introduce small-scale tourism. With the many charters in summer, this route via Corfu offers the prospect of a cost-effective way into the rest southern Albania as well, with attractions including the Roman, Illyrian and Byzantine remains of *Butrinti* with its acropolis, theatre and baptistery, mountain villages, its coastline and beaches.

Regent Holidays (15 St. John Street, Bristol BS1 2HR; tel 0117-921 1711; fax 0117-925 4866; e-mail 106041.1470@compuserve.com) is a long-established specialist in the formerly communist countries and offers 'individual arrangements, a one-week group tour and a longer one combining northern Greece and Albania.'

Doing Business

For Albania, the restoration of law and order – and a regional political settlement – is badly needed. This would encourage future development and more business opportunities. The etiquette for doing business will be formal, as for many other countries featured in this book. This will not be aided by the convention – as in Bulgaria – that a nod of the head means 'No' and shaking your head means 'Yes'.

Business and Industry Report

The *East European Trade Council* (tel 0171-222 7622; fax 0171-222 5359) has a business library, and can offer advice on business and trade throughout Eastern Europe. Another contact for business people is the British Government's *Know How Fund* which sponsors projects in Albania and its neighbours: *KHF*, Foreign and Commonwealth Office, Old Admiralty Building, Whitehall, London SW1A 2AF; tel 0171-210 0065. These projects are often administered by the *Overseas Development Administration*.

Bosnia-Herzegovina

Introduction

Bosnia-Herzegovina (or 'Hercegovina') has exactly the same borders as the former Yugoslav republic of the same name, even after four years of futile war between the federalists (who wanted a united country) and Serb nationalists – which became complicated by some Croatian and Muslim nationalism too. A united country where these communities often lived side by side has become divided, as if there had been a war in Northern Ireland, and neither side had won.

Here there were three sides: the Bosnian Muslims, Croats and Serbs (see also *Croatia* and *Serbia*); and the country itself is roughly triangular in shape, with Croatia on its western and northern sides – the disputed provinces of Western and Eastern Slavonia which are now back in Croatian hands – and Serbia and Montenegro to the east with just a small corrridor down to the sea and crossing Croatia which makes this also a 'Mediterranean' country.

The *Foreign and Commonwealth Office* advises against unnecessary travel to Bosnia; and you should take precautions to avoid theft and to ensure your personal safety. See BBC Ceefax p.470 onwards, or the Internet under the address http://www.fco.gov.uk/. Or call 0171-238 4503/4504 for their latest recommendations of their *Travel Advice Unit*.

Living in Bosnia

Climate

This is a continental climate – warmer on its short coastline – with warm summers and cold winters, and colder in the more mountainous north. It rains frequently in spring and autumn.

Residence and Entry

British and American passport holders presently do not require a visa to enter Bosnia; but these regulations may change. You are advised to contact the *Bosnian Embassy* (see below) for advice. To work or do business a letter of invitation will be required. Longer-term residents require a residence and work permit. You may also need the landing card you get on the plane as a kind of 'exit visa' as well; so keep this if you are given one, for your return. Entry may be difficult at some land border crossings; but is now safe if you travel via Sarajevo Airport.

Currency and Customs

This divided country now has a single currency – although the ones which work still tend to be deutschmarks and dollars. The new Bosnian currency is – or is intended to be – fully convertible; and pegged to the deutschmark. This came about because the IMF refused to allow loans to Bosnia until it had a fully functioning central bank and currency.

Getting There

This is possible by plane or coach nowadays. Contact *Austrian Airlines* which was the first non-Balkan commercial airline to return to Sarajevo after a four-year break; with a service operating on Mondays, Tuesdays and Thursdays. Or try *Croatia Airlines* from Zagreb (see *Croatia*) or *Adria Airlines* also via Zagreb (see *Slovenia*) and contact these airlines also for delivery of airfreight. From the airport there are now regular bus services to the city centre; and into the other Bosnian cities.

Rail travel to Bosnia is not recommended. Getting there by coach is easier and means contacting *Eurolines* in London (tel 0990-143219) which can get you to a surprising range of destinations: Donj Vakuf, Jaijce, Kakanj, Kiseljak, Sarajevo, Travnik, Visoko, Vitez and Zenica.

Another route is via Croatia, from Split or Dubrovnik; where you will still see signs to Sarajevo, and can reach Mostar and the western parts of the country by bus. The road to southern Dalmatia passes through Bosnia – where there are cursory customs checks – before you are back in Croatia again. If you are driving, bring all your documents, and an international driving licence is better, although your national or EU one may be accepted.

Communications

The country code is 387; and 99 is the international code out of the country. The city code for Sarajevo is 71.

Books and Maps

These may be obtained from *Stanfords* (12-14 Long Acre, Covent Garden, London WCE 9PL; tel 0171-836 1321 – which may send you its Eastern European catalogue; or the nearby *Zwemmer Bookshop* (28 Denmark Street, London WC2 8NJ; tel 0171-379 6253). One organisation which can mail books and their magazine to almost all Eastern European destinations is the *Good Book Guide* (see under *Books* in the *General Overview*.

A more unusual source of maps of Bosnia is the *CIA*; which British readers may be surprised to learn has to release this kind of declassified material: a catalogue can be obtained just by giving the CIA a call, at their *Public Affairs* office in the USA: tel 703-351-2053. To subscribe to all CIA declassified publications, the annual subscription fee in the USA is $500. To order, call 202-707-9527; or write to *DOCEX Exchange and Gifts Division*, Library of Congress, Washington, DC 20540-4230. Economic information as well as maps and other documents will be sent to you.

Embassies and Useful Addresses

British Embassy: 8 Tine Ujevice, 71000 Sarajevo; tel 71-204-781; fax 71-204-780.

US Embassy: Djure Djakovice 43, Sarajevo; tel 71-659-743 or 645-992 or 445-700.

Bosnian Embassy: 320 Regent Street, London W1R 5AB; tel 0171-255-3758; fax 0171-255-3760.

Bosnian Embassy: Suite 760, 1707 L Street, NW, Washington, DC 20036; tel 212-833-3612/3; fax 212-833-2061.
Ministry of Foreign Affairs: Vojvode Putnika 3, 71000 Sarajevo; tel 71-213-777; fax 71-653-592.

Working in Bosnia

Business and Industry Report

Bosnia is booming. Which sounds unlikely, but is more or less an accurate picture of the growing economy within the Muslim-Croat Federation according to those on the ground. There is building and reconstruction work going on, meaning that engineers and others are needed. A stable and convertible currency – if this is successful – will put Bosnia at an advantage compared to some of its neighbours. Life is returning slowly to normal in this country which was devastated by war, despite an abnormal political situation today which makes communications between the *Republika Srpska* part of the country and the *Muslim-Croat Federation* still difficult.

The *World Bank* has been coordinating this main $5-billion recovery programme. It found that '70% of productive capacity was intact, and management was still there, exempted from military service and maintaining contact with the West.' There is greater scope here, too, to start anew, and leave behind the old centrally planned economy – the destruction of which has been part of the tragedy of the country, but could also be an advantage. In Bosnia, they are starting again from scratch. It is moving to a market economy, like all its neighbours, and may be less rigid and bureaucratic than some.

The more enlightened donors are trying to organise their programmes within this free market context, so that these projects can also attract private investment. What Bosnia needs now is investment, and the federal government is making strenuous efforts to attract it. One example is the scheme of 'political risk guarantees,' a way of protecting joint ventures or export deals with Bosnian firms. The partners involved at present are German, Austrian and Italian, with some others, including some from Britain. This should take off, and so should more western airlines flying into Sarajevo. Improving internal communications, and a refurbished and retarmaced airport, are encouraging several to consider this (*Austrian Airlines* was the first) and there is a mini-property boom going on in the Bosnian capital too.

Commercial Contacts

The *Bosnia-Herzegovina* desk of the *Department of Trade and Industry*, (Kingsgate House, 66-74 Victoria Street, London SW1H) can provide an information pack (or can be contacted on 0171-215-4752 – 215-5000 for the switchboard). See the *General Overview* section, and also *Commercial Contacts* for *Romania* below for details of the *PHARE* programme providing aid for Central and Eastern European countries.

Bulgaria

Introduction

Bulgaria is located on the Black Sea Coast, between Romania to the north and Greece and Turkey to the south. Serbia and F.Y.R. Macedonia are its western neighbours. The population of about 8,500,000 is in an area of 43,000 square miles or so. The capital *Sofia*, in the west, has 1,200,000 inhabitants. The *Balkan* and the *Rhodope Mountains* stretch across the country to the Black Sea coast with its sandy beaches occasionally frequented by Britons. The climate is never extreme, with warm summers, and snow on the mountains in winter. The economy is traditionally agricultural; and Bulgaria is famous for its exported wine. Food-processing and packaging are important; and there are heavy industries like engineering as well as newer ones like biotechnology. But the transition to a market economy has been slow. There is high inflation here; and still high unemployment.

Handshaking is a common form of greeting in Bulgaria (as in France for instance) and as in much of the region small gifts from your country – and which say something about you – are also appreciated by the hospitable Bulgarians.

Living in Bulgaria

History

Bismarck's *Treaty of Berlin*, and his solution to the 'Eastern Question', caused immediate upheaval in Macedonia; with the Turks trying to salvage their position (and raping and exterminating the local population – see *Macedonia*). This is somehow where modern Bulgarian history begins, with the Russians advancing through the northern half of the country on the pretext of restoring order. They supported the Bulgarian claims to Macedonia and what is now Macedonian Greece.

It used to be all Bulgaria. The Bulgarians, in the tenth and then the thirteenth centuries, had advanced as far as the Aegean in the south; and all the way westwards to the Adriatic: a 'Greater Bulgaria' which many were dreaming of once again, but which this Treaty now denied them. History is Byzantine in this region. It moves around in circles in a way which makes it difficult to distinguish fact from fiction. All these myths of national greatness have sustained many Balkan peoples in their struggles for independence – and always there is this nostalgia for long-extinct empires.

Concentric circles, which meet other concentric circles... The great movements of a history which seem discontinuous and random have left whole populations behind; and brought others into view. This is one way Bulgarians see themselves today, as a great nation which was left behind by history, a tide which may one day turn.

There are the many tragedies of Bulgarian history. Where now are the all Bulgarians who used to live in northern Greece? Or the Turks who remained in

Bulgaria? Who now remembers the Sephardic Jewish community there – one of the largest in the world – which lived in Salonika in what is now Greek Macedonia, and which fared much better under the Ottomans than in independent Bulgaria?

This was all Bulgaria in the nineteenth century; and these peoples have been a part of Bulgarian history too.

A chronological account gives a more orderly impression. Here, it seems like a continuous development (the process of nation building which is the tale all these countries tell about themselves). So, the Bulgars – like the Magyars – and the Turks themselves – were originally from Central Asia. It was around AD 681 that about a quarter of a million of them came to this south-eastern corner of Europe, with their leader *Khan Asparuh*, and settled down, mingling with the Slavic peoples who had arrived 150 years or so before them.

In AD 865, the Bulgarians became the first of these Balkan peoples to accept Christianity. (The Macedonians dispute this claim, and say that this happened in Macedonia). The monks Cyril and Methodius set off from Bulgaria/Macedonia to convert the Russians – with their newly developed Cyrillic script. So Bulgaria (or Macedonia) was the birthplace of Christianity in the other Slavic or Slavicised countries in Eastern Europe as well – and is its oldest and most civilised nation.

The Bulgarian concept of nationhood was also quite pluralistic in those days: a Jewish community lived and flourished here (and its record in the Second World War of anti-Semitism was much better than that of most of its neighbours). In the early eleventh century, the Bulgarian *King Samuel* was defeated by the Byzantine Emperor at *Strumnitsa* (who then killed or blinded thousands of his Bulgarian prisoners). This was the beginning of the end of Bulgaria's independence and its greatest power, which was initiated by *King Boris*. The country was brought back into the Greek sphere of influence, although there was a national revival under Kings *Kaloyen* and *Assen II* in the fourteenth century. This was followed by Turkish rule from 1393 to 1877.

Who outside the Balkans has heard of *Vasil Levsky*, who led the nineteenth century guerila war against the Turks which resulted in the *Treaty of Berlin*? He is the Simon Bolivar of Bulgarian history. Or of these Bulgarian kings who carved out a vast empire from Albania to the Black Sea in the early Middle Ages, one which frequently threatened that of the emperors in Constantinople? It seems like ancient history, but these events are not quite like this for the locals – or British and American history may be more peripheral than we ourselves had known...

Great wars have started in the Balkans; and we can see the apparently unimportant question of Bulgarian relations with Macedonia (which it again claims as its own) as one which may again take centre stage in world affairs.

It was so on February 19, 1873, when their liberator and national hero Vasil Levsky was executed, sparking the guerila war which the Turks savagely suppressed. His hideout was in the Stara Planina (the *Old Mountain* more generally known as the Mountain – or *Balkan* – to the Turks which gave the whole region its name). Then, Oscar Wilde, Victor Hugo and Ivan Turgenev wrote in support of the nationalist Bulgarians and this was a *cause célèbre* thoughout Europe.

Residence and Entry

British passport holders require a visa to enter Bulgaria for more than 30 days, which authorised travel agents like *Balkantourist* (Boulevard Vitosha 1, 1040

Sofia, tel 2-43-331) can arrange. Or these may still be obtained at the border. US citizens require a visa to enter the country. A letter of invitation is required. Longer-term residents require a residence and work permit; and those working or looking for work in Bulgaria should register at the local police station. Enquiries about work and residence permits should also be made to a Bulgarian consulate or embassy abroad before departure.

The processing time for a multiple entry visa is currently around ten days: 'In cases where a foreigner is employed by a company or institution in Bulgaria he should apply with the letter from the Employer for his single or multiple entry visa with validity up to three months. Further in Bulgaria he can arrange with local emigration and labour employment authorities his working and residence permit...' (from the leaflet 'Basic Visa Information for Bulgaria' available from its Embassy). You may also need the landing card you get on the plane as a kind of 'exit visa' as well; so keep this if you are given one, for your return.

Getting There

This is possible by plane or coach or train. Contact any high street travel agency; or *Balkan Holidays* (independent travel tel 0171-543 5588). *Balkan Holidays* was set up in 1966 with the aim of establishing Bulgaria as a popular holiday destination. Based in Sofia, it operates in 17 countries – including the UK and USA – and from 13 UK airports. Scheduled flights are by *Balkanair, TAROM, Adria Airways* and charters run in conjunction with *Balkanair* and the Bulgarian airline *Air Via*. Recently it has expanded its operations to include Croatia and Slovenia as well as Romania (see the following chapters). *British Airways* and *Lufthansa* also have regular flights to Sofia. From the airport, there are regular buses to the city centre, much better than the taxis.

Rail Travel: Rail travel within Bulgaria is surprisingly straightforward. First class is recommended. The central railway station in Sofia (like many others) is a place to avoid if you can. Routes in are via Bucharest, Belgrade, Thessaloniki, and Istanbul. A metro is under construction in Sofia.

Coach Travel: This means contacting *Eurolines* in London (tel 0990-143219) which can get you by coach to Sofia.

Driving: If you are driving, bring all your documents with you, and an international driving licence is better, although your national one may be accepted. Allow extra journey time for crossing the various borders. Speed limits are 50 kph (31mph) in towns; 80 kph (50mph) outside towns; and 120 kph (75mph) on motorways. There is zero tolerance of alcohol; and traffic fines can be on the spot.

Car Hire: *Autotechnika Ltd*: (Hertz Franchisee) 10 Gurko Str., 1000 Sofia: tel 2-980-0461; fax 2-988-5729.

Travel Agencies

American Express: (representative: 'Megatours') 1 Levski Street, Sofia 10000; tel 2-9814201. American Express has two other offices in Bulgaria.

Liberty International (UK) Ltd: 11 Grosvenor Street, Chester CH1 2DD; tel 01244-351115; fax 01244-351116; e-mail liberty@chester.itsnet.co.uk. For full destination management services, including conference and meeting

organisation, guide and tour services etc. Associate office in Sofia.
Balkan Holidays: Sofia House, 19 Conduit Street, London W1R 9TD; tel 0171-543 5566 – or 0171-543 5555 for reservations – or 0171-543 5588 for independent travel; fax 0171-543 557. This longest-established tour operator specialises in summer and winter holidays in the region, mainly to Bulgaria, but also Croatia, Slovenia and Romania.
Overseas Business Travel Ltd: 8 Minories, London EC3N 1BJ; tel 0171-702 2468; fax 0171-488 1199. Offices in Moscow and Almaty; specialists in Romania, Bulgaria, Russia, and all Eastern European countries for business travel, flights and accommodation, visa support etc.

Removals

Corstjens Eastern Europe Movers: (head office) P.O. Box 71145, 1008 BC Amsterdam, The Netherlands; tel 31-2949-1514; fax 31-2949-3536. Offices in Bucharest, Sofia, Belgrade, Moscow, Budapest, Prague, Kiev and Warsaw.

A leading freight forwarding company with operations throughout Eastern Europe is *Eurogate International Forwarding Co. Ltd*: tel 0171-459 2900; fax 0171-588 9058. Also see the *General Overview* section for some UK-based international removers.

Health Service and Hospitals

See the *General Overview* under *Health and Hospitals* for the treatment you may receive free and what you have to pay for. There is a Reciprocal Health Agreement with the UK. Basic treatment is available but specialist treatments may not be. There are no international hospitals.

Culture and Daily Life

Festivals and Folklore:
'Balkan Folklore is part of the living fabric of village life. It documents the life and tribulations of a very proud nation – translated into lively verse, poetic songs, melancholic melodies, fanciful fairy tales...' and so on. See the brochure *Bulgaria, just unique* for information on city life, the countryside, its seaside resorts, and festivals and folklore – like the *Koprivshtitsa Folklore Festival* and the *Rose Festival* of Kazanlak. Contact *Balkan Holidays* or the *Committee of Tourism at the Council of Ministers of the Republic of Bulgaria*: 1, Sv. Nedelya Sq., 1040 Sofia; tel 2-84-131; fax 2-981-25-15.

Embassies and Tourist Offices

British Embassy: Boulevard Vassil Levski 65-67, Sofia 1000; tel 2-885-361-2 or 885-325.
US Embassy: Saborna Street 1, Unit 1335, Sofia; tel 2-884-801.
Bulgarian Embassy: 186-188 Queen's Gate, London SW7 5HL; tel 0171-584 9400/9433. General visa information tel 01891-171208; or for subsequent enquiries contact 0171-584 9433 from 2.30pm to 3.30pm.
Bulgarian Embassy: 1621 22nd Street, NW, Washington, DC 20008; tel 202-387-7969
Balkan Holidays (USA) Ltd: Suite 508, 41 East 42nd Street, New York, NY 10017; tel 212-573-5530.

Public Holidays

New Year's Day; March 3; Easter Monday; May 1; May 24; Christmas Eve; Christmas Day.

Working in Bulgaria

Business and Industry Report

Currency: 1 Lev (BGL) = 100 stotinki

Inflation in 1997 was 566%. It is projected to fall to 27% in 1998; so Bulgaria is experiencing a dose of economic realism. The *Comecon* markets of Eastern Europe and the FSU have come and gone; and the same prospect of privatisation and competition in world markets faces Bulgaria as it does all these countries; although it was more comfortable with the previous economic order than some others.

There was a banking and currency crisis in 1996, when protests against the former communist government began (inspired by demonstrations in neighbouring Serbia). This did not quite come to world attention; but did help to change the government. As in Romania, the anti-communists are now in charge, and *Petar Stoyanov* is the present pro-reform President. In the 1997 parliamentary elections, the *Union of Democratic Forces (UDF)* coalition came to power; and has been working since then with international organisations to create a more stable economic background; and a currency (like that in Estonia) which is now tied to the deutschmark.

Some of the problems are the relatively large percentage of pensioners; and a population 80% of which is said by the World Bank to live below the poverty line. The atmosphere today is more pro-western and pro-business than before as the previous system has been shown to have failed and a large number of major industries have been sold off; or shared out in the form of vouchers like those which were issued in Poland or Hungary. Bulgarian people are now more realistic about the change from communism to capitalism – and know from bitter experience that the latter does not always bring instant riches.

There are many business contacts being made now which will bear fruit in future. One venture which notably didn't was the *Rover* car factory in Varna; which has now ceased its operations.

The goverment insists this pro-western stance is not a barrier to good relations with Russia (which has adopted its own private sector policies too). In fact, there are good trading connections there which may be useful to British and other western investors and entrepreneurs; and give Bulgaria an important strategic position in the region. There is also a gas pipeline connection with Russia; and a new one being built to Turkey which ties the country to developments in that country; and beyond in the *Caspian and Central Asia* region. It will be the transit route for some of this natural gas into Serbia, Macedonia and Greece. Black Sea ports like *Varna* are already important for shipments of oil and gas exploration and drilling equipment to Azerbaijan and the Caspian region.

Employment

In the world of work, English is not very widely spoken; your colleagues are as likely to speak German, and more likely to speak Russian. The etiquette involves dressing neatly, much as you would in Britain or the United States, and learning to put up with the minor inconveniences of the bureaucracy; and a sometimes more informal way of doing things. There is a range of local agents and consultants (and some lawyers) who may be of assistance in your search for employment and business contacts; which may be contacted through your Embassy.

Teaching:
The *Central Bureau* (10 Spring Gardens, London SW1A 2BN; tel 0171-389 4004; fax 0171-389 4426) recruits a number of teachers for foreign language secondary schools in Bulgaria in a programme run by the Bulgarian Ministry of Science, Education, and Technology. *English Contacts Abroad* also provides a research and direct contacts service for EFL teachers in all CEE countries (PO Box 126, Oxford OX2 6UB, UK). Write in the first instance for a questionnaire.

Tourism:
Crystal Holidays (Crystal House, The Courtyard, Arlington Road, Surbiton, Surrey KT6 6BW; tel 0181-241 5111) requires a small number of representatives for skiing holidays in Borovets and Pamperova. Previous experience and fluent Bulgarian are desirable. So may *Balkan Holidays* (Sofia House, 19 Conduit Street, London W1R 9TD; tel 0171-543 5555). High street travel agencies are a source of brochures which will show you which of the major tour operators currently have operations there – and applications and/or enquiries should be made well before the next 'season'; at least by January for summer of the following year; and similarly for skiing. There will be an application form and information pack which most tour operators will send you.

Commercial Contacts

The *Bulgaria Desk* of the *Department of Trade and Industry* (Bay 756, Kingsgate House, 66-74 Victoria Street, London SW1E 6SW) can provide an information pack (for commercial or business purposes) which contains a list of UK companies with Bulgarian links. The *British-Bulgarian Chamber of Commerce* is at the Embassy address in London (above): tel 0171-584 8333. It has links with the *London Chamber of Commerce and Industry* (tel 0171-203 1828; fax 0171-489 0391). The *Bulgarian Chamber of Commerce and Industry* (Suborna Street 11A, 1040 Sofia; tel 2-872-631; fax 2-873-209) can also provide commercial advice and information. See the *General Overview* section – and *Commercial Contacts* also under *Romania* for details of the *PHARE* programme providing aid for Central and Eastern European countries. The *PHARE Coordination Unit* in Bulgaria is at the *Ministry of Finance* (102 Rakovski Str., 1040 Sofia; tel 2-869-219; fax 2-872-601). Or contact the *British Embassy Commercial Section* on fax 359-2-492-0345 which will have details of these and other investments and joint ventures.

Croatia

Introduction

Croatia is a southern Mediterranean country whose capital city Zagreb is just under two and a half hours' flight time from London. It is much closer to Italy, its neighbour to the northwest; and here, on the Adriatic coast, an Italian influence can be felt. Zagreb is inland; and has a more 'Central European' feel. The cultural influences here go back to the Austro-Hungarian Empire; and the more recent effects of communism which linger on. A country which rightly could be said to be one of contrasts, it looks to a Central European future; but its initial reluctance to comply with the terms of the Dayton Agreementhas has hindered its acceptance by the international community; and delayed its membership of the European Union.

Croatia is also once again welcoming British visitors and tourists who fondly remember holidays here, and have returned first of all to Istria in the north; and now to the whole of the Dalmatian coast. Its many attractions include food and wine, the 1,777km of coastline and many islands, and folk traditions like the Moreska dance on the island of Korcula – the more theatrical Croatian equivalent of English Morris dancing – as well as the largely restored architecture and city walls of Dubrovnik, the pearl in the Croatian tourism crown.

Economically, a Hungarian-style fast-track privatisation programme should see most state-run enterprises in private hands by the turn of the century. Many of its most important banks, hotels, utilities and industrial companies also represent significant investment opportunities, with a number already in partially foreign ownership. This programme, along with some greater acceptance of civil rights (for which Croatia now has an impartial Ombudsman) and some concessions by President Franjo Tudjman of the Croatian Democratic Union (HDZ) to the Social Democrat-led opposition (the SDP), are the main basis of Croatia's claim to membership of Nato and to be in the second wave of CEE entrants to the European Union.

Living in Croatia

Political, Economic and Geographical Structure

Although Croatia held elections in 1997 which gave the HDZ a majority in Parliament, the autocratic style of President Tudjman, and bias in the state-controlled media, are both obstacles to Croatia's acceptance as a fully democratic country. This political landscape is unlikely to change before the next general election in 1999; or when the ailing Mr Tudjman retires from the scene. The evolution of events does appear to favour the consolidation of liberal democracy; and there is now a more stable and prosperous middle class emerging. Most Croatians look north to Central Europe as their model (just as most Poles and Czechs are looking west and not east). But Croatia is one of these South-Eastern

European countries too, along with its neighbours in former Yugoslavia).

The current cultural and political scene is dominated by Croatian nationalism. The nation's ubiquitous symbol, the *sahovnica*, a red and white chequered shield crowned by the coats of arms of Illyria, Dubrovnik, Dalmatia, Istria and Slavonia – the principal regions – is everywhere; and like many other such symbols harks back to the Middle Ages. It has more sinister associations for those who remember the Nazi-backed Croatian government in the Second World War whose willing participation in the genocide of Serbian and Jewish people alike is sometimes glossed over by the local historians. This was a conflict which has echoes for Croatian and Serbian people today.

Perhaps a more mature democracy could remove this controversial *shovnica* from its red, white and blue tricolour flag – an unlikely prospect at present. But the climate is changing; and a more balanced reading of history which can accept all the complex strands of Croatian national identity should emerge, perhaps when the influence of the HDZ has declined.

Political Parties:
The other main party in Croatia is the *SDP*, supported at present by about 20% of the population; it is the heir to the former communist party; but as in the other formerly communist countries the nationalists (as represented by the *HDZ*) have also taken over some of the mantle of communism; and in its close relationship with the state the HDZ functions in some respects more like the old-style communist party than a liberal and democratic one.

Croatia does not have such long-established traditions of independence as some of its neighbours to the north; and the political scene is fragmented. Nevertheless, the country is now firmly set on a democratic course; and prospects for development are good as plans for economic reform are implemented and a new middle class emerges.

Pros and Cons of Moving to Croatia

For those considering living and working in Croatia, or those wishing to start a business there, the country has one enormous advantage: its location. Around the Mediterranean, France, Spain (and latterly Italy and Greece) have always been the traditonal destinations of expatriates getting away from it all to a life in the sun – and tourism originally led many to consider living and working there on a more long-term basis. Of all the central and eastern European countries featured in this book, Croatia is the only one with a similar advantage; ten million used to flock to is shores each year; and many are returning to enjoy the Mediterranean lifestyle and climate. Today there are many opportunities for investors and prospective residents to cater for the visitors who are returning to this enchanting and fascinating country.

Getting There

Charters:
At the time of writing, seat-only charter flights are available through some travel agents, notably Thomson which features several destinations in Istria in its 1998 brochure: *Thomson Tour Operations Ltd.*, Greater London House, Hampstead Road, London NW1 7SD; tel 0171-387 9321; fax 0171-387 8451 (or telephone 0990-502560).

Other charter and package tour operators include Palmair from Bournemouth to Dubrovnik and Cavtat on the Dalmation Coast: *Palmair*, 2 Albert Road,

Bournemouth, Dorset BH1 1BY; tel 01202-299299; fax 01202-294733; and Transun from Gatwick and Manchester to Dubrovnik: *Transun Holidays*: 70 St Clements, Oxford OX4 1AH; tel 01865-798888; fax 01865-793041. Saga Holidays are likely to expand its (so far successful) Croatian operations from April 1998: *Saga Holidays*, The Saga Building, Middleburg Square, Folkestone, Kent CT20 1AZ; tel 01303-711111; fax 01303-221638.

Bond Tours (tel 0181—786 8511) from Heathrow to the Dalmatian coast, *DIT* (tel 0171-379 6249) to the island of Korcula, and *Hungarian Air Tours* (tel 0171-437 9405), using BA scheduled services to Zagreb for their city breaks, complete this list of UK-based operators in Croatia. Most travel via Zagreb. Bond Tours goes to Split; and Palmair was the first and is so far the only UK tour operator to use the newly refurbished Dubrovnik Airport, the most direct route for those wishing to get to the Dalmatian coast and its islands.

Another operator flying direct to Dubrovnik is *Jet Air/Jet Tours* based in Brussels (which explains the large groups of Belgian holidaymakers to be found in the city's otherwise underoccupied hotels. Italians, Germans, Austrians and others tend to arrive by ferry, car or train; and these are other routes into the country for those travelling to Croatia through Europe). Also see the brochures of major tour operators like *Airtours*, *British Airways Holidays*, *First Choice*, *Panorama*, and *Skytours* for the latest packages featuring Croatia; and one which has included Croatia in its brochure is *Balkan Holidays*, Sofia House, 19 Conduit Street, London W1R 9TD; tel 0171-543 5555 (reservations); or 0171-543 5588 (independent travel). High street travel agencies are your best source of charter flights (which are generally in the summer season only).

Onward Connections:
Your onward travel, flight, hotel and other transfers, as well as excellent guiding services, can all be arranged by *ATLAS Travel* in Dubrovnik with branches throughout Croatia; they are best contacted direct by fax ('for the attention of Mr Tonko Kolendic'): 00385-20 41 11 00. Atlas can also be contacted on 212-697-6767 in New York (60 East 42nd Street, New York, NY 10165) or on 202-667-7411 in Washington (their marketing office). Ferry transfers on *Jarodrolinija* line for passengers and/or cars from Rijeka and Split down to Dubrovnik can be booked in the UK through *Dalmatian and Istrian Travel* in London (tel 0171-379 6249). Other local car ferries link the main islands like Hvar and Korcula; if you are travelling around in summer, it is also worth enquiring about the hydrofoil service which Atlas operates between Rijeka and Split; and to Rab and Hvar islands.

Scheduled Services:
Then there are the scheduled air services. *Alitalia* from London Heathrow via Rome can take you 'direct' to Dubrovnik. *Croatia Airlines* goes from Gatwick and Heathrow to Zagreb and Split (to the latter sometimes direct and sometimes via Zagreb) and is also another way of getting to Dubrovnik, with a connecting flight from Zagreb, or onwards to Pula in Istria: tel 0171-306 3138.

British Airways (tel 0345-222111) operates six times a week from Gatwick to Zagreb. Any onward connections have to be with Croatia Airlines but BA is at the time of writing also considering introducing flights to Dubrovnik (initially from May to October).

Guidebooks and Information:
There are no dedicated guidebooks to Croatia. Lonely Planet's *Eastern Europe on a Shoestring* is a possibility (head office: PO Box 617, Hawthorn, Victoria 3122, Australia; UK: 10 Barley Mow Passage, Chiswick, London W4 4PH; USA: 155 Filbert Street, Suite 251, Oakland, CA 94607). *Let's Go Eastern Europe* is another.

The Croatian National Tourist Board office in London (presently based at: 2 The Lanchesters, 162-164 Fulham Palace Road; tel 0181-563 7979; fax 0181-563 2616) will provide maps and brochures free of charge. In the USA this is at 300 Lanidex Plaza, Parsippany, NJ 07054; tel 201-428-0707; fax 201-428-3386.

The Croatian National Tourist Board head office can also be contacted: *Croatian National Tourist Board*, Glavni Ured, Ilica 1a, 10000 Zagreb; tel 1-4556-455; fax 1-428-674/430-858. They publish a range of brochures, a rather general *Passport to Croatia*, and the multilingual *Welcome to Croatia* tourist magazine (address: Trg bana Josipa Jelacica 1, 10000 Zagreb; tel 1-455-6455; fax 1-428-674), as well as brochures on all the main regions. They can also provide a useful *Croatia Tourist Map*.

History

We could begin with that map. Featuring as it must the arc of the Dalmatian coast and the northern part of the country stretching from the Istrian peninsula in the west to the Eastern Slavonia region (the scene of the most bitter fighting with neighbouring Serbia) it looks a little like a 'C' or a capital 'T', and includes some more space: Slovenia and Hungary to the north. The rest is Bosnia-Hercegovina – where the highways which criss-crossed former Yugoslavia used to continue – as they still do in fact today, on to Mostar and Sarajevo.

Only not on this map. Now these roads marked in red fade out into an edge of white – as this is now a map of Croatia, not of former Yugoslavia – and these have now been replaced by another smaller map where Bosnia used to be. Here there are now idyllic scenes of cathedrals and stags, and peasants in national costume, and green hills... it fades into another map of Croatia which has been inset into the larger one; and which itself then fades out into the former Yugoslavia, at second hand, into red and white again, then into the words Bosnia-Hercegovena, or 'Bosnia and Hercegovena'. We can imagine an almost infinite regression like this; from Croatia, into another Croatia, and into another one, and so on, which is not unlike the recent histories of the various nationalisms in the region.

The original map must have included all of Yugoslavia. This was the simple solution to the mapmaker's problem: how to have a map of Croatia without also including too much of Bosnia. In the war with Serbia/Yugoslavia (which continued until 1995) the objective was much the same. There were Serbian and Croatian regions of Bosnia; and many Serbs and Croats originally intended to carve up the country between them – when Bosnia declared itself independent – one solution to the patchwork of national allegiances which became apparent when the Yugoslav national identity broke apart. As with the former Soviet Union, and somewhat predating it in its break-up, Yugoslavia was really an artificial state; one which, paradoxically, was founded on the internationalist ideals of communism.

The wars in former Yugoslavia were all about maps; and involved many convenient simplifications like this. There is no consensus about such basic questions as language or national identity. There are different readings of history, and no agreement over national frontiers, or even the concept of nationality itself. Croatians are now a *narod* or people. But it was not always so. In 1929, there was an attempt to make a unitary state out of all the South Slav peoples, Slovenes, Serbs and Croats – as well as other regions like Macedonia – and 'Yugoslavia' was born. In this new state the use of the national names Serbia, Croatia and Slovenia was forbidden.

The Middle Ages:

Croatia did enjoy a period of independence in the Middle Ages. In 924 AD, King Tomislav led the expansion of his Croatian kingdom, free of the influence of the Frankish Holy Roman Empire to the west and of Byzantium to the east, to include most of what was then the Serbian *Raska* and is now Serbia. Some maps produced during 1991 war show this kingdom extending as far as Belgrade. Croatia's awkward 'C' shape represents these historical circumstances, the region becoming first of all the bastion of Charlemagne's Holy Roman Empire against Byzantium; and later of the Austro-Hungarian Empire against the Ottoman Turks.

Ancient events are important here. One of the first actions of the Croats in Bosnia, after this country declared its independence in 1992, was to rename the scene of King Tomislav's coronation there Tomislavgrad – which would be not unlike English nationalists deciding to rename Winchester after Alfred the Great, Alfredtown.

If the English had continued to nurture an ancient rivalry with the Vikings, and identified these with the modern states of Norway or Denmark, you would have an equivalent to the situation in former Yugoslavia. A closer parallel is in the rival and mutually exclusive nationalisms of Northern Ireland, each of which is identified with a larger neighbouring state.

Croatian history begins to be written during the nineteenth century, revived in part by the French occupation, and the romantic nationalism which was having its effect eleswhere in Europe. This was first of all an Illyrian nationalism, influenced later by the Pan-Slavism which was to have such an effect in Russia; and which was succeeded in its turn by a Yugoslav (or South Slav) nationalism. This was the somewhat confused National Reawakening which is now seen from the modern Croatian point of view as the beginning of Croatian nationhood.

Yugoslavia:

In the end, a kingdom uniting the Serbs, Croats and Slovenes was formed (in 1919) which developed along the lines of Yugoslav nationalism. After the Second World War, Yugoslavia (as it was christened in 1929) was refounded by the Croatian born communist Josip Broz Tito; and a federal solution to the country's apparent national and ethnic divisions was introduced. In each case rule was authoritarian and from the centre. In the war years there had been an Independent State of Croatia, but this was really heavily dependent on its Italian and German backers. Serbs and Jews were persecuted and massacred (at least half a million) as were any Croats who happened to disagree with the regime.

Then came Tito, and his partisans. It was his non-aligned People's Federal Republic of Yugoslavia which divided Yugoslavia up into the separate republics which are still recognisable on the map today: Bosnia-Hercegovina (or Herzegovina); Croatia, Kosovo (or Kossovo), Macedonia (or FYR – Former Yugoslav Republic of – Macedonia), Montenegro, Serbia, Slovenia and Vojvodina.

Independence and War:

A tense situation was dramatised further in January 1992 when the EU – with Germany taking the lead – recognised the newly independent states of Croatia and Slovenia. The British government had been pressing for a federal solution within Croatia in which the rights of the Serbian minority were officially recognised. This resistance was dropped in return for German agreement to the opt-out negotiated by Mrs Thatcher as part of the Maastricht Treaty, a *quid pro quo* which had some disastrous consequences.

A full-scale war had already begun in Slovenia. Here the government tried at first to preserve a federal Yugoslavia; but resisted the Yugoslav tanks when they came during its ten-day war of independence. Serbia (as opposed to Yugoslavia) had no real long-term interest there, and no Serbian community to defend. In Croatia – with its Serb minorities in Eastern Slavonia and Krajina – in the Dalmatian hinterland – the situation was different; and these 'Croatian' Serbs distrusted their Croat neighbours; and remembered the depredations of the fascist Croat regime. They had good reason to fear the reemergence of a state which said that everyone who lived in Croatia was Croatian and had revived some of the symbols of its fascist forerunner.

Those Serbs who dreamed of a Greater Serbia also played their part in this breakdown of law and order and helped to make it possible. There was the emergence (often from the Serb-led police force) of local militias. Attempts at mediation by the European Union were ill-conceived and ineffective (and are widely seen today in the region as hypocritical); the various international mediators failed to insist on a global solution to the break-up of Yugoslavia; or to agree a strategy which involved a guarantee of civil rights to the minorities as well as the recognition of pre-existing borders.

From then on it was war. Fighting had already flared up in Dalmatia and Slavonia between the local (Serb) militia on the one hand – supported by the Yugoslav National Army which was deployed, ostensibly to keep the two sides apart and defend Yugoslavia – and the Croatian police and their own improvised army on the other. Croatia was now committed to defending its newly declared independence within the borders defined by Tito's Yugoslavia; but the Yugoslav army had a different objective: to keep the Yugoslav state going. Yugoslavia was now identified with Serbia; and the Croatian Serbs were intent on seceding from Croatia, encouraged by nationalists in Belgrade.

The war between Serbia and Croatia was pursued from 1992 on a third front, in Bosnia, with the Muslims and Bosnian nationalists caught in the middle. In 1995, there was a large-scale Croatian military operation in Western Slavonia in which the Serbs were defeated. Eastern Slavonia was returned to Croatian control in 1997; and the country had won its war of independence.

Conclusion:

In any history of Croatia and its neighbours there are inevitably simplifications; but there are some conclusions we can draw. In each side's account of events it is often what is not said which is important – and many stories can exist side by side, often with an equal validity and each with at least a grain of truth – but really the feelings which underly this; and the emotions which recent events have inspired. These are difficult for many visitors to understand who have not had a close acquaintance with the country; and count for a great deal more than facts sometimes, throughout this complex region. In the end, vistors will have to judge for themselves; but it will be better not to jump to immediate conclusions in a country whose recent history is so tortuous; and whose past is not well-known to many Britons and Americans.

One real and tragic result has been the large-scale displacement of Serbian and Croatian people unlucky enough to be living in the wrong place at the wrong time; and many refugees live today with little hope of returning to their old homes; or have moved into the houses of their former enemies – a distasteful episode at this end of the twentieth century. Another has been the reappearance in Europe of a racial enmity which has not been seen since the Second World War.

There were many personal and cultural ties between the Serbian, Croatian and Muslim people in Yugoslavia which have been broken. Like the roads into Bosnia on the map of Croatia, they just fade out.

Economy

Croatia was the second-most prosperous republic in Yugoslavia (after Slovenia); and the economy has made a remarkable recovery after five years[a] of war. In some respects, a problem which affects other formerly communist countries has even been alleviated by the war. In many areas some of the existing industrial infrastructure was destroyed; and there is a greater sense in Croatia than in many other countries of starting again from scratch. New structures and new enterprises are appearing; and foreign investment is proceding apace.

For a list of British companies present in Croatia and sources of information in the UK, please see the *Business and Industry Report* in the *Working in Croatia* section which follows. The stabilisation programme implemented by the government has already been successful; a stable national currency, the kuna, was introduced in 1994; and many projects for privatisation are under way. Contacts are often best pursued at the local level first of all (where the staff may already be shareholders in the enterprise in question, along with government or other private investors like banks). Later the relevant government authorities can be notified. Personal contacts are an important part of doing business in Croatia, and making a trip there is advisable once these initial contacts have been made.

The *Croatian Chamber of Commerce* (Trg Rooseveltov 2; tel 1-456-1555; fax 1-448-618) can offer commercial information about Croatia. And see the *Doing Business in Croatia* section below.

Government

The Head of State is at present Franjo Tudjman. Under the President there is a bicameral parliament, the *Sabor*. The lower house is the Chamber of Constituencies (*Zastupnicki dom*) and the upper house the Chamber of Regions (*Zupanijski dom*). The legal system is based on the constitution of December 1900, amended in 1992.

Currency

The Croatian *kuna* (HRK), with banknotes from five to 1,000 kunas and coins for one, two and five kunas, as well as ten, 20 and 30 lipas (1 kuna 100 lipas). Foreign currency including pounds is readily exchanged in banks and travel agencies, exchange offices and post offices; and all the major credit cards are in use. Keep your receipt if you wish subsequently to exchange some of your kunas back into foreign currency.

The kuna is not convertible and so is only obtainable in Croatia.

Population

4,784,265, according to the 1991 census.

Geography

The land area is 56,538 square kilometres. There is a long coastal strip along the Adriatic; and its major ports are *Rijeka* and *Pula* in Istria, *Zadar*, *Split* and *Dubrovnik*. To the north-west lies Slovenia; to the north, Hungary; and to the east Serbia, Bosnia-Herzegovina and Montenegro.

Climate

Continental in northern Croatia, subalpine and alpine in the central parts, and mediterranean in the south along the Adriatic. An average sea temperature of 26°C is one of its attractions as a tourist destination. Spring and autumn are mild along the coast, while winters are cold in Zagreb and the north.

Cities and Regions

DUBROVNIK

Already, 70,000 or so visitors on cruise ships have stopped off during 1997 in this beautiful city surrounded by high medieval walls (which did little to protect it from Serb and Montenegrin grenades during the war). It was the capital of the ancient Republic of Dubrovnik which was first under Venetian and then Turkish influence. Most of it has been restored; most hotels are now in operation and many have been refurbished (although a few still house refugees); a stay in an 'A' or 'B' class hotel is reasonably inexpensive as the tourist industry is getting back on its feet. The *Atlas Travel Agency* can make arrangments for excursions and boat trips as well as private accommodation (Pile Gate, dr. A. Starcevica 1; tel 20-442-222; fax 20-411-100. These are also the *American Express* offices.

Atlas also owns the *Atlas Club Nautika*, a restaurant with a nautical theme which is suitable for entertaining business clients (Brsalje 3; tel 20-442-526; fax 20-442-525), outside the landmark which is also where the buses stop, the Pile Gate (and there is a small pizza restaurant opposite which is also recommended).

There are several branches of the *Dubrovacka Bank*; and they also have a tourist information service (tel 20-412-988). The *Zagrebacka Bank* (tel 20-432-893; fax 20-431-810) is at Put Republike 5 or at Placa 4, behind a pharmacy. (These are the two main banks in Croatia). There is also a marina; a lively café and restaurant scene (also inexpensive) and an Italian feel along its main street, the *Placa*, in the Old Town. The *Hotel President* is a large and reasonably comfortable hotel a bus-ride from the centre, with an extraordinary location, long corridors and unusual external lifts (tel 20-441-603; fax 20-413-819). The *Hotel Lapad* is a charming old-fashioned hotel on the waterfront (Lapadska obala 37; 20-432-922; fax 20-24-782). The *Hotel Croatia* (which has been completely restored) is noteworthy as the hotel which the Serbs used as their HQ; and launch their grenades at the city (tel 20-478-055; fax 20-478-213). It would now be a very suitable venue for package holidaymakers.

After reporting on the war there for the BBC, journalist and now MP Martin Bell returned to find in Dubrovnik that 'the charms that attracted so many holidaymakers have not gone away;' and recommends an ex-war zone as 'a fantastic place to have a holiday; the sun beats down on the ancient roofs and walls as it always did ... art galleries, courtyard restaurants and quiet bars all provide a hospitable protection, and many of these require a little hill-climbing: they are to be found up side-streets so steep and so narrow that the upper floors almost shake hands...'

Contacts: The *City of Dubrovnik* has an internet address: http://www.laus.hr/festival/Welcome.html. Also contact: *The Dubrovnik County Tourism Association*, Cvijete Zuzoric 1, 20000 Dubrovnik; tel 20-413-310; 20-413-745; e-mail tzzdu-ner@du.tel.hr.

SPLIT

In Split we move up to Middle or Central Dalmatia. This is a port; and a residence still for some of the peacekeepers working in neighbouring Bosnia; which means the hotels are often full; and the atmosphere sometimes frenetic. The 'A' category *Hotel Marjan* (tel 21-342-866/929; fax 21-342-930) opposite the harbour is where some of the soldiers stay. The history of Split is graphically represented by *Diocletian's Palace* which doubles as the old town. The ancient palace was founded by the Illyrian Roman Emperor of the same name who retired to Split as a convenient 'central' point in his empire – and who is distinguished as the only Roman Emperor to consider retiring at all. The palace and town became the dwelling-place of the Slavic tribes who came, and were rather peaceably integrated with the locals here.

It is not so much an ancient monument as a record of successive occupations which continue until today; and the ancient plan of the Palace is most visible in the recently excavated cellar. There is a market, some shopping streets, and some dubious-looking discoteques.

Middle Dalmatia. Middle Dalmatia boasts fine beaches shaded by pine trees along the 'Makarska Riviera' on the way to Dubrovnik, and hotels like the *Hotel Meteor* (tel 21-602-600, fax 21-611-419) in *Makarska*; there are others in the main islands of *Solta*, *Brac* and *Hvar* as well as access by ferry to *Korcula*, home of the *Moreska* dance (see above), and allegedly the birthplace of Marco Polo. A hotel there to which British visitors have returned and feel at home is the *HTP Korcula* (tel 20-726-336/306; fax 20-711-746). To the north is the historic Croatian capital at *Zadar*, the port of *Sibenik* with its Romanesque cathedral, and more islands. The ferry from *Dubrovnik* (tel 20-23-068) can take you to Hvar and Zadar as well as Split; or southwards arrives from *Rijeka* (tel 51-211-444). Other local ferries connect the larger islands (like Korcula) with each other.

Contacts: *Split and Dalmatia County Tourist Board Split* (Prilaz Brace Kaliterna 10/1, 21000 Split; tel/fax 21-362-561/40-853/40348; e-mail tzzup-st-dalm@st.tel.hr; http://www.dalmatia.mid.com); *Jadrolinija Split* (tel 21-355-399); *Croatian Railways* enquiries (tel 21-48-588); Bus Station, Split (21-345-047); Taxi (tel 21-47-777/49-999/551-88); *Croatia Airlines Split* (tel 21-362-202/551-993); Car Ferries Information (21-355-399). *Split Airport* (tel 21-203-506); *Croatian Automobile Club* emergency service (tel 21-587-259).

Also see *info 98* published by the *Split and Dalmatia County Tourist Board* (see above) for more practical and cultural infomration; a list of travel agencies; car hire firms; and other useful contacts.

ISTRIA

This is the peninsular in the north-west of the country which was the first area to reestablish itself as a tourist destination. Administratively it is a county, with around 200,000 inhabitants and covering 2,820 square kilometres. The Illyrians, Romans, Byzantines, Ostrogoths, Langobards, Franks, Venetians and Austro-Hungarians all came here. Porec, the biggest resort, with cobbled alleys and shady squares, is still laid out according to the Roman plan. *Trieste* (now in Italy) is not far away; and there is the resort of *Rovinj* half-way along the coast (where chess-player Gary Kasparov takes his annual vacation). It compares itself with St Tropez, but is certainly quieter.

Further south is *Pula*, which was the residence for a time of the writer James Joyce, who moved here when Trieste and its environs were part of the Austro-Hungarian Empire – to become an English teacher at the local Berlitz school. He paid an agency in Ireland, which did not come up with the promised job, and when he arrived at the Berlitz school in Trieste they recommended trying their school in Pula (or Pulj) – which is how he ended up living and working here.

The Gulf of Kvarner. Then there are the resorts of Rabac and Opatija in the Gulf of Kvarner on the other side of the peninsular, the so-called Kvarner Riviera.

In the twentieth century Istria has been Austro-Hungarian, Italian, and then, after the Second World War, Yugoslavian. It shows all these influences today; and has monuments from the Roman and Byzantine periods and some fine churches. There are presently 113 hotels and nine marinas. Cycling and horse-riding are alternative tourist activities; and the Croatia Open tennis tournament is held here. But the climate, and the long summer season (from May to October), is the main attraction for visitors.
Contact: *Tourist Association of the City of Rijeka/Tourist Information Centre*, Uzarska 14, Rijeka; tel 51-335-882; fax 51-214-706.

ZAGREB
The capital Zagreb is quieter than Prague or Budapest. It is in the same Central European area and shows the influence of the Austro-Hungarian Empire in its architecture and cuisine: one legacy of the Austro-Hungarian Empire throughout the region is the range of Viennese-style cakes and pastries which are available. Zagreb also has the same post-communist heritage of drab, barrack-block style housing in the suburbs. It is also the only Central or Eastern European capital known to the author without a McDonald's (after the belated arrival in Ukraine of the American fast food chain).

With a population of nearly one million it is by far the largest city in Croatia. Accommodation is good at the top end of the range; but there are as yet few hotels for budget travellers. The *Youth Hostel* is located at Petrinjska 77; tel 1-434-946; fax 1-434-962 and the *Studenthotel* (open from 15 July to 1 October) is at Cvjetno, Odranska 8; tel 1-530-609; fax 1-530-722.. De luxe hotels include the *Inter-Continental Zagreb* (tel 1-455-3411; fax 1-444-431) and the *Sheraton* (tel 1-455-3535; fax 1-455-3035).

Kaptol. There is a lively bar and café life. Going north towards the Kaptol district and the city's historic Upper Town there are cafés with terraces (and some of the aforementioned cakes) and performances by artists and street musicians. Kaptol was the original town, granted a charter by the Hungarian King Ladislas I Arpadovic in 1094, which is generally considered as the date of the foundation of the City of Zagreb. It was first mentioned as the capital of Croatia in 1557; and began to spread outside its medieval walls in the middle of the nineteenth century.

The *Mimara Museum* (Trg Rooseveltov 5; tel 1-448-055/234) contains works of art by Goya, Dégas, Leonardo da Vinci and Rembrandt. The twin spires of the *Cathedral of the Assumption* symbolise Zagreb for many. On the site of the medieval church and monastery we see today a striking late nineteenth century building in which some earlier frescoes have been preserved.

Contacts: See the *Tourist Guide Zagreb*, available from the Croatian National Tourist Board or the tourist offices mentioned above, for more on the history and culture; and hotels, cinemas, restaurants, shopping, public transport, garages, mechanics, hospitals; and generally where to go and what to do in Zagreb. Also see *Zagreb* under *Working in Croatia* below.

Accommodation

Croatia's *nouveaux riches* are busy purchasing desirable residences or plots of land outside Zagreb, or on the islands of Dalmacia, which means the prices have gone up. You are advised to seek advice at the *British Embassy* or *Consulate* about reputable agencies and lawyers who are able to handle all the paperwork. Many of the incoming travel agencies can also arrange private house or flat rental (see below).

Renting and Buying Property

Private accommodation in Zagreb can also be arranged by the *Turisticko Drustvo Novi Zagreb* (Tourist Association Novi Zagreb), Trnsko 15e, tel/fax 1-521-523; or by *Evistas*, Trg kralja Tomislava 19; tel 1-420-567/455-0262; fax 1-420-988. Along the Dalmatian coast, private rooms (often advertised in German, as 'zimmer') are to be found everywhere (meaning you don't really need to book if you are on a touring holiday or visiting by car – outside the busy summer season at any rate. Otherwise, contact the local tourist information office for advice on house rental and purchase agencies.

Hotels and Agencies

See the *Zagreb Tourist Guide* (contact listed under 'Zagreb' in this chapter's *General Introduction*) for a list of the various categories of hotel there. These are currently graded from 'A' to 'D'; although Croatia plans to move shortly – or has already moved – to the 'star' system which is better-known internationally. There are sometimes anomalies in the present grading system, so a refurbished 'B' class hotel can be better than an unrefurbished 'A' class hotel for instance. But standards are generally reasonably high.

The *Croatian National Tourist Board* (Trg bana Josipa Jelacica 1, 10000 Zagreb; tel 1-455-6455; fax 1-428-674) is the best contact for hotels and travel agencies. Of interest to business travellers and tourism professionals is their comprehensive guide to hotels, as well as suppliers, tourism trade events, camping-sites, marinas, airports, airlines, car rental agencies, cruises and travel agents across the country, *Tourist Offer for Croatia '99*, which is published annually by *Jam-mark d.o.o*, Trg kralija Tomislava 17, 10000 Zagreb; tel/fax 1-425-157; e-mail jammark@zg.tel.hr; http://www.netstudio.tel.hr/ns/crotour. The Tourist Board also publishes an annual *Hotel Rates* brochure which may be easier to obtain.

For youth hostel information, contact the *Croatian Youth Hostel Association Travel Section*, Dezmanova 9, 10000 Zagreb; tel 1-278-239/435-781; fax 1-426-201.

Utilities

Electricity: 220V, 50Hz. Tap water is safe for drinking throughout the country.

Removals and Freight

For a list of UK-based international removals and freight companies, many of whom specialise in Central Europe, please see *Removals*, in the *General Introduction* at the beginning of this book.

Import Procedures

Please contact the Croatian Embassy for these:
Croatian Embassy: 21 Conway Street, London W1P 5HL; tel 0171-387 1790; fax 0171-387 0574. *Consular Department*: tel 0171-387 1144; fax 0171-387 0574.
Croatian Embassy: 2343 Massachusetts Avenue NW, Washington, DC 20008; tel 202-588 5899; fax 202-588 8936.

The Language

Croatian is really the same as Serbian. This assertion, however, is loaded with political and cultural significance and would be denied by most Serbians and Croatians today. The situation is something like this: if Scotland ever became independent from the rest of Britain, it would naturally wish to emphasise that the Scots version of English has its own characteristics and literary history. Few would disagree. The Croatians have taken this one stage further, though, and say that their language is different from that spoken in Serbia or Bosnia, although their variant of Serbo-Croat (or Croato-Serb) is about as different from Serbian as Irish English is from British English.

Courses

The *BARBIC School for Foreign Languages* (Dioklecijanova 1, 21000 Split; tel/fax 21-341397) teaches Croatian as a foreign language, as well as English, Italian, German French and Spanish, and occasionally recruits RSA/Cambridge-qualified English language teachers, and translators. Contact Marija Barbic at the address above.

Transport and Communications

CNN is available in some hotels. The main local newspapers (in decreasing order of importance) are *Vecemyi List* (Zagreb), *Vjesnik* (Zagreb) *Slobodna Dalmacija* (Split), *Novi List* (Rijeka), and *Glas Slavonije* (Osijek). The state TV-radio sation *HRT* also produces programmes, including the news in English, for a worlwide audience via Eutelsat. The British Council is one place where you can find British newspapers; otherwise kiosks in the tourist centres will have some. The American Centre in Zagreb is at Hebrangova 2; tel 1-45-55-500.
Telephones: These are available in post offices (you pay after you talk); and phones requiring a card (*telekarta*) are becoming more common. The number for *British Telecom Direct* is 99-38-00-44; and for *AT&T Direct* for calls to the USA, 993-85-42-88. For the police, dial 92; for fire 93; and for an ambulance 94. 99 is the international prefix.

To dial a number in Croatia from the UK, prefix it with 00 and then 385. Within the country a nought is added before the first digit of the number with the regional code (e.g. numbers in Zagreb begin 01); calls are 25% cheaper between 4pm and 10pm; 75% cheaper between 10pm and 7am.

Public faxes are also available in many post offices.

Getting Around

Driving:
Speed limits are 50 kph in cities; 80kph outside cities; 120kph on motorways; or 40 kph in built-up areas front of schools or over bridges. In Britain there are wheel-clamps; in Croatia there are 'spiders'; you would do well to avoid one of these too; and if your wrongly parked car is now where you left it you are advised to contact the traffic police to check whether it has been taken by the 'spider'.

If you break down, the Croatian equivalent of the AA is the *Croatian Automobile Club (HAK)*. They can be contacted on 987 nationally; or 1-526-610 in Zagreb. RAC and AA members should not be charged if the repair takes less than four hours or if the vehicle has to be taken less than 40 kilometres. But in practise you are more likely to have to pay the full amount. Get a Lada, Yugo or Zastava in Croatia. Mechanics are on call twenty-four hours a day to carry out repairs free of charge. Call 1-566-225 in Zagreb. There are also secure garages in most areas for those afraid of car crime. See the *Zagreb Tourist Guide* (contact listed under 'Zagreb' in the *General Introduction*) for a list of some of these; and spare parts suppliers, car washes, 24-hour service stations and other car services.

To report a crime, the traffic police number is 1-770-170 in Zagreb; and the national police number is 92.

Car Rentals: *Hertz* car rentals can be contacted on 1-331-760 or 332-613. They have 20 offices nationally. The *Avis* representative in Croatia is *Autotehna Zagreb d.o.o.*, Republike Austrije 5, 10000 Zagreb; tel 1-172-133; fax 1-173-274. Contact *Europcar* in Zagreb on tel/fax 1-434-474 or tel 1-434-444. Their central reservations office is: M. Tita 200, Opatija; tel 51-272-993; fax 51-273-020. They also have 20 branches across the country.

Taxis: In Zagreb the main taxi phone numbers are 970, or 682-505 and 682-558. (Also see under *Split* above).

Trains: Trains arrive from Berlin, Munich, Vienna, Venice, Budapest, Paris, Geneva and Moscow. The Main Railway Station is Zagreb is located at King Tomislav Square (tel 1-45-77-111; and there is recorded information on 9830). (Also see under *Split* above). 1-9830 is the number for national railway information.

Buses: There are international coach arrivals in Zagreb from Germany, Switzerland, Hungary and Turkey. The Central Bus Station in Zagreb is in Marin Dnic Avenue (tel 512-331/515-037/510-609. Trams also run from 4am to 11.45pm; and tickets may be bought from the driver or (cheaper) at newsstands and cigarette kiosks. One ticket is for 1½ hours' travel by tram or bus. For coach enquiries, call 1-6157-111.

Boats: *Jadrolinija* ferries can be contacted in Rijeka on 51-330-899, or 211-444, or 335-418 (reservations).

Planes: Many flights arrive at Zagreb Airport, with an onward connection to places like Split and Dubrovnik. It is about 25 minutes from the airport city centre by bus. The flight information number is 1-6525-222 or 4562-222. Most airlines have offices and desks in the airports. In Zagreb their main offices are:

Adria Airways: Praska 9, tel 1-433-333/510; fax 1-425-399.
Aeroflot: Varsavska 13; tel 1-421-825; fax 1-423-819.
Air Canada: Mihanoviceva 1; tel 1-45-77-925.
Air France: Gajeva 12; te; 1-424-591.
Austrian Airlines: Trg S. Zrinskog 6; tel 1-420-255; fax 1-420-665.
Croatia Airlines: Nikole Tesle 5; tel 427-752 or 45-51-244 (the reservations number). Other reservations numbers are: 20-413-777 (Dubrovnik); 0171-306 3138 (London); 52-23-322 (Pula); 51-330-207 (Rijeka); 071-666-123 (Sarajevo); 091-115-858 (Skopje); 21-362-202 (Split); 23-314-272 (Zadar).
CSA: Trg N. S. Zrinskog 17; tel 1-434-355; fax 1-433-324.
Delta Airlines: Mihanoviceva 1; tel 1-45-77-277; fax 1-45-77-921.

KLM: Katanciceva 3; tel 1-415-445/433-107/207; fax 1-435-658.
Lufthansa: Krsnjavoga 1 (Hotel Inter-Continental); tel 1-445-655; 1-434-472/445-878.
Pan-Avia: Av. V. Holjevca 20; tel 1-65-52-632; fax 1-65-52-458.
Swissair: Trg N. S. Zrinskog 6; tel 1-420-255; fax 1-425-897.

Travel Agencies

American Express: Lastovaska 23; Zagreb; tel 61-24-422.
Astra International Tourism and Trade Co: Trg bana J. Jelacica 15/II, 10001 Zagreb; tel 1-421-479/428-856; fax 1-421-611.
Atlas Travel Agency, Zagreb and Dubrovnik: See *Banks* below.
Atlas Travel Agency, Split: tel/fax 21-355-833/43-055/362-012.
Croatia Express, Zagreb: Teslina 4; tel 1-421-216. Trg kralja Tomislava 17; tel 1-431-900. Ulica kneza Branimira; tel 1-45-77-752. Trg kralja Tomislava 12; tel 1-277-042 (the Main Railway Station branch, where there is an exchange bureau open daily from 6am to 10pm).
Croatia Express, Split: tel/fax 21-44-499/342-645/362-406.
Generalturist: Praska 5, 10000 Zagreb; tel 1-481-0033; fax 1-426-633. Thomas Cook representative. For individual and group travel, conferences, charters, air tickets etc.
Generalturist, Split: tel 21-45-183; fax 21-341-056.
Kompas Dalmacija d.o.o: tel/fax 21-342-993/587-280/42-491.
Kompas Zagreb: Gajeva 6; tel 1-423-545; fax 1-426-895.

Banks

The usual working hours are from Monday to Friday from 8am to 7pm; and on Saturdays from 8am until noon.

Atlas Travel Agency: Trg N. S. Zrinskog 17, Zagreb; tel 1-427-623; fax 1-432-394. To withdraw cash for American Express holders. Headquarters: Dubrovnik, Pile 1; tel 20-442-222.
Postanska banka: Berislaviceva 2, Zagreb. For Diners Club.
Splitska banka: Vlaáka 26, Zagreb; tel 1-273-650. For Visa cards.
Zagrebacka banka d.d: Savska cesta 66, Zagreb; tel 61-20-555. For Eurocard, Mastercard and Diners Club card. Also see under *Dubrovnik*.

The other main Croatian banks are *Croatia banka, Jadranska Banka Sibenik, Komercijalna Banka Zagreb, Gradska banka, Privredna Banka Zagreb, Promdei banka*, and *Rijecka banka*. There are several other regional and smaller ones.

In Zagreb, the branch of *Promdei banka* at the Central Bus Station is open daily from 8am until midnight.

Health and Hospitals

For emergency medical services call 94.
There is a list of hospitals and health centres in Zagreb in the *Zagreb Tourist Guide* (contact listed under 'Zagreb' in the *General Introduction*). 'Our physicians and other medical staff are obliged to provide their services to any foreign guest.' Information about private doctors may be obtained from the *Croatian Medical Board* (Subiceva 9; tel 1-416-820). Also see *info 98* published by the *Split and Dalmatia Tourist Board* (contact above) and the various other

leaflets available from the *Croatian National Tourist Board* for hospital, pharmacy and other medical contacts.

Manners and Customs

Cooking: Croatian cuisine has been influenced by the Austro-Hungarians; and a broad division between the Mediterranean and continental parts of the country inland. 'Mediterranean' means seafood, fish or shellfish served with fresh vegetables and grilled (*na gradele*); or cooked in olive oil, with herbs and the local fermented cheese. Black Rice Risotto is an Adriatic speciality. Another well-known Croatian speciality has a continental (or 'Pannonian') feel: *zagorski strukli* is a cheese strudel, boiled or baked, as a starter or desert.

Goat is often served in mountain villages. Fast food is still limited; but fresh produce generally excellent. Vegetarianism is a new idea in Croatia; and restaurants may not be sympathetic to your request for vegetarian food. In Dalmatia, there is smoked ham like that in Italy, and pasta; and everywhere delicious home-made bread.

Along the coast there are grape or herb brandies; and inland the famous *sljivovica* or plum brandy. Finally, there is wine; an important part of life for most Croatians – and the red and white wine which the islands and coastal areas produce is surprisingly good and som,etimes excellent. Croatia is already attracting the interest of Australian and Californian winemakers.

See the *Zagreb Tourist Guide* (contact listed under 'Zagreb' in the *General Introduction*) for a listing of the various restaurants and cafés there.

Religion: Roman Catholic (75% of the population with up to 20% Orthodox Serbs) although this number has diminished since the 1991 census.

Sport: *Croatia Zagreb* is the former Dynamo Zagreb football team (the name was felt to be too communist and, well, not Croatian enough). As well as its soccer stars, and basketball players, Croatia has produced two leading tennis players: Goran Ivanisevic and latterly Iva Majoli.

Shopping: Shops are open generally from 8am to 8pm, with some taking a break in the afternoon until around 5pm; and on Saturdays they are usually open only until 2pm. Some small shops are open on Sunday mornings. *NAMA* is the national chain of department stores. Handicrafts include hand-made folk items, embroidered tablecloths, hand-knitted woollen pullovers and carved wood. There are crystal items imported from Slovenia; and home-produced ceramics.

The wife of the first British ambassador, it is said, chose hand-made baskets as her souvenirs of Croatia. Ties are, of course, not exclusively Croatian, but the idea for cravates, as they were eponymously known, came from here, a word which derives its name from the Croatian horsemen who, in the seventeenth century and during the French Revolution, wore distinctive scarves. They then caught on as high-fashion items in Paris.

The main shopping mall in Zagreb is the underground *Importanne Centre*, with boutiques, galleries, cafés and fashion shops. The Dolac food market is by the cathedral, and well worth a visit. Croatia used to be cheap; but prices have risen and are now similar to Spain.

Public Holidays

These are: January 1 (New Year's Day); January 6 (Epiphany); Easter Monday;

May 1 (Labour Day); May 30 (Republic Day); June 22 (National Holiday); the Feast of the Assumpion (August); December 25 (Christmas Day); December 26 (Boxing Day).

Working in Croatia

Business Background

Language is not a great problem. English, as well as German and Italian, are quite widely spoken in the business community (which had many foreign contacts in the past). Etiquette means you should have a business card ready for formal introductions; and study your opposite number's card with an apparent interest in any professional and academic titles (which count for more here than in the UK). There is a range of local agents and cosultants (and some lawyers, see below) who may be of assistance; but it is better to approach one of these through a personal contact who can vouch for their efficiency and/or integrity.

There are also the UK-based organisations and *Croatian Chamber of Commerce* (Trg Rooseveltov 2; tel 1-456-1555; fax 1-448-618) mentioned in the *General Introduction*, and *Business and Industry report* below. The background to investment and business in Croatia is the 'fast-track' liberalisation and privatisation programme also mentioned above.

There are occasional special reports on the country in both the *Financial Times* and *New Markets Monthly*. (The *FT* can also be delivered to you in Zagreb: contact the Subscription Department, Europe on +49-69-156850; fax +49-69-596-4483). A book entitled *Investment in Croatia*, detailing rights and obligations of foreign investors and highlighting some specific areas of interest is available from *Masmedia* (Ulica baruna Trenka 13, 10000 Zagreb; tel 1-45-77-400; fax 1-45-77-769; e-mail masmedia@open.hr; http://www.open.hr/com/masmedia). They also have a business risk and business information service.

Masmedia can also supply an up-to-date copy of the Croatian *Zute Stranice* or Yellow Pages (in four volumes, and compiled according to the various counties). They are also the co-publishers of the previously mentioned *Tourist Guide Zagreb* along with the Zagreb tourist authorities.

The Austrian-based *RZB* bank has outlets throughout Central and Eastern Europe (in Bratislava, Budapest, Moscow, Prague, Sofia, Warsaw and Zagreb, with representative offices also in Moscow and Kiev) offering commercial and investment banking services. Their London branch number is 0171-929 2288 (http://www.rzb.co.at/rzb).

Employment

English is quite widely spoken in the business community and the workplace atmosphere is rather formal and involves dressing neatly (not unlike the Italians) in yoiur office or teaching job. 'Dressing down' here means dressing badly, as a stroll along the main street in Dubrovnik nowadays will show you. There is a range of local job agencies and consultants (and some lawyers) who may be of assistance in your search for employment; but it is better to approach business and employment contacts directly yourself; and preferably 'on-the-spot' if you can afford a week or two away in these congenial surroundings, on a package tour or charter flight perhaps, and also doing your own research. There is nothing like 'just being there' when it comes to getting a job, or really getting to know a country; and the same applies to many others featured in this book (although not many will be quite so easy to get to).

We have come back to one of Croatia's principle advantages, which is its location.

Tourism

Most of the business and work opportunities are in this important industry. See more about this in the *General Introduction* at the beginning of this book. The *Croatian Association of Marinas* has been set up as part of the *Croatian Chamber of Commerce* (see below); and currently has cooperation agreements with yacht clubs of Germany and Austria, but not so far with the UK. Various discounts for services and facilities are offered. Reconstruction of hotel facilities is a priority; as is customer service, with new 'special regulations' for catering currently being drawn up.

The sports and tourist centre at *Umag* in Istria (which hosts the *Croatia* Open and a racing yacht competition) is modernising its telephone network, computer systems, and tennis courts; and *Istraturist* (the main hotel enterprise) should be contacted in Umag. In Dubrovnik, a *Rebuild Dubrovnik Fund* is supported by, among others, *American Express*, and was praised by the then US Ambassador Richard Holbrooke in 1996: 'I believe there are tourist and travel opportunities in the former Yugoslavia, particularly on the Adriatic coast ... but in the long-run political stability is essential not just to tourism but much more basically for the people in the region.'

Incentives: There are also special subsidies for foreign tourist transport available to tour operators who contact the Ministry of Tourism and with a budget (in 1997) of 60 million kunas. These are 28% higher for air charters out of season; and 35% more for road transport (outside the period of 15 June to 15 September). The required level of booking of an aircraft or boat charter is 70% out of season; and 85% in the summer. Agents bringing less than 20,000 passengers receive 180 kunas per passenger in season and 230 kunas out of season currently; and the southern part of the coast has an additional five million kunas allocated to it; here operators may receive 40-50 kunas more.

English Teaching and Language Schools

Tourism is one of the preconditions of a growth in the English language schools and language travel markets (as in Spain or Greece). It means the locals have a perception that it is an advantage to speak English, even if they do not intend to work directly in tourism. So there are employment opportunities for English teachers – and business opportunities for entrepreneurs – in all the countries which have mass tourism; and Croatia has it.

There are already many private language schools; most of which are locally owned and run. British or American owned schools will be at something of an advantage, and all those employing 'native speakers' (putting the local teachers of English out of business, of course). Franchising is one of the opportunities, and an area where growth is occuring in the English language schools world (although it goes – mainly for tax or charitable status reasons – by a variety of different names, and some franchises insist that they be known as 'affiliates'... This all means opportunities for teachers as well of course; especially before the masses of British tourists arrive – and some stay behind – and teach English.

Croatia – with its easier connections to Britain – will be one of the fastest changing markets in this world of private education and 'language travel' both for schools, language holidays, and the employment of language teachers; all of which we can expect to take off here much as it did in Greece in the 1970s.

See below under *Other Employment Contacts* for more details; and some English language schools in Croatia.

Business Contacts

IBC UK Conferences Ltd. organised the 1997 *Doing Business in Croatia* conference at the Hotel Sheraton, Zagreb; tel 0171-453-2177; e-mail sarah.ritchie@ibcuk.co.uk (and for other trade fair contacts, see under *Zagreb* below). Currently seeking foreign investors and partners is the port of *Luka Ploce* (Trg kralja Tomislava 21, 20340 Ploce; tel 20-679-601; fax 20-679-836; e-mail luka-ploce@du.tel.hr). This is the port which deals mainly with trade to Bosnia, with facilities and a free zone open to development by 'manufacturers, merchants and other business partners'.

The Croatian National Tourist Board, Trg bana Josipa Jelacica 1, 10000 Zagreb; tel 1-455-6455; fax 1-428-674. Of interest to tour operators and investors is their comprehensive guide to hotels, suppliers, tourism trade events, camping-sites, marinas, airports, airlines, car rental agencies, cruises and travel agents across the country: *Tourist Offer for Croatia '98*. It is published by *Jam-mark d.o.o*, Trg kralija Tomislava 17, 10000 Zagreb; tel/fax 1-425-157; e-mail jammark@zg.tel.hr; http://www.netstudio.tel.hr/ns/crotour. The Tourist Board my also be able to supply its annual *Hotel Rates* brochure (which may not always be the final word for tour operators negotiating rates here).

The *Croatian Chamber of Commerce* (Trg Rooseveltov 2; tel 1-456-1555; fax 1-448-618) can offer commercial information about Croatia.

Running a Business

Consultancy Services:
Ceufin Brokers: an Anglo-Belgian consulting firm based in Croatia since 1991 which has in-depth knowledge of the economy; and advice in areas such as feasibility studies, market surveys, joint ventures, privatisation and mergers and acquisitions: tel 1-6114-730 (Croatia); 01732-459790 (UK).
Kaptol Investment Company: services include investment fund management, brokerage, company evaluation and analysis, and consultancy services (for professional investors) – Maksimirska 120, 10000 Zagreb; tel 1-23-91-916/7; fax 1-23-35-880.
Masmedia: Ulica barına Trenka 13, 10000 Zagreb; tel 1-45-77-400; fax 1-45-77-769; e-mail masmedia@open.hr; http://www.open.hr/com/masmedia. Business consultancy service.

Legal Services: The following are lawyers in Croatia speaking English (Source: *Tourist Guide Zagreb*):
Kresimir Anic: Gunduliceva 40, Zagreb; tel 1-440-827.
Jerina Malesevic: Poljicke poljane 19/1, Zagreb; tel 1-510-555.
Insurance Companies:
Adriatic: Vodnickova 13, Zagreb; tel 1-275-385.
Croatia: Trg bana Josipa Jelacica 13; tel 1-45-60-111.
Croatia Lloyd: Miramarska 22, 10000 Zagreb; tel 1-61-70-211; fax 1-61-70-366; e-mail crollyod@open.hr; http://open.hr./com/crolloyd.

Mediteran: K. Viseslava 14, Zagreb; tel 1-412-426.
Sava: Trg Francuske Republike 1; tel 1-175-281.

Business and Industry Report

The *British Embassy Commercial Section* provides general briefings for business travellers (Commercial Section, Vlaska 121, P.O. Box 454, 10000 Zagreb; tel 1-455-5310; fax 1-449-834. The DTI along with the Foreign and Commonwealth Offices publishes a *Croatia Market Menu* for exporters (Croatia Country Helpdesk; tel 0171-215 4849; fax 0171-215 8598) and maintains a database of UK companies interested in Croatia. Also see *Sources of Information – Finance and Advice for Trade and Investment in Central and Eastern Europe and the Former Soviet Union* (*DTI Export Publications*; tel 0171-510 0171; fax 0171-510 0197); or contact the DTI's resource and information centre (Kingsgate House, 66-74 Victoria Street, London SW1E 6SW, open from 9am to 8pm weekdays and until 5.30pm on Saturdays; tel 0171-215 5444/5445; fax 0171-215 4231; http://www.dti.gov.uk/ots/emic; e-mail EMIC@ash001.ots.dti.gov.uk). The *East European Trade Council* (tel 0171-222 7622; fax 0171-222 5359) has a business library and can offer advice on business and trade in Central and Eastern Europe.

Croatia is becoming an important market for trade with Britain; and is placing a high priority on modernising its infrastructure. A wide range of products as well as many consultancy services are actively being sought. Other than tourism and leisure, sectors which offer opportunities include consumer goods, retail and distribution, electronics and IT equipment, food products and the healthcare and medical equipment sectors. It is Britain's fifth largest export market in Central Europe.

Zagreb

The light engineering, electronics, textiles, food, wood-processing and printing industries are all concentrated here, in industrial areas like *Jankomir* outside the city, Trade and banking are important, as in any capital city. The historic *Zagreb Fair* today includes various business and trade fairs (like the *International Autumn Zagreb Fair*) for industry, crafts, science, tourism, and agriculture. Contact: *Zagreb Fair*, Avenija Dubrovnik 12; tel 1-612-3236; or the *Croatian Convention Bureau*, Ilica 1, 41000 Zagreb; tel 1-610-1111. The *Croatian Chamber of Commerce* is also based here (Trg Rooseveltov 2; tel 1-456-1555). Enquiries about forthcoming privatisations should be directed to the *Ministry of Privatisations* (Gajeva 30a; tel 1-456-9111).

English Language Schools

Zagreb and environs:
Centar Stara Vlaska: Vlaska 26/III; tel 277-998/270-678.
Centar za Strane Jezike: Vodnikova 12; tel 1-444-324; fax 1-444-516.
Ilmo: Pantovcak 9; tel 1-176-832; fax 1-176-353.
Lancon: Jurisiceva 1; tel 1-277-051; fax 1-424-895.
Octopus: Branimirova 25; tel/fax 1-439-938.
Parole: Poljicka poljana 19; tel 1-611-152.
Skola Stranih Jezika: Varsavska 14; tel 1-424-535; fax 1-435-692.
LS Lukavec: Skolska 27; 10409 Donja Lomnica; tel 1-734-469.
Narodno Sveuciliste Velica Gorica: Zagrebacka 37, 10410 Velica Gorica; tel 1-721-133; fax 1-721-270.

Zadar:
Langlia: A. Starcevica 19b, 23000 Zadar; tel/fax 23-438-581.
Split:
Centar za Strane Jezike: Trg Republike 2/1; tel 21-341-394; fax 21-361-444.
Narodno Sveuciliste Split: Dioklecijanova 7, 21000 Split; tel 21-46-662/361-524; fax 21-44825.
Rijeka:
Cosmopolitan: Pecine 10a, 51000 Rijeka.*Interlang*: Krizanicva 7, 51000 Rijeka; tel 51-428-347.*Linguae*: Radiceva 4; 51000 Rijeka; tel/fax 51-446-766.
Oxford d.o.o: Trg Jelacicev 1, 51000 Rijeka.
Poliglot: Wenzelova 2, 51000 Rijeka; tel 51-215-130.
Pula:
The English Workshop: J. Voltica 4, 52000 Pula; tel 52-20873.
Osijek:
Skola stranih jezika: L. Jagera 6, 31000 Osijek; tel 31-26-866; fax 31-26-629.
Cakovec:
ELC-English Language Centre: Ante Starcevica 55, 40000 Cakovec; tel/fax 40-315-883.
Otvoreno Sveuciliste Cacovek: Kralja Tomislava 52, 40000 Cakovec; tel 40-312-236.
Kolag-Trade d.o.o: L. Bezeredija 41, 40000 Cakovec; tel 41-311-625.
Skola stranih jezika Sever: Park Rudolfa Kropeka 2, 40000 Cakovec; tel/fax 42-812-971.
Bjelovar:
Skola stranih jezika Jeka: P. Zrinskog 12a, 43000 Bjelovar; tel 43-241-88.

Residence and Entry Regulations

UK citizens do not require a visa to visit Croatia; US visitors need a visa for tourism or business which can be obtained from the Croatian Embassy Consular Department or on arrival. A valid passport, completed application forms, the fee, and a letter of invitation from your contact in Croatia (if you are applying for a business visa) are required; and UK and US citizens and others should seek advice from the Consular Department about taxes, visas, work and residence permits (see below). It takes one day to process a tourist visa and up to three weeks for a business visa.

Embassies and Consulates

Croatian Embassy: 21 Conway Street, London W1P 5HL; tel 0171-387 1790; fax 0171-387 0574. Consular Department, tel 0171-387 1144; fax 0171-387 0574.
Croatian Embassy: 2343 Massachusetts Avenue NW, Washington, DC 20008; tel 202-588 5899; fax 202-588 8936.
British Embassy: PO Box 454, 2nd Floor, Astra Tower, Tratinska, 41000 Zagreb; tel 1-334-245; fax 1-338-893. Consulates in Split and Dubrovnik.
US Embassy: Unit 1345, Andrije Hebranga 2, 09213-1345 Zagreb; tel 1-455-5281; fax 1-455-8585.

F.Y.R. Macedonia

Introduction

Who are the Macedonians? This is a question of greater importance in modern European history than that of almost any other nation. Indeed there is in modern European history a 'Macedonian Question', which began ofter the Congress of Berlin. What is the answer? Alexander the Great was Macedonian by birth. So was Kemal Attaturk. The Macedonians are either Bulgarian, Greek, Yugoslavian, Serbian, or even not so long ago part of the Turkish Empire – according to your point of view. Only from the Macedonian point of view are Macedonians Macedonian.

Greece rejects even the name (which is why, in deferance to Greek sensibilities) the country is known today as F.Y.R. Macedonia, standing for the Former Yugoslav Republic of, and to distinguish it from the parts of Macedonia (or Bulgaria) which belong to Greece which are also called Macedonia.

For Bulgarians, this is Western Bulgaria. For Greeks, Alexander and all later Macedonians are really Greek. We can trace Macedonian nationalism back as far as we like, to Alexander the Great perhaps – and there are tribespeople today in Afghanistan claiming Macedonian ancestry – or more reasonably to the formation of an independent Macedonian patriarchate or church in the tenth century (which was also, it seems, and unfortunately for us, Bulgarian).

More recent manifestations of Macedonian nationalism include the world's first terrorist organisation, the *Internal Macedonian Revolutionary Organisation (IMRO)*, which inspired pre-war thrillers and grew out of the rising against the Ottoman Empire in 1878.

Living in Macedonia

History

Somewhere on the south-eastern fringes of Europe, and with many layers of history, this is a country which is difficult to get to – on a practical level – and difficult perhaps to understand, if you don't read up on your Balkan history a little. There are many minorities – and as many opposing points of view – but here are some official facts: 'The Republic of Macedonia was proclaimed as an independent nation after the referendum of 8 August 1991. The Macedonian state, nation and language were first sanctioned only after World War II by the *ASNOM*, the *Antifascist Brotherhood for the National Liberation of Macedonia* on 2 August 1944.'

The modern Macedonians claim to be descendants of the Slavs who invaded this territory during the sixth and seventh centuries – and we can see predated the arrival of the Bulgars in this part of the world. They 'got mixed up with the other local tribes, possibly including the ancient Macedonians (whose kingdom fell under Rome in 146 BC.' See the *Probing into the beauty of Macedonia* brochure published by the *Economic Chamber of Macedonia*.

Geography

The capital *Skopje* has 600,000 of the country's two million or so inhabitants, and dates back to the Roman and Byzantine Empires. Some ruins from the time of the earthquake of 518 AD can still be found, as can churches and mosques, frescoes, and some more modern buildings after a more recent earthquake in 1963... Macedonia's borders measure only 849km and it occupies an area of 25,713 square kilometres. There are Albanians, Turks and Serbs as well, and Romany people and Vlachs.

Climate

Like Bulgaria, it can be cold and rainy, even in spring and autumn. Snow falls in winter. This is a continental climate, but quite a mild one. With its mountains, rivers and lakes, this is not unlike a Balkan Switzerland.

Culture and Language

Bulgarians say Macedonian is a dialect of Bulgarian; but today this distinct language is being promoted in schools and public life, with a revival of Macedonian poetry and literature. In the ninth century, the two monks who invented the Cyrillic alphabet, St. Cyril and St. Methodius (regarded by the Greeks as Greek and by the Bulgarians as Bulgarian, but who could more properly be said to be Macedonian) were both born in what is now Greek Macedonia. In these Greek parts of the country, the Macedonian – or Bulgarian – culture was displaced by the invading Greeks after the Balkan Wars at the begionning of this century – yet another example of 'ethnic cleansing' in the region. The great Jewish community in Saloniki (or Salonika) also suffered, in what was formerly Bulgaria, or Macedonia. It was almost completely wiped out in the Holocaust.

Religion: The *Macedonian Orthodox Church* is known for its mediaeval churches and monasteries. It was reestablished in 1967 (as a sort of Yugoslavian buttress against the Bulgarians) and is seen as a lodestar of Macedonian identity, a kind of spirituality which the Macedonians themselves say is uniquely Macedonian (tinged by a kind of 'ethereal idealism' it is said). Macedonia sees itself as the place where Slavic Christianity was born.

Communications

The main international road route from Western Europe passes through Budapest and Belgrade to Skopje, and ends in Athens.

There are two airports, at Skopje and *Ohrid* – with its lake – which is one of the main potential tourist attractions of the country – and these are used by Macedonian as well as international airlines. The former are *Palair Macedonian* (tel 91-232-514/6; fax 91-233-155), *Makedonija Airways* (tel 91-112-410/2 or 119-565; fax 91-119-348) and *MAT Macedonian Airlines* (tel/fax 91-22-72-54). One of the latter is *Austrian Airlines* (27th March St. 12, 91000 Skopje; tel 91-233-333; fax 91-228-531).

Working in Macedonia

Business and Industry Report

There were several years of economic isolation due to the dispute about its name, which Greece refused to recognise after it declared its independence. The ingenious argument here – and a disingenuous one – was that Macedonia was in Greece – was really Greek – and therefore as a separate nation could not exist. Even if Macedonia only existed in the imagination of its people, we can see that this would be little different from many other nations in the region, and its claim to statehood is quite an ancient one. What the Greeks feared more than a name was the revival of the troubling 'Macedonian Question' which – for Macedonians – is a question about why the Greeks invaded Macedonia in the first place.

Bulgarians have exactly the same territorial claim. So we can see – as a matter of pragmatism – why this Pandora's box of rival territorial claims is better left unopened, and it has been better until now to stick with the status quo in this southern Balkans region.

The alternative – which could have happened after 1991 – and still could happen – would have been a kind of 'Bosnian' solution. The *quid pro quo* for the Macedonians should be that they have their independence recognised and guaranteed by the international community. This would be an almost stable solution, with only the sempiternal rivalry between Greece and Turkey to worry about. If this were also resolved there could be a more deeply established peace in the region.

Nowadays – and on all sides – there is a greater recognition of this country – and its importance in regional and European affairs. It is hoped it will lose the indignity of its 'Former Yugoslav Republic of' status, and Macedonia is already a member of the *OSCE (Organisation for Security and Cooperation in Europe)* and Nato's *Partnership for Peace*. The suspension of UN trading sanctions against Serbia – and of an embargo by Greece – would also help growth to resume. Much will depend on international efforts to consolidate peace in former Yugoslavia; and the maintenance for a while of a UN presence. But the government is optimistic about its intentions to become a major trading and communications centre in the southern Balkans.

Progress in industry and investment is being made, after its IMF-led restructuring; and GDP is now (slightly) up; with stronger growth forecast. Trade opportunities are in wine, vegetable production and cigarette manufacture. Then there are pharmaceuticals and textiles, where investment now could see rewards in future. Money is coming in from the many Macedonians working abroad, but unemployment is still high, up to 40%.

In the *DTI*, Macedonia – like most of the countries in this section – comes under their 'South East Europe' section. The general switchboard number for you to reach the *Overseas Trade Services* department on is 0171-215 5000. (Within these sections there are the various 'country desks', including someone specialisiing in F.Y.R.Macedonia).

Useful Addresses

British Embassy: Veljko Vlahovic 26, (4th floor), 9100 Skopje; tel 91-116-772; fax 91-117-005.

Macedonian Embassy: 10 Harcourt House, 19A Cavendish Square, London W1M 9AD; tel 0171-499-5152; fax 0171-499-2864.

Ministry of Economy: ul. Bote Bocevski, br. 9, 91000 Skopje; tel 91-220-655/112-628; fax 91-127-083/111-541.
Macedonian Chamber of Commerce: ('ATAM, Association of Tourist Agencies in Macedonia' and 'HOTAM, Hotel Association of Macedonia') ul. Dimitrija Chuposki, br. 13, 91000 Skopje; tel 91-116-652/118-088; fax 91-116-210.
Tourist Association of Skopje: ul. Dame Gruev, block 3, 91000 Skopje; tel 91-118-498/230-803.
Skopje Airport: tel 91-235-156; fax 91-116-334/711-019.
Ohrid Airport: tel 96-31-656/34-079 or 33-656 (info.); fax 96-33-16.

Moldova

Introduction

In Moldova, there are 4.3 million people in a relatively small and densely populated area, most of whom are Moldovians (meaning the Romanians in these parts who were brought into the Soviet Union in 1940 – this brought into being a separate Moldavian Soviet identity). When the Soviet Union was dissolved, in 1991, there was a large minority of Russians and Russian-speakers here, as in the Baltic States, who wanted to maintain the link with Russia. The Latin alphabet has been introduced once again (after the local Moldavians were encouraged to use Cyrillic) but Russian is still the main language in everyday use. 65% of the inhabitants are Moldovan; 14% Ukrainian; 13% Russian; 3% Gaguaz; and 2% Bulgarian.

The capital *Chisinău* (otherwise known as Kisinău, and formerly known as Kishinek) has nearly 700,000 inhabitants. The land area is 13,000 square miles (with a 130 per square kilometre population density). It is bounded in the east by Ukraine and the Dniester and in the west by Romania and the River Prut (or Pruth); to the south is the Black Sea; but also a part of Ukraine, which means this is a land-locked country. The port of Odessa is not far away; as is the Danube delta immediately to the south.

The *River Dniester* is also a boundary for another country which lies between it and Ukraine: the *Trans-Dniester Republic*, which seceded from Moldova in 1992 and fought its own bitter war of independence, with some help from Russia. This is also an outpost of Russian influence in south-eastern Europe (a little like Kaliningrad in the Baltic region).

Living in Moldova

History

At the entrance to Pushkin Park in the centre of *Chisinău* is the *Monument of Stefan cel Mare*, Stefan the Great. He was the *gospodar* (or ruler) of Moldova from 1457 to 1504 during its brief period of independence – much longer than that of neighbouring Ukraine – which is its main claim to be an independent entity today. Nowadays, it is separate from Romania, with which – before its annexation by Russia – it shared a language and a culture.

Do not go to Transdniestria (or the Trans-Dniester Republic) the British *Foreign Office* advises, on safety grounds; and you should take suitable precautions to to avoid theft, and for your personal safety in Moldova. See BBC Ceefax p.470 onwards, or the Internet under the address http://www.fco.gov.uk/ – or call 0171-238 4503/4504 – for their latest travel advice. In the United States – for all countries – telephone 202-647-5225 or fax 202-647-3000 for the US government's *Overseas Citizens Services* travel advice line and information service to find out what the authroities say about it; or contact the relevant Embassy or Consulate on the spot.

Visas and Customs

Britons and Americans require a visa; but these circumstances may change, so consult the Embassy or Consular Department of the Republic of Moldova in Brussels (for Europe) or in the United States.

Documents you need for a private visit are an invitation from a Moldovan citizen (written on the special *Ministry of the Interior* form which they can obtain). For tourism you need to have confirmation of the booked trip from a Moldovan travel agency (see below). For a business or commercial trip you should submit to the Embassy your official invitation from a governmental or non-governmental organisation written on headed paper, and signed by the head of that organisation.

Then you need your application form which the Embassy can send you; one recent photo; and your passport (valid for no less than six months subsequently). Fees range currently from 1,500 BEF for a one-month single entry visa to 4,000 BEF for a three-month multiple entry business visa. A one-way transit visa is 1,000 BEF. 'Urgent' visas can be issued for an additional 1,000 BEF in one day; or 500 BEF for three or four days. Otherwise submit all your documents – in person is better but for Britons this can be by recorded mail to Brussels – no later than 10 days before your departure, including the 'receipt for the payment transfer according to the type of visa' plus 500 BEF for administration, postage etc. You would be wrong to think this payment should go to the Embassy. It must be by bank transfer 'to the account number 210-0309063-73 (service consulaire) at *Générale de Banque* in Brussels; with a stamped envelope and the applicant's address.' A receipt for the bank transfer should be enough.

In Brussels, you can visit the *Moldovan Consulate* – at the Embassy address – every Monday, Tuesday, Wednesday and Friday from 10am to 12 noon; then from 2pm to 5pm. A trip there by Eurostar may be your way to sort out any problems.

Currency restrictions mean you will have to fill in currency declaration forms on arrival. The amount of foreign currency you take out may be limited to the amount you declare here – which should be accurate as you can make it – but foreign residents may take out up to US$500 provided this is declared on departure.

Travel Agencies

Moldova-Tur: tel 373-2-26-25-69; fax 26-25-86 (in Chishinău).
Moldsintur: tel 373-2-22-35-29; fax 24-02-68 (also in Chishinău -- these can both
  issue invitations and arrange accommodation).
CIS Travel Services: tel 0171-828 7613. Flights to Chishinău via Warsaw with *Air
  Moldova International* – can issue vouchers for invitations and offer general
  visa advice. *Tarom* is the other main airline going to Moldova (see under
  Romania).

There is a bus service to the city centre from *Chishinău International Airport* ten miles away; and taxis which are generally to be avoided. Contact *Moldova-Tur* to be met there or for car hire.

Culture and Language

It has its own tradition of folk music; and there are traditional instruments like the *cimpi* (bagpipe) and *tsambal* (like a large lute). There is a local cuisine, too; there are coffee shops and restaurants in Chishinău; and choral and opera performances; and a nightlife based around restaurants and discoteques and the hotels. Pushkin spent some time here (hence the park) and began composing his poem *Eugene Onegin*; so naturally there is *Pushkin House*.

Religion

This is mainly Eastern Orthodox, with other traditions like Armenian churches and Seventh Day Adventist, and also one remaining synagogue.

Communications

Post is subject to long delays (of up to six weeks). So are operator-assisted calls outside the country. To call Moldova the country code is 373. The Central Post Office in Chisināu is at 73 Stefan cel Mare, 277013 Chisināu. The city code is 2.

Working in Moldova

Business and Industry Report

Currency: 1 *leu* (plural 'lay') = 100 *bani*

The economy is 'moving towards the free market,' with the usual array of privatisations, joint ventures and investment opportunities. We would imagine companies and investors interested in Ukraine or Romania first would then continue to look at the (relatively) small Moldovan market; there are opportunities here mainly in the wine trade.

Moldovan wine can be of a high standard and has made an appearance on some international supermarket shelves. Most trade hereabouts is still with Russia and its neighbours, then with Germany. See many of the information contacts cited in other country chapters in this section. The *DTI Moldova Desk* number is 0171-215-4257 or 0171-215-5265.

Useful Addresses

British Embassy: The British Embassy in Moscow deals with Moldova (see under Russia).

Moldovan Embassy: Avenue Emile Max 175, B-1030 Bruxelles; tel 732-93-00 or 732-96-59; fax 732-96-60.

US Embassy: Strada Alexei Mateevici 103, Chisināu; tel 2-23-37-72 or 23-73-45 after hours; fax 2-23-24-94.

Moldovan Embassy: 1511 K Street, Suite 329, NW Washington, DC 20005; tel 202-783-3012 or 783-4218 (Consular Section); fax 202-783-3342.

Ministry of Foreign Affairs: 1 Piata Mani Adunāri Nationale, Chisināu 277033; tel 2-23-39-40 or 23-33-38; fax 2-23-23-02.

Moldovan Chamber of Commerce: 28 Eminescou, Chisināu; tel 2-22-15-52; 2-23-38-10.

Romania

Introduction

Romania lies between the Black Sea in the south-east, and Montenegro, Serbia and Hungary to the west, Moldova and Ukraine to the north, as well as Bulgaria to the south, covering an area of 91,700 square miles. The population is 22,800,000; and its density is 247 per square mile. It is divided into four parts: mountainous and forested Transylvania and Moldavia in the north, which is separated by the Carpathian Mountains from the flat Danube plain of Wallachia in the south and east; with the Black Sea coast and the Danube delta. The capital is Bucharest, with 2 million inhabitants. Business cards are widely used in business (as throughout Eastern Europe) and exchanges of presents are an important part of the etiquette for visitors. Agriculture supports a third of the population. Oil, natural gas and their products are important in the industrial sector. The economy remains fragile, with high inflation and unemployment. Romania's largest trading partner is Russia.

Living in Romania

The *Foreign and Commonwealth Office (FCO) Travel Advice Unit* recommends that travellers should take precautions to avoid theft and for their personal safety in Romania. See BBC Ceefax p.470 onwards, or the Internet under the address http://www.fco.gov.uk/; or call 0171-238 4503/4504 for their latest recommendations.

History

Romanians see themselves as a Roman people speaking a Romance language, cut off from France or Italy by the waves of invasion lapping to their borders. This feeling about themselves has something to do with their beleaguered history – and the forests which have been a refuge for Romanian culture down the ages – and for many Romanians a kind of spirituality developed which has nothing to do with the 'West' and much more with its dark forests and remote monasteries. Other Latin peoples – the French and the Spanish – are often struck by the similarity between Romania and their own countries. Britons and Americans tend to see more differences.

From the fourteenth century on – after many previous invasions and battles – the Romanians were kept in a constant state of fear by the Turks, who had occupied the rest of the Balkans, and were intending to invade Constantinople too. Some local *voivods* (the peasant chieftans) were powerful enough to make a deal with them and maintain some degree of self-rule. In 1391, *Mircea the Old* paid them a large tribute to go away.

This was also an aim of the much more vigorous *Vlad the Impaler*, who really did spend much of his time impaling tens of thousands of Turks – and many of his own countrymen as well. In the fifteenth century, Vlad – along with the Romanian

King known as *Peter the Great* – played politics with the Hungarians and others to keep the Turks out; and carved out kingdoms in what are now the regions of Wallachia and Moldavia.

It was the remoteness of some of these forests – a bit like the Montenegrins in Montenegro – that probably helped to save these remnants of Romania and this eastern Latin world from Muslim rule. When Constaninople fell in 1453, it was only in this remotest corner of its former Empire that this epochal scene could be recorded, in the frescoes of the famous monastery at Voronets, founded in 1488 by Peter the Great. This was in Moldavia – where today we can see the Turks with their turbans outside the ramparts, and the eleventh Emperor Constantine Palaeologus defending this last bastion of the Graeco-Roman world. These monasteries, at *Humor, Voronets* and *Moldovitsa*, with their painted frescoes, supposedly inspired the colours of the red, blue and yellow Romanian flag.

Readers may consult Robert D. Kaplan's book *Balkan Ghosts* (St. Martin's Press), with its perceptive account of both his own experiences there and the Romanian attitude to life, for more on the two great dictators who have marked its history in the twentieth century (with their two dictatorial wives): King Carol II and Nicolae Ceausescu.

Residence and Entry

British passport holders require a visa to enter; but Americans may stay for up to 30 days without one. Business visa applications should also include the name of the sponsoring Romanian company. Those working or looking for work should register at the local police station; they will require a residence and work permit. Enquiries about these should be made to a Romanian consulate or embassy abroad. Or travellers can buy visas on arrival (presently around £25). You need the landing card you get on the plane as an 'exit visa' so keep the slip you are given for your return.

Getting There

This is possible by plane or coach or train. Contact any high street travel agency, or the *Russian-Romanian Travel Agency*: 13B Addison Crescent, London W14 8JR; tel 0171-371 6367. *British Airways* and *TAROM* (the national airline) have regular flights from Heathrow to Bucharest. There are regular buses to Bucharest city centre from *Otopeni* airport which are cheaper and safer than the taxis: it may be better for business people to be met by a private car or limousine, though.

Rail travel (in first class) is comfortable and fairly straightforward. The central railway station, the *Gara de Nord*, is a place to avoid if you can. Getting there by coach means contacting *Eurolines* in London (tel 0990-143219) which can get you to *Arad, Brasov, Bucharest, Deva, Ploiesti, Sebes* and *Sibiu*. At the bus station in Bucharest and some other places you should find a board giving details of services.

If you are driving, bring all your documents with you and an international driving licence. Allow extra journey time for crossing this border too. Petrol stations are available there; if not always on the main roads. Seat-belts should be fastened even if the locals don't do this.

Travel Agencies

Balkan Holidays: Sofia House, 19 Conduit Street, London W1R 9TD; tel 0171-

543 5566; fax 0171-543 5577 – specialises in summer and winter holidays in the region, mainly to Bulgaria, Croatia, Slovenia and Romania – to Poiana Brasov.
Liberty International (UK) Ltd: 11 Grosvenor Street, Chester CH1 2DD; tel 01244-351115; fax 01244-351116; e-mail liberty@chester.itsnet.co.uk. For full destination management services, including conference and meeting organisation, guide and tour services etc. Associate office in Bucharest.
Marshal Turism: 20 Unirll Blvd., Bucharest; tel 40-16147951/4105304. *American Express* representatives.
Overseas Business Travel Ltd: 8 Minories, London EC3N 1BJ; tel 0171-702 2468; fax 0171-488 1199. Offices in Moscow and Almaty; specialists in Romania, Bulgaria, Russia, and all Eastern European countries for business travel, flights and accommodation, visa support etc.
Romania Travel Centre: tel 01892-516901; e-mail james@romtrav.demon.co.uk. For flights, hotels, car hire, business travel, meeting and greeting, tailored group tours, and insurance services.
Sepoy Intl. Tourism SRL: (Hertz representative) Hotel Dorobanti, Room 101-102, Calea Dorobanti no. 1-3, 71131 Bucharest; tel 1-210-6426; fax 1-210-6433.

Accommodation

For expats this is often in hotels. The 'international' one is the *Majestic Hotel* (11 Academia Street; tel 210-2746; fax 311-3363) with prices starting at around $200 presently. Less expensive are the *Hotel Manuc* (62 Iuliu Maniu Steet; tel 61-31-415; fax 61-22-811) or the *Hotel Venetia* (Piata M. Kogalniceanu; tel 61-59-149). If you are living there you are not supposed to pay more than the locals – and a special pass is issued to this effect which can reduce your hotel price from the international to the local rate – which it is worth making a fuss about.

Currency and Customs

1 *lei* (BGL) = 100 *bani*. Not more than Lei 5,000 can be exported. This is a non-convertible currency. As everywhere in the region, you should keep your exchange receipts as well, which you may be required to show when paying for your hotel etc. *American Express* is here (see above). But credit cards are accepted still in only the larger hotels and restaurants.

Culture and Daily Life

Foodwise, meat is a major part of the diet. You can try the *mititei* (spicy meatballs) or *tocanita* (which is a spicy stew); or have some *sarmale* (stuffed cabbage leaves). The *Bistro Atheneu* in Bucharest (3 Episcopei Street; tel 61-349-00) is popular with expatriates; and has an English-speaking owner. The *bera negra* or 'black beer' is a local speciality. Worth a try is the *Indigo Café* which has live jazz and a friendly atmosphere and some restaurants where you can find gypsy music.

In Bucharest, the Opera is also worth visiting, opposite the Orthodox Cathedral where orators gave their speeches during the revolution. The *Timis* cinema nearby is a place to see English-language films. There are open-air markets, dilapidated supermarkets, and the more expensive western-style shops with security guards and the richer locals.

Embassies and Tourist Offices

British Embassy: Strada Jules Michelet 24, 70154 Bucharest; tel 1-312-035.
US Embassy: Strada Tudor Arghezi 7-9, Bucharest; tel 1-210-0149 or 1-210-4042.
Romanian Embassy: Arundel House, 4 Palace Green, London W8 4QD; tel 0171-937 9666-8.
Romanian Embassy: 1607 23rd Street, NW, Washington, DC 20008; tel 202-332-4848 or 232-4747.
Romanian National Tourist Office: 83A Marylebone High Street, London W1M 3DE; tel/fax 0171-224 3692.
Romanian National Tourist Office: Suite 210, 342 Madison Avenue, New York, NY 10173; tel 212-697-6971.

National Holidays

January 1; January 2; Orthodox Easter; May 1; December 1; December 25; December 26.

Working in Romania

Business and Industry Report

Romania is disappointed not to have been accepted already for membership of the EU, and to be relegated to Eastern Europe's second division. According to the *European Bank of Reconstruction and Development (EBRD)*, '60% of its earnings are already generated by the private sector;' and 'free trade in industrial goods is being phased in over a ten-year period from 1995.' Romanians argue that their economic progress to date merits greater rewards. This was also one of the first countries in the region to dabble in trade with the West in the early 1970s, which then stopped as the regime became more isolated.

But the same elite was still running the country – according to the critics – until 1996 at least, when the former communists involved in the palace coup againts Ceausescu lost the elections and the liberal *Democratic Convention* came to power; and set off on a faster track towards liberalisation and privatisation which should bring it more into the Western orbit. So there was little time for Romania to prepare its case for for EU membership.

Employment

In the world of work, English is not very widely spoken; with your colleagues as likely to speak German, or Russian, or even perhaps Chinese. The etiquette involves dressing neatly, much as you would in Britain or the United States – not in shirt-sleeves – and 'learning to put up with the minor inconveniences of a sometimes bewildering set of rules and bureaucracy,' according to one correspondent from Bucharest. But the working environment is said to be relaxed and friendly – especially after work. There is a range of local agents and consultants (and some lawyers) who may be of assistance in your search for employment; but it will be better here, as in other countries, to make some direct contacts yourself – and preferably on-the-spot if you can afford to visit Romania in advance, or perhaps come on a holiday here.

Tourism:
Crystal Holidays (see *Bulgaria*) requires experienced representatives who speak Romanian to meet and look after skiers in Poiana Brasov and Sinaia. So may *Balkan Holidays* (Sofia House, 19 Conduit Street, London W1R 9TD; tel 0171-543 5555 – reservations – or 0171-543 5588 – for independent travel – and see above). High street travel agencies are a very good source of brochures which will show you which of the major tour operators currently have operations in Romania – and applications by resort representatives should be made early; at least by January for summer of the following year; and similarly for the winter ski season.

Voluntary Work:
Romania Information Centre: The University, Southampton, Hampshire – holds a register of voluntary work contacts in Romania.

Commercial Contacts

The *British Embassy* in Bucharest publishes a 'Commercial Newsletter' quarterly, with details of UK companies investing in Romania. The *Ministry of Commerce* (Str. Apolodor 17, 70663 Bucharest; tel 1-141-141) or the *Chamber of Commerce and Industry* (Boulevard Nicolae Balcescu 22, 79502 Bucharest; tel 1-615-4703) may also offer advice and commercial information. The *Romania Desk* of the *Department of Trade and Industry* (Bay 835, Kingsgate House, 66-74 Victoria Street, London SW1H) can provide an information pack for commercial or business purposes; and holds lists of foreign trade organisations and UK business representatives and companies in Romania.

Your local library or business library may hold copies of the *Official Journal* where the larger contracts and invitations to tender under the *PHARE* programme are published; or telephone 0171-873 9090 to arrange a subscription. On the Internet see *http://europa. eu.int/comm/dg1a/phare/index.html* where these are also listed; and see the *General Overview* section for details of the *PHARE* programme generally, providing aid for Central and Eastern European countries.

Also contact the *Romanian Development Agency:* (Foreign Relations and Economic Assistance), 7 Blvd. Magheru, Bucharest; tel 401-615-6686/8824; fax 401-613-2415/312-0371. The *RDA* aims to encourage and assist foreign investors in all aspects of their investment in Romania.

Slovenia

Introduction

Slovenia advertises itself as 'the green piece of Europe.' It is a small but not-quite-landlocked country skirted by Austria to the north, Italy to the west, Croatia to the south, and Hungary to the east. It has, however, a short but beautiful stretch of coastline along the northern Adriatic. Its capital *Ljubljiana* has a Central European feel, with street cafés and a cuisine not unlike that of Austria or Hungary, and an ancient castle. For much of its history Slovenia was part of the Austro-Hungarian Empire and today looks for trade and commercial contacts to its Central European neighbours. In the near future it will become a member of the European Union.

There are up-market resorts; and thermal centres on the coast. Other attractions inland include horse-riding; village inns and taverns; the Alpine scenery; its national parks, with forests and fast-flowing streams; skiing holidays; and a museum at *Kobarid* where Ernest Hemingway drove an ambulance during the First World War, it is said. The lake at *Bléd* was also a favoured resort of the Hapsburg royal family, and then Tito.

Slovenian people are relaxed and easy-going, and also courteous, interested in the outdoors and nature. Slovenians, like Austrians, like to go walking in the Alps. The reemergence of tourism is an important part of the economy and will be one important factor in the development of links with Central Europe, and further afield, and will encourage some holidaymakers – in the course of time – to consider settling down here.

Living in Slovenia

Pros and Cons of Moving to Slovenia

The people are friendly – but you will be closer to the the German-speaking part of Europe – and to Italy – than in some other parts of this Mediterranean, or Central, or South-Eastern region... This cultural situation is much the same as in Hungary and the Czech Republic, or even in Croatia, where German tends to be spoken before English. Tourism and trade may lead many to consider living and working here, especially those from neighbouring countries. The combination of Mediterranean and Alpine landscapes and climates is another plus.

History

A full-scale war in former Yugoslavia started here first. If we compare Yugoslavia to the USSR, Slovenia was the equivalent of the Baltic States, and the first to secede. But the Slovenian government had tried in the beginning to preserve a federal Yugoslavia, then resisted the Yugoslav army during its ten-day war of independence.

Geography

The population is 1,998,850 in an area of 7820 square miles. The capital Ljubljana has 320,000 inhabitants.

Getting There

Visas and Residence

UK and US citizens do not require a visa for entry. Foreigners who would like to be employed in Slovenia need a work permit (which may be obtained at the *Slovenian Bureau of Employment*, Parmova 32, 61000 Ljubljana; tel 61-321-041; fax 61-326-665 – applications usually to be lodged by the employer – and this work visa to be obtained at the Embassy prior to departure is valid for up to one year).

The Embassy needs: a letter of application with full employment details; description of the company and its main activity/object; number of employees; its official registration; and similar details; written evidence that you have a place to live; and an official statement by a regional bureau of employment that no unemployed Slovenian person can do that job. A work visa takes around 14 days, and the accompanying business visa 30-45 days. This is required by all those who have started a business there. More information – and a useful information sheet – should be sought from the Embassy or Consulate. The current fee in the UK is £86.

You may also enter as a tourist, for up to three months. You should register then with the local police, three days after arrival, and then apply for a temporary residence permit if you wish to stay as a resident, at the nearest *Office for Foreigners* (*Urad za tujce*) which will be in the town hall, or in Ljubljana at Proletarska 1/III: tel 140-12-44. This is a residence, not a work permit.

Customs and Currency

The currency is the Slovene *tolar* (SIT). One of these equals 100 *stotins*. This is fully convertible; and travellers cheques are widely accepted. The import and export of local currency is allowed up to a limit of DM 3000, and foreign currency may be taken out up to the amount declared on arrival.

By Plane

Charters:
Thomson features some holidays in Slovenia in its 1998 brochure: *Thomson Tour Operations Ltd.*, Greater London House, Hampstead Road, London NW1 7SD; tel 0171-387 9321; fax 0171-387 8451 (or telephone 0990-502560).
Other charter and package tour operators include *Balkan Holidays*, Sofia House, 19 Conduit Street, London W1R 9TD, tel 0171-543 5555 – reservations, or 0171-543 5588 – independent travel, and *Slovenija Pursuits*, 14 Hay Street, Steeple Morden, Royston, Herts. SG8 0PE, tel 01763-852646, fax 01763-852387, featuring many kinds of short and longer-stay holidays in the country and a Slovenia specialist. Also see the brochures of major tour operators like *Airtours*, *British Airways Holidays*, *First Choice*, *Panorama* etc. who may all include package tours featuring Slovenia. High street travel agencies are a good source of cheaper charter flight information too – these may be in the summer and winter seasons. 15 UK tour operators are already here, and more will come.

The national airline is *Adria Airways* – see below. Ljubljana is two hours' flying time (and less than a day's driving time) from London. Other airlines include *Aeroflot, Air France, Austrian Airways, Macedonian Airlines* and *Swissair*.

By Boat, Road and Train

Ferry Service: The *Prince of Venice* catamaran runs between Venice and Portoroz.

Road and Rail: By rail and road there are connections from the major European cities; and nowadays via the Channel Tunnel quite straightforwardly from London. There are direct trains from Germany (Munich and Leipzig), Italy (from Venice and Trieste) and Austria (via Vienna and Villach); and Croatia (Zagreb), as well as from Budapest in Hungary. Inter-city travel is run by *TTG* and is generally inexpensive.

Speed limits are 120kph (75mph) on motorways, 100 kph (62mph) on other roads, and 60kph (38mph) in cities, where one rule is that 'school buses cannot be overtaken.' There is a low alcohol limit, so no drinking and driving here.

Useful Addresses:
Adria Airways: ('The Airline of Slovenia') SL-1000 Ljubljiana, Kuzmiceva 7; tel (0)61-133-43-36; fax (0)61-323-356. London tel 0171-7344 630; fax 0171-2875 476.
ABC Rent-a-Car: Aerodrom Ljubljiana, 61000 Ljubljana; tel 64-261-684; fax 61-261-669.
Kompas-Hertz Rent-a-Car: Celovska 206, 61000 Ljubljiana; tel 61-156-1311; fax 61-572-088.
Automobile Association of Slovenia: Dunaijska 128, 61000 Ljubljiana; tel 61-341-341; fax 61-342-378. Assistance: 987.
Airport Ljubljiana: 64210 Brnik-Aerodrom; tel 64-222-700; fax 64-221-220.
Railway Station: Trg OF, 61000 Ljubljiana; tel 61-131-51-67; fax 61-319-141.
Bus Station: Trg OF 4, 61000 Ljubljiana; tel 61-133-61-36; fax 61-133-63-00.

Communications

Radio Slovenia: Tavcarjeva 17, 61000 Ljubljiana; tel 61-321-655; fax 61-132-72-76. Traffic information and weather news on channels 1 and 2 in English, German and Italian: AM 549 Khz; FM 92.4, 93.5, 98.9, 99.9...

Post/Telephone information: tel 988. Stamps available in bookstalls and post offices (open weekdays until 7pm). The country code is 386, plus 61 for Ljubljana. Outgoing international calls begin 00; there are token or phonecard phones.

Newspapers: The main local newspaper is *Delo*. English-language publications include *Ars Vivendi, MM Slovenia, Slovenian Business Report, Slovenija*, and *Slovenija Weekly*.

Accommodation

There are 175 hotels throughout the country, and a two, three, four and five-star system, as in the rest of Europe. Further information from the *Tourism and*

Catering Association of the Chamber of Economy of Slovenia (Slovenska cetsa 51, 1000 Ljubljana; tel 61-132-72-83; fax 61-302-983); or the *Slovenian Tourist Board*, see below, which has an annual directory of hotel rates for travel agents.

Rental agencies in Ljubljana can be found through the newspapers or on a stroll through the centre. Some telephone numbers for these are 126-407, 1339-454, 1258-141, 1251-262, 345-361, 1234-792. Rental contracts should be checked at the *Housing Department*, Zarnikova 3, tel 61-171-0600/0651, the British Embassy advises.

Travelling Around

For more information, contact the *Slovenian Tourist Board* or the *Ljubljiana Promotion Centre*, Dunaijska 156, 61000 Ljubljiana; tel 61-1881-165; fax 61-1881-164. Also see the *Tourist Map of Slovenia* produced by the *Centre for Tourism Promotion*, which is part of the *Slovenian Tourist Board*: Dunaijska 156, 1000 Ljubljana; tel 61-1891-840; fax 61-1891-841; and the various brochures entitled *Slovenia, the green piece of Europe* all available from tourist offices: *Slovenian Tourist Office*: 2 Canfield Place, London NW6 3BT; tel 0171-372-3767; fax 0171-372-3763; 345 East 12th Street, New York, NY 10003; tel 212-358-9686; fax 212-358-9025.

Culture and Daily Life

The language is Slovene, which in addition to singular and plural has a dual. 'No, it is not the same in Slovene if one, two or more people are talking...' they insist. It is a rural country with some cultural and scientific highlights (of which all these CEE/South-Eastern European countries seem proud). These are, respectively, the *Slovene Academy of Sciences and Arts* (going back to the 17th century) and the *Slovene Philharmonic* orchestra (going back to 1701, one of the oldest in Europe).

Sport means skiing (and other winter sports) and remarkably, we are told, the 'autochtonous Bloke skis are considered some of the oldest means of transportation in Europe.' Mountaineering and hiking are practised. Across the countryside you will see, looking like small wooden houses, the *kozolecs*, which are racks for drying hay, and some beehives which have been painted in true Balkan manner – one of many local folk traditions, as are the *Mardi Gras* costumes, harking back to pre-Christian times and decked out with greenery like moss and leaves... so you could visit when the carnival comes to town.

Cuisine has an Austrian/German flavour. Sauerkraut or grilled sausages and apple strudel are the kind of thing the locals like. Bread can be stuffed with sweet fillings, meat or vegetables. In the north-east there are some excellent white wines.

Shopping is from 8am until late; and the nightlife and its symphony orchestra are attractions of the capital Ljubljana.

Embassies and Tourist Offices

Slovenian Embassy: Suite One, Cavendish Court, 11-15 Wigmore Street, London; tel 0171-495-7775; fax 0171-495-7776. Visa section open 10am to 12am.
British Embassy: 4th Floor, Trg Republike 3, 1000 Ljubljiana; tel 61-125-71-31; fax 61-125-01-74.
Slovenian Embassy: 1525 New Hampshire Avenue, NW, Washington, DC 20036; tel 202-667-5363; fax 202-667-4563. Consulate in New York, tel 212-370-3006.

US Embassy: Prazakova 4, 1000 Ljubljana; tel 61-301-427/485; fax 61-301-401.
Slovenian Tourist Board: Dunaijska 156, 1000 Ljubljana; tel 61-1891-840; fax 61-1891-841.
Slovenian Tourist Office: 2 Canfield Place, London NW6 3BT; tel 0171-372-3767; fax 0171-372-3763.
Slovenian Tourist Office: 345 East 12th Street, New York, NY 10003; tel 212-358-9686; fax 212-358-9025.

Public Holidays

January 1, 2; February 8; Easter; April 27; May 1,2; Whit Sunday; June 25; Assumption; October 31; November 1; Christmas Day; and Boxing Day (Independence Day).

Working in Slovenia

Establishing a Company

These can be *Limited Partnerships, Joint Stock, Limited Liability Companies* and so on, much as in the USA or UK. A minimum founding capital for a Limited Company is SIT 1.5 million, with the fees payable on incorporation etc. Agreements like this all have to be notarised; and there is a legal framework for bankruptcy and liquidation, accounting and auditing, very much as in Britain. For more information see the leaflet *Slovenia, Establishing a Company* available from the Slovenian Embassy, and some of the *Useful Addresses* below.

Employment

There is a range of local agents and consultants (and some lawyers) who may be of assistance in your search for employment; and the British or US Embassies may have some contacts for these. But it is certainly better to approach business and employment contacts directly yourself, and preferably on-the-spot if you can take a week or two to have an exploratory holiday there.

English Teaching:
English Contacts Abroad provides a research and direct contacts service for EFL teachers in Slovenia and all CEE countries: PO Box 126, Oxford OX2 6UB, UK.

Teacher Agents:
This is a way for English as a Foreign Language teachers and others to bring their group (usually of secondary school or university-level students, and usually in the school holidays) to Britain, often having their expenses paid or earning a small commission. This is sometimes for one, two, or three week-courses in the summer; but can be all the year round. One excellent organisation offering courses like this in Oxford is *Speak English* (PO Box 126, Oxford OX2 6RU, UK). Write to the Director for more details.

Income Tax

You will need to have lived there continuously for six months to have to pay income tax in that tax year, and to have a permanent residency there. A double tax convention has been signed with Britain, meaning you don't pay tax on income you earned elsewhere which you have already paid tax on.

Business and Industry Report

The *British Embassy Commercial Section* may provide general briefings for business travellers. They inform us that they will send their *Registration Pack* for those doing business or who are resident there – with a very wide range of English-speaking and British community contacts, like English Church Services, the *Slovene-British Society*, English-speaking lawyers, doctors, dentists and so on, which make this an invaluable document for all those considering living, working or doing business there. All expats should always register their presence with the Embassy as well. The Embassy can also send its *List of British Companies* and briefings on the economy. They suggest also contacting the *DTI* (see previous chapters). Also see all the research and background contacts under *Business* and *Employment* in earlier country chapters in this section.

Useful Addresses

Slovenian Chamber of Lawyers: Trdonova ulica 8, 1000 Ljubljiana; tel 61-312-979; fax 61-301-956.
Chamber of Notaries: Tavcarjeva 6, 1000 Ljubljana; tel 61-301-454.
Ljubljana Court Register: Tavccarjeva 9, 1000 Lubljiana; tel 61-303-040.
Trade and Investment Promotion Office: (Ministry for Economic Relations and Development) Kotnikova 5, 1000 Ljubljana; tel 61-178-35-57; fax 61-178-35-99.

Yugoslavia

Introduction

The *Foreign and Commonwealth Office (FCO) Travel Advice Unit* recommends that travellers should take precautions to avoid theft and for their personal safety in Serbia and Montenegro. For their latest recommendations, see BBC Ceefax p.470 onwards or the Internet under the address http://www.fco.gov.uk/. The *FCO* advice line telephone number is 0171-238 4503/4504.

Living in Yugoslavia

Politics

One piece in this Balkans jigsaw puzzle has been the 'western-style' democracy which has been introduced in almost every country, including Serbia/Yugoslavia. But in its recent history – and we should make a distinction between the politicians and many of its ordinary people – Serbia has sometimes abandoned this in favour of a chauvinism based more on race and history, which is not quite 'democratic' and certainly not liberal.

This is not a unique tendency in all these countries of this South-Eastern Europe region, stretching from the shores of the Mediterranean to the Black Sea. By an accident of their geography, perhaps, these have all have known invasion and the threat of oblivion, have resisted empires, and reinvented themselves many times over, in the course of a long and troubled history. So it is in Serbia, where this newly discovered – or recreated – national identity is based especially on the Orthodox religion, and memories of defeats and former greatness.

As yet, politics here is not quite as it is in Western Europe. At present, Slobodan Milosovic is still the President of the Yugoslav Federation (his latest manoeuvre to hang onto power after he gave up the Serbian Presidency). Serbia and Montenegro are the two partners in this larger Yugoslav Federation. But now even some of the much less numerous Montenegrins (650,00 as opposed to ten million Serbs) are demanding equal political status with Serbia, and 'to destroy autocratic political conceptions and their representatives,' as one of their leaders puts it.

One rivalry which Serbs and Montenegrins can share is with the mainly Albanian residents of the Province of Kossovo (or Kosovo) in the south. This is where the present unrest in the Yugoslav Federation is located. The key to solving this dispute – in this byzantine region where all is not what it seems – may not lie in the various efforts at international mediation, involving Albania, Macedonia and others, but mainly in the resolution of this tension between Serbia and Montenegro which is one of its indirect causes. This could be inside or outside the context of the Yugoslav Federation.

Economy

Some UN sanctions against Yugoslavia have been lifted as a result of the Dayton peace accord. Others have been reimposed, after the Serbian crackdown in Kosovo, an 'outer wall' of measures which looks like continuing. This is one of many drawbacks for those thinking of living or working there. Serbia/Yugoslavia is not a member of the *IMF* for instance (and see the *Business and Industry Report* below). Although the Montenegrin President says he wishes to preserve a connection with a more democratic Serbia, the Dayton Agreement has, paradoxically, given the Montenegrins another reason to take a more independent line – counterbalanced by the much greater Serbian military and economic strength.

Geography

Along with Serbia and the provinces of Kosovo and Voijvodina this is all that is left of the Yugoslav Federation. If Montenegro were to secede and Kosovo to revolt, then Yugoslavia would be no more; and the process of disintegration would be complete.

Business and Trade

Conditions and circumstances can change quite quickly in this region. The *British Embassy* replies to our enquiry there that: 'Conditions are changing all the time ... In this market any advice offered now may well be out of date even before the book hits the shops. We tailor our advice to the needs of the individual business caller,' so this is what readers are advised to do, and to contact the *British Embassy Commercial Section* in Belgrade.

History

When the first Serbian state was carved out of the Byzantine Empire by the tribal chieftan Stefan Nemanja in the twelfth century, it was one of the most civilised in Europe. Its leader at least could write his name, unlike many of his neighbours; and Serbia preserved the traditions of the Greek Orthodox Church in its own version of it which became known as the Serbian Orthodox Church, founded by Stefan's successor and son, the travelling monk who became known as Saint Sava.

The fourteenth century was certainly Serbia's heyday. King Milutin (and later his grandson Stefan Dushan) had conquered territory to the south, east and west, and created a new Orthodox empire, wealthier even than the one based in Constantinople. King Milutin married and left wives with as great an enthusiasm as Henry VIII (including the six-year old daughter of the frightened Byzantine Emperor Andronicus II Palaeologus). Unlike Henry VIII, though, he didn't have any of them put to death.

The Turks conquered Byzantium, renaming it Istanbul; and they put paid to the Serbian Empire too. But because the land here was more wooded and inhospitable, the Serbs were never so completely subjugated as the Bulgarians or the Greeks, especially in the mountains of Montenegro, where a slightly different sense of national identity grew up and where foreign domination was never quite as complete.

Climate

Northern and central parts have a continental climate, with short springs and hot summers; the coastal part of Montenegro has a mediterranean climate.

Population

10,394,026

Visas

The British Embassy advises that visas are still required and 'despite the advice given by some travel agents, under no circumstances can they be obtained at the border.' Applications should be well in advance to avoid the risk of delay, and 'the Yugoslavian Embassy can now issue multiple-entry visas.'

Currency

This is the *dinar* (YUD), divided into 100 *paras*. Officially, this is the only legal tender, but in practice deutschmarks and dollars will be very useful. Credit cards are not widely accepted.

Getting There

By Air:
British Airways flies from Gatwick six times a week; so does *Yugoslav Airways (JAT)* (tel 0171-629 2007) from Heathrow. *JAT* and other international operators also fly to the major European destinations.

By Sea:
There are container services to the port of *Bar* in Montenegro.

By Rail:
There are direct, but slow services to Vienna, Athens and Istanbul as well as all neighbouring countries (excluding Croatia, Bosnia and Albania).

By Car:
There are generally good roads. Foreign driving licenses are accepted for short visits but third party insurance and temporary registration must be paid for at the border (costing DM 90 and DM 50 at present). Take all your insurance, ownership and driving license details.

Communications

From the UK, Yugoslavia is 00-381 plus 11 for Belgrade, 21 for Novi Sad, Nis, 18, and Pristina, 38. The code for Podgorica is 81. Banks and post offices are open until 7pm on weekdays; and until 3pm on Saturdays.

For drivers, there are some tolls on major roads. The emergency number for the *Automobile and Motorcycle Club of Serbia* if you break down is 987, for help and information.

Serbia on line: www.serbia-info.com. For information an all aspects of Serbia.

Cities and Regions

BELGRADE
In this region of mixed ethnic identities, the Celts founded the first known settlement at the confluence of the *Danube* and *Sava* rivers in the third century B.C. This was overlaid by Roman, Byzantine, Serb, Turkish and Austro-Hungarian settlements at this meeting point of these two rivers and many cultures. The frontier today is between the old communism and the new capitalism. There are parks with gardens, and broad avenues (which were the scene of student demonstrations as recently as the winter of 1996-7).

There are theatres and concert halls; and monuments like the *Kalemegdan* fortress, constructed mainly in the 12th and 14th centuries but founded by the Romans. The *Gallery of Frescoes* houses a permanent collection of copies of these frescoes from medieval monasteries. The skyline of the capital is dominated by its two cathedrals. The population of Belgrade is two million. Other large cities in Serbia are *Novi Sad* (278,700) and *Nis*.

REGIONS
'Get away from it all into the centre of the world...' says the tourist brochure (*Serbia, landscape painted from the heart* – available from *TOS, National Tourism Organization of Serbia*, Belgrade, Dobrinjska 11, tel 11-235-27-66, 11-68-68-04). 'People in Serbia suffer from incorrigible idealism,' and you can share some of this, from its church architecture to the national parks. 'Roam through Serbia. You won't lose your way, no matter what city you get to!'

The many skiing resorts include *Kopaonik*, the largest, where UK tour operators like *Thomson Holidays*, *Crystal* and *Inghams* go, the sports centre of *Brzovica*, and *Zlatibor* with gentler slopes – and you can also skate on its frozen lake. One agency to contact, which offers a range of skiing and summer holidays and specialises in this region, is *Balkan Holidays*: Sofia House, 19 Conduit Street, London W1R 9TD; tel 0171-543 5566.

Rural tourism is another opportunity for travel agents and tourists, with the kind of farm holidays where you can get away from it all in picturesque surroundings. The specialist operator *Folk Tours* (Freepost Lon7933, London SE16 1BP; tel/fax 0171-231 5782) offers a visit to one folk music festival, in the town of *Gucha* in Yugoslavia in August.

MONTENEGRO
It has its own *National Tourist Organisation*, which will also be a very good source of some primary information about the country, at: 81000 Podgorica, Stanka Dragojevica 26; tel/fax 81-41-591/45-95. *Podgorica* is the regional – or national – capital, with 620,000 inhabitants. 'Contrary to popular belief' – according to its brochures – 'The Republic of Montenegro was never involved in war and has a totally unspoilt natural landscape.' Mountains, beaches and national parks give it some of the same appeal as Croatia, and some Britons will also have holidayed along this 150 miles or so of Montenegrin coastline in the 1970s and 80s. Holiday bookings can be made through *Pilgrim Holidays*: tel 0171-495 1323.

Business and investment from abroad is welcomed, and 'a legal base has been established to guarantee foreign partners the safety of their investments.' Some are investing today in this Montenegrin Riviera, which has the greatest scope for tourism development. Transfers presently to Podgorica or the coastal town of *Tivat* are from Belgrade, but there will be some scheduled services and charters into Tivat soon. The historic and cultural capital of Montenegro is *Cetinje*.

Working in Yugoslavia

Business and Industry Report

Serbia/Yugoslavia has begun its slow journey from isolation to reintegration into the international community; its endorsement of the Dayton Agreement in 1995 was the most important first step on this road. The political situation is unstable, but the economy has picked up of late. It couldn't have got any worse. The war with Croatia helped to give Yugoslavia what will probably continue to be the world record inflation rate: 313 million per cent per month.

Banks are burdened by bad debt; but agriculture holds out some prospects for trade and exports. Key companies and personalities of the Serbian commercial world are the *Zastava* car factory, *Galenika* pharmaceuticals, *Rudnik* textiles, *Simpo* furniture, and the *Karic* brothers, whose interests range from television and communications to banking.

From 1948, Yugoslavia under Tito took what became known as a 'middle course' between isolationism and the free market – which is why western tourists could come – and some companies had a form of ownership supposedly based on workers' management. This system, too, collapsed, not only because of war (which began in 1991) or sanctions (which started in May 1992) but because it was as inefficient as the Soviet model. The first economic reforms and privatisations had been introduced in 1988, before the war started, and before the break-up of the larger Yugoslavia.

Sources of Information

British Embassy: Commercial Department, Ul. Generala Zdanova 46, Belgrade; tel 11-645-055.
Department of Trade and Industry: tel 0171-215-8560; fax 0171-215 8598. The Yugoslavia desk.
Embassy of Yugoslavia: 5-7 Lexham Gardens, London W8 5JJ; tel 0171-370-6105; fax 0171-370-3838.
Embassy of Yugoslavia: 2410 California Avenue, NW, Washington, DC 20008; tel 202-462-6566; fax 202-797-9663. New York Consulate: tel 212-879-8700/535-2154.
Tourist Office – JAT: Prince Frederick House, 37 Maddox Street, London W1R 0AQ; tel 0171-629 2007/409 1319; fax 0171-493 8092.
TOS, National Tourism Organization of Serbia, Belgrade, Dobrinjska 11; tel 11-235-27-66; fax 11-68-68-04.
Yugoslav Chamber of Economy: Ul. Generala Zdanova 13-15, 11000 Belkgrade; tel 11-339-461; fax 11-631-928.
Chamber of Economy of Montenegro: Novaka Miloseva 29/11, 81000 Podgorica; tel 81-31071; fax 81-34926.

The Caspian and Central Asia Region

Armenia
Azerbaijan
Georgia
Kazakstan
Kyrgyzstan
Tajikistan
Turkmenistan
Uzbekistan

Caspian and Central Asia Region

Introduction

The Caspian Sea is bordered by five states: *Russia, Kazakstan, Turkmenistan, Azerbaijan* and *Iran*. Of these, the Russian Federation, *Kazakstan* and *Turkmenistan* may also be considered as belonging to Central Asia, a region which includes *Kyrgyzstan, Tajikistan* and *Uzbekistan*. Most of these Central Asian countries have languages, civilisations and much of their history in common. *Azerbaijan* (on the other side of the Caspian Sea) also has this Turkic or Central Asian heritage.

The common thread in this tapestry is 'Turkestan'; the name which was given to this entire Central Asia region as it was slowly being incorporated into the Russian Empire in the nineteenth century. There are also three countries in Transcausia: *Armenia* and *Georgia* as well as the above mentioned, and potentially the most prosperous country in the region, Azerbaijan.

Culture:
The cultural situation in Central Asia and Transcaucasia is post-colonial, with responses to the retreat of the Soviet Union ranging from complete rejection to nostalgia for the 'good old days' which now have gone. Many old traditions have been forgotten. Others were assimilated by the old order and became a form of propaganda.

All this may explain the high hopes many have of a rapid modernisation along East Asian lines, and international trade and consumerism, a kind of global economic solution to their specific cultural problems.

Economy:
Azerbaijan is at the head of the league table of these former Soviet, Asian economies. In Central Asia proper, *Kazakstan* and also *Uzbekistan* have made the greatest progress economically, with *Turkmenistan* not far behind. The *Caspian Sea* and its environs contain the third greatest reserve of oil in the world – which is an advantage to all these countries – this is after the Persian Gulf and Siberia, and far ahead of the North Sea. Proven reserves of oil in the Caspian basin amount to 20 billion barrels (with an estimated 10 or 15 billion barrels on top of that; and 7 billion billion cubic metres of natural gas.

This has created a complicated political and economic situation; and there are some difficult decisions to be made. Where should the oil pipelines go, for instance? The Russians say from Baku through Russia to the Black Sea through the existing pipeline (which is currently being repaired). *Chechnya* (which considers itself a *de facto* independent state) wants to earn money from this pipeline too.

The West prefers a route going through its Nato ally *Turkey*, and ending up at the Mediterranean port of Ceyhan, a project which is currently still under consideration. Partly for this reason, the West would prefer Turkey to improve its own domestic human rights situation as well.

The most logical route, from a practical point of view, is through *Georgia* to its Black Sea port of Soupsa – a pipeline which has been built and will come on stream at the end of 1998. Logical, but there are other political instabilities to consider, and we can see the potential for instability here is very great indeed.

Armenia

Introduction

Armenia is not the most positive pattern for development in the region. It is a country recovering from a war with its neighbour and – as Armenians see it – from thousands of years of persecution too.

The *FCO* Travel Advice Unit warns that the border with Azerbaijan should be avoided; as should travel by night outside Yerevan (or Erevan). 'Use officially marked taxis which you should not share with strangers. When travelling by train, keep you valuable in the compartment under the bed/seat,' all advice which will be familiar to those who have been to former Soviet Union. Armenia, in other words, is in a not dissimilar position to many of its other ex-republics – but is developing more slowly than some.

There is an unresolved conflict over this border with Azerbaijan, which is the reason for the negative travel advice. This is the greatest political and economic problem. Another parallel could be with the more stable European CIS states of Ukraine and Belarus, where the economy will also take years, and probably decades, to readjust.

Living in Armenia

Geographical Information

It borders on Turkey in the south-east, Iran to the south, and Georgia to the north (which is one indirect way into the country from Azerbaijan), with Azerbaijan in the east separating it from the Caspian Sea and making this a kind of Christian enclave in a mainly Muslim area. The southern border of the Russian Federation is further to the north.

This is how many Armenians see their country; as an island surrounded by enemies; there is a kind of siege mentality – and a certain resignation to losing out once again – which certainly predates the recent war with Azerbaijan. It suffers from its landlocked position but is now a relatively safe and easy country to visit – despite the above advice – apart from its eastern border and Yerevan by night. But it is not a recommended destination for those without travel experience in the region.

The population is nearly four million, in an area of 11,500 square miles. There are hot summers and extremely cold winters, a continental, mountainous climate as nearly 80% of the country is 1,000 metres above sea level. The landscape is of high mountains and bare rocky hills with few trees. Sheep breeding and vegetable or fruit production are the main forms of agriculture. The capital, Yerevan, has a population of 1.2 million.

Residence and Entry Regulations

Contact the Armenian Embassy in the UK or USA or your home country. You will need your original passport, photo, invitation and visa fee. They advise that 'visas can be obtained from the Armenian consulates in Moscow, Tbilisi, Ashkabad etc. Generally visas are not granted at the borders. The nearest you can apply is Tbilisi.' Other Armenian Embassies can do this too, but 'generally speaking visas are issued for a stay of 21 days inside Armenia and if the person intends to stay longer or work then the sponsor/employer applies to the *Ministry of the Interior* to obtain extension of leave to stay.'

Useful Addresses

British Embassy: 28 Charents Street, Yerevan; tel 15-18-42; fax 15-18-07.
Armenian Embassy: 25A Cheniston Gardens, London W8 6TG; tel 0171-938 5435; fax 0171-938 2595.
US Embassy: 18 Marshal Baghramian Street, Yerevan 375019; tel 15-11-44; fax 15-11-38.
Ministry of Foreign Affairs: 10 Marshal Baghramian Street, Yerevamn 375019; tel 52-35-31; fax 56-56-16.
Chamber of Commerce and Industry: 39 Alevardyan Street, 375010 Yerevan; tel 56-54-38; fax 56-50-71.
Ministry of Foreign Economic Relations: tel 56-21-57.
British Council: (Yerevan) tel 58-24-75; fax 15-18-03.

Working in Armenia

Business and Industry Report

The *British Embassy Commercial Office* can provide general briefings for business travellers on different sectors, exports and matching UK companies with local firms etc. (see British Embassy address above). The *DTI* has a desk for the region and some general publications for exporters (*Transcaucasia Helpdesk*: tel 0171-215 4771 for Armenia; or 215-5000 for the switchboard) and also has information on UK companies interested in the region. For a full tailor-made destination or country report with many direct contacts for businesses and/or expatriates or an extensive background briefing write in the first instance to *English Contacts Abroad*, PO Box 126, Oxford OX2 6UB, UK, a direct contacts service for businesses and expatriates.

'Brochures regarding some basic facts about Armenia are available at the Embassy in Britain, at the cost of £2 each,' the Armenian Embassy tells us; and see the *Armenian Chamber of Commerce* and other useful addresses above.

Azerbaijan

Introduction

There is great potential for trade and investment here; and Azerbaijan has become the most popular destination for expatriates in the region, working in the oil industry, transport and services. So Baku has its pubs and expat social life along 'Oilmen Boulevard', with bars, boutiques and jazz clubs – and some internationally known jazz musicians hail from this part of the world. This really is becoming a 'second Kuwait': reserves are twice or three times as large as those in the North Sea; and the giant multinationals – Amoco, Exxon, Mobil, Chevron, BP and others – have all signed multi-billion dollar deals with the government – the 'deal of the century' it was called when the American companies moved in.

President Heidar Aliyev is an ex-KGB boss who was number two to Leonid Brezhnev. Now, times have changed; and today he tries to balance the rival claims of his larger neighbours like Russia and Iran by sharing out the oil concessions. In the end, this should all help to bring stability, but Azerbaijan's neighbours are already squabbling about where the pipelines should go: this was one reason Russia fought so hard to hold onto Chechnya. Many Azerbaijanis today – apparently – are hanging a dried plant called the 'camel flower' in the front of their Merc or BMW. It is meant to ward off envy.

Living in Azerbaijan

History

Azerbaijan has never quite been a centralised state along the lines of Armenia or Georgia; but also has its former empire, stretching from the Caucasus to Tehran and the Caspian Sea to Turkey. Later it came under the influence of Persia, and Turkey. In Azerbaijan, the influence of Europe has been weak; and its people came from the east not the west. To the east it turns into lowlands and is easily accessible and 'open'. It is the threshold of Central Asia.

Geographical Information

The population is 7.5 million. The climate is temperate; and cotton and wine are also produced.

The Language

Azeri, a Turkic language which Turkish people can quite easily understand, and also Russian.

The Currency

The currency is the *manat* – introduced in 1991 – which has quite a stable exchange rate. US dollars are the most useful currency to take with you; and may be the only currency accepted in some places. The manat may not be imported or exported. Credit card facilities are becoming available in some restaurants and hotels.

Getting There

The train from Moscow might be the longest way to get there. The most popular indirect route is through Moscow with *Aeroflot*, or with *Transaero*: tel 0171-828 7613/393 1210/393 1211 – *CIS Travel Services*; or via Amsterdam with *KLM* (UK reservations: 0990-750900. *Lufthansa* has regular flights from London and Frankfurt (airport office: tel 412-90-08-13; Baku city office tel 412-98-12-34 – in the UK tel 0345-737747 for reservations). *British Airways* (tel 0345-222111) and *Turkish Airlines* also offer flights to Tbilisi in Georgia, from London and Istanbul. In the country itself, you can contact *IMAIR Airways*: 115, Azi Aslanov str., Baku 370000; tel 98-23-76; fax 93-04-78.

Travel Agencies

Improtex Travel: 16 Samed Vurgun, Baku, 370000 Azerbaijan; tel 931728/932279/934243; fax 927520. Services from hotels, visas, tours, transfers to car hire.

Hotels

The *Hyatt Regency Hotel*, Bakuranov Street, is the local five-star one. Building new apartment complexes for expatriates is also one of the business opportunities here. Prices are very high, from $500 for a very modest two-room flat to $5,000 for something furnished to international standards. Hotels can be anything from $100 to $400 a night.

Residence and Entry Regulations

Contact the Embassy of Azerbaijan in the UK (tel 0171-938 5482) or your home country. You will need your original passport, photo, visa fee (£37 currently in the UK); and to make this application well in advance. Business and private visas also require a letter of invitation from the company or individual concerned, or from the *Ministry of Foreign Affairs*: Genjler Meydani 3, 370000 Baku; tel (+994-12 or +99-412 – satellite phone code) 92-56-06/97-56; fax 65-10-38 or 98-73-27 (information department) or 93-56-43 (consular department); or an official letter or invitation from any other state organisation will do.

Transit visas need your visa or invitation and/or air ticket for your country of destination. These procedures are often best done in person at the Embassy. Contacting local travel agencies, or those like *Intourist* in London and New York who know the visa situation, may be advisable but is not always necessary to organise your visa for Azerbaijan.

Customs

On arrival you need to fill in the currency declaration forms for foreign currency; there are no restrictions on items for personal use; and visitors should also declare all these, and keep the slips for their departure.

Utilities and Communications

Electricity is 220 volts AZ, 50Hz as throughout the CIS countries, so a standard continental-style plug can be used.

The country code from the UK is 00-994, and as in all these countries there are sometimes different satellite phone codes. Letters to Western Europe can take four or more weeks. The code for Baku is 12.

Health Service and Insurance

Worldwide emergency evacuation health cover is recommended; but there are also the *OMS* clinic and *Western Medical Clinic* in Baku. The former has an annual membership fee of $350, and you should have private insurance cover.

Schools and Education

There is also an *International School* in Baku.

Cultural Background

Religion:
This is Muslim; with some other more ancient traditions like Zoroastrianism.

Social Life and Entertainment:
There are now a large number of Britons and Americans living in Baku working for international oil and trading companies, along with Germans, Japanese, Italians, and other foreign nationals, and including of course many Russians. The beaches and sailing are popular with expats, as are eating out and other tourism-related activities.

Shopping and Restaurants:
The local markets are the best supply of food like bread, vegetables, meat, cheese, and other produce, although there are some dollar supermarkets (with guards) for westerners, with every kind of imported item. Some construction and other workers live like this, in guarded camps away from local people; others prefer the purpose-built apartment blocks which are currently being built. You meet the locals over a cup or tea or Turkish coffee, or vodka and 'champagne' drunk in the Russian way.

Food specialities are similar to those of the Central Asian countries, with seafood and fish dishes too. Some drinkable wine is also produced here. You can eat Russian-style or Azeri-style cuisine as you prefer, and along with the expats have come all kinds of international restaurants too.

Useful Addresses

British Embassy: 2 Izmer Street, 370065 Baku; tel 92-48-13; fax 39-13-41; e-mail office@britemb.baku.az. Satellite tel +873-144-6455. Satellite fax +873-144-6456.

Embassy of Azerbaijan: 4 Kensington Court, London W8 5DL; tel 0171-938 5482 (visa); 937-2097 (commercial); fax 0171-937 1738.

Azertaj State Information Agency: Bulbul Avenue 18, 370000 Baku; tel 93-54-45/98-60-79; fax 93-81-38.

Working in Azerbaijan

Business Contacts

Contact the *Department of Trade and Industry Central Asia and Transcaucasia Desk* in London (757 Kingsgate House, 66-74 Victoria Street, London SW1E 6SW; tel 0171-215 4771; fax 0171-215 4817) for a general background briefing; and a database of British and international companies operating there, including construction companies, investors, insurance brokers, oil and gas companies; as well as contacts for local ministries and firms. Also contact the *Oil and Gas Projects and Supplies Office* (*OSO* – Room 33, Tay House, 300 Bath Street, Glasgow G2 4DX, Scotland; tel 0141-228 3626) for details of oil firms. The *World Aid Section* (Room 117 at the Kingsgate House address for the *DTI* above) holds a list of contacts for development projects in Azerbaijan.

The *British Embassy Commercial Officer* in Baku can provide general briefings for business travellers on different sectors, exports and matching UK companies with local firms etc. For a comprehensive research service, and destination reports with many direct contacts for businesses and/or expatriates, write in the first instance to *English Contacts Abroad*: PO Box 126, Oxford OX2 6UB, UK.

Courier and Freight Forwarding Services

DHL Baku: Tbilisi Prospekti, Palace of Sports, entrance 7; tel 95-12-40.
Inter-Logistic Worldwide Courier: Unit 7, Craufurd Business Park, Silverdale Road, Hayes, Middlesex; tel 0181-569 0616; fax 0181-569 0616; e-mail XK241@DIAL.PIPEX.COM.
Inter-Logistic PLM, Apt 60, 11 Nrami Street, Baku 370010.
Murphy International World Carriers Ltd: Rasul-Rza St. 8 15/26. Baku; tel (994 12) 98-34-22; (994 12) 93-93-15.

Georgia

Introduction

This is the third of the Caucasus or Trans-Caucasus or Transcaucasian countries, bordering the *Black Sea* and not the Caspian, and really a part of this Black Sea region as well. It is the destination of at least one of the pipelines bringing oil from Azerbaijan (see the *General Introduction* to this section). The most notable recent event, following its secession from the Soviet Union, was the secession of the north-eastern province of *Abkhasia* from Georgia, a conflict which is presently being resolved by more peaceful and diplomatic means. The Russians have played a part in the talks between the Georgian President Shevardnadze (formerly the Soviet foreign minister, and one of the better known CIS leaders) and the current Abkhasian leader Vladislav Ardzinba. In 1997 they met for the first time for talks.

Georgians are at the same time gregarious and laid back; with an even more formal style of welcoming guests than their Russian neighbours. The climate also encourages a kind of 'Mediterranean' lifestyle where you may while away the evening in long discussions in a roadside café – making Georgia to Russia what the south of France is to Britain. Most of the hundred or so British expats who are there say they enjoy it.

The resorts combine the mountains and the sea, and there is also great potential for tourism – when Western Europeans and others can be persuaded that it is really safe to come – which some tour operators are now taking up. The Russians are already returning in some numbers as well – although many have now discovered the competing attractions of the Canary Islands or the Côte d'Azur.To the south is another Georgian 'Autonomous Republic' known as *Adzhania*, whose capital is the port of *Batumi*.

With its strong agricultural sector, and the high level of education and training in what was formerly one of the richer places in the USSR, Georgia now needs only a period of stability to be prosperous once again. There is great potential here for trade and investment, and some British and American expatriates here who are discovering it is an enjoyable place to live and work.

Living in Georgia

Residence and Entry Regulations

Contact the Georgian Embassy in the UK or USA. You will need your original passport, photo, visa fee (up to $100 for a multiple entry visa) at least seven days in advance. Business and private visas require a confirmation from the *Ministry of Foreign Affairs*; or an official letter or invitation from any other state organisation. Transit visas need your visa or invitation and/or air ticket for your country of destination. This is all best done in person at the Embassy. Or entry visas can be obtained at Tbilisi Airport on arrival.

Useful Addresses

British Embassy: Metechi Palace Hotel (room 339), 380003 Tbilisi; tel (995 32 or +7-8832) 99-84-47/98-87-96/95-54-97; fax (995 32) 00-10-65.
Georgian Embassy: 3 Hornton Place, London W8 4LS; tel/fax 0171-937 8233.
US Embassy: 380026 Tbilisi, 25 Atoneli Street; tel (995 32) 98-99-67/8; fax (995 32) 93-37-59.
Georgian Embassy: Suite 424, 1511 K Street, NW, Washington, DC; tel/fax 202-393-5959.
British Council: 380079 Tbilisi, Chavchavadze Avenue 13, 2nd floor (British Council Resource Centre); tel 25-23-60.

Working in Georgia

Economy and Trade

See above for a general overview of living and working there, and the sources of information in the *Business and Industry Report* below. There are tax benefits for foreign investors nowadays; and Georgia's development will be depend on that in the Caucasus and Trans-Caucasus region as a whole.

The Tax System

Residents are those there for longer than 183 days in any one year and will have to submit a tax return before their departure, or before 31 March each year. Some expenses expatriates receive, like bonuses, are also liable to be taxed; and you should check with the Commercial Section of the British or US Embassy for up-to-date information on this. The tax year is from 1 January to 31 December.

Doing Business

The currency, the *lari*, is not yet convertible; and there are no branches of international banks here just yet (although some have set up joint ventures with local banks). Business etiquette means bearing gifts (often to an extravagant extent if you are trying to match the hospitality of the locals). A few hotels and restaurants also take credit cards. Communications to Tbilisi are good by telephone and fax nowadays.

Business Contacts

Research is important before you go. The Commercial Officer at the British Embassy (see above) recommends contacting the Central Asia and Transcaucasia desk of the *DTI* beforehand for a general background briefing, and holds an up-to-date list of British companies operating there ranging from *BP, British Airways, BAT* and so on to less well-known investors, insurance brokers, and oil and gas companies, as well as contacts for local firms.

Also see *Sources of Information – Finance and Advice for Trade and Investment in Central and Eastern Europe and the Former Soviet Union* (DTI Export Publications; tel 0171-510 0171; fax 0171-510 0197); or contact the DTI's resource and information centre (Kingsgate House, 66-74 Victoria Street, London SW1E 6SW, open from 9am to 8pm weekdays and until 5.30pm on Saturdays; tel 0171-215 5444/5445; fax 0171-215 4231; http: //www.dti.gov.uk/ots/emic; e-mail

EMIC@ash001.ots.dti.gov.uk).

Save the Children has also compiled a useful *Directory of Humanitarian, Aid and Development Contacts (Georgia)* available from your embassy or their field office in Tbilisi (tel 22-77-24; fax 22-77-24/23-40-59); e-mail frank@save.ge). For a tailor-made destination or country report with many direct contacts for businesses and/or expatriates or an extensive background briefing write in the first instance to *English Contacts Abroad* (PO Box 126, Oxford OX2 6UB, UK) who will send you a questionnaire.

Kazakstan

Introduction

These are the deserts and steppes of Central Asia, stretching from the Caspian Sea, and the sadly polluted Aral Sea all the way to China, in the largest of these Central Asian and trans-Caucasian states: Kazakstan. These were the cottonfields of the former Soviet Union, originally wild steppe but brought under cultivation by Stalin in a process which saw about a third of its population die. The ethnic minorities, mainly Russians, but also Tartars, Kurds, the Volga Germans – and the whole panoply of former Soviet Union peoples – were transplanted here, meaning there are 120 ethnic groups in this country which is vast in area if not in population (some 16,763,000 at the last count). These are mainly Kazaks, who still remember their ancient tribes and lineages; and their own class-system which just survived the mass starvation of the 1930s.

The dream of the Kazaks is to be the Central Asian 'tiger' economy which leads the region to western-style prosperity in the next century. This very far from being a reality; but has some realistic chance of success as many western and international firms have also realised. Liberalisation has been faster than in some other countries; and privatisation has often breathed new life into the old industries.

Living in Kazakstan

Residence and Entry Regulations

Contact the Kazak Embassy in the UK (tel 0171-244 0011) or USA for a form; and they will need your original passport, photo, visa fee (up to $100 for a multiple entry visa) at least seven days in advance. Business and private visas require a confirmation from the *Ministry of Foreign Affairs*; or an official letter or an invitation from any other state organisation. For private visits to friends or relatives an invitation letter issued by the Department of the Ministry of the Interior is required, as well as a letter from your friends to get this permission in the first place. Transit visas need your visa or your invitation or itineray and/or air ticket for your country of destination. This is all best done in person at the Embassy.

All foreign travellers to Kazakstan must also register their passports with the Passport Department.

Useful Addresses

British Embassy: 173 Furmanova Street, Almaty; tel 50-61-91; fax 50-62-60.
Embassy of Kazakstan: 3 Warren Mews, London W1P 5DJ; tel/fax 0171-3871 047.
US Embassy: 99 Furmanova Street, Almaty; tel 63-39-05/36-39; fax 63-38-83.
Embassy of Kazakstan: 3421 Massachussetts Avenue, NW, Washington, DC 20008; tel 202-333-4504 or 333-4509 (Consular Section); fax 202-333-4507.

British Council: 158 Panfilov, 1, Almaty 480064, Kazakstan; tel 633339; fax 633443.
Ministry of Youth Affairs, Tourism and Sport: 48 Prospekt Abaya, Almaty; tel 67-39-86; fax 67-50-88.
National Company for Foreign Tourism 'YASSAUL': 73 Gogolya Street, Hotel 'Otrar', Almaty; tel 33-00-02/11-55; fax 33-20-56/13.

Working in Kazakstan

Economy and Trade

There are tax benefits for foreign investors ranging from manufacturing and construction to tourism, as the country seeks markets for its vast natural resources. Trade routes are opening up to the west, and latterly to China which is emerging as the largest trading partner; and growth areas for the future are oil and gas, minerals and metal mining, electricity equipment and telecommunications, wool, textiles, food processing, and transport. The economy is growing (albeit slowly) and inflation is around 15% and falling, creating the right conditions to make its currency, the *tenge*, fully convertible in the near future.

Business, Legal and Recruitment Contacts

Cameron McKenna: Mitre House, 160 Aldersgate Street, London EC1A 4DD; tel 0171-367 3000; 0171-367 2000. 2nd floor, 45 Khadzi-Mukana Street, Almaty 480099, Kazakstan; tel 650049/650515; fax 811518. Mosenka Plaza III, 24-27 Sadovaya-Samotechnaya Street, Moscow 103051, Russia; tel 501-258 5000; fax 501-258-5100. 90 Acad. Vosit Vokhidov Street, Yakkasasayskiy District, Tashkent 700031, Uzbekistan; tel 406946; fax 406185. '40 CIS specialists working for Europe's eighth-largest law firm.'
English Contacts Abroad: PO Box 126, Oxford OX2 6UB, UK. For a tailor-made destination or country report with many direct contacts for businesses and/or expatriates and an extensive background briefing. Also English teaching opportunities.
Investconsulting Company Ltd: 480072 Almaty-72, PO Box 50, Satpaev Street 9; tel 54-35-53; fax 50-74-46.
jib Express: (recruitment agency); tel Almaty 42-14-74; e-mail jibexpress@asdc.kz.
*Kazakhoi*l: (National Oil and Gas Company), Bogenbay Batyra 142, Almaty; tel 62-60-80; fax 69-54-05. Largest oil and gas company.
'Kazakstan on the Internet': www.kazecon.kz.
KPMG: Abylai Khan Avenue 105, 480091 Almaty; tel +7-327-581-1662; fax +7-327-581-1663.
Law Firm 'GRATA': 157, Schevchenko str., Almaty, 480008; tel/fax 530-999/925 or 538-830; e-mail grata@grata.almaty.kz; internet www.grata.kz. Oil, gas, mineral and other opportunities researched, and legal expertise.
Telstra: (Kazaktelecom) 6th floor, 22 Zenkov Street, 480100 Almaty; tel 636432; fax 638769. Or telephone +7-327-581-1546; fax +7-327-581-1419. International telecommunications services for companies and businesses.
Terminal: 480008 Almaty, Manas str.22b; tel/fax 42-67-16/74-66/52-83. For imports, exports, customs clearance and regulations etc. with 80 offices around the country.

Kyrgyzstan

Introduction

Although its currency is not yet fully convertible liberalisation has been faster in Kyrgyzstan than in some other countries in the region. National advantages are its educated workforce, natural resources and relatively liberal regime.

Living in Kyrgyzstan

This is a small country on the same latitude as Britain, whose climate is much more extreme. It is mountainous and criss-crossed with rivers and gorges which give it water and hydro-electric power, valuable commodities in a generally dry region. The mountains – and *Lake Issyk-Kul* in the north-east – are its main tourist attractions. There are beaches on the shore of this lake surrounded even in summer by the snow-capped *Tien Shan* (Heavenly) mountains.

Residence and Entry Regulations

A completed visa application form is needed (the Kyrgyz Embassy in the USA may send this to the UK on receipt of a s.a.e. and International Reply Coupon). In addition the Embassy requires a letter of invitation of some sort, original passport, photo, visa fee (which ranges from $25 for a single entry visa to $120 for a multiple entry visa valid for over a year) all at least five working days in advance for it all to go through, or the price goes up. Letters of introduction are not needed for stays of up to one month. Business and private visas require either confirmation from the *Ministry of Foreign Affairs* or an official letter or an invitation from any other officially recognised organisation, stating confirmation of the trip, the purpose, dates etc. For private visits to friends or relatives a letter of invitation issued by the Department of the Ministry of the Interior is required instead, as well as a letter from the friends or relatives (and they will have to do some queuing for you to get this permission which they can fax or send a copy of to you).

Useful Addresses

Embassy of the Kyrgyz Republic: Suite 706, 1732 Wisconsin Avenue, NW, Washington DC 20005; tel 202-338-5141; fax 202-338-5139.
Ministry of Foreign Affairs: 720003 Bishkek, ul. Abdumomunova 205; tel 22-05-45; fax 22-57-35.
Ministry of Trade and Industry: 720000 Bishkek, pr-kt Chui 106; tel 22-38-66; fax 22-97-03.
Commission on Foreign Investment and Economic Assistance: 720874 Bishlek, ul Kievskaya 96; tel 22-14-35; fax 22-03-63.
Ministry of the Economy: 720874 Bishkek, Blvd. Erkindik 58; tel 22-89-22; fax 22-74-04.

Ministry of Education and Science: 720040 Bishkek, ul. Tynystanova 257; tel 26-31-52; fax 22-86-04.
US Embassy: (Bishkek) tel 22-29-20; fax 22-35-51.
British Embassy: 173 Furmanov Street, Almaty, Kazakstan; tel 50-61-91; fax 50-62-60.
British Council: 158 Panfilov, 1, Almaty 480064, Kazakstan; tel 633339; fax 633443.

Working in Kyrgyzstan

Economy and Trade

This was one of the first countries in the region to reform its economy. Not quite as dependant on cotton as its neighbours, it supplies water, another valuable commodity, to some of them. A lot of trade is routed through nearby Almaty (the British Embassy of which also deals with Kyrgyzstan) so see the previous chapter on *Kazakstan* for some business and trade contacts. There are now at least 50 private travel agencies in Kyrgyzstan; the relevant state authority is the *State Committee for Tourism and Sport*, tel 3312-22-06-57, fax 3312-21-28-45.

Joint ventures and 100% ownership are both possible vehicles for investment. For more information on this obtain the leaflet *Trade and Investment* from the Kyrgyz Embassy in Washington.

Tajikistan

Introduction

Tajikistan is still a lawless country. At present the *Foreign and Commonwealth Office Travel Advice Unit* advises against all travel there (see BBC Ceefax p.470 onwards, or the Internet under the address http://www.fco.gov.uk/; or call 0171-238 4503/4504 for the current situation). There are Tajiks in Afghanistan to the south, as well as in Uzbekistan to the west. Kyrgyzstan is the northern neighbour, with China and Pakistan to the east and south-east. There is also a large Uzbek minority within the country; and a much smaller Russian population. The country contains the famous *Pamir Mountains*, including the tallest peak of the former Soviet Union, Mount (or 'Peak') Communism, which no-one has as yet got around to renaming. The Afghan border is the most unstable and is presently closed. There are few hotels outside the capital Dushanbe.

The Tajik economy has suffered first from the break-up of the USSR, and then from its 1992-3 Civil War. Natural resources include gold, aluminium, mercury, coal and natural gas; and hydro-electric power would in itself be enough in more peaceful times for the country to be self-sufficient. The population is just over five million. The currency is still the Rouble and the preferred hard currency is the dollar.

Living in Tajikistan

Residence and Entry Regulations

Residence is not advised. There is no British Embassy; but the USA is there (see the useful addresses below). A completed visa application form, passport, photo, visa fee etc. need to get to the *Ministry of Foreign Affairs* in Tajikistan, or *Intourist Tajikistan* who can give you permission to enter the country (they will need your itinerary as well). The way this then works is through your nearest Russian Embassy, which is where the Tajik authorities will send their fax of confirmation.

Useful Addresses

Ministry of Foreign Affairs 42 Rudaki Pr., Dushanbe 734051; tel 211-808; fax 232-964.
Tajikistan Mission to the United Nations: 136 East 67th Street, New York, NY 10026; tel 212-744-2196; fax 212-472-7645.
US Embassy: Octyabrskaya Hotel, 105a Rudaki Pr., Dushanbe 734001; tel 210-356/270/211-280.

Courier Service:
Inter-Logistic Worldwide Courier, Unit 7, Craufurd Business Park, Silverdale Road, Hayes, Middlesex; tel 0181-569-0616; fax 0181-569-0616; e-mail xk241@dial.pipex.com

Working in Tajikistan

Economy and Trade

Little is working in Tajikistan, in fact. One contact for business people may be the British Government's *Know How Fund* which sponsors projects in the Central Asian countries (Know How Fund, Foreign and Commonwealth Office, Old Admiralty Building, Whitehall, London SW1A 2AF; tel 0171-210 0065. These are often administered by the *Overseas Development Administration* (write to their Contracts Branch (COMIND), Abercrombie House, Eaglesham Road, East Kilbride, Glasgow G75 8EA; tel 0135584-4000; fax 0135584-3499) if you wish your firm to be considered for registration. In Tajikistan itself contact the *Chamber of Commerce and Industry* (21 Mazayeva str., 734012 Dushanbe; tel 279-519) or the *S-T Industrial Association*, PO Box 48, Rudaki Prospekt 25, 734025 Dushanbe; tel 232-903; fax 228-120.

Turkmenistan

Introduction

It became a republic (along with its Central Asian neighbours) in 1924; and achieved independence in 1991 with the failed coup against Mikhail Gorbachev and the break-up of the former Soviet Union, although there were few changes at the top. Previously it formed part of the mainly Turkic-speaking Turkestan conquered by the Russians in several stages in the nineteenth century; before then it was known for the *Silk Road* from China to the West.

Large numbers of its peasants and Muslim clergy were repressed during Stalin's rule and replaced by the local and Russian bureaucrats who in many respects are still running things today; although this became more like the sytem of indirect rule employed by the British in India, with a local clan-system and various compromises with the local tribes, all of which continues alongside a more democratic style of government. Turkmenistan is the Central Asian republic which is the most free from ethnic tensions; and one of the most stable.

Living in Turkmenistan

Residence and Entry Regulations

A completed visa application form, original passport, photo, visa fee (currently $20 for a single entry visa; $50 for multiple entry visa) are required by the Embassy at least seven working days in advance. Business and multiple entry visas may require a confirmation from the *Ministry of Foreign Affairs*; or your letter of invitation/hotel booking may be enough; visas can also be issued at the border, if you have one of these invitations and a valid passport etc. Applications for temporary residence for business reasons are handled by the *Interior Ministry* and for residence for other purposes by the *Consular Affairs Office* in the *Foreign Ministry*. For transit visas you need details of your travel arrangements and the visa issued by the country you are going to through Turkmenistan and/or air ticket for your country of destination. Contact local travel agencies or your local contacts; or *Intourist* in London and New York (tel 0171-538-5902; fax 212-757-3884 respectively) which will have details of visa requirements in all the CIS countries.

Useful Addresses

There is a Turkmen Embassy in Washington, but not London; and a US but not a British Embassy in Ashgabat: tel 24-49-25 or 51-13-06; fax 51-13-05.

Working in Turkmenistan

Business and Industry Report

SME's (small and medium-sized enterprises) have been privatised. Other industries will take longer to bring into the private sector; but the government has set up some Free Enterprise Economic Zones providing tax breaks for companies (which may be 100% foreign-owned; elsewhere they must be joint ventures). This kind of investment must go through the *Commission for External Economic Affairs* in the capital, Ashgabat: tel 297 511; fax 297 524 (92 Kemine Street). For a tailor-made destination or country report with many direct contacts for businesses and/or expatriates and an extensive background briefing write in the first instance to *English Contacts Abroad*: PO Box 126, Oxford OX2 6UB, UK. For more on business and trade opportunities in Turkmenistan, contact the *Commission for External Economic Affairs*.

Uzbekistan

Introduction

We imagine deserts or arid steppe with caravans following the oases of the Silk Road, impressive mausoleums, mosques and minarets (in Samarkand, Bhukara, Khiva and the Fergana Valley) and eastern bazaars. The capital is Tashkent, with a population of over two million – one of the largest cities in the region, with many tourist attraction in its own right, along with the Chimghan Mountains which attract some hardy skiers from the capital. This is also a modern country with highly developed industry and agriculture, a world leader in gold mining, cotton production (number four in the world), gas, silk and sheep breeding, which is however suffering from too great a dependence on these primary goods, and the old-fashioned industrial infrastructure left behind by the former Soviet Union. After a crisis in 1996 (when cotton prices fell and there were bad wheat harvests) inflation is down to 35% and GNP is recovering. The currency is not yet fully convertible; and liberalisation has been slow. Advantages are its educated workforce and natural resources.

The big state industries are scheduled to be sold under a programme sponsored by the World Bank, with 25% to go to employees, 25% to the state, and the rest to private investors. Copper mining and aircraft production facilties are some of the first for sale. The most notable foreign investor is the Korean conglomerate Daewoo (producing cars, TVs, and building a business centre as well as installing Tashkent's new telephone network). UK companies investing there include BAT (British American Tobacco) making cigarettes, builders John Laing, Cargill Commodities and A. Meredith Jones, processing cotton, Rank Xerox (selling their xerox machines and office equipment) and Marconi Instruments (electronics).

Living in Uzbekistan

Geographical Information

This is the third largest Central Asian country, with a population of 23 million Uzbeks and others, and nowadays only a few Russians. Koreans also came here, after the Second World War. The *Great Silk Road* (followed by the earliest western travellers like Marco Polo and Sir John Mandeville) unwinds from Nukus and ancient Khiva in the north down to Bukhara, Navoy, Samarkand, Djizak, and then Tashkent, and on into Tajikistan like a ribbon on the map, one which tied medieval Europe to ancient China; it crosses 32 towns and cities in Central Asia today. Tashkent (to the east) was famous once for exporting its own gold, precious stones, fruits and horses to neighbouring cities, but is now an industrialised and somewhat bleak metropolis, extensively rebuilt during this century, with the usual museums, art galleries, institutes, and so on, in a Soviet style. Samarkand is famous for the Silk Road and its ancient Islamic architecture. It contains the gravestone of Tamberlaine, a name which echoes down the ages – and which has a curse attached to it, like Tutankhamen and his tomb. Some Russians disturbed his resting place, and are now, the locals say, doomed.

Like Genghis Khan in Mongolia, Timur here is the national hero, and the *Registan* is perhaps the best-known square in all of Central Asia, reminiscent of the Alhambra in Spain or the citadels of Mogul India. This whole medieval city is being restored, as is the old city of *Bukhara* (also conquered by Alexander the Great) with mosques and fortresses. *Khiva* was the capital of the Khoresm Khanate in the fourth century BC; and also has an old town, called *Ichan-Kala*, with a citadel and palace and towering monarets, giving a clear idea of a medieval Central Asian city. The *Fergana Valley* has some breathtaking views and is famous in this desert region for its fast-flowing river and wildlife.

The Language

This is Uzbek, a Turkic language closely related to those of its neighbours – who can understand it, as can speakers of Turkish in Turkey.

Residence and Entry Regulations

A completed visa application form, original passport, photo, visa fee (currently $50 in the USA for one-year multiple entry visa) are required by the Embassy at least seven working days in advance (or the price goes up). Business and multiple entry visas require a confirmation from the *Ministry of Foreign Affairs* in Uzbekistan (see below) which must be communicated to the Embassy; and for private visits an invitation letter issued by the Department of the Ministry of the Interior of the Republic of Uzbekistan is required. Transit visas don't need this; but you do need your visa and/or air ticket for your country of destination.

Useful Addresses

Embassy of Uzbekistan: 72 Wigmore Street, London W1H 9DL; tel 0171-935 1899; fax 0171-935 9554.

Embassy of Uzbekistan: 1748 Massachusetts Avenue NW, Washington, DC 20036; tel 202-530-7291; fax 202-293-6804.

British Embassy: 6 Murtazayeva Street, Tashkent 700084; tel 3712-345-652; fax 873-340-465.

US Embassy: Chilanzarsaya 55, Tashkent 700084; tel 3712-771-407/772-231; fax 3712-771-081.

Republic of Uzbekistan Tourist Information Centre: 60 E. 42nd St., New York, NY 10165; tel 212-983-0382.

Ministry of Foreign Affairs: 87 Gogolya Street, 700047 Tashkent; tel 336-475; fax 394-348.

Working in Uzbekistan

Economy and Trade

See the *Introduction* above. A trade and double taxation agreement was signed with Britain in 1993; and the UK is the second largest of the EU countries in terms of its trade with Uzbekistan (worth US$474 million in 1996). There have been various trade missions – most notably a British festival in Tashkent which promoted trade and tourism in 1997. The latter is also a priority area; and the

Great Silk Road and its ancient monuments of world importance mean that there is a real and not imagined potential for tourism. There are now at least 150 private travel agencies in Uzbekistan. *Uzbektourism*, the relevant state authority, has offices in London and New York.

Business Contacts

American Business Centre: 82 Chilonzor Street, Tashkent 700115; tel 33-28-80; fax 89-16-92.

Bukhara Regional Department: 8, 40-Let Oktyabraya, 705016 Bukhara; fax 37550.

DHL Worldwide Express: 42 Druzhba Narodov str., Tashkent; tel 781436; fax 780134.

English Contacts Abroad: PO Box 126, Oxford OX2 6UB, UK. Business briefings and direct contacts for all the CIS countries, including Uzbekistan.

Ministry of Foreign Economic Relations: 75 Buyak Ipak Yulli Street, Tashkent; tel 689-256; fax 687-231.

Appendix I

Personal Experiences – Former Soviet Union

Ukraine

Richard Creagh

Dick Creagh, 53, was a senior executive with the Irish airline Aer Lingus before he was offered his position as an airline executive with Ukraine International Airlines by the Irish company which invested in it. It means he has lived in the country, and worked closely with Ukrainian people. His working life there he describes as 'very interesting, very challenging and occasionally frustrating.'

'Adapting to understand a different cultural and behavioural background is essential,' he says. So how easy was it to adapt and settle in to this new culture? 'The Ukrainian people are very intelligent, well educated, cultured and very warm and hospitable (when you get past their initial suspicious facade). So social life can be pleasant – and expats should avoid the trap of only mixing with each other,' he says.

What about living conditions for expats? 'Here apartments are all in multi-storey blocks. Hallways and stairs and lifts are often dark and dirty. There is much variety in prices, so shop around..' Flats refurbished to western standards are expensive, he says. His advice for business people will also be useful. There is 'bureaucracy and red tape' here;' and he advises that you seek your own advice – from people who have 'been through the hoops already' – if you are thinking of doing business or starting a company.

What are the advantages of doing business there? Richard Creagh says it is 'having an experience of a different world, before it becomes westernised.' And there are 'real opportunities' for investment as the economy grows. Small business must 'beware of the local mafia' though.

When he took the job, he prepared for it, he says, 'with an open mind.' And the experience of living and working in the former Soviet Union turned out to be 'better than expected.' He advises a full health check before you go; but 'most goods and foods are available in supermarkets,' so it may not be necessary to stock up too much before arriving. On the other hand it can be expensive, at least in the restaurants and bars, although the local beer is cheap, and so is travel, on trams, buses, and the metro. 'Buy a monthly ticket,' he advises, 'but very often it is packed, at least in the peak hours.'

Overall, living and working in Ukraine has been 'very positive'. 'We have participated in and steered the development of a quality international airline,' he says. 'Getting out is important for expatriates;' and all flights and travel there and back can be arranged with this modern joint venture, with Irish, Austrian and Swiss partners. The creation of a new company – in somewhat difficult circumstances – is a challenge which Richard Creagh has enjoyed.

Contact *Ukraine International Airlines* directly in Kiev at Prospect Peremohy

14, 252135 Kiev; tel 44-221-82-85; tel 44-216-79-94. They can arrange all flights and travel to Ukraine at the most competitive rates.

Azerbaijan

Richard McGeough

Richard McGeough, 28, worked in the UK and before that in Turkey as an English language teacher. He is now in Azerbaijan where he finds his teaching and working conditions to be 'great' and the experience mainly positive. I asked him about teaching there:

'The students are highly motivated, well educated and almost embarrassingly hospitable and generous. I'm working in newly modernised premises now, but until recently in our old premises we had to contend with alternately unheated and unventilated classrooms and regular electricity cuts in winter.'

How easy is it to mix with the people and what kind of social life is there?
The Azeris are very friendly and concerned about you, and they often dismiss the Russians as cold and inhospitable. I often get invited to students' homes for dinner, or on class picnics. Foreigner/Azeri relationships are rare. It's a fairly traditional (but not religious) place. I'm one of the few exceptions.

Social life in Baku is steadily improving, but a lot often depends on your own initiative. If you just want to mix in a bar it's fine. There are a few OK bars, often with live music (too loud!). There's a sizeable foreign community here because of the oil, so the bars are often full of oil types: it can be quite laddish at times. Most Azeris haven't got the money to go out to bars so this is a 90% foreign pastime. There are plenty of restarants: Turkish (all over the place); Chinese, Indian, Mexican, Italian, French, all good. Again, an almost exclusively foreign clientele.

There's ballet, opera, theatre, all quite cheap and very popular. Cinemas are the pits, showing usually Indian films poorly dubbed into Russian. You'll need a video if you're staying any length of time.

There's a video rental shop, with a good selection of (pirated) English language videos in town. It's not dead by any means, but it's quiet enough for most of us occasionally to feel that the best years of our lives are hurtling by, while life goes on elsewhere.

What about travelling around? Have you been out and about?
In Azerbaijan, yes. There's a law here that prevents any foreigner from driving a vehicle that isn't their own, so car hire involves hiring a driver too, and is expensive. Long-distance buses are usually 1960s relics and real boneshakers. I haven't tried the inter-city train but I've heard it's pretty uncomfortable with no heating in winter.

If there are enough people hiring a car for the day it's generally the best option. Anyone who comes to work here can easily find a willing driver through their company. The other options are probably best tried once, for the experience.

What about accommodation?
Hotels are very difficult to come by. Outside Baku, I only know of two so far, a great restored *caravanserai* in Sheki at the foot of the Caucasus in the north-west (great atmosphere, no heating, $15 a head). In Lenkoran near the Iranian border there's an old decrepit Intourist hotel (Soviet atmosphere, no heating, occasional water and electricity – and whatever they feel like charging). They told us $10

beforehand, and on the night we paid about $2. Still, it's a good base for exploring the mountains around Lerik, right on the Iranian border, where some of the oldest people in the world are said to live. (Someone who died recently was said to be 160 plus, but because his date of birth was only recorded on the back page of the family Koran and not on any official birth certificate, it doesn't count).

You can't travel much past Gence in the west without speciial permission as you're nearing Nagorno-Karabakh and other occupied territories. If you want to visit Armenia, you'll need to go via Georgia. Quite a few foreigners have done this. I flew to Tblisi with *Azerbaijan Airlines* (AZAI): questionable safety standards, but we got there and back in one piece.

What are your living conditions like in Baku?
Flats are expensive for what you get ($400 to $1000 a month). On the plus side, there are a lot of old flats (pre-Soviet) with lots of charm. On the minus side, most areas of the city have a sporadic water supply, and electricity is occasionally a problem in winter. But foreigners have a good pick of flats. Well organised, English-speaking agencies have sprung up to cater for the demand and it's possible to view a good number of places before making a decision. These are furnished; and may have central heating. Personally, I'm very happy with my flat, although most of my colleagues have moved on at least once because of problems with water, heating etc.

What are the advantages of living and working in Russia/CIS?
My primary motivation for coming here was the salary my post offered. For an EFL teacher I'm on extremely good money here (£15k – as much as you'll earn anywhere outside Japan or the Middle East). There is the chance to see somewhere and meet people who it would have been impossible to meet before, bearing in mind what life was like in the Soviet Union; and to realise that people aren't so different and that hardly anyone believed in the communist system.

What about preparation, and the rules and regulations?
I read a couple of books, one of which *A Dry Ship to the Mountains* by Daniel Farson (Penguin) had a useful chapter on Baku. Also, it's not easy to get good clothes at a reasonable price here (Benetton and Levi's have come by the way). The red tape is no worse than elsewhere. One problem, though, is you can't take more cash out of the country than you brought in. As a result, some foreigners end up flying out with several hundred dollars in their socks.

What about shopping and the cost of living?
It's not cheap, unless you seriously want to restrict yourself. I reckon on $100 to $150 a week (excluding rent) which would include a good meal out, a couple of bar visits, and shopping at a western supermarket. It can be done a lot cheaper. Virtually all Azeris have to get by on a fraction of that.

Is Baku a safe place to live?
Yes. Azerbaijan is one of the safest places I've been to. Having said that, a few foreigners have been mugged downtown, and flats have occasionally been burgled. But it's far safer than most cities of comparable size. Women out alone after dark will routinely be considered on the game.

Has it been a positive experience for you?
80% positive, 20% negative. Hugely positive in that the people are great and want to tell you so much about themselves, their view of the past and hopes and fears

for the future. Slightly negative in that, as I said before, it can be too quiet sometimes (although a Turkish acquaintance of mine who lived in Ashkhabad, Turkmenistan, for two years says that Baku is like Paris compared to there).

It may not always be a beautiful place, but what it lacks in beauty it makes up for in interest. And Baku – if you're living close to the centre – the Oil Town and the Old Town – is beautifully rustic and charming, and not at all what I'd expected of the USSR. Having lived in Istanbul before this, historical Baku was like a return to the 50's before the ugly modern apartment buildings were put up.

What else do short and long term travellers and residents need to know?
The war in Karabakh hasn't really affected the rest of Azerbaijan in terms of safety. New hostilities can break out, but you will hear little about it. Then, if you're going to be here a while and need to get money transferred from the UK, the *British Bank of the Middle East* currently have the only cash machine in town (next to the *Hyatt Regency Hotel*). If you're living in the centre *Most-Bank Azerbaijan* are infuriatingly inefficient and petty, but only ask for a minimum balance of $20.

Malaria is making a comeback in Azerbaijan, and a few cases have been diagnosed in Baku. The foreign medical community have been advising people to stick to long sleeves and trousers, especially from dusk onwards. Malaria aside, mosquitoes can be a real problem here. Thankfully you can buy zappers and tablet supplies in some of the western-style supermarkets. Like many places, be careful with bottled water too. I'm certain someone somewhere is making good money from refilling old bottles with tap water. Always check that bottles come properly sealed.

Lithuania

Barbara Hyde

Barbara is an ELT (English Language Teaching) consultant in Lithuania working with local teachers and organisations. Before, she worked in Hungary and Albania; and says that 'adapting largely depends on language, and the willingness to make efforts to get to know local people. Without a knowledge of the language you remain largely outside the culture.' We asked her:

How easy is it to mix with people?
On the surface not difficult, i.e. no hostility. But to really become involved in people's lives is very difficult. There is a social life for young people in clubs, bars, discos etc.

Are there any problems with personal safety?
The dangers tend to be exaggerated for Vilnius. Violent crimes, mugging and theft are on the increase, but attract more attention than they would do in the West. You should just take normal care as anywhere.

What are living conditions like?
As with many expats, my flat was found by my employer. Many flats are available, but at high prices to foreigners: $500 plus monthly. Problems are hot water sometimes, and rubbish disposal. With car registration, residence and medical matters there are no problems, just with customs, for example, when things – even books – are sent into the country.

The cost of living in Lithuania is low for Westerners. Don't drink wine in restaurants, it is greatly overpriced.

How did you prepare before you came?
By reading about it; and I asked people who'd been – for example clothing needed, flat equipment etc. (extra heaters much recommended for spring and autumn for instance). Bring plenty of books to read. And good footwear. Be prepared for the winters too.

What are the advantages of living and working here?
In Lithuania – many. Vilnius, the capital, is a green and relaxed city, not over-westernised. People are reserved but friendly. Cultural life is good. There is space. You can keep a low profile. This has been a positive experience for me. Vilnius particularly offers a genuinely functioning multi-ethnic multi-cultural society – Lithuanian, Polish, Russian – without conflict or prejudice. This is rare.

Estonia

Sara Wadsworth

Sara is 27 and teaching English in Rapla, Estonia. Her sister worked for a year there with a Christian organisation working in Eastern European countries: 'she told me about the need for English teachers, and in a school in Rapla in particular. I taught at a state school here, and then at a Music High School in Tallinn where I commute.' She applied for four jobs in Estonia, and was offered three – and the other school said they didn't want an English teacher anyway, despite having placed an advert. Good places to look for jobs, she says are *Opetaja Lent* (the teachers' newspaper, for teaching in state schools, and the British Council. International House has a school in Tallin; and the Peace Corps has English teachers in state schools.

'Recently I have taught evening classes at a Folk High School which is paid and came through word of mouth. It is possible to find a job without being qualified, but I would really encourage people to get a TEFL/TESOL qualification.'

Her teaching at the high school was at times 'frustrating' (when she didn't have much responsibility, and sometimes students didn't show up to her voluntary conversation classes). 'Getting the work and residence permits took a lot of time and patience, and was quite expensive, about £60. The main problem was finding out what papers were needed.' Her impression of the facilities and teaching materials is a rather mixed one; but communication with her colleagues – this was her first teaching job – was OK when she found a helpful English-speaking person, something she says is 'essential'.

'Making an effort to get to know the rest of the staff on a social as well as professional level is a very good idea but there is a need to be sensitive in relationships,' she says. 'Being prepared to listen and learn' is important: 'a culturally imperialistic attitude won't win you any friends.'

'In Tallinn and major towns there are many leisure options; but outside towns there is not much to do; and social activities have to be self-made. I am very involved with the local free church, which takes up most (but not all) of my time.' Rapla is a 'typical' country town, she says; but with quite a range of facilities: bars, cafés, restaurants and a new library, at least three sports halls, and a culture centre containing a video rental shop, sauna, and showing plays, films, concerts and so on; with an adult education centre and swimming pool nearby.

'Some facilities can be difficult to find – consulting the phone book helps – and it can also be difficult to find out about the existence of various social clubs.' Being without a TV (due to lack of funds) has been a good thing for her, she suggests; meaning she listens to the BBC World Service and is able to go to friends' occasionally and watch their TV. Otherwise, satellite and cable can be found here. But activities like country walking, cross-country skiing, outdoor skating and sledging are all popular in Estonia.

'Estonia has a low crime rate but Estonians have a big fear of crime,' Sara says, 'which has gone up since independence – but it was very low to start with. The Russian mafia is here, but as far as I can tell it doesn't affect daily lives.' Other social problems include 'drunks in public,' and some areas of Tallinn can be 'dangerous late at night.' She has 'never felt unsafe walking around Rapla.'

She has travelled around Estonia – mostly by public transport – and to neighbouring Finland. 'Travelling is more difficult during winter (November to April approx.) especially in private transport, with vehicles very often getting stuck in snow, and icy roads.' Public transport is 'quite good at running during winter, but can sometimes be affected.' But timetables change frequently, i.e. about every three to four months, without warning.

These are some of her impressions of Estonia. She has bought a car – these range from Russian to imported second-hand western ones of all prices and types – but there are many 'which will break down the day after you buy them,' as she knows now from personal experience. Insurance is not expensive (£3.50 a month); registering a car is 'bureaucratic' and expensive (£100); and you need a residence permit for this. There is no road tax but a mechanical check is required every two years. The police are quite strict; and 'a fire extinguisher, first-aid kit and warning triangle are compulsory.'

Last summer she drove with her parents home, through Estonia, Latvia, Lithuania, Poland, Germany and the Netherlands; and then back to Britain. Along the Via Baltica (as it is known) there were few problems. 'In a few places the road was not very good but we saw many roadworks, especially around the borders.'

Appendix II

Personal Experiences – Central Europe

Czech Republic

Keith Bates

Keith Bates has been living in the Czech Republic and working as a lecturer in English for five years. He stresses that his comments 'probably only apply to this area – i.e. Northern Moravia, and particularly to the town of Oprava.' His detailed comments will be of interest to all those considering moving to the Czech Republic and will find some echoes for all of those who have lived and worked in CEE and the CIS. Originally, he came here through the auspices of the VSO and their Eastern European Partnership. He stayed at the University post they found him for two years, then moved to another by request. 'Appointments in the sphere of education are often done by word of mouth and/or reputation,' he says.

Initially it was easy to fit in, despite having no Czech, 'as I had the support of a very good Czech boss.' What of the situation for foreigners and expatriates in the Czech Republic now? Keith Bates has noticed a decline in enthusiasm since 1992: 'In 1992 and in the subsequent years there was a keen enthusiasm for change in the country, together with a curiosity and great friendliness towards foreigners. This enthusiasm has gone, and there is now a suspicion of foreigners, a view supported by a Dutch businessman who has been here for the same length of time'.

'He puts it down to the lack of expertise that business advisors brought with them, and a natural reticence by the Czechs for any sort of change now. Perhaps a more significant thing is that, in 1989, ex-communists were forbidden to hold positions of authority for five years. Those five years passed quickly, and they are now back in those positions, both in industry and education. It is certainly the case here in Oprava, and also in the University of Oprava.'

'There is still a huge demand for English here, as reflected in the number of applications for places at our University – some 850 for 45 places. Working here is easy if you are self-reliant and have experience, but otherwise difficult if you are conscientious and want to do a good job. In this part of the Czech Republic, you need Czech or at least German. English is still not widely spoken in shops etc. In the tertiary educational sector there are shortages of photocopiers and, more importantly, paper.'

'We have a brand new building and lots of new furniture,' he says, but a lot of this 'is show'. 'Underneath there are severe shortages, especially in library facilities and text books. No new text books have been bought since a British Council donation in 1992. There are also difficulties concerning the adaptation by traditionalist Czechs to new teaching methods and this can extend to obstruction in some cases.'

'On the other hand, the workload is far from demanding; and you can be left alone to get on with your job if you display success. It is necessary to adapt to the slow speed at which things happen here, and also to the lack of communication from those in charge about what is happening, cancellations and so on. There is little planning ahead, and it is not unusual for classes to be cancelled the day before they are due to take place. The telephone system is expensive and far from reliable. It cannot be depended on for e-mail or Internet facilities...'

Social Life. We also asked Keith about the social and cultural life in the Czech Republic: 'Generally speaking, Czechs are friendly so long as there is something in it for them. They want to speak English and will be happy to invite you to their house for that purpose. Often that friendship is short lived. They are devious people with little loyalty except to themselves, not as a group but individuals. Social life revolves around sports and the pubs. There is 'higher' culture in the performance of opera and symphony concerts, but these are now becoming expensive compared to local wages. There are swimming pools and local gyms too.'

'Generally speaking, there is nothing to worry about,' is his comment about personal safety. 'People in the city of Ostrava will tell you that there are problems with the ethnic minority gypsy population, and I do know personally of two women who had money stolen in the streets there, but they were not physically harmed. The general advice is as for all countries – make sure your money is well hidden etc. Credit cards can be used in Prague and Brno, but are not generally accepted elsewhere. This applies particularly to Visa.

Bureaucracy. 'Red tape then was not a problem, but I had a lot of help from my institution. The real problem is that rules change and no-one knows what these are. When I first came the work permit was a green booklet which was stamped annually. This was changed to a plastic card for one year, and has now reverted to the green booklet again. Each year of stay requires a stamp which costs 1000kc – about £25 or so. There is little red tape in the job itself. In fact, Czechs have found ways around most of it. There are clear lines of command in the work place; but people are reluctant to take responsibility even where there is status attached. One university here had four heads of their English department in as many years. People are genuinely frightened by anything that looks remotely official and written down, and needless pieces of information are required for some simple things like booking a package holiday...'

Preparation. He points out that 'there are no longer any shortages as there were in the past, but it's an advantage to speak a little Czech, or at least some German. No injections are required and the water is safe to drink, if a strange colour at times. There is confusion about whether the work permit should be set up in the home country or not. If it's possible, it's probably a good idea, but the Czech Embassy in London gives conflicting advice to that given here...'

Cost of Living. 'When I first came in '92 the country was very cheap to live in. It was possible to eat out virtually every night and not to worry about it. Similarly travel was cheap. It is now becoming more expensive, and Prague, in particular, is becoming as expensive as any European city. As mentioned above, rents are expensive, but this has to be put in the context of my salary as a teacher, which is relatively low. Cinema tickets, concert tickets etc. have doubled in price in four years but my salary is broadly the same as when I came. Food prices are still relatively low, but alcohol has virtually doubled in price. Petrol is still slightly less than in the UK, but in terms of salary earned, of course, it is much more expensive.

Daily Life. 'The country, in this area at least, is dirty and polluted. Pavements are in poor condition. Coal dust is used in the winter to help clear the snow and ice and the resulting mess is around for days. Shoes should be appropriate to this. There is also a lot of pollution in the form of cigarettes from smokers in restaurants and bars. People should be prepared to come out smelling like an ashtray as there are few non-smoking restaurants, or smoke-free areas. Many people smoke on the streets. Drivers do not stop for pedestrians on zebra crossings though the law says they should. If a driver does stop, he will be overtaken by the car behind so it is still unsafe to cross...'

Advantages and Disadvantages. Keith Bates says he is planning to extend his stay, 'so I must be finding it rewarding.' He considers the 'pace of life and the relative independence' the greatest advantages of his life in Ostrava: 'The understanding of what constitutes a day's work is very different from that in the UK. Work is an incidental part of life, not its *raison d'être*. Given the caveats above, it's relatively easy to make friends; and if you work for an organisation that pays pounds – the British Council for instance – living is cheap. The culture is still a 'foreign' one, but not so much as, say, China so there's a chance to be in a foreign culture, but one which is still fairly European and familiar. In my particular area, I found the students a great joy, the best reason for working here.'

Czech Republic

Jon Holmes

Aged 33, Jon was an MA student before going to the Czech Republic, by that well-known route into employment for EFL (English as a Foreign Language) teachers, an ad in the 'Guardian'. Adapting and cultural difference were not a problem, he says; but he has found three 'possible culture attitude differences': first, 'rudeness, or lack of customer service (as perceived by westerners);' then 'Czech pessimism;' and finally 'the perception of all foreigners as cash cows' (which chimes with many other personal experiences as they have been recounted to us throughout this CEE/CIS region).

This 'Czech pessimism' may be a problem in personal relations too; he reports that 'of the teachers at my school, most have found partners but few have found friends.' On the plus side, there is an 'excellent social life;' but 'if you don't like drinking or smoky pubs then think twice about coming here, despite all the opera, ballet etc.' And 'asthmatics should not attempt to live here due to the inversion, trapping pollution.'

There is a minor, not a major problem with theft, he says: 'but not violence.' Tips are to 'hold your bag in front of you on any public transport, or put it firmly between your legs when taking photos in touristy places, not next to you or in front of you,' and another good one: 'putting your bag strap inside a chair leg in restaurants.' The pickpockets here are very skillful, he says.

For travelling around, he advises 'throwing away your guide and asking your students/Czechs where they go, and then go for it. This is a beautiful country away from the tourist centres.' In restaurants, 'waiters have a tendency to rip foreigners off. So find honest restaurants – they write the cost on the bill at the time of ordering – and stick to them if this bothers you.'

'If the menu does not say cover charges – check the small print at the foot of the page – then it is illegal for the restaurant to charge it.' His other main tip is more straightforward: 'don't take taxis.' A problem for foreign workers is that the accommodation agencies cater for foreign businessmen. So 'limited budget workers need help from Czechs, i.e. school secretaries.' Another warning is 'do not have sent or send small packages in or out of the Czech Republic. Many do not arrive; and two out of two of mine were stolen.'

Jon Holmes says his English teaching job and life in the Czech Republic have been 'both a positive and a negative experience. 'But political discussions with Czechs, and the current economic situation, do not fill one with any great hope for the future.'

Poland

Overall we had the greatest number of responses to our survey of expatriates in Central and Eastern Europe from Poland; we sent out questionnaires to British Council offices in the country; many came back; and it seems that this largest Central/Eastern European country is also now where most Britons, Canadians, Americans and Irish citizens live and work.

Raymond Flynn

Raymond (26) went to university in Cork, Ireland; and completed his MSc in Rural Development. His university was organising a PHARE project in Krakow and Czestochowa, and he went to the former to work on this; and found, he says, that 'culturally coming to Krakow was a wonderful experience.' As far as working conditions were concerned, though, these were less familar:

'I found it quite unrelated to what I had experienced in Ireland. Conditions were poor and sometimes communications presented problems.'

The way of life is much more congenial and 'relaxed', though, with 'friendly' and 'hospitable' people, and many cultural activities being accessible 'due to their inexpensiveness.'

'It is much safer than the 'West'. Obviously the stations, i.e. bus and train, and local 'pubs', are best avoided after dark.' Many other respondents and expats in Poland have also stressed this positive safety aspect to living there; with only one or two disagreeing. 'And people won't rip you off,' Raymond says.

But what are the drawbacks? 'If you are a student and intend to travel by rail (which accesses most towns) be aware that the ISIC card will not work, although some guides claim it will (there were conflicting reports about the usefulness of these cards in Poland). Buy tickets well in advance during the summer as it's too hot to queue for hours on end!'

Does he have any regrets? 'No, I just went unprepared. In retrospect I wouldn't have changed much. If you can get a reliable local contact, then use it, because as a native English speaker, you will tend to be exploited for your language.' A good – and a bad – point is the accommodation, which is 'OK' in 'student-type hostels' in the short-term – and 'OK' too in 'tower blocks for longer term stays.' But in Krakow the apartments are 'too expensive for what's offered.'

On an average wage of around £220 a month, Raymond says, 'it is possible to save money in some places, but not much; and not if you want to lead any sort of social life.' Working hours in Poland are 'less'; and one advantage in the workplace is 'the choice to do what you want without outside interference.' Travellers need to be prepared for the weather, though, which can be extreme.

Rathna Muthukumaran (Poland)

Rathna would recommend Poland as well. She is 25, and was a student at Loyola

University of Chicago, receiving her BA in Biology and minor in Sociology before 'moving out here to join a one-year American programme in Poland.' We asked her about settling in, which 'got easier as time went on,' she says: 'At first everything was very different, especially the language, but as my stay continued, I learned to adapt very easily to the customs and culture.'

'The Polish people in general are very friendly and kind; I feel very welcome here. And I enjoy the many pubs and restaurants, as well as the student clubs.'

What about personal safety? 'My only concern with safety is pick-pockets. A few students in my group were robbed. Despite this, I believe Poland is relatively safe. It is important to be careful anywhere you live.'

'As for travelling around, I have been to Prague, Czech Republic, and Frankfurt, Germany. It's rather inexpensive for students (especially with a Student – International – Identity card) and 50% discounts. It is most exciting to explore the cities on your own rather than join an organised group.'

Her advice to others is simple: 'to get the most out of visiting Europe by experiencing all the possible opportunities – easy travelling, meeting people, and exploring the culture. She prepared for her stay by 'reading about Poland, and then we just brought what we needed for our stay here, books, clothes, etc.'

Priya Patel (Poland)

One expatriate who responded to our survey who has 'no idea' about working there before she arrived was Priya Patel (24) who was living in Nairobi, Kenya, before she came with her husband who is a chartered accountant and who got a job with an American company here.

'It was difficult to adapt initially,' she says. And she has noticed a difference in attitude between the old and the young: 'the younger generation are more friendly while the older people hesitate to approach and talk to a foreigner.'

'I don't find safety as such a problem; but there is a lot of pick-pocketing and mugging which some of my friends have faced. So my advice would be to be careful about your purse when in a crowded place.'

'I have travelled around quite a bit. The mountains around Zakopane are really very beautiful. The Lake District and Sopot (which is near Gdansk) is a beautiful place, with old buildings and churches... Cracow is so full of history and there is a lot of old world charm and an aura about the place.

'The living conditions are not great, but they are acceptable. As for bureaucracy, I find there is a problem if you do have a foreign passport because then you have to go through a lot of hassle every time you travel and there are endless formalities for a foreigner. It is not expensive to live here, not as expensive as London, or any other European country for that matter. Eating out is reasonably priced and the food is cheap.'

'Generally,' she says, 'this has been a positive experience for me and Polish people are friendly when you get to know them.'

Lily Anne Latham (Poland)

Lily Anne Latham is another who has had a positive experience of the country. She got her job in an unorthodox way: 'I came on holiday to visit a friend in February 1990 and returned for a second holiday in June 1991. During that second fortnight I was introduced to the founding members of a new Social School, who asked me to find three native British speakers – I did, but then one couldn't come, and I asked if I would do.' The answer was yes!

Lily has been a nurse, midwife, counsellor and natural health practitioner in the

NHS and the private sector. She is 72; but found it 'very easy to adapt.'

'I and my two British colleagues were surrounded by an increasing number of friends and would-be students of English. There were some unusual happenings in the first year. The new school buildings had no heating during the winter, and renovation continued alongside lessons, but everyone coped happily, even if wearing outdoors clothes indoors.'

It is 'easy to mix, and the people are extremely friendly, helpful and courteous,' she says. She has travelled a lot, although less in the last couple of years due to disability. She lived at first in a bungalow which her school provided (and found ingenious uses for packing cases there apparently, as furniture) and then moved to flats; this is her fifth – and best so far – with two rooms, bathroom, kitchen and telephone, on the first floor and 'in a quiet part of town, and surrounded by friends and friendly children!'

She advises that work permits – which are harder to obtain than they were – should be applied for in advance; and you should be ready for cold winters and hot summers: 'winter clothes are a must.'

She has some experience of hospital treatment in Poland, too, which differs markedly from what most of the guide-books say: 'I couldn't have received kinder, more professional and thorough treatment. Everything during thisa five-week stay was looked after for me by friends.' This was following 'an allergic reaction to something after eating some spinach!'

'More things are available, but the cost of living has risen dramatically.' Lily gets by giving private English lessons (a native English speaker is very quickly discovered and still in great demand for private lessons to supplement the low teachers' salaries at schools or universities). She recommends the food, and local customs – the Polish ways of celebrating Christmas and Easter, and All Saints Day.

What is her overall impression? 'I'm still amazed at the courtesy and general helpfulness I find everywhere.'

Ray Riley (Poland)

Ray is a university professor, aged 65, who came from Portsmouth University to Lodz to teach his own subject – in English – there. For some years he has been researching Polish manufacturing and is familiar with the economic environment. Mixing with people, the social life, and travelling around all get a strong recommendation. Once he was not 'mugged' but 'forcibly approached' for money, and he was told once that 'you should never travel in an empty train or railway compartment' which 'seems reasonable,' he says. His tips for travel are 'never carry your wallet in your back pocket' and 'never carry your camera over your shoulder, rather in a plastic bag.'

Eating cheaply is possible: 'Banks, universities, town halls all have canteens where wholesome food may be bought at subsidised prices.' The university accommodation there is 'a trifle spartan but satisfactory: with fridge, telephone and radio in situ and so on.' He learnt enough Polish to get around before he left to take up his new job, and left his car in the UK, but his warning is more a cultural than a practical one, and would apply to all those considering going to live in Central/Eastern Europe:

'The general danger is applying British culture to a foreign country. An open mind is absolutely essential. The British approach is not 'right'. It applies in the UK only.'

Other Information and Advice

Some other useful information and advice for those thinking of living working in Poland has come from respondents to our survey. This seems to fall into two categories, the cultural and the practical.

The friendliness and hospitality is one feature of Polish expatriate life. But it can be 'difficult to find family activities to do.' The main focus of another respondent was learning the language, which was 'difficult for the first six months. 'But if you have kids, they too experience more; it broadens their thinking.'

David Morgan (married to Barbara, who is Polish) found 'mixing socially easy' as a result. He has three jobs, based around his experience as a recreation manager and then in business; he also says his Polish experience is a positive one. The language and local salary levels are a difficulty and speaking French or German can be a help, he says. Keeping your bank account in dollars or pounds is his other practical advice. If you want to start a business, go to the British Embassy Warsaw. They have a Commercial Department with experts willing to help.

Frances Gregory observes that 'social life tends to be very home-based;' and advises taking your English-language cassettes and videos with you as 'living in a foreign-language environment can be wearing.' Small town life is different, according to *Michael McCabe* from Canada: 'Little social life is not church-based. For an agnostic in Poland, pariah status is assured – outside of Warsaw anyway.' He is one of a large number of correspondents who have had their wallet stolen incidentally. He found Poland 'more expensive than the Czech Republic in almost every area.'

Margaret Coll- found her social life through the Church, and colleagues in the secondary school where she teaches (where teenagers are 'extremely polite and respectful'). Very few said they had made any special preparations for their stay in Poland; and most recommend that you should.

Slovakia

Adrian Ash

Adrian Ash is living and working in Banská Bystrica after teaching English as foreign language in Japan. Aged 24, he took a short Introduction to TEFL course at Aston University and then applied to the VSO's East European Partnership who interviewed and 'assessed' him; and then offered him several postings. He is teaching now at the university in the town. We asked him:

How enjoyable is it to teach in the Slovak Republic?
In my experience the teaching is enjoyable – students are usually keen, and glad to have native speaker tuition – but it is often frustrating as well. Communication with colleagues is poor; there is a lack of meetings involving non-Slovak staff and an inability to inform me of impending events (holidays, exam periods etc.). The marking scheme is still an issue of contention – students have a lot of class hours and so lack the time for self-study. Academic standards are relatively low.

What about life outside work?
Students are friendly and enjoy socialising, which usually means one of Banská Bystrica's several 'pubs'. It has a few nightclubs, usually cheesey Euro-house but

a few dance parties have been held in the town's larger community centre. Cinemas are good, operas have a varied repertoire.

What about getting around?
I haven't done much (lack of money) but would advise caution with timing of longer rail/bus journeys. Delays are very likely. Buses are very crowded – where possible try to reserve a seat. As for foreigners, I have heard of physical attacks on some, especially non-white. Skinheads are a growing feature in Slovakia. But I have not had any problems myself besides the obvious Friday/Saturday night drunkards.

What kind of accommodation do you have?
I am living in a university dormitory – single room, own bathroom, shared kitchen – and the room is 'cleaned' once a week. It's fine, but catering facilities are poor. Heating is overpowering and turned on or off according to the calendar, not the weather.

Were bureaucracy and red tape a problem?
Greencard arrangements should begin before arrival – application for clean criminal records (UK and Slovak) via the Embassy especially – but many colleagues had no problems being paid before they received theirs. Medical tests are best left until arriving – the police won't recognise foreign documentation.

What about preparation?
I was briefed by EEP at short notice and couldn't find any language material in Britain, but was given a lot of political/economic background.

What are the advantages and disadvantages of living and working there?
The scenery is stunning, hiking excellent. This winter has been relatively mild, so skiing was poor. Most towns have some historical centre and some – Bystrica, Banska Stiavnica – are well worth visiting.

Going out is relatively cheap (especially beer) although restaurant prices are increasing now. General food prices are becoming comparable with the UK for many things and there is an influx of German products. Overall, this has been an enjoyable, interesting experience, and hopefully useful in the future as well.

Do you have any other tips?
If cashing cheques, try to get some small denomination notes: shops and bars often don't carry enough change. Always check your change and receipt.

Jonathan Brown (Slovakia)

Jonathan Brown and his partner were hotel managers before trying their hand at teaching in Slovakia. The way this worked for them was meeting a Language Link representative in North Yorkshire where they lived who arranged everything. We asked them:

How have you found living and working there?
It was quite easy to adapt to the Slovakian way of life; the language obviously is a huge barrier but on the whole the way of life and work is fairly relaxed; and quite often wine is more important than work, which isn't such a bad thing! Slovakians are very friendly, and we have mainly enjoyed the experience.

What is your advice about personal safety?
Relax, blend in, and be respectful as in any country. There seems to be little problem in this area. The town we are living in is quite small and it feels safe, better than home.

What about travelling around?
We haven't had much time for this as we have been mainly working; buses and trains to distant places run fairly infrequently, maybe once a day. The main local sights are the High and Low Tatras; and we have made occasional trips into Poland and Hungary.

Did you make many arrangements in advance?
Our employer made most of these when we arrived. Our flat is warm and cosy and very nice, in a well-kept block of flats. The visa was a big problem for our employer – we had to go to the police station many times, and it took three months for it to come through. We were still working and getting paid during this time, though.

Do you have any other advice for those thinking of working in Slovakia?
It's not expensive to live, in comparison with the wages you receive. If you are there in winter it can be bitterly cold, so take warm outside clothes, but beware as most buildings are heated 24 hours a day so inside it can be hot. Most things are available, e.g. toiletries/food, but don't forget to pack as many tins of baked beans as possible!

Arrange work before you come, and try to learn a little of the language. Now we are working, we don't seem to have time! It's not easy to save money if you are earning a Slovak salary, so not really worth trying when you come to Slovakia.

Slovenia

Sharina Calveley

Sharina Calveley, 28, is enjoying living and working in Ljubljana as an infant teacher after doing a similar job in the UK. She saw an ad in 'The Guardian'; and participated in our survey organised with the assistance of the *British Council* there. We asked her

How easy was it to adapt to your new working environment?
Because I have already had experience of teaching children the transition has not been too difficult. In fact teaching English is easier than primary school teaching – and the classes smaller – but I have had to learn quite a lot which was new.

What about the social life outside work?
Mixing with people is not really a problem; and I believe your social life is what you make of it – although a couple of my other British friends thought it was very hard to make friends here, and that Ljubljana socially was a bit boring.

How did you organise accommodation?
In my first year my boss organised accommodation for me and in the second year I have done this myself with the help of my Slovene boyfriend – otherwise I might have found more problems.

What about personal safety in Slovenia?
You feel much safer than in Britain – and it makes a nice change from London. The streets are much cleaner too.

Where can you go if you are travelling around in Slovenia?
I've been to Italy, Austria and Croatia – three out of the four borders – and seen lots of Slovenia. You need to go with some of the locals who know the untouristy spots.

What about bureacracy? Is this a hassle?
Yes it is. Getting visas and permits takes time and at the moment I'm working illegally as the Foreign Office won't give me a work permit until I have proof that I've been actually working for a month – which means working initially without a permit.

What about accommodation and the cost of living?
The prices in shops and cost of accommodation are far lower than in England but salaries are much much lower here too, so this is quite a hurdle for me as I find the standard of living much lower.

What are your impressions of living and working in Slovenia?
It is a beautiful country – and it's easy to get away to the beautiful spots when you want to. My job is generally quite satisfying and easier that it was working in the UK. Also, people tend to be very nice to you here if you are English and you can get away with all sorts of things!

On the whole it's been a very positive experience, and I don't regret coming as it gives you a less blinkered view of life if you travel – a real education. Sometimes I feel a bit frustrated for financial reasons, but that's about all.

Patricia Robison Bechi (Slovenia)

Patricia is originally from the United States, where she taught ESL (English as a Second Language) before moving to Romania, then Slovenia, under the auspices of the Soros Foundation. She says working conditions are 'quite like those in the USA; the conditions are good and the expectations are high.' We asked her:

How did you prepare; and what do you recommend?
I didn't do much. Buy your dictionary and books in the US as books printed in Slovenia cost a ton.

What are the advantage of working there?
The salary is higher than most or all countries in Central and Eastern Europe and similar to those in Western Europe. Conditions in schools are excellent; and there are many many English teaching jobs for qualified teachers.

What about the people?
It's not so easy to mix with the Slovenes; I, at least, have found them to be reserved and very family-oriented. Neighbours do not necessarily know each other (neighbours in Romania were much more open and hospitable). The people are not unkind – I have a few very good Slovene friends – but I found myself mixing much more with other expats – although I do have a few very good Slovene friends.

Do you have any advice for personal safety?
There are no particular problems if you take the usual logical precautions – avoid the train station and dark areas alone at night, etc.

Have you travelled around? And do you have any tips?
Mostly hiking in the hills. My tips are, bring hiking shoes and skis. Hitch-hiking is common and believed to be very safe; students do it regularly. It's also expensive here, so be prepared.

Do you have any other observations about living and working in Slovenia?
In my experience the living conditions have been very good, just like Western Europe. Bureaucracy was no worse – there is some, but not to the point of being a hassle. When shopping you should compare prices, which can vary drastically, and buy clothes and electronics elsewhere.

Samuel Willcocks (Slovenia)

Aged 24, Samuel did his BA degree course in Cambridge before heading off to the Czech Republic, Germany and then Slovenia, where the *Central Bureau* arranged 'teaching assistant' work for him. He found this more fun than previous jobs he did in the Czech Republic and Germany. We asked him:

What is living in Ljubljana like?
In Ljubljana there is a surprisingly rich array of scenes and subcultures – gay, theatrical, student, expatriate – but individual Slovenes can be very standoffish.

What about personal safety? Any problems? Advice?
A drug-crazed Frenchman tried to break into my flat at 4am with a knife. The natives are calm and kindly people, however. My advice? Avoid Francophone flatmates...

What about bureacracy and red tape?
Ignore them and they often go away. My employers were very useful here, fixing me up with a current account, health insurance etc. Other individuals have traumatic problems.

What other practical difficulties were there?
Mainly getting somewhere to live. My employers were no help at all in finding suitable lodgings. Learn Slovene to read the small ads!

How did you prepare? What advice do you have?
Four years studying modern and medieval Czech surely helped, as would any other Slavonic language, but this is not essential. For other travellers – make sure your friends at home can find you on the map. My wage packet does vanish quite quickly every month, so do like the Slovenes do and work in the grey economy, not declaring all your earnings for tax.

What advantages have you found living and working there?
Anyone with an interest in early or medieval Slavonic history, or a philologist, will have a good time here. otherwise, Slovenia is very well located for further travel – I often visit my brother in Budapest. This has been an ultimately positive experience for me after many setbacks. Much as I like this country, I would recommend it for a holiday rather than working though.

Other advice from expatriate 'Slovenes' is to 'buy a car' (I. Harvey) to 'stay legal' and 'befriend lots of Slovenes'; to 'talk to people' and 'be fairly outgoing' and 'get a bicycle' (D. Clarke – who says 'the young people I have met in Slovenia are the most friendly I have ever met').

This survey in Slovenia was carried out with the assistance of *Romana Gasperlin* in the British Council library, Ljubljana. She says that administration is very often the biggest problem for foreign people coming to work in the country: 'Be prepared to have administration problems! Even where people there are nice and do their best there is also the Slovene law – and there is a long procedure for getting visas. For example, even if a Slovene takes a degree abroad it will take him up to two years to get the foregn diploma validated in Slovenia.'

'People enjoy speaking English, and are happy to hear a foreigner speak some Slovene. My advice to newcomers is to have attitude and show patience!'

Appendix III

Personal Experiences – Eastern Europe

Bulgaria

Ruth Cherrington

Ruth is a university lecturer who has worked in both Bulgaria and China. She got her job in Bulgaria through the British Council. Getting along and adapting, she says, 'was quite easy.' The bureaucracy and red tape are 'not so bad, but then I used to live in China.' We asked her:

What is your working environment like?
It is quite easy to get along with the students; but the education system is different from the UK – and the educational 'environment' – so that was problematic. Time and patience are needed, and an understanding of the historical/political/economic background of a 'post-communist' society.

What tips do you have for personal safety and getting around?
This is not a great worry outside the major cities. Sofia is not so safe – so avoid it! Travel by train – especially at night – is not very advisable. Sit in compartments with others, especially families and older people. Avoid dark streets and don't talk to strangers at train stations. And don't go to places with strangers either, especially if no-one knows where you are.

I have travelled around quite a lot. The buses (run by the private company 'Group') tend to be quicker than the trains, but more expensive. Don't rely on guidebooks too much – some hotels/guest houses have closed. But this is a very good place to explore. Trains are reliable if slow.

What about accommodation?
Mine is quite good as a university lecturer, but there is deterioration recently in the environment due to economic problems, a lack of money for repairs.

How did you prepare for your trip? What should other people do?
I didn't I'm afraid, as it all happened at the last minute and it was all a bit of a hurry for me. It depends how long you are coming for. Bring foreign currency in ample supplies, especially US dollars. Some words in Bulgarian are helpful, or Russian, but then some people might think you are Russian and treat you impolitely. Some knowledge of recent history, especially political and economic changes, will be useful.

Did you find it expensive to live in Bulgaria?
No, it was very cheap, but prices are going up, and we've had hyperinflation. It is still cheap for tourists due to rising exchange rates, but living here on a local salary would now be very difficult.

What are the advantages of living and working there?
Bulgaria has beautiful countryside and mountains plus the coast to be enjoyed, and all relatively cheaply. It is not so consumerist (yet) as Britain and there are lots of traditional folklore and customs remaining, plus lots of holidays. My experience of living and working here has been generally positive, but since the economic crisis, it is becoming less so. Everyone is so depressed due to financial worries and it is sad to see hope fading.

John Charles Lopez (Bulgaria)

John Lopez is a British Gibralterian working for the Direct Teaching Operations Department in Sofia, after living in Belgrade, and previously working in London, teaching English and Spanish. The Spanish department of his school in London was due to be axed, so he decided to look elsewhere, saw an ad in the 'Guardian', and applied. This was for qualified teachers who wanted to work in Bulgaria.

He got the job, after an 'on the spot' interview and sending his school and university references. He also had previous experience of a kind which would be useful for all those thinking of developing this kind of career in Eastern Europe. He had completed his BA at Thames Valley University in Ealing, in Russian, and spent some time studying at different universities in former USSR (Vladimir, Krasnodar and Leningrad) and also in Havana in Cuba. 'Speaking Russian means I have no real problems in communicating with people who speak other Slavonic languages,' Mr Lopez says, 'as long as it isn't too complicated.'

He worked from 1990 with Yugoslav Airlines (JAT) as their customer services representative; had a training course in London and Belgrade – and visited cities all over the ex-Yugoslavia – before the war worsened in 1992; and foreign workers were sent back to their 'home' office. He returned to London, where sanctions meant after a few months that the JAT office had to close down. 'Therefore, applying to Bulgaria was not new to me, and I found that as I already had an Eastern European language and had worked in the Balkans before, adapting to Sofia was no real problem for me. The British Council had a flat ready for each individual teacher, and I moved in.' We asked him:

How easy is it to mix with people? And what are Bulgarians like?
If I compare the Bulgarians with the Serbs, I could honestly say that the Serbs are much more open and friendly although at the same time they can be very rude and aggressive. The Bulgarians (known to the Serbs as *brato* – brothers) are the complete opposite. They are cold at first, but they do open up – eventually – once they feel they can trust you ... I honestly think they are a very gentle people, kind-hearted and helpful. Friendship takes a long time to develop, but once it is there it is there for ever.

What about the social life?
One of the problems Sofia suffers from is transport. After midnight there are no trams, trolleybuses or buses, and night buses don't exist here (unlike Belgrade). So many people depend on taxis, which are now charging incredible prices. These are expensive for the average Bulgarian, hence the limited nightlife around the city. Sofia's main street, Vitosha, has a good selection of western-style shops and there are many cafés, restaurants and bars to choose from. At night, Vitosha becomes a quiet place and night clubs are usually found in the little side streets by or behind Vitosha Street. At the end of Vitosha Street is the NDK (National Palace of Culture) which houses several cinemas, theatres, bars and a splendid view of Sofia from the top. Just outside the NDK, during the day until late

evening, there is an abundance of little cafés and bars. Well worth a visit.
The social life in Bulgaria revolves around the economic situation of the country. Just after 1989, people earned low salaries, around $5 a month, and spending money was somehow difficult in the few bars and restaurants during that time. Now, the economic situation has started to improve. People are on better salaries and there has been a sudden boom in the social life. Unlike Belgrade, where there is a very lively nightlife around the Knaz Mihailova – the main street of Belgrade – here in Sofia nightlife is concentrated in different parts of the city. There are about 10-15 discos and a good selection of clubs with live music. Once again, they are all dispersed around Sofia. Recently a gay bar and a gay disco have also opened in the centre of Sofia.

What about personal safety and getting around?
In principle, Bulgaria is a very safe country, and Bulgarians are very helpful and honest people. However, groups of gypsies are now a safety problem for foreigners. They also tend to hang around outside big hotels like the Sheraton. Young girls carrying babies and looking rather scruffy approach you for money. Avoid going near them. They tend to glue themselves on you if they hear you speaking a foreign language ... Also be careful when you are going around certain suburbs of Sofia, such as Lulin, Mladosts, Nadezhda, and others further out.

And I should say that Bulgaria is not as bad as Bucharest. The last time I went my Bulgarian friend managed to have his bag stolen within seconds at the train station while we were looking for a café to have some coffee.

What about travelling around in the country. Do you have any other useful tips?
Trains go to many places. they are comfortable, and if you wish to travel by night there are sleeper carriages too. It takes around 8 hours to go from Sofia to Bourgas on a night train. Day trains take around 8 hours too. The scenery on the way there is breathtaking! Flights within Bulgaria consist of flights from Sofia to Varna and Sofia to Bourgas, both on the Black Sea coast. One way costs around $40. It's cheaper to buy a return. Ask at any local travel agency in Bulgaria. Flights to Varna and Bourgas take around 35 to 40 minutes. Well worth the money for a quick weekend on the Black Sea.

There are several bus companies which operate around the country. These are comfortable, and a journey from Sofia to the Black Sea takes around 6 hours. Tickets for trains and buses can also be bought at any local travel agency in Bulgaria. Rent-a-car is also available. There are many companies. Try to avoid hitch-hiking around Bulgaria – it could be dangerous.

Bureaucracy and red tape? Were these a problem?
In 1995, the British Council arranged a one-year multi-entry work visa for me. That was no real problem. Once we arrived in Bulgaria, we had to fill in a statistical card at the airport and then we had to register with the local police within 48 hours of arriving. Then began the painful process of acquiring a blue passport which is a foreigner's identity card in Bulgaria. The British Council arranged this for us, and after three trips to the police station, once with our landlords, we were given the famous blue passport. Every friend or family member arriving in Bulgaria, and going to stay with you and not in a hotel, once had to go through the same painful process.

Now, things have changed. For all European citizens (and those from the EEA countries) there is no need for a visa if you are going as a tourist for one month or less. However, at the airport or point of entry (by train, bus or boat) you still have to fill in a statistical card and get yourself registered within 48 hours at the local police station if you are staying with friends or family already living in Bulgaria. However, if you are staying in a hotel, ask the reception to stamp your statistical card, and that will be sufficient. You will not need to go to the local police station.

Do remember that these statistical cards are very important (they go back to an old law about thirty years ago) and must not be lost or tampered with as you have to give them in when you leave the country. If you lose it, you may be fined on the way out, and the fine could be anything the control people want. So take care!

How did you prepare beforehand? What would you recommend to others?
I bought myself various guidebooks and read up on the history of Bulgaria. Bulgarians love talking about their long and interesting history, so it's best to know something about it. I also visited my GP and had the vaccinations required for the area. Not so much for Bulgaria, but in case you decide to venture into neighbouring areas where certain vaccinations are needed, i.e. the Middle East or some of the ex-Soviet republics. You can buy just about everything you need here, although certain things are a little more expensive, like deodorants or cornflakes. So, if you want to play it safe before you go, go into your local Sainsbury's or Boots and buy things that you really need – i.e. cornflakes, deodorants, condoms, toothpaste etc.

What about living conditions and accommodation? What are these like?
When I arrived the British Council had several flats to choose from. They were very spacious, in the centre of Sofia, and had either two or three bedrooms. All the flats had a washing machine, telephone, cooker, cable television, video, central heating and general furniture in every room. Since arriving in Bulgaria, I have moved on to another flat and will possibly be moving to another one during this summer.

The same has happened to colleagues of mine and other foreigners living in Sofia. Prices for flats tend to be between $100 to $500 a month for a reasonable flat. A $100 one will probably be on the outskirts, while $300 upwards will find you a decent flat in the centre. Those that do not have a boiler for hot water have the hot water cut off in May or June for maintenance work. This has happened to me two years on the go. So always check to see if your flat has a boiler; if not, try and convince the landlord to install one.

There are now plenty of agencies with flats to rent. People are generally friendly and helpful, although you should always try to get a second opinion or help from a local Bulgarian friend or colleague. You never know who might be wanting to rent out a superb flat in the centre, someone who does not want to have to go through an agency, that charges around $300 agency fees.

What about the cost of living? Has it gone up?
Yes it has. Life here was not expensive when I arrived, however things are now changing and in the past few months certain things have gone up to western prices. The post went up in February, central heating has been going up every month, and the telephone shot up in March. The government is also saying that electricity, gas, water and prices of flats will also go up over the next twelve months. Despite this, you can live reasonably well on a British salary, although care must be taken.

What about going out?
Restaurants are generally nice and clean and serve good food. You have a wide variety, between Bulgarian, Chinese, Spanish, French, Macedonian, Serbian,

Japanese, Greek, Turkish and even Mexican cuisine to choose from. Drinks, especially wine and beer, are very cheap while clubs and discos tend to charge more. Shopping varies, from the very cheap to the very expensive; and transport is cheap: it may be a good idea to have a weekly or monthly pass.

What are the advantages of living and working in Bulgaria? And what else do short and long term residents need to know?
In a way, it is an experience not to be missed. You can save money if you want to. There's plenty to do and see. You have the chance of meeting and sharing so much with the Bulgarians. The Balkans is also an interesting area of the world and from Bulgaria you can visit Romania, Serbia (with certain restrictions), Macedonia, Greece, Turkey and then venture further south or north... Employment is difficult at the moment. Students wishing to study here will find it great, but forget employment unless you decide to give private lessons. Bulgarians are very good students and enjoy attending private classes in order to improve their English. You can start up your own business now. It's a lengthy process, so it's worth getting in touch with a good Bulgarian English-speaking lawyer. Banks now change money, and there are plenty of exchange bureaux. All banks and many shops now accept credit cards.

For me it has been a positve experience in many ways. One, I had the chance to return to the Balkans and work in an area of Europe I am interested in and truly love. I also enjoy my work as a teacher and examiner. During my first year here, I had to go to Sevlievo, a small town smack in the middle of Bulgaria where I taught teenagers in a secondary school. It was fascinating. I have met lots of interesting people, from Bulgarians working on the land to Bulgarians who are very rich and famous. I have taught at the Ministry of Defence, at the Sheraton Hotel, and even people from the Bulgarian government. I have met other teachers, other foreigners working here, and of course diplomats from the many foreign embassies and consulates.

You must remember that Sofia, although the capital city of Bulgaria, is in fact a small village where practically everybody knows you. So be careful!

Romania

Michael Frost

Some travel notes on Romania:

Overall, I have found this one of the most interesting places I have visited. You can have experiences there which you will not have in Western countries, or even other Eastern European ones. It can come as a shock at times – for example amputees begging, poverty, street urchins – and travel is not easy – but it is worth it.

I would advise against travelling solo – less vulnerable – but that is a personal preference. Security is an issue, so be on your guard, but not paranoid. As Romania opens up, things will get easier. It is worth seeing, if one is prepared to put up with the inconveniences and the absence of some western comforts.

Bucharest:
This was the least impressive part of my trip. Dirty, dusty, unpleasant. One of the least enjoyable places I have visited in my entire travels. I chose the *Dimbovita Hotel* (Strada Schitu Magureanu) for around £16 – they wouldn't be beaten down,

despite pleas of poverty – it was a dingy and grotty room. It is slightly better (i.e. marginally less tatty) than its sister hotel the *Venetia* where the breakfast is served.

This was poor value for money compared to what you can get elsewhere in Romania. If tourism in Bucharest is ever to take off, they must tackle the poor quality of some of the hotels and abolish the higher prices for western tourists (also see the *Romania* chapter).

Metro tickets are issued for two rides. There are some reasonable cafés along Bul Margheru, and cinemas mainly along Boul Kogalniceanu or Boul Balescu, 75p for a seat, and book in advance for Friday and Saturday when they are very popular. Service with a smile in the city's two McDonald's restaurants includes 'Yes! have a nice day!'. The staff seemed delighted to have a Westerner to serve, but the Romanian cover version of fast-food is not so good!

Brasov:
Hotels were very expensive. Far better value was the private room I was offered. I was met at the station by a room tout, initially sceptical, but pursued the offer after checking out the hotels. Maria and Grig Bolea act as agents for several people with rooms to offer: tel 68-31-19-26. they are helpful and reliable.

Good restaurants are the *Gustari* (excellent value – £6 gets you a filling meal with a bottle of red wine. Sit outside on the terrace and be pestered by kids for change while enjoying the view), the *Intim* (better value, but less impressive inside), and *Mammamia* (Strada Muresenilor) sells good ice cream in a variety of styles. Beware pickpockets in Brasov. I went for a stroll along the Strada Republicii, and was followed into a shop by three youths. I felt someone tugging at my daybag, and turned to face the culprit. When I did so, one of the others had a go at getting inside my bag. I spoke loudly to them in English and walked away. They didn't get anything, although they had managed to unzip one of the pockets. One of the youths had a coat over his arm – the weather didn't merit it – which I think would have been to conceal anything stolen.

Timisoara:
The Opera is worth catching – equivalent of £1.50. Productions in Romanian and Italian are good quality. Don't miss the view of the square below from the balcony in the interval. The cinema is dirt cheap. Best is the *Timis*, opposite the Cathedral. A bookshop – not a very good one – stocks English-language and French-language books off the Lupa Capitolina. The open-air market is worth a visit: and the vegetables are good (when available). The best exchange rates I found were at the *Cina* exchange, near the Cina restaurant. The brewery (some way out of town, on tram route 20?) is worth a trip. It has good beer with reasonable food, and good waiter service. The 'bera negra' or black beer is the local kind.

Sibiu:
Not recommended is the small pension at Strada Anton Pann 12, off Calea Dumbravil, reached by trolleybus 1: noisy thin walls, and about £7 or £8 a night as far as I recall. Breakfast is extra and poor. Much better is the *Hotel Bulevard* (Piata Unirii 10) for around £16 a night. Not cheap, but better value than the pension.

A good restaurant (by local standards anyway) was *Restaurant Bufnita*, Balescu 45 – the waitress spoke some French and German, quite friendly. Food not great, but then Romanian food rarely is. Around Piata Mare are several cafés – the one on the corner of Balescu served tasty snacks (ham rolls etc. microwave heated). The *cofeterias* around the square had good service and reasonable coffee.

Lovely to sit outside in the morning sunshine and enjoy a good breakfast, while watching the locals go about their business.

The *Brukenthal Museum* was very good and worth an afternoon. A good bookshop with a wide range of English books is off Piata Mica – *Libraria Thausib* (Piata Mica 3; tel 69-21-57-74). Stocks Penguins, novels and academic books. The best selection I encountered in Romania.

Sibiu was much friendlier than larger cities, and felt safer than Bucharest or Brasov. The best place I visited in Romania!

If you have your own personal experience to contribute or observations to make about living or working in any country covered in this book, please contact the author at: 'Live and Work in Russia and Eastern Europe', Vacation Work, 9 Park End Street, Oxford OX1 1HJ, UK: fax 01865-790885.

Vacation Work publish:

	Paperback	Hardback
The Directory of Summer Jobs Abroad	£8.99	£14.99
The Directory of Summer Jobs in Britain	£8.99	£14.99
Adventure Holidays	£7.99	£12.99
Work Your Way Around the World	£12.95	£16.99
Working in Tourism – The UK, Europe & Beyond	£10.99	£15.99
Kibbutz Volunteer	£8.99	£12.99
Working on Cruise Ships	£8.99	£12.99
Teaching English Abroad	£10.99	£15.99
The Au Pair & Nanny's Guide to Working Abroad	£9.99	£14.99
Working in Ski Resorts – Europe & North America	£10.99	–
Accounting Jobs Worldwide	£11.95	£16.95
Working with the Environment	£9.99	£15.99
Health Professionals Abroad	£9.99	£15.99
The Directory of Jobs & Careers Abroad	£11.95	£16.99
The International Directory of Voluntary Work	£10.99	£15.99
The Directory of Work & Study in Developing Countries	£8.99	£14.99
Live & Work in Russia & Eastern Europe	£10.99	£15.95
Live & Work in France	£10.99	£15.95
Live & Work in Australia & New Zealand	£10.99	£14.95
Live & Work in the USA & Canada	£10.99	£14.95
Live & Work in Germany	£10.99	£15.95
Live & Work in Belgium, The Netherlands & Luxembourg	£10.99	£15.95
Live & Work in Spain & Portugal	£10.99	£15.95
Live & Work in Italy	£10.99	£15.95
Live & Work in Scandinavia	£8.95	£14.95
Travellers Survival Kit: Lebanon	£9.99	–
Travellers Survival Kit: South Africa	£9.99	–
Travellers Survival Kit: India	£9.99	–
Travellers Survival Kit: Russia & the Republics	£9.95	–
Travellers Survival Kit: Western Europe	£8.95	–
Travellers Survival Kit: Eastern Europe	£9.95	–
Travellers Survival Kit: South America	£15.95	–
Travellers Survival Kit: Central America	£8.95	–
Travellers Survival Kit: Cuba	£10.99	–
Travellers Survival Kit: USA & Canada	£10.99	–
Travellers Survival Kit: Australia & New Zealand	£9.99	–
Hitch–hikers' Manual Britain	£3.95	–
Europe – a Manual for Hitch-hikers	£4.95	–

Distributors of:

	Paperback	Hardback
Summer Jobs USA	£12.95	–
Internships (On-the-Job Training Opportunities in the USA)	£16.95	–
Sports Scholarships in the USA	£12.95	–
Making It in Japan	£8.95	–
Green Volunteers	£9.99	–

Vacation Work Publications, 9 Park End Street, Oxford OX1 1HJ
(Tel 01865–241978. Fax 01865–790885)
Web site http://www.vacationwork.co.uk